The Japanese Central Banking System Compared with Its European and American Counterparts

Yoshiharu Oritani

The Japanese Central Banking System Compared with Its European and American Counterparts

A New Institutional Economics Approach

 Springer

Yoshiharu Oritani
Meiji University
Hayama, Kanagawa, Japan

Translated by
Kazuyo W. Tanimoto
Kunitachi, Tokyo, Japan

ISBN 978-981-13-9000-5   ISBN 978-981-13-9001-2   (eBook)
https://doi.org/10.1007/978-981-13-9001-2

This Springer imprint is published by the registered company Springer Nature Singapore Pte Ltd.
The registered company address is: 152 Beach Road, #21-01/04 Gateway East, Singapore 189721,
Singapore

Foreword

In any country, a central bank is an organization deemed intriguing, one that at times is considered more mysterious than necessary. Reflecting this or not, there are a countless number of studies and books on central banks. I have had opportunities to read such writings from time to time since I joined the Bank of Japan, but through experiencing various workplaces within the Bank, I have come to feel a perception gap between the central bank as I understand it and as it is perceived and presented in books. This gap seems to have widened with the passage of years.

Such a gap not only is about monetary policy, such as how one evaluates the effect of quantitative easing, but also is about the very existence of a central bank. My perception gap may be summarized under the following three points: first, while a central bank is an organization whose principal objectives are to supply money and maintain its value, various operations related to having bank deposits work as deposit money, especially tasks in the field of payment and settlement systems, are not recognized or analyzed as much as they should be. Second, while central bank tasks, including monetary policy, are conducted through actual transactions and not in the form of administrative directives or orders, such a perspective is not abundant in the literature. Third, surprisingly enough, people seem simply unaware of the self-evident fact that a central bank is an organization like any other. Two factors characterize an organization: (a) various governance mechanisms that influence the behavior of an organization and its components and (b) morale and ethos that are not necessarily included in governance. Even when we limit the topic to the mechanism of governance, researchers' interests are focused on what in this book is called public governance and rarely go beyond that to a discussion of governance within central bank organization.

The three points mentioned above are, at a glance, small practical themes. However, as the saying goes, "the devil is in the details." If we do not recognize these points, my experience tells me that no matter how grand the policy is, any discussion of it is likely to be hollow. I am not suggesting that economists have neglected these themes. Over the past 20 years, new institutional economics such as transaction cost economics has developed significantly, as exemplified in the awarding of the 2009 Nobel Prize in Economics to Professor Oliver Williamson.

Such a new wave of studies could bring about considerable development in central bank theory, but I am afraid such challenges have not been fully accepted and pursued. Someone must fill this vacuum and Professor Yoshiharu Oritani does just this in his book titled *The Japanese Central Banking System Compared with Its European and American Counterparts: A New Institutional Economics Approach*. This book most fit for the task and one that directly challenges the subject with a refreshing tone and approach. I have not come across a book of similar flavor either in Japan or overseas to date.

I joined the Bank of Japan in 1972 (the same year as Yoshiharu), and we worked side by side in Foreign Department (the current International Department) and the Special Research Office (currently the Institute of Monetary and Economic Studies). Yoshiharu studied monetary economics that applied time series analysis and then became involved in the banking area of a central bank such as bank examination and payment and settlement systems. He also has ample experience in the international arena and has contributed to developing central banking and payment and settlement systems in Central and East Asian countries and transition economies. This book reflects the diverse experience Yoshiharu had while he worked for the Bank of Japan.

It is important for researchers to continuously provide new perspectives. Throughout this book, the reader will be presented with unique ideas and interpretations based on his 30 years of experience at the Bank of Japan and research at Meiji University. Readers will inevitably agree or disagree with them, but I believe that developing and deepening this kind of research will lead to the further progress of central banks. As one of the central bankers who along with Yoshiharu dedicated a long career to the Bank of Japan, my fondest hope is that this book will be read by as many readers as possible who are interested in central banks.

Tokyo, Japan   Masaaki Shirakawa
                                                      Former Governor of the Bank of Japan

Preface

This book has three objectives. The first is to attempt to apply new institutional economics (NIE), especially transaction cost economics (TCE), organizational economics, and public choice theory to central banking such as the governance structure, functions and services provided by central banks. Application of these theories to central banks means to test whether they have the same analytical viability as when applied to other systems and corporate organizations. Until now, past experience and political decision have been the only tools in designing the governance and scope of functions and services provided by a central bank, and institutional economic theories have not been referred to.

The second objective is to place special emphasis on the Bank of Japan (BOJ), in particular to clarify the cause of a problem (how to maintain independence) that the bank is facing by applying NIE. When the BOJ Act was revised in 1998 for the first time in 50 years to strengthen its independence, it was generally seen in a positive light. However, once Prime Minister Abe took office in 2012, the administration made what should be an independent central bank adopt monetary policy that was in line with the administration's ideas, namely bold quantitative easing. The lesson learnt is that central bank independence cannot be defended solely by law and a mechanism to be able to reject advances from politicians needs to be embedded within the governance structure. Here, it should be noted that the author is well versed in various aspects of BOJ based on a 30-years career and 'participant observation.'

The third objective is to apply NIE to central banks in Europe and in the US to be able to make comparative analysis with the BOJ. The analysis covers governance structure (board structure and capital), as well as functions and services provided by the central bank (the supervisory authority of financial institutions, foreign exchange rate policy, and payment and settlement services). In this connection, the book analyzes the global financial crisis of 2007–09 that stemmed from the US by applying behavioral economics. Public choice theory is applied to consider measures to strengthen the central bank's role so that such crises can be avoided in the future, e.g., to retain seigniorage within the central bank. The comparative analysis provides useful insights when considering questions such as whether a central bank should issue electronic money and whether something akin to the European System of Central Banks (ESCB) could be established in Asia.

In the first place, a central banking organization and system are considered particularly unique within the economic arena. For example, Paul Samuelson and William Nordhaus (2010, p.475) quotes in their famous economics textbook (at the beginning of Chapter 24 entitled "Monetary Policy and the Economy") from writer/humorist, Will Rogers (1879–1935):

> There have been three great inventions since the beginning of time: fire, the wheel, and **central banking** (emphasis by Oritani).

And M. Mitchell Waldrop (1992, p.243) introduces Brian Arthur's words in his book *Complexity* in Chapter 7 entitled "Peasants Under Glass" as follows:

> Now, my earlier interests had been how economies change and develop in the Third World....I had this notion that you could have within your office in the university a little peasant economy developing under a bubble of glass. Of course, it would really be in a computer....Then in this dreamlike idea, you'd go in one morning and say, 'Hey, look at these guys! Two or three weeks ago all they were doing was bartering, and now they've got joint stock companies.' Then next day you'd come in and say, 'Oh, they've discovered **central banking**' (emphasis by Oritani).

Note that both authors, whether intentionally or not, say "central banking" and not "money." Indeed, a central banking organization and system that provide central banking services are, in various aspects, an interesting entity.

First, a central bank is a 'bank of issue' that issues banknotes as a major cash currency under a fiat currency system. After inventing money, mankind liberated it from natural materials such as gold and silver, replacing it with inconvertible notes which are bank debts, and, in due time, a central bank was established as the only entity that could issue such notes. Second, a central bank plays the role of 'bankers' bank,' taking deposits from financial institutions (i.e., private banks, 'banks' hereafter) and providing credit. The deposits are used for interbank settlements, and therefore, central banks are deeply involved in payment and settlement systems. On the other hand, central bank credit encompasses not only simple lending to banks but also liquidity provision to overall financial markets through the purchase of various financial assets. Moreover, considering that a central bank has the ability to provide liquidity, is involved in payment and settlement systems, and has a close relationship with private banks, it plays the role of maintaining financial system stability as well as regulating and supervising banks. Third, a central bank holds government deposits as the 'bank for the government' and at the same time extends lending to it and purchases government bonds. Besides the provision of banking services, a central bank stands in a complex and diverse relationship with the government that involves the appointment of high officials of the central bank and management of monetary policy.

Central banking systems, at the core of which is the central banking organization (simply 'central bank' hereafter), are undergoing comprehensive reform worldwide having seen the transition to a market economy of former socialist republics of the Soviet Union and the global financial crisis of 2007–09. For example, the European

Central Bank (ECB) was established in 1998 prior to the introduction of the euro in 1999 and its role is the subject of heated discussion in light of the Greek financial crisis (2009–12) in Europe. Following the global financial crisis of 2007–09, the roles of the Federal Reserve System (FRS) and the Bank of England (BOE) in the prudential policy area have been strengthened in both the US and the UK. In Asia, many countries underwent central banking system reform after the Asian financial crisis in the late 1990s. For example, the BOJ Act was revised in 1998 for the first time since World War II.

These central banking system reforms, excluding discussion on central bank independence, have been implemented without due consideration being given to institutional economic theories and rather decided from historical and political perspectives or experiences of the pertinent officials concerned. In order to adapt to changes in the financial and economic environment as well as financial systems, discussion and reform of central banks should be a continuing topic for the future. In this regard, analysis of central banking systems applying institutional economic theories can provide those concerned with what an optimal central banking system might look like based on efficiency and rationality and at the same time is itself expected to become a springboard for objective argument regardless of the positions of the parties.

Hitherto, the main reason why central banking systems were not analyzed based on institutional economic theories is that in traditional economics necessary tools to explore organizations and systems were not available. However in recent years, economic tools for discussing organizations and institutions have developed significantly. In particular, transaction cost economics developed by two Nobel Laureates, Ronald Coase (1991 winner) and Oliver Williamson (2009 winner), became the nucleus of new institutional economics, organizational economics, comparative institutional analysis, and public choice theory. Among them, NIE differs from old institutional economics prior to World War II in that while it basically respects instruments of traditional economics as much as possible, it utilizes the recent development of microeconomics such as information economics. By linking a system and transactions among agents that comprise it, NIE enables the exploration of subjects surrounding the institution based on economic theories. Similarly, organizational economics uses almost the same fundamental theory as NIE which allows discussion of various organizations (i.e., corporate organization that used to be a theme of business management in the past) based on economic theories. Moreover, comparative institutional analysis provides economic theory that could compare and discuss corporate organizations, economic systems in various countries, and historical background. These economic theories differ in purpose and subject analyzed but have many aspects in common regarding theoretical framework, and therefore, we regard them all as NIE.

Recently, various issues regarding the financial system, from raison d'être of financial institutions (i.e., banks) to issues regarding the Japanese main bank system, have been researched applying NIE. However, to date, there is no full-fledged research on central banking systems based on NIE. From NIE, this book will mainly apply TCE, as well as public choice theory and agency theory to analyze central banking systems (organizational culture theory and sociology of culture are also partially applied).

In this regard, for readers who are not well versed in the above theories, and also to clarify my own understanding of them to readers, an outline of all applied theories is first given before applying them to central banking systems. Practitioners as well as scholars and students are the intended audience for this book. Practitioners include those in the financial industry, especially central bankers and those working in organizations similar to central banking organizations. Intended scholars and researchers are those studying either money and banking or NIE. In addition, this book is written so that undergraduates interested in the subject will be able to understand with minimal knowledge of financial systems.

There are various benefits in applying NIE to analyze central banking systems. First, we can confirm the efficacy of NIE. A central banking system is a unique entity within a financial and economic system, and to know to what extent NIE is valid in analyzing such an important economic system would be useful for the future development of NIE.

Second, to confirm the efficacy of NIE in the study of central banking systems would also mean discussing to what extent NIE is useful in analyzing organizations and systems that have similar characteristics to a central bank. The central bank is a unique organization that is neither government nor private but has both features. Therefore, we could in turn consider whether NIE could be applied to the research of various types of exchanges such as stock exchange as well as semi-governmental corporations and banks.

Third, studying central banking systems based on economic theories could correct my biased view, if any. This book comprises research based on my experience at the BOJ and observation of overseas central banking organizations and systems. This type of research is similar to a research method termed 'participant observation' where research is conducted by actually participating in a target organization or society. While this method allows the researcher to collect detailed information on the target organization and society, it entails the risk of a biased view, either affirmative or critical of the target organization. I have tried to be as objective as possible and to be neither critical nor affirmative of central banks and the views of the BOJ. However, nothing can be completely objective. Thus, recognizing the possibility of value judgments on my part coming through, I believed that applying economic theories would minimize any negative aspect of participant observation-style research.

Fourth, economic theories are constructed with clear premises and logical consistency and therefore can be useful as communication instruments between myself and readers. This book provides my views and opinions on governance structure and roles of a central bank based on economic theories. If readers read through the book following the logic of various theories, they should be able to understand my views and opinions and recognize any fallacies.

The book does not clearly differentiate between 'central banking system (=institution)' and 'central banking organization' although NIE has separate definitions: "Note that the term 'institution' refers to the rules of the game, whereas 'organization' refers to players of the game" (*Glossary for New Institutional Economics*, The Ronald Coase Institute website).

If we adapt this to a central bank, a 'central banking system (=institution)' comprises the overall rules that players in a socioeconomic system including a central bank abide by, and a 'central banking organization' is the central bank itself, a player that operates under such an institution. However, within an organization, there are also players such as managers and employees that act abiding by the organization's rules of the game. Therefore, a central banking organization can be regarded as an institution as well as a player (managers and employees) meaning that NIE can be applied to the issues of a central banking organization.

I have been planning to write this book ever since working at the Bank of Japan (BOJ). Joining the Bank in 1972, I became especially interested in central banking systems, an interest which deepened after I worked in the fields of bank supervision and examination as well as payment and settlement systems. However, I soon discovered that the traditional economics I studied at university and at the Institute of Monetary and Economic Studies (IMES, BOJ) could not assist me in engaging in theoretical analysis of central banking systems. Then, in 1991, when I was in charge of researching financial systems at the Institute, Professor R. Coase received a Nobel Prize which prompted me to research the development of Coase–Williamson type new institutional economics and think about the possibility of applying it to central banking systems since the theory challenged the organizational and institutional issues head-on. I subsequently became involved in a project that made me think about the very existence of central banking systems, both directly and indirectly. Specifically, from 1993, I was engaged in technical assistance regarding central banking systems and their operation to central banks of former republics of the Soviet Union that were established after its collapse. And, after the Asian financial crisis, I became member of the World Bank mission to the Bank of Thailand (led by E. Gerald Corrigan, Former President of the FRB New York) in response to the request by the then Thai Minister of Finance regarding revision of the Bank of Thailand Act.

Through these experiences, I became very aware of the necessity to analyze central banking systems theoretically. Therefore, after I moved to Meiji University in 2002, I wrote research papers on central banking systems that applied new institutional economics which were released in succession in *The Bulletin of the Faculty of Commerce* (in Japanese), Meiji University, based on the ideas I had developed during my days at the BOJ.

In the meantime, I had also been deeply involved in payment and settlement systems since I first stepped into the field in 1984. At the BOJ, I researched payment and settlement systems at the IMES, took part in technical assistance in International Department to construct payment and settlement systems for the Kyrgyz Republic, and later took a post in the Financial System Department. Meanwhile, I became member of the Committee on Payment and Settlement Systems (CPSS) at the Bank for International Settlements (BIS), and chaired the Working Group on Payment and Settlement Systems of the Executives' Meeting of East Asia-Pacific Central Banks (EMEAP). For my seminar at Meiji University,

I had been taking up the study of financial information systems as the theme, the focus of which was payment and settlement systems.

This book is comprised of roughly two parts. The first part (from Chap. 1 to Chap. 3) discusses the fundamental structure of a central banking system which begins with the rationale of central banks and followed by the governance structure and public governance of central banks. The latter part (from Chaps. 4 to 7) explores the relationship between the main central bank functions and its organization/system. As the main central bank functions, monetary policy, prudential policy, financial crisis management, and payment services are discussed. However, we do not cover central bank functions comprehensively, but rather focus on major functions that are often the subject of discussion. The main discussion points of each chapter are as follows:

Chapter 1 applies TCE, namely theory on three modes of economic systems (market mode, hierarchy mode, and hybrid mode), to examine the fundamental raison d'être for the existence of a central bank within a banking system. We conclude that a two-tiered system with both a central bank and commercial banks coexisting could minimize the transaction costs of interbank transactions. From this analysis, implications are drawn to consider the significance of establishing a supranational central bank such as the ECB and the supervisory role of a central bank.

Chapter 2 focuses on central bank organization and considers its governance structure, rather than as just a central bank within the financial system. Features of goods and services provided by the central bank are first analyzed based on the theory of club goods. Then, TCE is applied to explain that the governance structure of a central bank contains features of both public and corporate governance. And, in order to incorporate these two features, it is appropriate to adopt a multiboard system for the central bank's supreme decision-making body where several boards coexist to take on different responsibilities. Central bank governance structure has two aspects, 'ownership' and 'organizational governance,' just like the governance structure of a private company. This chapter will also consider the characteristics and role of a central bank's capital stock as part of central bank ownership.

Chapter 3 discusses public governance of a central bank based on the theory of bureaucracy cost, agency theory, and public choice theory from new institutional economics. The importance of probity in central bank governance structure as well as central bank independence under representative democracy is explained.

Chapter 4 looks at two aspects of governance (ownership and organizational governance) by applying the theory of organizational boundaries, multitask agency theory, and theory of organizational culture. The analysis explicates the appropriateness of a central bank to be responsible for monetary policy management and issues related to managing monetary policy together with foreign exchange policy and prudential policy. As for the latter, the design and management of a board system are considered to mitigate such issues.

Chapter 5 discusses the relationship between a central bank and prudential policy such as regulating/supervising financial institutions using the theory of organizational boundaries and agency theory. We conclude that a central bank needs to manage prudential policy and that duplicate supervision by various supervisory authorities is important.

Chapter 6 analyzes the failure of the US monetary authorities in terms of their financial crisis management during the global financial crisis of 2007–09 by applying behavioral new institutional economics that integrates behavioral economics and new institutional economics. From the analysis, rationale is offered for the necessity of providing risk money in times of crisis and also an explanation of issues related to the decision-making process under representative democracy. Then, based on public choice theory, the role of a central bank in time of financial crisis will be discussed from the perspective of utilizing central bank seigniorage.

Chapter 7 deals with payment and settlement systems. First, the theory of organizational boundaries is applied to discuss the role of a central bank in providing payment and settlement services. We point out that the central bank needs to own securities' settlement systems as well as be involved in retail payment systems, including electronic money. Next, we look back on how Continuous Linked Settlement Bank (CLS Bank) was established for interbank foreign exchange transactions applying the theory of peer group association from TCE and consider the need to realize the globalization of central bank payment and settlement systems by linking systems among central banks. Lastly, the theory of bureaucracy cost from TCE is applied to consider governance of payment and settlement systems managed by a central bank, especially with regard to the relationship between the governance of central bank payment systems and design/management of a board system.

Hayama, Japan   Yoshiharu Oritani

Acknowledgements

This book is a translated and updated version of Japanese version of the book titled *Chuo Ginko Seido no Keizaigaku (Institutional Economics of Central Banking Systems)* published by Gakujutsu Shuppankai in Tokyo (November 2013). Chapters 1 and 3 in the original Japanese book (and this book) are taken from the following sources:

Institutional Economics of Central Banks, *Proceedings of the 21st SEANZA Central Banking Course*, People's Bank of China, 1997.

Public Governance of Central Banks: An Approach from New Institutional Economics, *BIS Working Paper*, No. 299, March 2010.

    Other chapters are based on 12 research papers written for *The Bulletin of the Faculty of Commerce,* Meiji University, which were subsequently revised for the original Japanese edition of this book. Then, in compiling this English edition, they were revised and updated.

    I wish to thank Kazuyo W. Tanimoto who translated this book from Japanese into English, Bernard Grace who edited the English version, and those who have kindly given permission for the use of copyright materials.

    My heartfelt appreciation goes to Masaaki Shirakawa, Former Governor of the Bank of Japan, for his long-term friendship and for kindly writing a foreword in the Japanese version of this book. I would like to thank Eikichi Saito, President of the Bank of Toyama that is located in my hometown, for giving me a precious opportunity to observe the central bank from a commercial bank side as Outside Director of the Bank from 2012 to 2018. Finally, I would also like to express my sincere gratitude to Juno Kawakami, Editor of Springer, for her helpful advice to compile the book.

Contents

Abbreviations

ACH	Automated clearing house
BIS	Bank for International Settlements
BOE	Bank of England
BOJ	Bank of Japan
BOT	Bank of Thailand
CCP	Central counterparty
CLS Bank	Continuous Linked Settlement Bank
CPSS	Committee on Payment and Settlement Systems
CSD	Central securities depository
DTCC	Depository Trust & Clearing Corporation
DVP	Delivery versus payment
ECB	European Central Bank
ECSDA	European Central Securities Depositories Association
ESCB	European System of Central Banks
FCA	Financial Conduct Authority
FOMC	Federal Open Market Committee
FPC	Financial stability policy committee
FRB	Federal Reserve Bank
FRS	Federal Reserve System
FSA	Financial Supervisory Agency
FSOC	Financial Stability Oversight Council
MOU	Memorandum of understanding
NCB	National Central Bank
NIE	New institutional economics
OCC	Office of the Comptroller of Currency
PRA	Prudential Regulation Authority
PVP	Payment versus payment
RBA	Reserve Bank of Australia
RBV	Resource-based view
RTGS	Real-time gross settlement system

SCB	Supranational central bank
SEC	Securities and Exchange Commission
T2S	TARGET2-Securities
TARGET	Trans-European Automated Real-Time Gross Settlement Express Transfer System
TBTF	Too big to fail
TCE	Transaction cost economics
UK	United Kingdom
US	United States

Chapter 1
Rationale of Central Banks

1.1 Overview

This chapter will examine why central banks exist within the banking system, and then study the institutional issues currently facing central banks, for example: the evolution of central bank cooperation and supranational central banks, bankers' associations versus central banks in providing payment and settlement services, the supervisory role of central banks, and the clients and business scope of a central bank.

In studying these issues, we will apply the theories of New Institutional Economics (NIE), particularly transaction cost economics (TCE[1]). TCE began to spread in the 1970s, primarily thanks to the contribution of Oliver Williamson. In 1991, one of the founders of TCE, Ronald Coase, won a Nobel Prize for his work; then in 1993, Douglas North won a Nobel Prize for his application of TCE to economic history; moreover in 2009, Oliver Williamson was awarded a Nobel Prize. TCE is, therefore, a recognized and powerful force within the discipline. In contrast with old institutional economics, NIE, represented by TCE, supports the basic attitude of respecting the traditional tools of microeconomics whenever possible. Based on recent developments in microeconomics, which includes information economics and organization theory, TCE can provide a much better understanding of many interesting institutional issues.

Although TCE is not hostile to orthodox economics, it operates at a more microanalytic level than is customary in economics. Williamson (1996, pp. 6–7) says "the transaction is the basic unit of analysis, whereas orthodoxy is concerned with composite goods and services…. Discrete structural rather than marginal modes of analysis are therefore employed. First-order economizing (getting the basic align-

---

[1] For an introduction to TCE, see Williamson (2013), Brousseau and Glachant (2008).

This Chapter is based on the paper titled "Institutional Economics of Central Banks," *Proceedings of the 21st SEANZA Central Banking Course*, People's Bank of China (pp. 625–667), by Y. Oritani, 1997.

© Springer Nature Singapore Pte Ltd. 2019
Y. Oritani, *The Japanese Central Banking System Compared with Its European and American Counterparts*, https://doi.org/10.1007/978-981-13-9001-2_1

ments right) rather than second-order refinements (adjusting the margins) is therefore featured."

First, we will briefly survey the earlier studies on the rationale of central banks in Sect. 1.2. Then, we will apply Williamson's three modes of economic systems to identify three types of banking systems seen historically worldwide in Sect. 1.3. In Sect. 1.4, we will analyze transaction costs in these three types of banking systems and explicate why it is the two-tiered system with both a central bank and commercial banks that has survived. Section 1.5 provides an explanation of four recent changes in institutional environment that has strong influence over central bank diversification and governance. From this analysis we go on in Sect. 1.6 to consider implications for the institutional issues that central banks currently face. As examples, we take up such issues as the evolution of a supranational central bank, a bankers' association versus the central bank in providing payment services, the supervisory role of the central bank, and the clients and business scope of the central bank.

1.2 Earlier Studies

There have been many, if we include related research, studies on the raison d'être of a central bank. This section introduces four generally well-known ones including the relatively direct raison d'être of a central bank and that by Hayek that considers a central bank to be unnecessary. Economic theories applied in these studies are demand-supply theory from microeconomics and the quantity theory of money from macroeconomics, both of which are limited to traditional economics. As for institutional economics, neither old nor new are applied.

1.2.1 Bagehot's Study

Bagehot (1873) wrote a book entitled *Lombard Street: A Description of the Money Market*. In the book, Bagehot clearly illustrated the code of conduct of a central bank, especially as a lender of last resort (LLR) in financial crises taking the BOE (established in 1694) as a model. This code of conduct was proposed at a time when there was no concept of central banking, much less that of LLR, and became well-known as 'Bagehot's Dictum.'

'Bagehot's Dictum' states that central banks should lend freely to solvent depository institutions in times of financial crisis only if they have sound collateral and at high interest rates to discourage borrowers that are not truly in need. In Bagehot's own words (Bagehot, ibid, pp. 78–79):

> First. That these loans should only be made at a very high rate of interest. This will operate as a heavy fine on unreasonable timidity, and will prevent the greatest number of applications by persons who do not require it. The rate should be raised early in the panic, so that the fine may be paid early; that no one may borrow out of idle precaution without paying well

for it; that the Banking reserve may be protected as far as possible. Secondly. That at this rate these advances should be made on all good banking securities, and as largely as the public ask for them. The reason is plain. The object is to stay alarm, and nothing therefore should be done to cause alarm. But the way to cause alarm is to refuse someone who has good security to offer....No advances indeed need be made by which the Bank will ultimately lose. The amount of bad business in commercial countries is an infinitesimally small fraction of the whole business....The great majority, the majority to be protected, are the 'sound' people, the people who have good security to offer. If it is known that the Bank of England is freely advancing on what in ordinary times is reckoned a good security — on what is then commonly pledged and easily convertible — the alarm of the solvent merchants and bankers will be stayed. But if securities, really good and usually convertible, are refused by the Bank, the alarm will not abate, the other loans made will fail in obtaining their end, and the panic will become worse and worse.

In addition to 'Bagehot's Dictum,' it is important to note that Bagehot suggested that central banking systems evolve with time. In the UK, historically, many banks deposited pay-off reserves with a larger bank and thus a credit system in the form of a pyramid of currency reserves was established. And, based on such a historical background, a central banking system in the form of the BOE emerged. Bagehot wrote in detail about how the BOE as an institution came to be positioned at the top of such a pyramidical structure.

1.2.2 Sayers' Study

R. S. Sayers (1957), renowned for studying the history of the Bank of England (BOE), published *Central Banking after Bagehot*. This book is a collection of his research papers appearing in various journals and lecture manuscripts, although the only content that is in line with the book's title is Chap. 2 on "The Development of Central Banking after Bagehot." Nevertheless, this book holds a significant historical meaning in studying the rationale of central banks.

First, he clarified the essence of central banking in various sections of the book, stressing the need to recognize that central banking is an act of discretion by men, and that a central bank can never be "a mere machine" for carrying out rules. This is an argument in line with the aforementioned Bagehot's Dictum and, more importantly, his book was published when many still favored "a more automatic system" as represented by Milton Friedman of the University of Chicago (for example, Friedman proposed the central bank should supply money constantly based on the 'k-percent rule').

Second, as a conclusion to Chap. 2, he showed how the BOE evolved after Bagehot's Dictum to embody the concept of central banking that he himself clarified. However, as mentioned in the following quote (ibid, pp. 18–19), the evolution of the BOE was not achieved consciously but "stumbled into central banking in a fit of absence of mind."

Although Bagehot's *Lombard Street* clearly, and to the satisfaction of almost everyone, laid the foundations of modern central banking theory, neither the men who had to seek a solution of the contemporary practical problems, nor most of the commentators, were at all conscious that they were developing a theory of central banking....We might almost, amending the old saw about the British Empire, say that England stumbled into central banking in a fit of absence of mind. And though I have argued in this paper that the process was largely completed in the generation after Bagehot, there is something to be said for the view that genuine central banking is a highly self-conscious business, and if this view is accepted, I have perhaps been guilty of anachronism in entitling this paper 'The development of central banking after Bagehot.'

Third, in Chap. 9, "Central Banking in Underdeveloped Countries," Sayers provided manuscripts of lectures sponsored by the National Bank of Egypt in 1956. This chapter consists of three sections and Section A (p. 108) entitled "Are Central Banks Universally Necessary?" raises an especially interesting argument. Back in 1956, according to Sayers, "The need for central banks in the major financial centres of the world is now generally accepted, but whether a central bank should be established in every independent political unit is much an open question." In response, he argued that a central bank should be established and that "The central bank should have the monopoly of legal-tender currency and should be the ultimate source of 'emergency credit.'"

He explained the role of a central bank in more detail in sections B and C. In section B (p. 115), "The Central Bank as a Banker," he stated that "The banking business to be cultivated falls into three parts: the central bank can be a bank for the general public, it can be the government's banker, and it can be the bankers' bank." With regard to "a bank for the general public" he assumed that there would be criticisms that were already pointed out by the experts in the 1920s "that the central bank should confine itself to the second and third field." At the same time, he understood that a central banker "may sometimes find his duty as central banker conflicting with his duty as a commercial banker." However, he believed that in underdeveloped countries where commercial banks are not fully functioning, it would be necessary for central banks to provide banking services to the general public (including firms) to achieve economic growth. As for the bankers' bank, he said "More fundamental, and universally acknowledged, is its duty to serve as the bankers' bank. This is basic to its authority as controller of the financial system....The central bank has a duty, as lender of last resort, to support the market with adequate loans to relieve a liquidity crisis." This argument endorses Bagehot's Dictum.

Sayers not only just endorsed Bagehot's Dictum but he also pointed out the necessity of a central bank's role in regulatory and supervisory functions, as he wrote, "It has no duty to support everybody alike. It is entitled to say that it will channel its help only through institutions that have conducted their business on healthy lines." For example, when a central bank considers regulating commercial banks, he stated that "The central bank must make up its mind about the principles on which commercial banking ought to be conducted. That is, the central bank as a regulator makes regulations that commercial banks should comply with." As for the supervisory function of a central bank he noted "An authority — sometimes the central bank, sometimes another branch of government — is charged with detailed inspection of the commercial banks. This supervision of banks, if conducted in a spirit of positive guidance rather than bare prohibition, can be an important factor in ensuring the healthy development of commercial banking."

In Section C (p. 123), "The Central Bank as a Controller," he laid out his views on how a central bank should consider and implement monetary policy in countries where securities markets and/or commercial banks are not fully developed. Specific instruments and methods include bank rate policy (official discount rate policy) and open market operations. Also, in other chapters of this book, he provided detailed historical accounts of monetary policy instruments and methods utilized until the 1950s based on the UK.

1.2.3 Smith's Study

Smith (1936) wrote a book titled *The Rationale of Central Banking*. The book was a doctoral dissertation at the London School of Economics written under the supervision of F. A. Hayek. Her dissertation was quite balanced in the discussion of central banking versus free banking considering that Hayek, her supervisor, was a very clear proposer of free banking as will be introduced in Sect. 1.2.4.

Smith reviewed banking history and surveyed debate in England, Scotland, France, Germany, and the US. She found that discussion of central banking versus free banking was linked with that of the currency school versus banking school. The currency school argues that money should be created exogenously out of the economic system, while, vice versa, the banking school argues that money should be created endogenously in the banking system. The currency school prefers central banking, in other words, the monopolistic issuance of banknotes, because it is easier to control the quantity of money. In contrast, the banking school is against monopolistic banknote issuance since it believes that the quantity of money should fluctuate automatically reflecting demand from commercial activity.

Smith thought that the central banking versus free banking argument should be considered separately from the discussion points between the banking and currency schools. In conclusion, Smith pointed out the following five arguments behind the rationale of central banking.

The first is that, with free banking, individual banks may fail from time to time. Through circulation, banknotes issued by a failed bank will be in the hands of third parties who have no immediate connection with it—those unfortunate enough to be holding notes of such a bank at the time of its failure will suffer a loss. Therefore, the community is burdened with the task of distinguishing between good and bad banknotes. Smith concluded that the government should intervene and introduce some uniformity into note issuance to protect those holding banknotes.

The second argument concerns monetary expansion and contraction leading to inflation and depression under a free banking system. Smith (ibid, p. 192) wrote as follows:

> Any attempt to make a final evaluation of the relative merits of alternative systems of banking must look primarily to the tendencies they manifest towards instability, or more particularly to the amount of causal influence they exert in cyclical fluctuations.

Opponents of free banking argued that aggressively expanding banks might impose the burden of restraint, or even the necessity of going out of business, onto more conservative banks. However, the central banking school has also cast doubt on the realism of "the concept of the so-called conservative bank" and has submitted that the profit motive may lead all banks to join in expansion.

The third argument holds that a central bank is better equipped to gain public confidence and to cope with crises by serving as LLR. Unless free banking can prove that it could entirely eliminate the trade cycle and general runs on banks, the argument for the LLR remains a very powerful instrument in defence of central banking.

The fourth argument, a secondary argument in favor of central banks, is that some form of central monetary authority is essential to pursue what is called a 'rational' monetary policy. The founders of the currency school considered the policy of the central bank to be automatic, but it is no longer so. The efficacy of central bank control is gaining importance, and, as such, demand for concentrating more control in the hands of the central monetary authority is rising.

The fifth argument, another secondary argument in favor of central banks, is that it is indispensable for international monetary cooperation. This is partly due to a situation where stable exchange rates among countries may not always be in line with a stable price level within each country. International cooperation in monetary policy could be a useful countermeasure in tackling the problem. Another reason is stretching the concept of the LLR to the international arena. Where the banking system of any country is faced with a run by foreign depositors, what the central bank of that country can do for the deposit-taking banks involved may be limited.

1.2.4 Hayek's Study

Hayek came into the spotlight against the background of discussion that economic cooperation in Europe should pursue currency integration through development of the EEC (European Economic Community). Hayek (1976), who was a strong proponent of free banking, wrote *Denationalisation of Money*. In this book he made a concrete proposal that the countries of the Common Market mutually bind themselves by formal treaty not to place any obstacles in the way of the free dealing in one another's currencies. This proposal was not only contrary to currency integration among EEC member countries that was beginning to be discussed, but also, in the first place, was against the monopolistic issuance of currency by respective central banks. He argued that national currencies should compete against each other, and said that this was a proposal more practicable than "utopian European currency." But in fact, the European Monetary Union was ratified and the euro introduced in 1999.

Other than national currency competition, Hayek also argued that it will be possible to establish a number of institutions in various parts of the world which are free to issue notes in competition and proposed the competitive supply of money by private banks. He pointed out the following reasons why private money can maintain stable value:

- a money generally expected to preserve its purchasing power approximately constant would be in continuous demand so long as the people were free to use it;
- with such a continuing demand depending on success in keeping the value of the currency constant one could trust the issuing banks to make every effort to achieve this better than would any monopolist who runs no risk by depreciating his money;
- the issuing institution could achieve this result by regulating the quantity of its issue; and
- such a regulation of the quantity of each currency would constitute the best of all practicable methods of regulating the quantity of media of exchange for all possible purposes.

Hayek's proposal utterly denies the raison d'être of a central bank and in fact, in Chap. 18 entitled "Monetary policy neither desirable nor possible," he has a section named "The abolition of central banks" and wrote as follows (ibid, p. 105):

> Perhaps a word should be explicitly inserted here about the obvious corollary that the abolition of the government monopoly of the issue of money should involve also the disappearance of central banks as we know them, both because one might conceive of some private bank assuming the function of a central bank and because it might be thought that, even without a government monopoly of issue, some of the classic functions of central banks such as that of acting as 'lender of last resort' or of 'holder of the ultimate reserve', might still be required.

1.3 Three Types of Banking Systems and Three Modes of Economic Systems

In this section, we will apply Williamson's three modes of economic systems—market mode, hierarchy mode, and hybrid mode—to identify three types of banking systems—commercial banks only with no central bank, central bank only, and both central bank and commercial banks.

1.3.1 Three Types of Banking Systems

History shows that the banking system found in the modern market economy is not the only kind possible. This is especially true if we focus on central banks; there have been times when no central bank existed. There have also been times, as under socialist economies, when only central banks comprised the banking system. Thus,

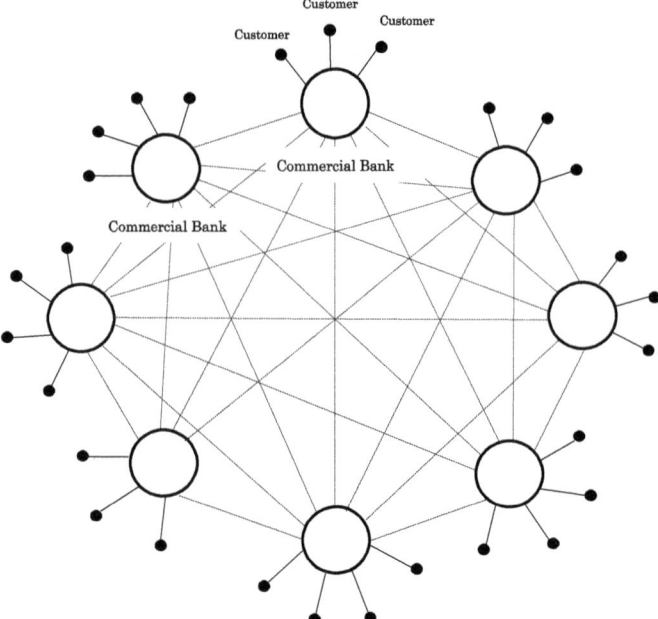

Fig. 1.1 Commercial banks only

historically, there have been three types of possible banking systems, one of which is the current two-tiered system in which commercial banks and a central bank co-exist.

Type A: No Central Bank, Commercial Banks Only (Fig. 1.1)
Before central banks came about, only commercial banks existed in the banking system. Historically, similar types of systems evolved in many different countries. This type of system was seen in the US until 1913, and in Japan from the Meiji Restoration in 1868 through to the establishment of the BOJ in 1882 (see Sect. 1.4.2). According to White (1984), a similar type of system was found in Scotland from the early eighteenth century through to the mid-nineteenth century. England also had this type of system until the establishment of the BOE in 1694.

Type B: Central Bank Only (Fig. 1.2)
In this system, there are no commercial banks; commercial and central banking functions are integrated. Historically, a similar type of banking system actually existed in socialist economies and was called 'monobank system.' For example, in the Soviet Union, which collapsed in 1991, there was only one central bank, Gosbank, for all of the federated republics as late as 1988. A similar system existed in China until 1983.

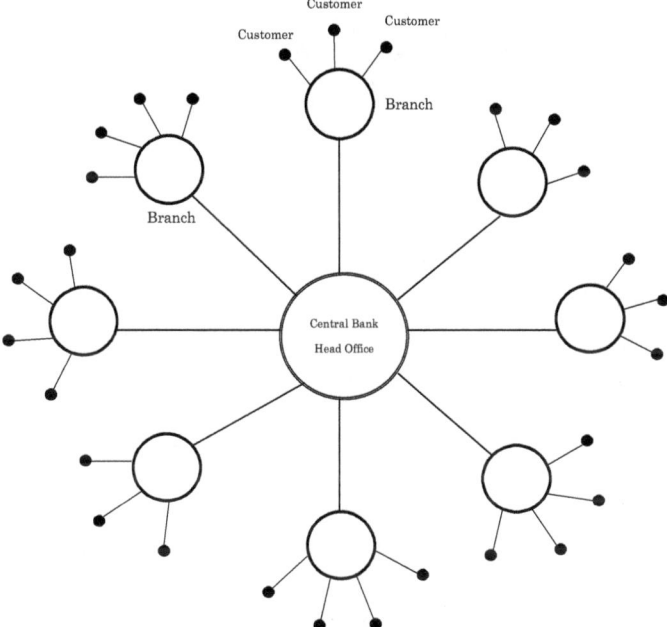

Fig. 1.2 Central bank only

Type C: Both a Central Bank and Commercial Banks (Fig. 1.3)
This is the system employed by modern market economies, and is also known as the
'two-tiered banking system.' Under this system, the central bank does not, in principle, engage in transactions directly with individuals or non-financial corporations.
Instead, it functions as 'the bankers' bank,' and it is this function that distinguishes
it from the central bank in Type B.

From a theoretical perspective, this is the logical categorization since it covers all
the basic types of banking systems that could exist, at least in terms of whether or not
there is a central bank. It therefore serves as an important starting point in our study;
why are there central banks? Of the three possibilities, Type C, the co-existence of
a central bank and commercial banks, has survived. Analyzing the reasons why this
came about may help us to understand the reasons why central banks exist.

Table 1.1 gives a summary of the three types of banking systems[2] and an outline
putting them in perspective for considering the banking systems discussed.

These three types of banking systems, categorized based on presence or otherwise
of a central bank, provide the following considerations for our analysis of the rationale
for a central bank.

---

[2]Note, however, that the three types are only a model. While, historically, there have been systems
similar to each type, no system has perfectly matched the table.

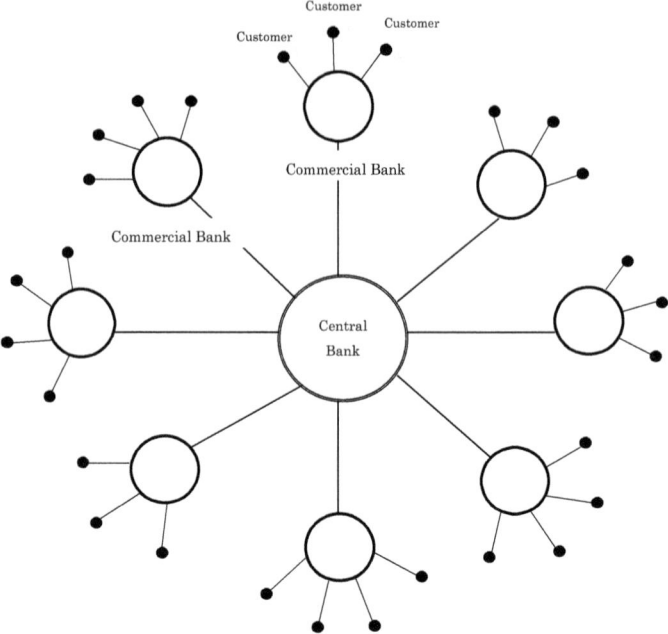

Fig. 1.3 Both a central bank and commercial banks

Table 1.1 Three types of banking systems

	Type A (no central bank)	Type B (central bank only)	Type C (both)
Participants	Only private financial institutions, including commercial banks	Only central bank, no private financial institutions	Both central bank and commercial banks
Financial markets	Financial markets exist, including interbank market	No financial markets	Financial markets exist
Financial assets	Cash exists	Cash exists	Cash exists
Payment and settlement system	Settlements between financial institutions by cash, clearing houses, and/or bilateral correspondent service	No need for settlements between financial institutions	Possible to use central bank accounts for settlements between financial institutions

First, we must examine why central banks emerged from a banking system in which only commercial banks existed. Although Goodhart (1988) analyzes this from a historical perspective, there has never been an analysis based on economic theory. This is related to the question first posed by Coase (1937) as to why firms emerged out of markets.

Second, our analysis will be insufficient if, as Goodhart (ibid) said, we consider only why central banks emerged out of a banking system in which they originally did not exist. As there was a banking system comprising only a central bank, we also need to explain why such systems could not survive and why the two-tiered system became the norm instead. Once again, this is related to an issue raised by Coase (ibid): if firms are superior to market transactions, why does the size of firms not become infinitely large? This question corresponds to why the central bank only system disappeared with the collapse of socialist economies.

1.3.2 Examples of Type Change from Type A to Type C in Japan and the US

1.3.2.1 Example in Japan

In Japan, the National Banking Act of 1872, modelled after the National Banking Act of 1863 in the US, was enacted, and, based on this Act more than a hundred private banks were established (Type A). As these banks were allowed to issue banknotes under relatively easy conditions, the balance of issued banknotes increased dramatically. At the same time, the government also issued a large volume of government notes to fund the Seinan Civil War that began in 1877. Hyperinflation ensued, and, to turn the situation around, the government established a central bank in Japan, the BOJ, in 1882 (Type C). As a result, the private banks were forbidden to issue banknotes and the government also stopped issuing government notes, allowing the BOJ to be the sole issuer of notes. As a consequence, hyperinflation following the Seinan Civil War subsided. Hyperinflation again flared up after World War II, and, from the end of the 1980s to the beginning of the 1990s the so-called bubble economy and its subsequent bursting transpired. The BOJ was criticized for failing to implement adequate monetary policy, which failure was considered to be one of the causes behind post-war hyperinflation as well as the 1980/90s bubble economy.

The BOJ was also established to serve another purpose. That is to integrate regional financial markets, divided until the establishment of the BOJ, to facilitate financing. Ohnuki (2006) examined "the role played by the Bank of Japan in the process of financial market integration in Meiji Period Japan, using interest-rate data and documentary evidence of financial transactions." The conclusion of her study is as follows (Ohnuki, ibid, (abstract)):

> The analysis finds that, from the perspective of reducing inter-regional interest-rate differences, there was indeed significant progress towards financial integration in the latter half

of the 1890s. It also finds that the Bank of Japan may have played a role in promoting financial market integration because the expansion of its networks (correspondent network with private-sector banks and branch office network) served to facilitate the movement of funds between regions through the funds transfer services it provided.

1.3.2.2 Example in the US

In the US, historically, the establishment and dissolution of a central bank was witnessed on two occasions, and, until the establishment of the Federal Reserve System (FRS) in 1913, the country's financial system did not feature a central bank for 66 years. The first national (akin to a central bank) bank was established in 1791 under the name "The First Bank of the United States" based on a 20-year charter, but it ceased operations when it expired. In 1816, "The Second Bank of the United States" was established, also with a 20-year charter, but which was similarly dissolved when it expired. The US financial system was without a central bank (Type A) until 1913 when the FRS was established, and both a central bank and commercial banks have coexisted since (Type C).

When we look at the payment and settlement systems of the US financial system in the era that there was no central bank, while clearing houses were provided within regions, payment systems using clearing houses and checks did not exist for distant transactions. As such, settlement between distant regions relied on the transportation of cash, but the cost was extremely high. One of the major objectives in establishing the FRS was to reduce the cost of collecting bills and checks. The role has not changed thus far, and FRS (2016) holds that the central bank "Fosters payment and settlement system safety and efficiency through services to the banking industry and the US government that facilitate US-dollar transactions and payments" as one of its five objectives.

As for monetary policy implemented by the FRS, Milton Friedman and Anna Schwartz (1965) criticized the FRS saying that the Great Depression worsened as an outcome of restrictive monetary policy. Even after the stock market crashed in 1929, the FRS continued to restrict money supply and refused to take action to save banks that were struggling from bank runs. Critics charge that such an erroneous monetary policy propelled a relatively mild recession into a catastrophe. Also, some economists assert that the FRS was responsible, or at least partially, for the subprime loan housing bubble that occurred prior to the global financial crisis of 2007–09. They claim that if the FRS had not kept interest rates so low after the 2001 mini recession, the housing bubble would not have led to such a credit crunch (see Chap. 6, Sect. 6.2).

1.3.3   Three Modes of Economic Systems

Williamson (1985, 1996) defines three economic system "modes"[3]: "market mode," "hierarchy mode," which are alternative extremes, and "hybrid mode" in the middle.

Market Mode
The market is the arena in which autonomous parties engage in exchange. In market mode, transactions are made by spot (short term) contracts. The parties are in pure competition. Markets can promote high-powered incentives and restrain bureaucratic distortions more effectively than hierarchies.

Hierarchy Mode
In hierarchy mode, transactions are placed under unified ownership (buyer and supplier are the same enterprise) and are subject to administrative control, such as an authority relationship. Authority is a solution to the complex problem of coordination, and it arises out of mutual consent. Auditing/monitoring are important instruments of governance. Hierarchy mode is also referred to as 'internal organization' or 'vertical integration.'

Hybrid Mode
In hybrid mode, transactions are long-term contractual relations that preserve autonomy but provide added transaction-specific safeguards compared with the market. A franchise network is an example.

The three modes of economic systems classified by Williamson correspond to the aforementioned three types of banking systems:

Economic systems	*Banking systems*
Market mode	$\rightarrow$ Type A (no central bank)
Hierarchy mode	$\rightarrow$ Type B (central bank only)
Hybrid mode	$\rightarrow$ Type C (central bank and commercial banks)

The basic reason we can draw these parallels is as follows: while Williamson's classification assumes that components of the system are individual persons, our analysis assumes that they are individual banks. Therefore, the mode, system, or organization that we are analyzing is the entire banking system. Individual persons in the market or organizations are not the subject here. Organizations such as non-financial corporations or banks are components forming part of the banking system and can be handled as economic agents. Comparison of each type yields the following analogies.

Relation Between Market Mode and Type A
When there is no central bank, as in a Type A banking system, there are no vertical relations between commercial banks; transactions take the form of spot transactions in the market. This is the same as the relationship between market participants and the transaction methods they employ in the market mode.

---

[3] Modes are also termed 'organizations,' 'systems,' or 'institutions' in this book.

Relation Between Hierarchy Mode and Type B

This mode bears similarities to a Type B banking system in which the central bank and commercial banks are integrated into a single entity like the vertical integration that is seen in a hierarchical economic system.

Relation Between Hybrid Mode and Type C

Being a combination of the first two modes of economic systems, the hybrid mode corresponds to a Type C banking system, which is a mixture of types A and B. When we analyze transactions between a central bank and commercial banks in Sect. 1.4, we will see that they possess the nature of being both market transactions and a hierarchical relationship.

1.3.4   Transaction Costs and Modes of Economic Systems

TCE assumes that the optimum mode will be selected out of the three modes according to each institutional environment existing at the time. The basic factor in making that selection will be the relative efficiency of each mode, which is expressed in terms of transaction costs. In other words, modes evolve based on 'transaction cost-economizing' to offer the greatest efficiency. Modes are also the 'governance structure' that suppresses transaction costs; the transaction costs of a particular governance structure are considered its 'governance cost.'

The basic reason why there are transaction costs is because contracts are incomplete—they might be broken, or costs are incurred to ensure that they are not broken. Williamson (1996, p. 379) defines 'transaction cost' as "the ex ante costs of drafting, negotiating, and safeguarding a contract and, more especially, the ex post costs of maladaptation and adjustment that arise when contract execution is misaligned as a result of gaps, errors, omissions, and unanticipated disturbances."

The issue of incomplete contracts arises because the following two factors and information asymmetries[4] interlink under uncertainty. One factor is that economic agents act based on opportunism[5]; the other is that economic agents possess 'bounded rationality.'[6] When these factors are present, a contract loses its usefulness being blemished with contractual hazards, and transaction costs can thus no longer be ignored.

The concept of 'asset specificity' is a factor that has a large impact on the size of transaction costs. Williamson (ibid, p. 377) defines asset specificity as "a specialized investment that cannot be redeployed to alternative uses or by alternative users except

---

[4]Williamson (1975) uses the term "information impactedness" as a broad concept including information asymmetries. However, the term "information asymmetries" is more commonly used in microeconomics and we have adopted it in this book.

[5]"Opportunism" refers to seeking self-interest with guile, including calculated efforts to mislead, deceive, obfuscate, and otherwise confuse.

[6]'Bounded rationality' refers to behavior that is intentionally rational but only limitedly so. All complex contracts are unavoidably incomplete because of bounds on rationality.

at a loss of productive value. Asset specificity can take several forms, of which human, site, and dedicated assets are the most common. Specific assets give rise to bilateral dependency,[7] which complicates contractual relations."

1.3.5 Asset Specificity and Modes of Economic Systems

Williamson (1996) analyzes transaction costs as being "expressed as a function of asset specificity and a set of exogenous variables." Below is the relationship between different degrees of asset specificity and economic modes:

Low Degree of Asset Specificity
The transaction cost (governance cost) is lowest in the market mode and highest in the hierarchy mode. The hybrid mode is in the middle. Therefore, the market mode would be chosen to economize transaction cost.

This case also describes the economy assumed in neoclassical economics. There being no bilateral dependency, almost no hazards are involved, even in spot transactions in the market. The high-powered incentives of the markets work efficiently. On the other hand, in hierarchy mode, bureaucratic costs rise and there is little advantage in employing governance instruments, such as auditing and monitoring.

High Degree of Asset Specificity
When asset specificity is high, hierarchy mode is selected from the perspective of transaction cost economization. This is the case where serious problems occur in market mode. Governance instruments under hierarchy mode must be used to control hazards, or otherwise transaction costs become extremely high. Vertical integration has advantages that outweigh bureaucratic costs. Shifting transactions from the market to an internal organization with hierarchies, therefore, makes transaction cost economization possible.

Medium Degree of Asset Specificity
This is in between the first two cases, where hybrid mode is selected. This analysis illustrates the selection of market mode versus hierarchy mode which is really a trade-off between contractual hazard and bureaucratic cost. Therefore, the fact that neither a banking system without a central bank (market mode) nor one with only a central bank (hierarchy mode) survived, whereas a banking system where a central bank and commercial banks co-existed (hybrid mode) did survive, indicates that from the perspective of asset specificity, central bank services are provided using assets of medium specificity. To verify this will require further investigation into the backdrop of this hypothesis, entailing examination of banking transactions as units of analysis.

---

[7]The concept of "bilateral dependency" is defined as: "An ongoing dependency relation obtains between a buyer and a supplier when one or both have made durable specialized investments in support of the other. Although sometimes this condition exists from the outset (familiar bilateral monopoly condition), often it evolves during an ongoing contractual relationship. Such dependency poses contractual hazards in the face of incomplete contracting and opportunism, in response to which contractual safeguards are commonly provided" (Williamson, 1996, p. 377).

1.4 Analysis of Transaction Costs in Interbank Transactions

This section will show the reasons for the evolution and survival of the two-tiered banking system where both a central bank and commercial banks exist in the modern market economy by comparing transaction costs of the three types of banking systems.

1.4.1 Methodology

The unit of analysis in TCE being the transaction, analysis of the banking systems based on this theory should take banking transactions as the unit of analysis. In the two-tiered banking system, banking transactions can be classified into transactions with customers (individuals and non-financial firms) and interbank transactions. Since a central bank deals almost exclusively with commercial banks, it will be sufficient to analyze only interbank transactions.

This means that we will only be analyzing a central bank's function as the 'bankers' bank.' The central bank also functions as the 'bank of issue' and the 'bank for the government,' and, while these functions are deeply interrelated with 'bankers' bank' services, we have chosen to ignore them in this analysis.

Even when limiting the scope of analysis to the interbank market, the central bank is involved in a wide variety of transactions. Focus will be on two specific types: 'interbank payment transactions' and 'interbank money market transactions.' We will also analyze 'deposit transactions,' in which a commercial bank holds deposits at another commercial bank or the central bank. Deposit transactions usually involve either 'correspondent deposits' that are for making payments, or 'interbank loans' in which a deposit is made as a means of lending funds. As the first is a payment transaction and the latter a money market transaction, we have not analyzed deposit transactions separately.

1.4.2 Transaction Costs of a Banking System with No Central Bank

Our first analysis considers the transaction costs for payment transactions and money market transactions in a Type A banking system as described in Sect. 1.3. The Type A banking system corresponds to the market mode of TCE, and our analysis will assume similarities between transaction costs in this type of banking system and those in a market mode economic system.

A basic characteristic of this banking system is that commercial banks must engage in transactions in the interbank market with other commercial banks, but these same commercial banks compete with each other in the customer market. Goodhart (1988) says that there is considerable historical evidence of conflicts of interest among commercial banks. The competitive relationship means that commercial banks incur hazards when they sign contracts with one another. These hazards work as a built-in mechanism for increasing transaction costs. We may therefore conclude that this type of banking system is not viable.

1.4.2.1 Transaction Costs of Interbank Payment Transactions

Asset Specificity of the Interbank Payment System
Even in a banking system that does not have a central bank, there is still need for interbank funds transfers between commercial banks. Commercial banks will be asked to send funds from their customers to the customers of another bank, and they will also need to settle funds traded on the interbank money market. Assuming that there is some form of cash—say, pieces of gold—even if there are no central bank notes, then settlements will to some extent be possible by physically transporting cash. This is, however, inconvenient when large value funds transfers are involved. Banks are therefore likely to come up with the idea of establishing a clearing house; indeed, clearing houses were in fact established in banking systems that did not have central banks.[8] Or a specific bank might serve as the "central commercial bank" (Goodhart, 1988), with payment services provided via deposit accounts with that bank.

The asset specificity of interbank payment systems like clearing houses is extremely high because it is difficult to redeploy the dedicated physical assets (including computer software) of the payment system to other purposes. In addition, payment system experts have a high degree of 'human asset specificity' since they learn their jobs through 'hands on' work. Another factor with respect to asset specificity is 'brand name capital' which reflects a system's reputation.

Contractual Hazards Attaching to Payment Transactions
Given the high asset specificity of the payment system, the contractual hazards discussed in Sect. 1.3 are inherent for both the providers and buyers of services.

Hazards for Service Providers
One hazard that providers of payment services face is that after having heavily invested in a system, they might lose customers (commercial banks) to another payment system before they can recover investment costs. There is high asset specificity because it is difficult to redeploy the physical assets and human resources invested in a system. This is particularly true for computer-based payment systems because there is practically no possibility of redeploying software developed (for payment services) to other purposes.

---

[8]The New York Clearing House was in operation before the US Federal Reserve System was established.

The reason why providers may lose most of their customers is because, as TCE teaches, the action of customers is governed by opportunism. Because of bounded rationality, providers are unable to design contracts to completely prevent this. One strong incentive for customers to act opportunistically is that the provider of the service is itself a commercial bank, thus a competitor. Historically, there have been cases of systems with no central bank having a large commercial bank act as a central commercial bank in providing correspondent banking services including payment services. The hazards we described were inherent in these systems. Nor are they completely avoided by having a bankers' association own and manage the payment system (clearing house) because it is also a group of competitors (see Sect. 1.6.2).

Hazards for Customers
There are also hazards for the customers (commercial banks) in a payment system that lacks a central bank. When a commercial bank utilizes a specific payment system, it adapts its computer systems and operational procedures to that system. It would therefore incur substantial damage should the provider of the system suddenly cease to provide services for whatever reason or should the customer commercial bank be discriminatorily refused services. Further, even if services continue, it has little choice but to pay service charges if a hike is demanded.

These hazards are high when services are received as part of correspondent banking services provided by a central commercial bank, because the service provider is a competitor. The central commercial bank is likely to act opportunistically, but the customer commercial bank will, because of bounded rationality, be unable to design a contract that entirely prevents this. Like the provider hazards, the customer hazards are not completely alleviated by having a bankers' association own and manage the payment system (clearing house) because the bankers' association is a group of competitors (see Sect. 1.6.2).

Even if the provider does not intentionally stop services, they may be brought to a halt by bankruptcy. When a central commercial bank provides payment services, the hazards are further compounded by the credit risk attaching to the deposits held with it for settlements. Any payment system that does not use real time gross settlement (RTGS) will also incur systemic risk because bankruptcy or failure to make payment by one customer commercial bank could adversely affect a large number of customer commercial banks. If the service provider also provides liquidity support, these risks could be prevented from emerging, but the provider is also a competitor and may selectively refuse liquidity support to specific customers for competitive purposes. This is related to the arguments concerning interbank money market transactions that will be discussed in Sect. 1.4.2.2.

Governance Structures of Payment Transactions
There are basically two types of governance structure to deal with these hazards. The first is to use bilateral correspondent accounts. Commercial banks remain competitors, but they open accounts with each other ('nostro' and 'vostro' accounts) to facilitate interbank payments without having to depend on a specific commercial bank (central commercial bank). This governance structure corresponds to the "cred-

ible commitment"[9] described by Williamson (1985, 1996). Since both hold accounts of the other, contractual violation by one commercial bank can be responded to in tit-for-tat fashion by the other.

This method was actually used in banking systems that had no central bank (the US prior to the establishment of the FRS) and also in systems in which the central bank did not provide sufficient interbank payment services (before establishment of the BOJ, the Kyrgyz Republic after independence).

But this is extremely inefficient. It requires commercial banks to open correspondent accounts with a large number of other commercial banks and maintain idle balances for payments. The banks must also use different procedures for payment transactions involving different banks. This raises transaction costs.

The other structure is to establish a bank that does not compete with commercial banks (i.e., a central bank), and use it as a payment service provider. This banking system corresponds to types B and C (systems with central banks) in Sect. 1.3.

1.4.2.2 Transaction Costs of Interbank Money Market Transactions

Information Asymmetries of Money Market Transactions
Money market transactions are a type of interbank transaction in which a commercial bank with a surplus lends money to a commercial bank with a shortage. Compared to payment transactions, this type of transaction has low 'physical' asset specificity. There is not that much in the way of physical assets that needs to be dedicated to these transactions. In point of fact, the market for these transactions is well-known and called the interbank money market.

But this is for a money market transaction in a normal situation. In an abnormal situation, information asymmetries between a lender bank and a borrower bank lead to extremely high 'informational' asset specificity for money market transactions. Thus, money market transactions are not made in the interbank money market in an abnormal situation. A money market transaction in an abnormal situation is, for example, when concern about the financial condition of a particular borrower bank is high, or a borrower bank is obliged to suddenly borrow a large amount just before market closing time.

Information asymmetries are a significant problem for money market transactions in such abnormal situations. A lender bank does not have as much information regarding a borrower bank's ability to repay as the borrower bank itself has (i.e., information is distributed asymmetrically between the lender bank and borrower bank). Not having enough information about the borrower bank's financial situation, the lender bank may refuse the loan on the basis of rumors that the borrower bank

---

[9]Williamson (1996, p. 377) defines a "credible commitment" as "a contract in which a promise is reliably compensated should the promisor prematurely terminate or otherwise alter the agreements. This should be contrasted with noncredible commitments which are empty promises and semicredible commitments in which there is a residual hazard. Credible commitments are pertinent to contracts in which one or both parties invest in specific assets."

is close to bankruptcy, even thought it might not be, because the lender bank has no way to judge the truth or falsehood of the rumors.

To deal with this problem, prospective borrower banks must dedicate the following resources to assets with high specificity. First, they must inform possible lender banks about their management conditions, even in a normal situation. Vice versa, possible lender banks must audit and monitor prospective borrower banks in order to accumulate information. Because this information that the lender banks demand is not general information, asset specificity of the information is high. Second, prospective lender banks must build a long-term relationship with the prospective borrower banks. Since this relationship cannot be redeployed to others, asset specificity of the relationship is high. Third, prospective borrower banks might provide collateral to prospective lender banks. Shifting collateral that has been pledged to one lender bank to another is not easy. In this sense, asset specificity of collateral is high.

Contractual Hazards of Money Market Transactions in Abnormal Situation
As mentioned, prospective borrower banks must dedicate assets with high specificity and, moreover, even if a contract for money market transactions is signed, it is difficult to ensure that this will be a complete contract. The lender bank may act opportunistically and suddenly demand that the contract be interpreted much more strictly, or might even refuse to lend at all. Due to bounded rationality, the borrower bank will be unable to design a contract that completely covers every imaginable situation, and, given the time value of money, there is no time to take the issue to court. Also, it is difficult for the borrower bank to shift the dedicated assets from the lender bank to another bank in a short period of time considering the high specificity of assets, which means that the borrower bank faces a bilateral dependency problem with the possible lender bank.

To make matters worse, there are incentives for the lender bank to refuse loans. The lender bank and the borrower bank compete with each other in the customer market, so the lender bank will tend to want the borrower bank to go under. Goodhart (1988, p. 38) says the following about this attitude among commercial banks in correspondent relationships:

> Moreover, there may always be, or it may be feared that there would be, a temptation for the central commercial banks to take the opportunity of a crisis to force a competitor out of business by not providing the loans/assistance that in more normal times a correspondent could have expected as a natural concomitant of the relationship.

Governance Structure of Money Market Transactions in Abnormal Situations
As was not the case for payment transactions, for the borrower bank it is impossible to find a credible commitment to avoid these hazards. The only way is to set up a bank that does not compete with commercial banks (i.e., a central bank), and borrow from it. This is the lender of last resort (LLR) function that central banks provide. This banking system corresponds to types B and C in Sect. 1.3.1 (systems with central banks).

1.4.3 Transaction Costs of a Banking System with Central Bank Only

In this part we analyze the transaction cost associated with a Type B banking system as described in Sect. 1.3.1. The Type B banking system corresponds to the hierarchy mode (internal organization) in TCE and can therefore be assumed to have similar transaction costs. In this type of banking system, all transactions are considered to be internal transactions in a single organization.

1.4.3.1 Advantages Over Commercial Banks Only System

Let us first examine some of transaction costs advantages this system has over a banking system in which there is no central bank (Type A).

In this banking system, payment transactions involve no hazards for either the provider or the customer of services since they are both part of the same bank. In other words, there is no risk that customers will move to another payment system before invested costs can be recovered, or that the provider will suddenly cut one off from services. Likewise, there are no credit risks stemming from the possible bankruptcy of the provider or systemic risks from the bankruptcy of a customer.

In this system, the relationship between the head office and branches of a single bank may correspond to that between providers and customers. One of its advantages is that the "internal organization can be more effectively audited" (Williamson, 1975, p. 29) should there be improprieties. Likewise, "when differences do arise, internal organization realizes an advantage over market mediated exchange in dispute settling respects." (ibid, p. 29).

Meanwhile, in money market transactions, the fact that this is a single bank turns interbank money market transactions into 'inter-branch money market transactions.' There need be no prior contracts to provide for a loan from branches with a surplus to those with a shortage. Money market transactions can be engaged in flexibly according to circumstances. As Williamson (ibid, p. 25) says, "Internal organization often has attractive properties in that it permits the parties to deal with uncertainty/complexity in an adaptive, sequential fashion without incurring the same types of opportunism hazards that market contracting would pose."

1.4.3.2 Disadvantages Compared with the Other Types

The most serious problem with respect to this type of banking system is bureaucracy costs. In a commercial bank only system where there is no central bank, competition among commercial banks provides the "high-powered incentives of markets" (Williamson, 1996). But in the central bank only case, there is no competition and therefore no incentive to be efficient; high-powered incentives are necessarily degraded when transactions move from Type A and Type C to Type B banking systems. This causes bureaucracy costs to rise, and potentially to exceed the advantages just discussed. In this connection, Williamson (ibid) suggested the reason why the central bank only system could not survive as "almost surely, the added costs of bureaucracy are responsible for limitations in firm size."

1.4.4   Transaction Costs of a Banking System with Both Central Bank and Commercial Banks

Finally, we will analyze the transaction costs for Type C banking systems. Type C corresponds to the hybrid mode in TCE, so we will assume that the transaction cost analysis of the hybrid mode can be applied.

This type of banking system is a mixture of types A and B, combining the strong points of both. It appears that at the current time only this type of system has survived. The two-tiered banking system corresponds to the hybrid mode economic system, of which Williamson (1996, p. 107) has said, "…the hybrid mode is located between market and hierarchy with respect to incentives, adaptability, and bureaucratic costs. As compared with the market, the hybrid sacrifices incentives in favor of superior coordination among the parts. As compared with the hierarchy, the hybrid sacrifices cooperativeness in favor of greater incentive intensity."

Certainly, this type of banking system provides for competition among commercial banks, but the central bank does not compete with them. This is what Goodhart (1988) describes as "a noncompetitive non-profit-maximizing role that marked the true emergence and development of proper Central Banking."

In other words, the central bank is the provider of services for payment transactions, while commercial banks are the customers of services. Even though the central bank and commercial banks are different entities, they do not compete with each other, which makes it possible to avoid the hazard seen in Type A that customers will shift to another payment system before the costs invested in the system are recovered. Likewise, there is no possibility that the provider (central bank) will suddenly cut off customers from services for any reason. The credit risk of bankruptcy for the central bank is also non-existent. At most, credit risks involve the problems raised by the bankruptcy of an individual commercial bank. This the central bank can also prevent, to some extent, by using its supervisory functions to audit and monitor commercial banks in much the same way as internal sections are audited in hierarchy mode. The LLR function of the central bank can provide liquidity support to a troubled bank in order to prevent systemic risk.

As for money market transactions, the auditing and monitoring functions of the central bank also relieve to a great extent information asymmetry issues. As a supervisory organization, the central bank is able to use its auditing and monitoring functions during normal times to gain information about financial conditions at commercial banks. Should a commercial bank require a large sum of money that it is unable to borrow on the interbank money market, the central bank is able to provide the loan as the LLR. Obviously, as a noncompetitive, non-profit-maximizing organization, the central bank has no incentive to drive the borrower bank out of business, and, as the bank of issue, the central bank enjoys an unlimited supply of funds.

The Type B banking system also has these advantages, but Type C combines them with the high-powered incentives of the market that Type B does not have. This is because the central bank and commercial banks do not compete, but commercial banks compete with each other. Compared to both A and B, Type C is clearly more efficient in terms of transaction costs. This is because Type C is the best governance structure of banking systems given the degree of asset specificity of interbank transactions. In other words, the banking system is one in which commercial banks engage in fair competition under the high-powered incentives of the market, while the central bank uses its auditing and monitoring functions to gather appropriate information on commercial banks, and provides required payment and lending services.

As we have discussed above, we must conclude that the superiority of their transaction costs compared to the other types is the reason why central banks exist in a two-tiered banking system. In the future, there may be new banking systems that evolve so as to adapt to new institutional environments and the economization of transaction costs will be a key factor determining what these systems will look like.

1.5 Importance of Institutional Environment and Recent Changes

Section 1.3.5 introduced Williamson's theory that considered asset specificity as one of the key factors that determines mode of economic system, and, based on such recognition, explanation is made that asset specificity determines type of banking system in Sect. 1.4. This Section provides explanation of the institutional environment that has strong influence over central bank asset specificity. Then, four recent changes in the institutional environment are discussed.

1.5.1 Institutional Environment and its Influence

1.5.1.1 What is "Institutional Environment"?

"Institutional environment" is a concept formulated by Williamson (1996, 2000),—it is a formal rule of the game that determines governance structure such as property law and contract law. Williamson also notes that there are informal rules that build the foundation of such formal rules, namely, customs, traditions, culture, and religion. He calls them "embeddedness," but, in this book, we will not differentiate between the two and regard them comprehensively as the institutional environment. Under a certain institutional environment, transaction cost is determined, and, in turn, to economize such transaction cost, the mode of economic system, governance mechanism, and degree of diversification are determined.

1.5.1.2 Main Effect of Institutional Environment on Transaction Cost

Transaction cost is a concept corresponding to production cost and encompasses various costs such as cost to collect information and cost to have a party sign a contract and implement it. Coase (1937) was the first to point out the importance of transaction cost but it was Williamson (1975, 1985, 1996, 2013) who analyzed it in detail and classified what generates it into four factors. And, by clarifying the relationship among the factors he made transaction cost economics operational. The four factors generating transaction cost are:

- human behavioral factor (bounded rationality, opportunism).
- transaction factor (asset specificity, uncertainty including complexity, and transaction frequency including limited number of transaction counterparts).
- fundamental factor (uneven distribution of information, atmosphere <Williamson provided the concept of "atmosphere" which is very similar to organizational culture in his book of 1975 (see Chap. 4, Sect. 4.5.1.2)>).
- intra-organizational factor (incentive, bureaucracy cost).

All of these factors change through various routes once a change in institutional environment occurs, which in turn changes transaction cost structure and also asset specificity as well as degree of central bank diversification.

1.5.2 Recent Major Changes in the Institutional Environment

The following four changes in the institutional environment have influenced governance structure and diversification of central banks.

1.5.2.1 Emergence of Serious Financial Crises

The most important change in the institutional environment surrounding central banks is the repeated occurrence of serious financial crises that were unprecedented since World War II. In the latter half of the 1990s, the Asian financial crisis and financial crisis in Japan emerged. And, starting from the subprime loan problem in 2007, the Lehman shock was seen in 2008 which then developed into a global financial crisis. Moreover, in 2009, the Greek financial crisis prompted the emergence of the European debt crisis in 2010–12.

Such repeated occurrence of financial crises affected central banks in various ways. First, the importance of a central bank's prudential policy such as regulatory and supervisory function as well as function to maintain financial system stability became widely recognized (refer to Chap. 5, Sect. 5.4). Second, political pressure over central bank independence increased. One of the specificities of a central bank's organizational structure is central bank independence and this forms part of the core competence of a central bank. Such central bank independence was strengthened around the world in the 1990s having experienced inflation and the bubble economy during the 1970s to 1980s. However, against the background of the rise of populism in politics in addition to financial crises, currently there is a strong urge from the political side for central banks to implement monetary easing and offer financial support, e.g. the Abe administration in Japan (refer to Chap. 3, Sect. 3.4.2.1, vote-maximization behavior hypothesis and politicians).

1.5.2.2 International Cooperation and Competition Among Central Banks Through Development of Global Financial Markets (See Sect. 1.6.1)

In recent years, with the development of global financial markets and increase in the international activities of financial institutions, the impact of financial crises has also become globalized. This is an important change in the institutional environment that affects the diversification of central banks. While central bank services are basically provided within the borders of a bank's home country, financial market participants such as financial institutions, who are recipients of such services, are not necessarily confined to domestic financial markets. And, what is more, domestic financial markets are now closely connected with global financial markets.

Such a situation is the cause of various issues that are arising both in domestic and global financial systems. For example, a central bank that acts as LLR in domestic financial systems does not exist for the global financial system, and therefore it is difficult to prevent a global financial crisis by providing international liquidity compared to the case of a domestic financial system. Since the impact of monetary policy spills over to global financial markets and, on the other hand, the trends of global financial markets influence domestic financial markets, it is becoming impossible for a central bank to make decisions on monetary policy and its various functions based only on domestic financial and economic conditions.

One way for central banks to cope with such a change in the institutional environment is to establish a supranational central bank within regions and merge the currencies as in the case of the ECB. To be more extreme, if we could establish a 'Global Central Bank,' many of the issues facing global financial markets could be solved. However, numerous obstacles stand in the way of establishing a supranational central bank that exist above the various national sovereignties and central banks (currencies) involved. Thus, it is considered practically impossible to realize such a supranational central bank even within an interrelated region (for example Asian countries), let alone a 'Global Central Bank.' Therefore, realistically speaking, to at least mitigate the problem, not to say the entire problem, it is all the more necessary for central banks to cooperate with one another. From a different perspective, this means that each central bank should enhance its central bank functions on an international basis and, through developing the network integration[10] of various central banks, we could suppress transaction cost and realize both economies of scale and economies of scope.

Changes in the institutional environment such as development of global financial markets prompt central banks to cooperate with one another, but at the same time, they intensify competition among them. From the perspective of global market participants, it implies that they are given more choices, i.e., they can choose safer, more inexpensive and user-friendly central bank banking services from among various central banks. Moreover, users have more of a free hand in deciding which currency to hold and use. As a result, central banks are placed under market pressure which prevents inefficiency that accompanies organizational expansion. At the same time, such market pressure will also provide an incentive for central banks to offer safer and more user-friendly banking services.

1.5.2.3   Development of Information Technology

The development of information technology is having a big impact on every aspect of society and the economy. This significant change in the institutional environment is expected to have various effects on financial transactions and eventually central bank functions for years to come. As the impact is huge and may well last for a long period of time, we cannot foresee at this point how it might influence the boundaries of central bank organization. But there is already a sign of the impact. For example, changes in central bank settlement services, such as the computerization of payment and settlement systems, and the development of electronic money that may substitute for or compete against cash currency (i.e., banknotes and coins, see Chap. 7, Sect. 7.2.2.3).

1.5.2.4   Changes in Human Behavioral Factor

The opportunistic behavior of humans that Williamson (1985) supposes as behavior of "contractual man" brings about change in the institutional environment in the form of changes in tradition and culture in the long run. This may affect the diversification of central bank organization. If, for example, the tendency for politicians to take opportunistic behavior increases, central bank governance will need to change as well. In some cases, society may strongly urge that the aspect of 'governance as probity' (see Chap. 3, footnote 3) should attach to a central bank and that the bank may need to broaden the boundaries of its organization (of course, vice versa, it may need to narrow its boundaries). Whatever the case, if embeddedness (such as customs, tradition, norms, and religion), which is considered the most fundamental factor by Williamson (2000), changes, so do the boundaries of a central bank.

---

[10]According to Williamson's definition (1985), this is one type of hybrid mode of governance that is placed between the market and the organization.

1.6   Implications for Institutional Issues of Central Banks

We have been able to use TCE to provide a theoretical explanation for the existence of central banks. We will now try to apply TCE to some issues central banks face today given the change of institutional environment in the Sect. 1.5.2.

1.6.1   Evolution of a Supranational Central Bank

1.6.1.1   Issue Identification

Up until now, a central bank has existed within the banking system of a specific country. In other words, the central bank of one country does not open branches in another country, offering central bank services through them. Central banks have been defined as 'national central banks' (NCBs) and there has been no 'supranational central bank' (SCB). In contrast to central banks, large commercial banks do cross national borders to set up branches and offer banking services. They are not limited to a specific country. As a result, interbank transactions cross national borders too. This has been even more so the case in recent years as financial globalization has enabled cross-border transactions to flourish.

The questions for us, in the context of financial globalization, are: (a) What international financial services should central banks offer? And, (b) Why is cooperation among them necessary? We will examine these questions applying the theoretical conclusion for the rationale of central banks discussed in Sects. 1.3 and 1.4.

1.6.1.2   Solution of Issues

The TCE of central banks implies that central banks will need to globalize in response to the globalization of financial markets. As we have seen, central banks evolved to economize transaction costs in the interbank market. But, while financial markets have globalized—many interbank transactions now cross national borders—central bank services have not. Therefore, what we have is a global market with no central bank services, resulting in large transaction costs to the global banking system, just as with the commercial banks only system.[11]

Many of the problems encountered in the global banking system are easy to understand when viewed in the following terms. For example, 'Herstatt risk'[12] comes

---

[11]Oritani (1991a) pointed out the globalization of risks resulting from the globalization of payment networks.

[12]On 26th June 1974, Herstatt Bank had received deutschmarks from some of its counterparties, which expected to receive their side of the transaction in US dollars later in the day. However, Herstatt's banking licence was revoked due to insolvency and all outgoing USD payments were suspended. Although the counterparties had fulfilled their obligations to Herstatt, the bank was

about in cross-border interbank settlements because two currencies involved in a foreign exchange transaction cannot be settled by one central bank (see Chap. 7, Sect. 7.3). Or, there is the question of who, in the context of interbank borrowing and lending, is to provide liquidity support to overseas branches of commercial banks—the central bank where the branch is located (the host central bank), or the central bank where the head office is located (the home central bank)? A similar question could be put with respect to which central bank is responsible for monitoring the foreign branches of commercial banks.

1.6.1.3 Globalization of Central Banks

In order to deal with these problems and economize transaction costs in the overall global banking system (i.e., to economize the transaction cost of interbank trans-actions in global markets), a new type of central bank will need to evolve, just as it did within the banking system of one country. This new central bank will be a 'supranational central bank' or SCB, rather than a central bank within the banking system of a specific country (national central bank, NCB). TCE yields the following insights into the SCB concept.

Three-Tiered Banking System
Figure 1.4 illustrates the basic hierarchical structure of a global banking system with an SCB. There are three distinct tiers because an SCB is added to the two-tiered banking system. As this structure is only a prototype, the variations below are possible.

Central Bank Cooperation
We do not necessarily expect that an SCB will, from the beginning, be an established central bank integrating all NCBs. Rather, the degree of integration will gradually rise keeping pace with the globalization of financial transactions, with the establishment of an SCB as the ultimate goal. Over the course of time, central banks will cooperate to provide substitute services that the SCB will eventually be able to provide. We have already seen how there are two types of banking systems, depending on whether there is full integration between commercial banks and the central bank (fully integrated systems are Type B and non-fully integrated ones, Type C). Similarly, there can be many variations in the degree of integration between an SCB and NCBs in the international banking system.[13]

---

closed down before being able to make the offsetting payments. The counterparties lost the entire value of their payments to Herstatt, resulting in three days' disruption to FX settlements in New York.

[13]When an SCB and NCBs are not fully integrated, there will be competition among NCBs. For example, NCBs may compete to gain wider usage of their respective currencies and settlement systems in global markets so they can enjoy greater seignorage. However, competition will not be as intense as that between commercial banks because NCBs have little, if any, pressure to pursue the profit motive.

Fig. 1.4 Three-tiered
banking system

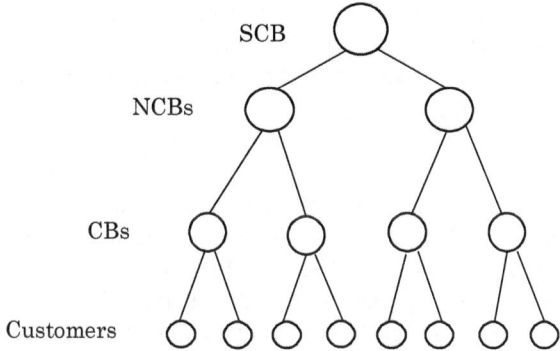

SCB: Supranational Central Bank

NCB: National Central Bank

CB: Commercial Bank

Regional SCBs and/or Central Bank Cooperation

We also do not expect that there will, from the beginning, be just one global central bank that covers all the countries in the world. Rather, expectations are that SCBs will be established in regions where central bank cooperation is already advanced, with financial market linkages then becoming stronger before a single global central bank is established.[14]

1.6.1.4 Developments

These trends are evidenced by recent events, the most forceful of which is the establishment of the ECB and ESCB in 1998. The aim of the ECB is that it becomes the SCB for Europe. The globalization of financial transactions within the area had already resulted in the gradual strengthening of cooperation between the NCBs of EMU members, which have reached a level of integration of NCBs, the ultimate form of cooperation. The ECB linked the payment and settlement systems of NCBs to provide payment services (known as 'TARGET') and supplies them with liquidity.[15] It also serves as the bank of issue, printing the 'euro.' And, the ECB has integrated banking supervision responsibilities for the euro area (see Chap. 5, Sect. 5.4.3.1).

Though not in a true sense, the Bank for International Settlements (BIS), established in 1930, provides services as both an SCB and a forum for central bank cooperation. Recent trends towards globalization in financial markets have caused it to reinforce those services. As an SCB, it provides investment services for the

---

[14]This corresponds to the optimal currency area theory. While the theory focuses on currency, our concept emphasizes the central bank as a 'bankers' bank' rather than the 'bank of issue.'

[15]Oritani (1991b) pointed out the importance of payment system linkages among EU members for success of the European Monetary Union.

foreign reserves of NCBs and functions as an LLR to NCBs experiencing liquidity problems. As a forum for central bank cooperation, it has been instrumental in
many areas including banking supervision, coordinating regulations on issues such
as capital adequacy.

An example of the substitute services provided by central bank cooperation that
an SCB will eventually provide is payment system linkages between NCBs, or a
'payment versus payment system' (PVP system). A PVP system enables the simultaneous settlement of two currencies involved in foreign exchange transactions and
reduces Herstatt risk. The CLS Bank has already started PVP payment services;
however, the CLS Bank is owned by a kind of bankers' association and central banks
can also provide such services by linking their RTGSs (see Chap. 7, Sect. 7.3).

1.6.2   Bankers' Associations Versus Central Banks

1.6.2.1   Issue Identification

In the banking system of most countries, commercial banks have organized bankers'
associations,[16] which are similar to central banks in that they provide services all
commercial banks require. A central bank should probably be seen as the 'guardian of
the bankers' club.' Its services as a bankers' bank are neither private goods nor public
goods; rather, they are 'club goods'[17] as will be discussed in Chap. 2, Sect. 2.2.2.

The service of bankers' associations that most interests us is the interbank payment
facility. It has long been common practice for bankers' associations to run clearing
houses. In most countries, bankers' associations today operate 'automated clearing
houses' (ACHs) utilizing computers. This has led to a debate with respect to payment
system policy as to who should provide ACH services (see Chap. 7, Sect. 7.2.2)
and/or the international payment system (see Chap. 7, Sect. 7.3), the private sector
(bankers' associations) or central banks. Debate has for the most part focused on risks,
noting that they are higher for netting provided by clearing houses because, unlike
the payment services of central banks, they have no finality. It is also necessary to
compare the nature of the two organizations, bankers' associations and central banks,
that provide payment services.

In addition to payment services, bankers' associations provide services similar to
the banking supervision of central banks, setting regulations among members. Corresponding to the LLR function of central banks is the signing of mutual assistance
agreements, providing for the extension of emergency loans to one another. Some
bankers' associations, such as the central institutions of credit unions, have also
been established to pool the deposits taken in by their members for joint investment.

---

[16]For our purposes, a 'bankers' association' does not need to be so named. Any organized association, joint-stock bank, or similar institution to which commercial banks (deposit-taking institutions)
belong or in which they have invested is considered a 'bankers' association' in this book.

[17]Goodhart (1988, p. 69) described the central bank as "arbiter of bank clubs."

Services provided by bankers' associations that are not provided by central banks include the exchange of information and training for member employees.

The questions raised are: What is the difference between a bankers' association and a central bank? Or, in what sense are bankers' associations regarded as 'private sector entities'? And, what sort of division of labor should exist between a bankers' association and a central bank? It will therefore be worthwhile to examine the two organizations, bankers' associations and central banks, in terms of TCE, especially in the provision of payment services.

1.6.2.2 Peer Group Theory

Chapter 3 of Williamson (1975), "Peer Groups and Simple Hierarchies," uses TCE to analyze peer groups and peer group associations. He defines 'peer group association' as a perfectly flat organization that, although not a market, does not recognize any hierarchies among members. Therefore, a peer group association is a kind of hybrid mode, but close to the market mode. In analyzing employment relations, he explains peer group association as a kind of "non-market organization" that "may have attractive properties in relation to the market." He also analyzes the choice between peer groups or simple hierarchies. As was defined in Sect. 1.3.3, 'markets' signify spot transactions in the markets and 'simple hierarchies' long-term relationships in the internal organization.

As was studied in Sects. 1.3.1 and 1.3.3, we can regard banking systems without central banks as markets, bankers' associations as peer group associations, and central banks as simple hierarchies, which enables us to adopt Williamson's peer group theory to compare bankers' associations and central banks.

Advantages of Peer Group Associations
Williamson (ibid) argues that there are three advantages to the services of peer group associations compared to spot transactions in the markets:

Indivisibility
Economies of scale are gained in terms of the physical assets and information that members acquire, which makes it advantageous to organize peer group associations.

Risk Bearing
There will be a kind of insurance in the form of providing income guarantees to buffer the effect of unanticipated contingencies on members.

Involvement Relations Between Group Members
This refers to productivity increases among members who feel a sense of responsibility to do their fair share as members of the group. In other words, the members tend to contribute to the joint interests of the group voluntarily based on a kind of friendship. Peer group associations enable valuable 'involvement relations' that are upset, in some degree, by hierarchies. As the degree of hierarchy increases, involvement relations become less pronounced. In other words, the degree of bureaucracy increases.

Limitations of Peer Group Associations
However, peer group associations do have their limitations because of the following
reasons and these limitations prevent the group from fully displacing other modes of
organization, according to Williamson (ibid):

Limitations to the Communication of Information
A peer group association is limited for reasons of bounded rationality with respect to
both communication and decision-making. Figure 1.5(a) illustrates the information
processing that occurs in a peer group association. It is an 'all-channel network.'
Everything should be communicated to everyone and joint decisions reached. Since
the number of linkages in all-channel networks increases as the square of members,
the size of a peer group association is inevitably restricted. These limitations become
serious when disputes between members must be settled or when the peer group
association attempts to adapt to new circumstances. If, for example, a leader is chosen
in order to resolve these issues, then the association becomes essentially the same as
a hierarchy. It will in any case have to face the trade-off between performance and
peer group democracy.

Loose Auditing and Monitoring
A free-rider problem is inevitable in peer group associations since opportunism and
information asymmetries exist among members. Indeed, we might go so far as to
say that peer group associations are vulnerable to free-rider abuses because the peer
group is inherently limited as an auditing and monitoring instrument. If the peer
group tries to perform the necessary audits, it would violate both the letter and spirit
of the peer group, which would, in turn, negate involvement relations, one of the
most important advantages of a peer group association.

Competition Problems
Williamson does not directly lead with competition in his peer group theory, but,
following his TCE (discussed in Sect. 1.3.3), it is reasonable to conclude that there
will be inevitable competitor-problem limitations similar to the market mode. This
is because peer group associations are flat organizations whose members are also
competitors and who may be just as opportunistic in their activities as they are in
their market transactions.

Fig. 1.5 Information flow
network (Williamson, 1975)

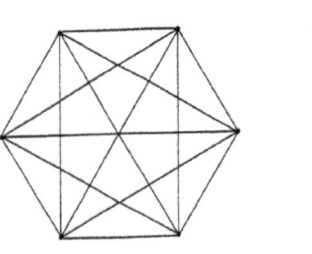

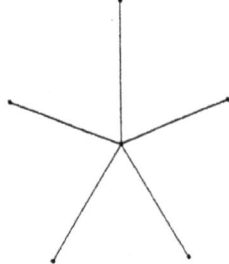

(a) All-Channel Network   (b)Wheel Network

Advantages of Hierarchies

Williamson (ibid) points out the advantages of hierarchies in comparison with the limitations of peer group associations:

Economies of Information

Hierarchical organizations make it cheaper and more efficient to transmit all information because both information and decision-making are centralized. This is illustrated in Fig. 1.5(b), which shows that supplanting the all-channel network in a peer group association with a wheel network (in which each member is connected only with the center) yields savings in terms of both information transmission and decision-making.

Auditing and Monitoring

Hierarchies have clear advantages because a supervisor is assigned the task of auditing. Auditing serves to overcome opportunism and information asymmetries, and also solves the free-rider problem.

Fair Treatment of Competitors

While Williamson (ibid) does not treat this point specifically, 'leaders' or 'coordinators' in a hierarchy mode are not in a competitive relationship with members (unlike the relationship among the members of a peer group association) and therefore have the advantage of being able to treat competitors fairly.

Choice of Peer Group Association or Hierarchy

In the real world, a choice must be made between peer group association or hierarchy as to which mode of organization best serves the purpose of economizing transaction costs.

Williamson (ibid) says, "It would appear that the simple hierarchy can do everything the peer group can do and more." And to the question, "What then prevents the peer group from being fully displaced by a simple hierarchy?", he suggests "involvement relations" as the main reason. As we have already noted, when the degree of hierarchy increases, involvement relations become less pronounced and therefore the degree of bureaucracy increases. Along with it, bureaucracy costs increase.

Figure 1.6 provides a simple illustration of this relationship. As the degree of hierarchy increases, the costs inherent in peer group associations (information cost, loose auditing and monitoring cost, and cost associated with competition problems) declines (Line P). However, at the same time, involvement relations also diminish, so bureaucracy costs increase (Line H). Therefore, the optimum degree of hierarchy h is determined at the point of minimum cost c according to the nature of the transaction.

From a different viewpoint, this indicates that a hierarchical organization might be superior to a peer group association. Even with a higher degree of hierarchy, if involvement relations are strengthened, bureaucracy costs do not rise. This would involve the downward shift of Line H to Line H' in the Fig. 1.6, therefore, the optimum degree of hierarchy h would shift to h* and the minimum cost c would shift to c*. On the other hand, it is difficult for a peer group association to take advantage of hierarchical organization for the purpose of reducing costs inherent within itself. This is because even a very small degree of hierarchy goes against the essential nature

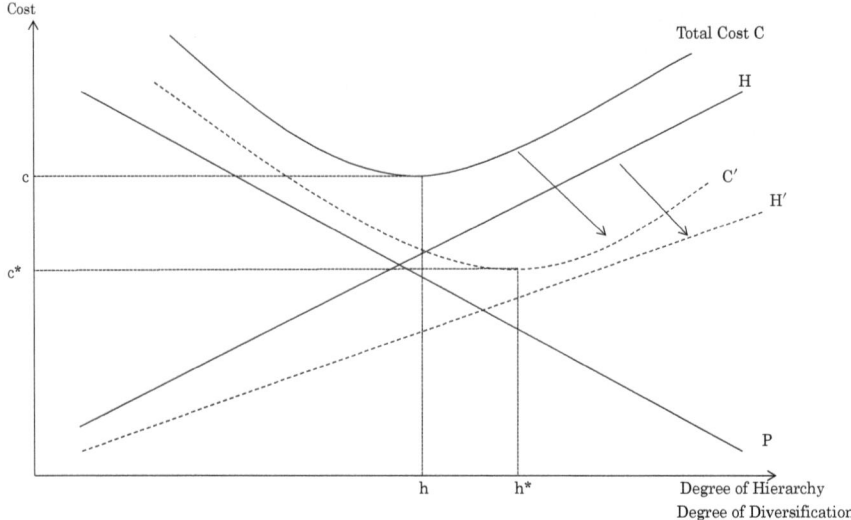

Fig. 1.6 Relationship between bureaucracy cost and the degree of hierarchy/diversification

of the organization i.e., involvement relations. According to Williamson (ibid), the introduction of leaders and auditing to peer group association are understood as "whatever it may be called, it is functionally equivalent to introducing hierarchy."

1.6.2.3 Application to Banking Systems

It can be easily understood from the foregoing peer group theory that a bankers' association is a kind of peer group association. However, it may require some explanation to understand that a central bank is a hierarchy. In Sect. 1.4.4 we saw the banking system with both a central bank and commercial banks as a hybrid mode economic system located somewhere between the market mode and hierarchy mode. However, when comparing the two organizations, a bankers' association and a central bank, a central bank has a considerably higher degree of hierarchy in its relations with commercial banks than it does with a bankers' association. Unlike the bankers' association, commercial banks do not control the management of the central bank, nor are central bank executives chosen directly from among commercial bankers. In addition, most central banks also function as the supervisor of commercial banks (see Sect. 1.6.3 and Chap. 5, Sect. 5.4).

Let us proceed from this analogy to examine the advantages and limitations of bankers' associations, and the advantages of central banks.

Advantages of Bankers' Associations
The three advantages that Williamson found for peer group associations appear to apply to bankers' associations as well:

Indivisibility
There are obvious economies of scale associated with payment systems such as clearing houses. There are also economies of scale in information, which is why members use bankers' associations to exchange information and train staff.

Risk Bearing
For example, in Japan, regional bankers associations have a mutual assistance fund endowed with contributions from members. Should a member bank experience business difficulties, it can turn to the fund for financial assistance.

Involvement Relations
Although the positive impact of involvement relations on members' management policies is unmeasurable, one can assume that if there were no positive effects bankers' associations would not be viable.

Limitations of Bankers' Associations
Limitations on the Communication of Information
   As with peer group associations, this could be a serious problem for bankers' associations, but generally it is not too serious by means of appointing leaders and executives to centralize information and decision-making. Naturally, this brings a corresponding diminution in involvement relations, and some amount of bureaucratic slack is indeed observed in most bankers' associations.

Loose Auditing and Monitoring
Many bankers' associations formulate self-discipline and regulations, but few are strict. In almost no cases do they perform on-site examination. As Goodhart (1988, p. 103) says, there are "doubts whether the group of central commercial banks, or the clearing house(s), could be sufficiently independent to act as arbiter for the 'club' of banks, limiting entry and monitoring behavior, so as to cope with the free-rider problem."

Competition Problems
This is the most serious problem, for as Goodhart (ibid, pp. 38–39) has noted with respect to clearing houses, there is competition among commercial banks and they may take the opportunity a crisis affords to force a competitor out of business;

> Since it is now argued that support/supervisor quasi-Central Banking activities may be provided by clearing houses....It is as well to note that such commercial conflicts of interest may also exist in this latter case (clearing houses) . Such conflicts appeared to play a part in the 1907 financial crisis occurring in New York.

   Though not as serious as the concern above, Goodhart (ibid, p. 37) also notes the potential for action that goes against the principle of fair trade; "One of the main functions of the clearing house was to maintain discipline....Insofar as that function is carried out by one main bank, the conduct of that discipline may be seen by competitors as, and may indeed in some cases actually be, unfair, and certainly unwanted, competition."

Because these competition problems are serious, Japanese credit unions, whose cooperative relationships are so deep that they have established central institutions, make some agreements limiting business territory.

Advantages of a Central Bank

Economies of Information

Though central banks are not pure hierarchies, they have a higher degree of hierarchy than bankers' associations and so enjoy one of the advantages of hierarchical organizations, economies of information. In terms of Fig. 1.5, the information flow and decision-making structure of bankers' associations is closer to that of an 'all-channel network,' while that of central banks is closer to a 'wheel network.'

Auditing and Monitoring

Just as with a hierarchy, even if central banks audit and monitor commercial banks, this does not contradict the substance of a central bank. In fact, most central banks do indeed function as the supervisor of commercial banks and are responsible for activities from on-site examination to regulations. This is an effective way to avoid the free-rider problem of commercial banks. For example, when a bankers' association runs a payment system, it is unable to sufficiently monitor members. Thus, there is systemic risk that 'bad' members will, via the payment network, cause trouble for 'good' members. Bankers' associations therefore have a much harder time running payment systems than do central banks. Additionally, both the mutual assistance funds of bankers' associations and the LLR function of central banks may present moral hazard to commercial banks. However, central bank supervision is an effective way to avert moral hazard (see Sect. 1.6.3).

Fair Treatment of Competitors

As in a hierarchy, central banks are not in competition with commercial banks and therefore do not experience the competition problem that bankers' associations would.

Choice of Bankers' Association or Central Bank

We have shown Williamson's peer group theory to be applicable to financial transactions. Therefore, arguments over the choice of peer group association or hierarchy apply to the debate on bankers' associations versus central banks. Therefore, let us interpret within the context of the bankers' association/central bank debate, the idea of strengthening involvement relations so that bureaucracy costs do not rise even though there is a higher degree of hierarchy (i.e., the shift of line H downward to line H′ in Fig. 1.6).

With the payment system provided by the central bank, strengthening involvement relations means arriving at an appropriate design for the central bank governance structure so that bureaucracy costs can be lowered. More specifically, this involves improving central bank transparency and accountability vis-à-vis commercial banks who are the users of the interbank payment system, seeking out the opinions of commercial banks, and providing tailored services to commercial banks at arm's length. One idea might be the good use of a 'national payment committee.' Were central banks to make these kinds of efforts it would in many cases be appropriate from the perspective of transaction cost economization that they, rather than bankers' associations, provide such services as ACHs and PVP systems (see Chap. 7, Sects. 7.2.2 and 7.3.3).

1.6.3 Central Bank as Supervisor

1.6.3.1 Issue Identification

One issue in the two-tiered banking system that has received a great deal of attention recently is who should supervise commercial banks, the central bank, a government agency, or the deposit insurance agency? Studies must take into account a wide variety of contentions, including consistency with the purposes of the agencies involved and independence from political pressure (see Chap. 5, Sect. 5.4).

In Sects. 1.3 and 1.4 we have considered the banking system as a single system and applied TCE to uncover new perspectives on the relationship between central banks and commercial banks. Let us now use these arguments to consider the issue.

1.6.3.2 Application of TCE

To jump straight to the conclusion, the central bank is the most appropriate supervisor. There are at least three reasons:

First, TCE shows that when the market mode is compared with the other two modes (hierarchy and hybrid), the main reason they are more advantageous than the market mode in terms of transaction costs is that they have auditing and monitoring functions that the market mode does not.[18] Applying this to the banking system, the main reason types B and C are more advantageous than Type A in terms of the transaction costs of interbank transactions is that the central bank is able to engage in auditing and monitoring, i.e., banking supervision.

Second, this is especially true for interbank money market transactions. In Sect. 1.4.2.2, it has been pointed out that prospective lender banks must audit/monitor prospective borrower banks in order to accumulate information about their conditions even in a normal situation. As the central bank is the best possible lender bank in an abnormal situation in terms of transaction costs, the central bank is the most appropriate supervisor.

Third, TCE shows that internal auditors are better than external auditors. Says Williamson (1975, pp. 29–30), "The auditing advantage of internal organization in relation to inter-firm organization is attributable to constitutional and incentive differences which operate in favor of the internal mode. An external auditor is typically

---

[18]The advantages of hierarchy, in which the supervisor is expressly assigned the task of auditing, have also been discussed by Alchian and Demsetz (1972).

constrained to review written records and documents and in other respects restrict the scope of his investigation to clearly pertinent matters. An internal auditor, by contrast, has greater freedom of action, both to include less formal evidence and to explore the byways into which his investigation leads."

It is possible to see the 'internal auditor' as the central bank and the 'external auditor' as the government agency. The reason for this is that when the monobank system of Type B is divided into the two-tiered system of Type C, what has taken place is a separation of the central and commercial banks. In this sense, the central bank is still an organization within the banking system. By contrast, the government agency is outside the system in Type B, and in Type C only becomes more of an outsider. The central bank has emerged from the market of commercial banks.

Being in the banking system, the central bank enjoys more efficient communication with commercial banks than the government agency, which is an outsider. In TCE, "A further advantage of internal organization is that, as compared to recurrent market exchange, efficient codes are more apt to evolve and be employed with confidence by the parties. Such coding also economizes on bounded rationality. Complex events are summarized in an informal way by using what may be an idiosyncratic language" (Williamson, 1975, p. 25).

Certainly the central bank, being a bank itself and therefore engaged in banking operations, has the advantage of being able to understand the "codes" used by commercial banks better than an organization not so engaged. This becomes even more apparent when Type C's two-tiered system is seen as a division of the single-tiered Type B system into the central bank and commercial banks.

1.6.4 Clients and Business Scope of Central Banks

1.6.4.1 Issue Identification

A central bank's clients are institutions that have opened accounts with it, have entered into borrowing agreements with it, use services provided by it, or enjoy some other similar relationships. While there is a broad consensus that commercial banks ought to be clients of the central bank, there is still much argument over whether to include other financial institutions and non-financial firms. Among financial institutions, the question hinges on the inclusion of, for example, securities companies, securities brokers, and small-scale depository institutions such as credit unions.

There are also the issues concerning the scope of the central bank's business. For example, should it engage only in financial business, or should it engage in the same kind of commercial business as non-financial corporations and, if so, under what standards?

1.6.4.2 Application of TCE

Applying TCE to both these issues, a single principle indeed serves to answer both questions. That principle is that central banks should choose their clients and businesses so as to avoid competition. As we have seen in Sect. 1.4, when there is competition there are also opportunistic and contractual hazards that raise transaction costs. One of the basic advantages of the Type C two-tiered banking system is that the central bank is not a competitor.

Applying this principle to the question of central bank clients, we find that when financial institutions and non-financial firms compete with commercial banks, it is meaningful to include them as clients of the central bank. For example, if a securities company competes with commercial banks, it is not desirable for it to have to depend on the banking services of a commercial bank because that will make the commercial bank privy to contact information about the securities company's transactions. The central bank needs to take the securities company on as a client in order to ensure fair competition between it and the commercial bank. In an extreme case, were a non-financial firm to compete with a commercial bank, then the central bank should allow the non-financial firm to become a client.

Applying the same principle to the scope of central banking business, the central bank should avoid competition with its clients. For example, it should avoid taking on as clients securities companies and non-financial firms because they are the clients of commercial banks. This can lead to conflicts with the first point we made, and in such cases the yardstick to be used is the intensity of competition between commercial banks on the one hand and securities companies and non-financial firms on the other. If competition is intense, then the central bank may be justified in taking them on as clients.

There can be no justification for the central bank entering businesses conducted by non-financial firms. Doing so would bring it into competition with such firms, and this is far different from the argument that the central bank (from a position of neutrality) should provide banking services to non-financial firms when commercial banks are in direct competition with them.

1.7 Conclusion

We have applied Williamson's three modes of economic systems—(a) market mode, (b) hierarchy mode, and (c) hybrid mode—to identify three banking systems (a) commercial banks only with no central bank, (b) central bank only, and (c) both a central bank and commercial banks. Then, by analyzing transaction costs in these three banking systems, we have explicated why it is the two-tiered system with both the central bank and commercial banks that has survived.

It has been very useful to apply NIE, particularly the theories of TCE, to the institutional issues of central banks. Indeed, this theoretical approach to these issues deserves to be explored more deeply, perhaps by applying other theories stemming from TCE. For example, the corporate governance theory based on TCE would surely contribute to studying the governance structure of central banks (see Chap. 2).

Our study has focused on the central bank's function as a 'banker's bank,' but the central bank also serves as the 'bank of issue' and the 'bank for the government.' TCE may have much to say about the institutional issues involved in these aspects of central bank functions as well. In other words, the economies of scope theory re-interpreted from TCE as Teece (1994) did would be useful in analyzing the relationships between the different functions of central banks (see Chaps. 4, 5 and 7).

Chapter 2
Governance Structure of Central Banks

2.1 Overview

While Chap. 1 discussed central banks within the framework of the overall financial system, this chapter focuses on individual central banking organization and governance structure. Governance structure of a central bank has two aspects similar to governance structure in a private corporation: 'ownership' and 'organizational governance.'

The ownership aspect deals with the question, 'Who owns the organization?' which decides the basis of its governance structure. The owner of an organization is an important stakeholder and holds a special position within the organizational governance structure. When we look at the ownership of central banks from this perspective, all central banks in major countries have 'capital stock' and 'stockholders' like private corporations do. However, the rights of central bank stockholders are limited in various ways and they cannot really be considered the owners of a central bank like they would for a private corporation. So, why do central banks have capital stock? Is it even necessary for central banks to have capital stock? This chapter will examine these questions regarding ownership of a central bank and discuss features and roles attaching to central bank capital stock.

Next, the 'organizational governance' aspect deals with a governance structure that is based on a specific ownership. Since the most important internal body within a central bank is the 'board,' we will consider organizational governance of a central bank from its board structure. The Bank of Japan (BOJ) adopted a so-called 'single board' structure (Policy Board) as stipulated under the new BOJ Act in 1998, but many central banks have a 'multiboard structure' where, for example, a 'policy board' and 'executive board' or 'monetary policy committee' and 'prudential policy committee' co-exist. We will examine reasons for these differences in this chapter.

In discussing the governance structure of a central bank, we need to analyze the basic characteristics of 'goods and services' provided by a central bank. In doing so, we should not limit central bank functions to monetary policy but should adequately incorporate the fact that a central bank also provides banking services such as deposit

© Springer Nature Singapore Pte Ltd. 2019
Y. Oritani, *The Japanese Central Banking System Compared with Its European and American Counterparts*, https://doi.org/10.1007/978-981-13-9001-2_2

taking, lending, and payment. In this chapter, we will mainly use transaction cost economics (TCE) by Oliver E. Williamson and the 'economic theory of clubs' developed by James M. Buchanan to discuss features of central bank banking services. Additionally, with regard to a central bank's capital stock, the theory of organizational culture that incorporates 'organizational symbolism' and 'cultural sociology' will be applied. The theory of organizational culture will also be applied to monetary policy governance in Chap. 4.

2.2 Governance Structure Theory of New Institutional Economics

In this section, we will explain two theories from New Institutional Economics (NIE) that are helpful in considering the governance structure of a central bank. One is governance structure theory based on TCE by Williamson and the other is the economic theory of clubs developed by Buchanan.

2.2.1 Williamson's Governance Structure Theory

Williamson developed a detailed theory on organizational governance structure based on TCE. The basic framework, namely the differences between 'public governance' and 'corporate governance,' and 'ownership' and 'organizational governance' are explained, and then Williamson's theory on corporate governance is introduced.

2.2.1.1 Basic Concept

This section will explain the basic framework of Williamson's governance structure theory. First, this theory explains that the governance structure of an organization/system aims at economizing transaction costs and, based on the features of the entity involved, can be roughly divided into public governance of public organizations[1] or corporate governance of private corporations. Then, we explain that each governance structure has the dual aspect of 'ownership' and 'organizational governance.'

Governance Structure as a Means of Economizing Transaction Costs
Chapter 1 introduced Williamson's TCE as being a mode selection problem concerning economic organization and applied it to the selection problem of banking systems whether they have a central bank or not. This chapter will look at TCE not from the

---

[1] We also use 'public bureau,' 'public agency,' 'bureaucratic organization,' and 'public sector' but they all mean the same.

viewpoint of the overall economic system, but in terms of a selection problem of the governance structure of a specific organization.

That is, according to TCE, transactions, including economic transactions, generate 'transaction costs' through various independent factors or factors that are interrelated. The theory defines 'governance structure' or 'governance mechanism' as a mechanism to economize, as much as possible, such transaction costs in the form of a 'contract' or 'arrangement' or collective form such as 'organizational framework' or 'institution.'

There are various modes of organizational governance structure and the most adequate is selected from the perspective of efficiency in the long run. The optimum organizational governance structure is not fixed, and changes according to transaction cost factors and 'institutional environment.'[2] And, based on the institutional environment of a society and current events, governance structure that could minimize transaction costs will be selected.

Differentiation Between Public Governance and Corporate Governance

Williamson's governance structure theory classifies various modes of governance structure between 'public governance,' that is governance structure of a public institution, and governance structure of a private institution. Initially, Williamson considered two types of organizations, namely, 'market mode' and 'hierarchy mode,' but then proposed 'hybrid mode' that falls between the two. However, all three types are, basically, governance structures of private organizations that are determined by transaction cost from the efficiency point of view. Among them, the hierarchy mode governance structure of private corporations will be discussed as 'corporate governance.'

Moreover, Williamson (1999) newly proposed a 'bureaucracy mode' governance structure that is determined by transaction cost from the perspective of 'probity' (see Sect. 3.2.1). This type of organization is considered to be the last resort since it deals with transactions that the above three types (that envisage private organization) are incapable of. That is, bureaucratic organization has a low incentive to pursue efficiency, prefers extensive administrative controls, and prioritizes employment stability of organizational staff, all of which imply that the organization has efficiency problems. However, for a specific transaction that especially necessitates 'probity,' bureaucracy mode is utilized as 'governance as probity' since it does not pursue profit (this is called 'public governance' in this book and will be introduced in Chap. 3, Sect. 3.2.1).

Differentiation Between Ownership and Organizational Governance

There are two aspects to an organization's governance structure. One is the 'ownership' aspect of 'Who owns the organization?' and the other is the 'organizational

---

[2]The institutional environment is conceptualized by Williamson (1996, 2000) and is the official rule of the game that decides governance structure, e.g., property law and contract law. Williamson states that such official rules are, in turn, based on unofficial rules such as customs, tradition, culture, and religion which he calls "embeddedness." We will not differentiate between official and unofficial rules, and, in this book, include "embeddedness" in the institutional environment concept.

governance' aspect of 'What sort of internal organization should make fundamental decisions?'

Williamson's theory mainly discusses the latter 'organizational governance' aspect and the ownership aspect is discussed only from its effect on transaction costs. On the other hand, 'property rights theory' clearly differentiates ownership from organizational governance and stresses the importance of the ownership aspect.

2.2.1.2 Williamson's Corporate Governance Theory

Based on the above basic framework, this section will take up private organizations that are determined by transaction costs from the perspective of efficiency. We will highlight the governance structure of private corporations known as 'corporate governance.' Corporate governance is a mechanism where corporate stakeholders (interested individuals) control corporate managers and their employees. Williamson (1985) thoroughly examines corporate governance based on TCE in Chap. 12 entitled "Corporate Governance."

Relationship Between 'Transaction Specificity' and 'Safeguard'

The major feature of Williamson's corporate governance theory is the idea that within a corporate governance framework, specific stakeholders such as stockholders should not be given a large role unilaterally, but that each stakeholder be given a role. Moreover, the degree of role played by each stakeholder should be determined by a specific criterion, namely the degree of 'transaction specificity'[3] of assets (including human assets) provided by the stakeholder when engaging in transactions with the corporation concerned.

This is shown as a relationship between transaction specificity and 'safeguard'[4] in Fig. 2.1. Corporate organization is composed of numerous 'constituencies'[5] such as stockholders, business managers and employees. Transactions between such constituencies and corporations can be classified by whether they include transaction-specific assets. k shows the degree of transaction specificity of transaction assets, and, if $k > 0$, it is transaction specific and, if $k = 0$, it is not. Assets that do not have transaction specificity are assets that are used for general purposes and are traded as spot transactions in the market. Therefore, governance of these assets need not be considered (node A, p_1).

On the other hand, transaction specific assets are assets used for specific purposes or that are difficult to be redeployed for other means once used for such specific purposes. Transaction specific assets (including the labor force that does not initially

---

[3]Transaction specificity in this section can be considered as degree of stakeholders' interests. Assets that have transaction specificity (including both material and human assets) are called 'transaction-specific assets.'

[4]'Safeguard' is terminology used in Williamson's theory and otherwise known as 'credible commitment.' This concept is included in governance structure and governance mechanisms, both of which minimize transaction costs.

[5]Among 'constituencies,' stakeholders are those that trade transaction-specific assets.

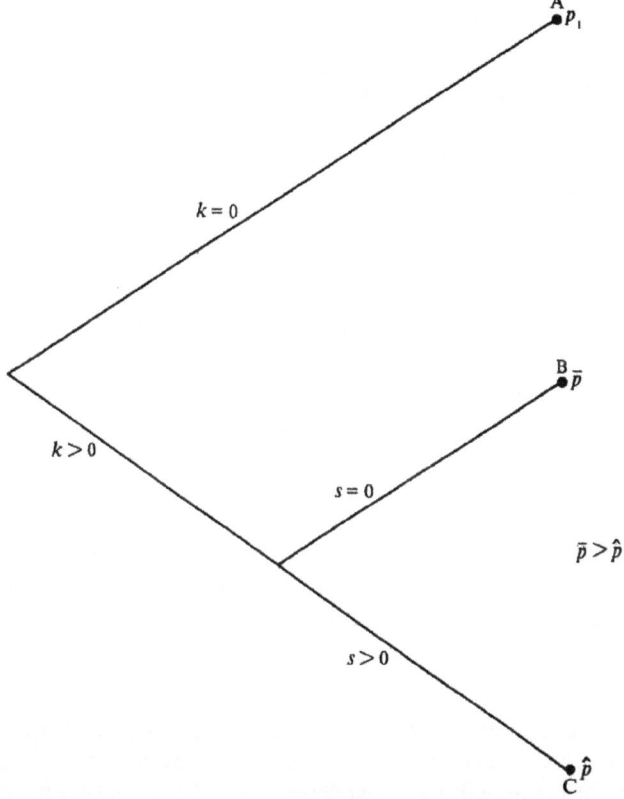

Fig. 2.1 Transaction specificity and safeguard (Williamson, 1985)

have transaction specificity but gains such over the years) can be divided into those with or without safeguards. The most important safeguard for those concerned is to govern business managers and employees through participating in a 'board of directors.' There are other safeguards and the overall system of safeguards is the governance structure.

For transaction specific assets that do not have a safeguard (node B), a cost that would cover the risk incurred during the contract will need to be added to the transaction price (p_1). Therefore, when we compare transaction price with a safeguard (node C, $s > 0$, $\hat{p}$) and that without (node B, $s = 0$, $\bar{p}$), the latter is higher than the former ($\bar{p} > \hat{p}$). A higher price is necessary to cover the risk of asset specificity that does not have a safeguard. In other words, a safeguard needs to be in place to lower the transaction price (which can be considered transaction cost) where there is transaction specificity. And, if the transaction price is fixed, the safeguard should be strengthened as the degree of transaction specificity increases.

Therefore, stakeholders that have transaction specific assets when trading with a corporation would participate in corporate governance (e.g., sit on the board of directors) based on the degree of transaction specificity as a safeguard to reduce transaction cost.

Stakeholders Within Corporate Governance
As explained above, how to treat major stakeholders within a firm's corporate governance should be decided by a specific criterion, namely the degree of 'transaction specificity.' Based on this, Williamson explains the transaction specificity of major stakeholders and how it is considered in corporate governance as follows:

Stockholders
Stockholders have a unique relationship with a firm and are considered most important within corporate governance. This is because transactions between stockholders and the firm have strong transaction specificity. Since stockholders have such strong transaction specificity, a secure safeguard needs to be in place for the transaction to become node C rather than node B. If it becomes node B, equity funding cost using the firm's shares becomes high. The most important safeguard is considered to be establishment of a board of directors and control over the firm through it.

However, stockholders are not the only stakeholders that make transactions with transaction specificity. In varying degrees, management, suppliers, customers, lenders, and moreover employees are stakeholders that conduct transactions with transaction specificity and need to play a certain role within the governance structure.

Management
According to simple principal-agent theory, management is thought to be just a responsive agent of the stockholders. However, TCE considers that management also shoulders a portion of corporate governance and it is rational for them to give feedback regarding governance to the board of directors. That is, skills provided by management gradually develop into assets with transaction specificity through the years in a specific company. Based on such a relationship between management and the company, if we are to establish a governance structure encompassing a safeguard for management (node C), the transaction price for stockholders to employ management will become lower than those without a safeguard (node B). Therefore, from the perspective of economizing transaction costs, governance structure that includes management as a member of the board of directors can economize even more on transaction costs.

Suppliers and Customers
Suppliers of raw materials and intermediate products and customers that can change supplier without too much cost are included in node A and a safeguard is not necessary. However, for those that depend heavily on a certain company and trade transaction specific assets, they should be placed under either node B or node C. If included in node B, a high price for each transaction should be considered to cover the loss incurred during the contract. Or, it may be rational to select node C and establish a safeguard from a transaction cost perspective. In this case, the customer company should participate on the board of directors.

Banks (Lenders)

Short-term and long-term loans against earmarked assets are classified under node A and do not require a safeguard. Other loans will have transaction specificity and the lender needs to cover the possibility of loss through a high interest rate (node B) or participate on the board of directors of the borrowing company and play a role in its corporate governance.

Labor

Workers with general purpose skills and knowledge do not have transaction specific features like management. Nevertheless, there are workers who accumulate firm-specific skills over the years, and thus increase transaction specificity, like the employees under life-time employment in Japan. In this case, a safeguard needs to be in place according to degree of transaction specificity.

Williamson's Corporate Finance Theory

After proposing the above corporate governance theory based on TCE, Williamson (1996) presented the following theory concerning corporate finance in Chap. 7 titled "Corporate Governance and Corporate Finance."

Transaction Specificity and Corporate Finance Theory

Williamson criticized the Modigliani-Miller theorem (hereafter MM theorem) with respect to corporate finance theory. The MM theorem suggests that, under a certain precondition, how a firm raises funds, whether through debt (borrowing, bond issuance) or equity (stock issuance), does not affect its corporate value. However, in reality, the precondition for this theorem cannot be fulfilled (because of, for example, the influence of taxation), which invited numerous counterarguments that the way in which a company raises funds (debt vs. equity) does affect its corporate value.

Williamson examined these counterarguments and proposed a theory that looked closely at the relationship between how funds are used and a company's corporate governance. While debt is usually used to hold "redeployable assets,"[6] equity is invested in transaction specific assets such as capital investments that are specifically used for manufacturing a certain product. Should a company go bankrupt, it is more difficult to recover original value of transaction specific assets than redeployable assets. Therefore, stockholders, as important stakeholders, need to have strong safeguards to reduce transaction costs through participating in a company's corporate governance such as establishing a board of directors. In this regard, there is a big difference between debt and equity from a corporate governance perspective and it is considered that the precondition for the MM theorem cannot be fulfilled.

Pecking Order Theory of Finance

Williamson proposes his own unique ideas on the 'pecking order theory of finance' based on the above theory. This theory states that when a company wants to raise funds, the order of priority regarding how they should be raised would be (a) retained earnings, (b) debt, and (c) equity. Williamson basically follows this priority. However, the reason why he chose this order of priority is not simply based on how easily

---

[6]Assets that can be put to a different use without large loss of value; cash is the most redeployable asset, real estate the least; antonym of transaction specific assets.

funds are raised, but, similar to his criticism of the above MM theorem, based on how they are used (that is, the features of assets bought by those funds <transaction specificity>) and what degree of safeguard is necessary (corporate governance). Therefore, although equity generally has low priority, when raising funds to purchase assets with high transaction specificity, its priority could be ahead of others.

The above pecking order is the priority of how funds are raised by corporations that are already established. When establishing a new company, equity (capital stock) comes first, in compliance with legislation. According to Williamson, the existence of such legislation can also be considered as a measure to determine a newly established company's corporate governance.

2.2.2   Theory of Club Goods and Governance Structure of Club Organization

Buchanan's theory of club goods that is included in organizational economics in a wider sense, does not classify goods and services between public goods and private goods. It adds the concept of 'club goods' in between. The theory of club goods is beneficial in discussing the governance structure of a central bank that is neither a government agency nor a private entity. In the following, we will first look at the definition of club goods and then the governance structure of three types of suppliers of goods and services including club goods.

2.2.2.1   Club Goods

Sandler and Tschirhart (1980) say that the concept of 'club goods' may have its origin in the theory by A. C. Pigou and Frank Knight but consider Buchanan (1965) to be the first to clearly put forth the concept. Buchanan defined club goods as an intermediate concept between 'purely private goods' and 'purely public goods.' With the development of public economics, research into goods and services that fall under such an intermediate category progressed and it became widely accepted to classify goods and services into three categories: private goods, public goods, and quasi-public goods that come in between the first two.

Public economics usually considers the 'publicness' of goods and services from the two aspects of 'non-excludability' and 'non-rivalness' as shown in Fig. 2.2. First, non-excludability shows the degree of difficulty in limiting the buyer of goods and services to a certain economic entity. For example, if it is difficult to eliminate a specific buyer from buying the goods and services from other consumers at a low cost, then the non-excludability of those goods and services is considered high (upper part of the Y axis). On the other hand, non-rivalness means how much a person's consumption of certain goods and services reduces other people's consumption. If a certain person's consumption does not affect other people's amount of consumption,

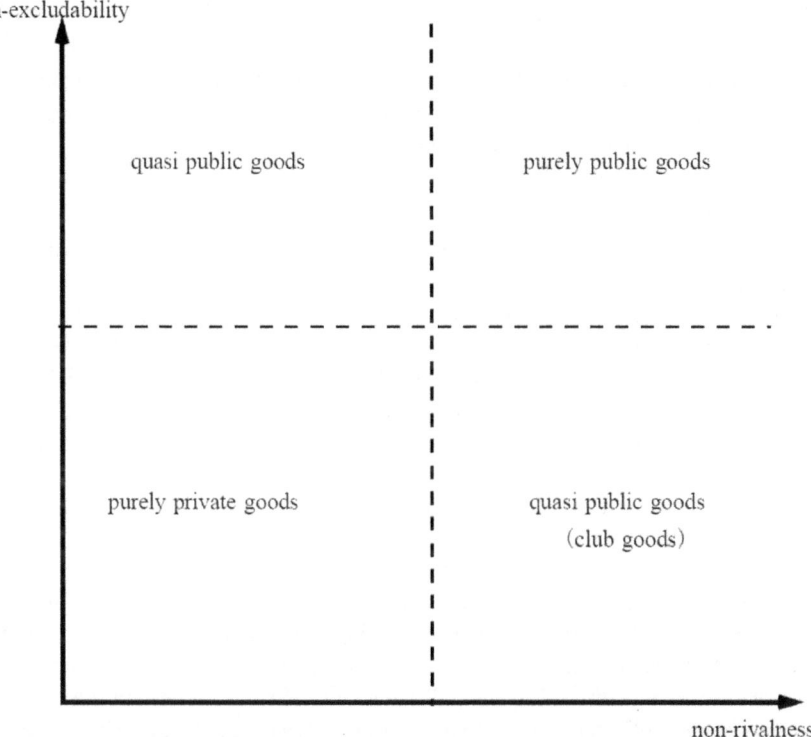

non-excludability

quasi public goods

purely public goods

purely private goods

quasi public goods
(club goods)

non-rivalness

Fig. 2.2 Three types of goods and services

then the non-rivalness of those goods and services is considered high (right part of the X axis). In this sense, non-rivalness is also called 'collectiveness.'

If the goods and services have high non-excludability and high non-rivalness, they are purely public goods, and vice versa, purely private goods. Club goods are those with low non-excludability but with high non-rivalness. That is, considering that club goods can be supplied to only a specific person, they are similar to private goods but, with respect to the fact that they have a certain level of collectiveness, are similar to public goods. Common examples of club goods are members-only golf clubs and tennis clubs.[7]

---

[7] As you can see from these examples, once club members increase beyond a certain level and become too many, non-rivalness (collectiveness) decreases and the peculiarity of club goods is diminished. Therefore, in club theory it is important to ascertain the optimum number of members that could maintain the peculiarity of club goods while taking into consideration the club goods' feature of non-excludability and the ability to limit members.

2.2.2.2 Supplier of Club Goods and Governance Structure

Below we look at suppliers of club goods by comparing the two organizations of 'clubs' and 'government' and discuss the features of suppliers that provide goods and services other than club goods such as public goods and private goods. Then, the governance structure of various suppliers of goods and services will be discussed.

Suppliers of Club Goods

Looking at the three types of suppliers of goods and services, suppliers of purely private goods and purely public goods are evident. For purely private goods, private corporations (including individuals) are the most efficient suppliers, and purely public goods can only be provided by public organizations due to free-rider problems.

On the other hand, for suppliers of club goods, there is no clear answer like there is for purely private goods and purely public goods as the features of goods and services they provide are somewhere in between. But, from the perspective of whether club goods should be provided by a profit or non-profit organization, many believe it would be more efficient for a private company to provide club goods through competitive supply than public organizations.

According to Ng (1973), "government intervention is necessary to achieve efficiency, since members will maximize average rather than total net benefits." However Sandler and Tschirhart (1980) refute this saying "there is no reason why the members of the club cannot form their own centralized authority to collect the proper tolls because efficiency gains will result."[8] Buchanan (1965) also states that just because club goods have collectiveness, it does not necessarily mean that they should be supplied by cooperatives or public organizations, and that profit-seeking organizations can efficiently manage club goods since they could bring about benefits. Hillman (1978) also comes to the conclusion that it is more desirable for profit-seeking organizations under market competition to manage club goods than non-profit cooperatives since this could better achieve an efficient market solution.

Features of Goods and Services and Governance Structure of Suppliers

Based on the three types of goods and services and their relationship with their suppliers, their respective governance structure is as follows:

Governance Structure of Suppliers of Private Goods (Corporate Governance)

Suppliers of purely private goods have the governance structure of a private organization according to Williamson's classification. And, looking at the governance structures of private organizations, it might not necessarily be a "hierarchy mode" structure but could also be a "market mode" one. In the case of a "hierarchy mode" governance structure such as in corporations, the theory of corporate governance will be applied.

Governance Structure of Suppliers of Public Goods (Public Governance)

As aforementioned (Sect. 2.2.1.1), Williamson (1999) discusses in detail the governance structure of public organizations ("public bureau" type). He explains that

---

[8]This discussion can be considered as an inefficiency issue of a peer group with no hierarchy from the perspective of TCE (see Chap. 1, Sect. 1.6.2).

the governance structure of public organizations is basically 'hierarchy mode' like corporate governance but differs in the sense that it places importance on 'probity.' Such governance structure of public organizations is called 'public governance'[9] vis-à-vis 'corporate governance.'

Governance Structure of Suppliers of Club Goods (Corporate Governance)
As mentioned, while suppliers of club goods cannot be clearly defined like those of purely private and purely public goods can, it is the majority view that club goods could be more efficiently supplied by a private company than a public organization. Therefore, if suppliers of club goods are private companies, the theory of corporate governance for private firms can be applied in considering their governance structure.

However, in the case of club goods, suppliers often become the consumers (that is, club members become its owners). In such a case, two stakeholders, namely stakeholder as a consumer of club goods, and stakeholder as an owner of the supplier of club goods, become identical. The governance structure of suppliers of club goods needs to incorporate this fact.

And, when comparing the governance structure of 'clubs' and government (public organization) there are the following differences. Government rules and activities influence people and force them to comply, so the government needs to be governed by the public. For this governance structure, a presidential and parliamentary political system is applied. This is 'public governance.' On the other hand, the rules and activities of 'clubs' can only be forced on their members so it is adequate that 'clubs' should only be governed by their members. Therefore, discussion on 'corporate governance' regarding a private organization's governance structure will be applied to suppliers of club goods.

2.3   Application to Central Bank Governance Structure

This section will apply corporate governance theory and corporate finance theory that are based on Williamson's TCE as well as Buchanan's theory on club goods to a central bank. First, we will discuss central bank services and organizational features followed by the question of a central bank's governance structure. This will be a preliminary step to discussing the multiboard system of a central bank in Sect. 2.4 and a central bank's capital stock in Sect. 2.5.

---

[9]As we will explain in Chap. 3, Sect. 3.2.1, Williamson does not use the term 'public governance' but Bevir (2007) uses it as the title for his book.

2.3.1 Central Bank Services and Organizational Features

The following section will discuss central bank services and their organizational features as a necessary preparation for discussing the governance structure of a central bank.

2.3.1.1 Features of Central Bank Services

First, we discuss what might be the central bank equivalent of a corporation's inputs and outputs. Then, the theory of club goods will be applied to the features of services provided by a central bank.

Inputs and Outputs of Central Bank Activities
The inputs of central bank activities (equivalent of materials, parts, intermediate products in manufacturing industry) are physical goods such as computers, stationery, buildings, and vaults as well as human capital, and, intermediate goods and services that are provided within the central bank organization. Next, with regard to central bank outputs (or in other words, products, goods and services) it is quite difficult to clearly define them compared to general manufacturing companies. In the first place, defining the outputs of a commercial bank in itself involves a discussion of money and banking theory and no consensus has been reached yet. Against such background, if we are to define central bank outputs, they could be categorized into two: 'attainment of an overall goal' such as price stability and financial system stability, and 'specific concrete services' to attain such goals (e.g., payment, lending and supervisory services).

Classification of Central Bank Services Under the Framework of Theory of Club Goods
When we consider the features of central bank services and classify them according to the theory of club goods, the following findings can be made. First, there are almost no central bank services that can be considered purely private goods. Second, services considered as club goods are those offered as a 'banker's bank' and are at the core of a central bank's banking services. For example, private financial institutions (hereafter 'private banks') have a deposit account with the central bank through which funds are transferred to effect interbank settlement (interbank settlement services). Moreover, private banks can withdraw cash money from this account. And, if approved, private banks can also borrow funds from the central bank. The central bank provides these services to private banks but whether they utilize such services is left to their discretion and not mandatory (a central bank can also have the right to refuse). In this regard, private banks are considered members of a 'club' organized by the central bank. Indeed, private banks that have a deposit account with the Federal Reserve Bank are called 'member banks.'

Third, central bank services that are considered purely public goods are those offered as the 'bank of issue' and 'bank for the government.' Central bank services that issue and control banknotes as 'bank of issue' historically started as being more considered as private goods since 'banknotes' are literally securities issued by the bank. However, as these banknotes started to circulate widely as money, their feature as public goods strengthened. Now that the central bank has sole authority from the government to issue and control banknotes that are legal tender, such services can be considered purely public goods.[10] And, central bank services to stabilize the value of the currency through macro monetary policy can also be considered purely public goods.

As for services provided as 'bank for the government,' there are some services that can be delegated to private banks (services with low non-competitiveness and non-rivalness). However, a central bank should basically be the sole provider of most services (services with high non-competitiveness and non-rivalness) which are considered purely public goods.

As above, central bank services can be classified either as club goods or public goods but such classification is neither decisive nor fixed.[11] That is, central bank services are deeply interrelated and it is not possible to classify each individual service definitively. From another perspective, it might be more appropriate to consider services classified as club goods as public goods. For example, among central bank lending to private banks, there are cases where it is appropriate to consider such lending as purely public goods rather than club goods. Central bank lending is sometimes used to prevent a borrowing private bank from going bankrupt. However, this type of lending also has the aim of preventing the said financial institution's bankruptcy from affecting other private banks (the so called manifestation of 'systemic risk'), thereby securing the stability of the overall financial system. The effect of securing financial system stability extends beyond club members (member banks) to non-club members and moreover to the general public, and, in this sense, such lending can be considered as purely public goods.

To the contrary, though banknotes are usually classified as purely public goods, there are cases where they are considered as club goods. For example, should most people stop using banknotes under hyper-inflation, those still using banknotes could be regarded as members of a club that opted to use banknotes. So in this case, it would be appropriate to regard banknotes as club goods.

2.3.1.2 Two Features of Central Bank Organization

Based on the above classification of central bank services, we now look at the features of central bank organization. First, central bank organization related to providing club goods can be considered a private organization as discussed in the previous section

---

[10]This is not necessarily in line with the 'state theory of money.' While private money that is used as currency may exist without government approval, there could be legal tender that would not be used due to inflation.

[11]Even with respect to the sole right of the central bank to issue banknotes, the legal tender, Hayek (1976) and others suggest that private banks should also be allowed to do so freely. Therefore, the nature of central bank services may change over time for reasons other than those mentioned here.

(Sect. 2.2.2.2) on suppliers of club goods. That is, a central bank may compete against a peer group (such as a bankers' association, see Chap. 1, Sect. 1.6.2). For example, its interbank payment systems compete against payment systems operated by a bankers' association.

On the other hand, central bank organization responsible for providing public goods is a public organization. For example, a central bank influences interest rates through various market transactions and thus has an impact on the macro economy. Central bank decisions on interest rates for lending to private banks and its guidance of interbank market interest rates are basically implemented through business transactions between it and private banks. However, its scope of influence extends beyond the parties concerned. Interbank market interest rates affect various other interest rates and also influence income distribution among a wide range of lenders and borrowers. As long as an organization exists within the same economy, it is difficult for it not to be influenced by interbank market interest rates which evidences their prescriptive effect. Such strong influence over income distribution is a feature of government activities and therefore one reason for the central bank being a public organization.

Also, the central bank does not, in principle, pay interest (or only at an extremely low rate) on funds collected through banknote issuance and reserve deposits. On the other hand, it could gain profits through managing such funds (such central bank profit is called 'seigniorage,' see Chap. 6, Sect. 6.3.3). Seigniorage is not taxation, but profit gained from the general public (individuals and firms that have banknotes and reserve deposits). And, the amount depends on market interest rates that the central bank can control. That is, the central bank has a profit similar to taxation and, in this sense, has the feature of a public organization.

In providing such public goods-related services, a central bank should abide by 'probity,' emphasized by Williamson (1999), and 'governance as probity' is indispensable. In this regard, a central bank is a bureaucracy mode organization and thus has the feature of a public organization.

However, the above classification is only conceptual and the central bank cannot actually be divided into two parts—private organization and public organization. This is because central bank services are deeply interrelated with one another. Just because one service is club goods, it is difficult to make the related department into a private organization.

2.3.2 Arguments on the Governance Structure of Central Banks

In the previous section, we looked at central bank services and related organizational features. In this section we show that the central bank falls under the category of hierarchy mode among the basic modes of Williamson's governance structure. Then, we explain issues regarding a central bank's governance structure. Specifically, a central bank's governance structure involves the dual aspects of public governance and private governance, as well as the fact that central bank ownership cannot be determined from central bank capital stock investors.

2.3.2.1   Necessity of Hierarchy Mode Governance Structure

Let us first examine why a central bank is neither a competitive market mode nor a mixed mode but a hierarchy mode among the basic modes of Williamson's governance structure. The question is, while it is apparent that one person alone cannot provide central bank services, why is it not possible for that person to purchase necessary human assets and goods competitively in the spot market to provide central bank services even without formulating a hierarchical organization?

Let us first look at central bank services in line with Williamson's theoretical framework. Assets that are necessary for a central bank to provide its services are human assets and goods. Human assets comprise senior officials (in the case of a multiboard structure, all board members) and staff that perform actual operations. Among their various jobs, there are those that do not require expertise and could be effected by temporary employees. However, most central bank operations need expertise and so the central bank's skilled labor force has 'transaction specificity.' Moreover, central bank staff that trade their expertise with the central bank (in return for a salary) exhibit bounded rationality and opportunism. So, under the competitive market mode governance structure that procures staff through spot contracts, transaction costs become high. Therefore, central bank organization is a hierarchy mode governance structure where staff are bounded by long-term contracts.

Next, central bank goods include business equipment and IT systems such as payment systems. Many of these have been transformed to meet the needs of central bank operations and it is difficult to simply redeploy them to be used for other purposes. This means that goods also have transaction specificity and transaction costs will be high if purchased competitively from the spot market. Therefore, from the perspective of transaction costs, the central bank needs to adopt a hierarchy mode governance structure.

2.3.2.2   Two Features of Public Governance and Corporate Governance

In light of the definitions of public governance and corporate governance under Sect. 2.2.1.1, central bank governance structure cannot be grasped by a single governance structure. It has features of both public and private governance structure.

Central bank services (a feature of a central bank) are characterized by their being the provision of purely public goods, from which we can grasp governance structure (of the organization providing such services) from the perspective of public governance of a public organization (bureaucracy mode). Similarly, central bank services also involve the characteristic of club goods and the related provider, and organizational governance structure here can be grasped from the perspective of the corporate governance of a private organization.

When we deem a governance structure is based on the features of corporate governance, the transactions in question would be those related to central bank services that have the features of club goods. Namely, transactions between a central bank and member private banks. On the other hand, when we deem a governance structure is based on the features of public governance, the transactions in question would be those related to central bank services that have the features of public goods. In the latter case, transactions with the central bank encompass a wider scope than club goods services. Specifically, transactions with the legislative and executive branch of government that include monetary policy that determines the raison d'être of central bank services as well as appointment of senior officials. Of course, as mentioned before (Sect. 2.3.1.1), the central bank directly enters into transactions with the general public by providing services such as stability of currency value and maintenance of a stable financial system through which central bank officials and staff earn their salaries.

As such, central bank governance structure has two features and it is necessary to integrate them within a single central bank organization. It is not rational to completely divide the central bank organization into two. Central bank services are deeply interrelated with one another and therefore just because a certain service is a club good, if we cut off that department from the central bank, the service may no longer be provided.

2.3.2.3 Ownership Issue of a Central Bank

As explained in Sect. 2.3.2.2, the organizational governance aspect of central bank governance structure has mixed features of both corporate and public governance. On the other hand, if we look at ownership, the more basic aspect of central bank governance, all central banks of major countries have, as will be mentioned under Sect. 2.5.1, 'capital stock,' similar to a private firm. But, while stockholders of capital stock exist, we cannot consider them owners of the central bank like those of private firms. To consider that a central bank's capital stock represents its ownership is a misinterpretation in thinking that stockholders of a central bank are simply the same as those of private firms.

If central bank ownership cannot be ascertained from stockholders of its capital stock in the first place, there remains the question of how we determine central bank ownership. One idea is, based on Williamson's corporate governance theory, to consider central bank stakeholders as its owners and regard them as partially sharing central bank ownership depending on their degree of transaction specificity. Based on this idea, central bank owners would be the general public that use banknotes (and their representatives, the legislature and the government) and member private banks that utilize banking services such as payment systems offered by the central bank. This is in line with the idea that central bank governance structure has two features—public governance (governance by the public's representatives) and corporate governance (governance by member private banks).

Of course, it is a little bit of a stretch to consider central bank stakeholders as the owners. As Williamson (1985) mentions, owners (stockholders) hold a special place among the stakeholders and have more of a stake than other owners. That is, shares held by stockholders have transaction specificity and once persons/entities become stockholders they cannot withdraw without risking depreciation of the value of their holding.

Therefore, a natural idea would be to not consider central bank stakeholders as owners but simply think that central banks do not have owners. Generally, there are not a few organizations without owners in the form of 'investor.' This type of ownership exists by accumulating past profits in the form of 'funds' and making them the organization's capital, thus not having any specific stockholders. For example, among life insurance companies, there are those that do not have stockholders but instead the funds accumulated from profits are a proxy for their owner.

2.4 Designing a Central Bank Board Structure

Of the two aspects of central bank governance structure, namely ownership and organizational governance, based on the analysis in the previous section, here we will discuss the latter. Discussion will especially focus on the core issue, namely designing a central bank board structure. With regard to the former, the ownership aspect of central bank governance structure, capital stock only plays a symbolic role as will be explained in the next section and does not directly relate to ownership as in a private company. Therefore, the other aspect of governance structure, organizational governance, and especially designing a board structure, holds considerable significance.

There are other issues pertaining to organizational governance such as how internal organizations in a central bank should be managed other than via designing a board structure, which will be taken up in Chap. 4 (Sect. 4.4.2.3). And more discussion will be made on designing a board structure in Chaps. 6 and 7 from different perspectives.

2.4.1 Multiboard Structure

2.4.1.1 What Is a Board Structure?

A central bank board is a decision-making body comprised of senior officials that have authority and responsibility to make important decisions such as appointing executives and formulating basic principles. They could be considered a 'committee.' Nicholl (2009) points out that a board is established within a central bank to reflect the feature of a private corporation. There are various board compositions:

(a) both non-executive and executive members participate and someone from the former group becomes the chairperson, (b) the same as (a) but the governor (executive member) becomes the chairperson, and (c) only executive members participate (the chairperson is undoubtedly the governor). As for the board's functions, some have a policy executive function while others only supervise ('supervisory board') lower boards.

According to BIS (2009), there are three types of board: policy board, management board, and supervisory board. A policy board can be established for each policy or united in one (for example, the BOJ). If there is only one board, it is called a 'single board structure,' and if two or more, a 'multiboard structure.'

2.4.1.2 Types of Multiboard Structure

As shown in Fig. 2.3, there are various types of multiboard structure in central banks, an outline of each of which is as follows:

Prototype A
This is a multiboard structure where the upper board is superior to the lower board. The upper board is equivalent to the 'board of directors' of a private corporation

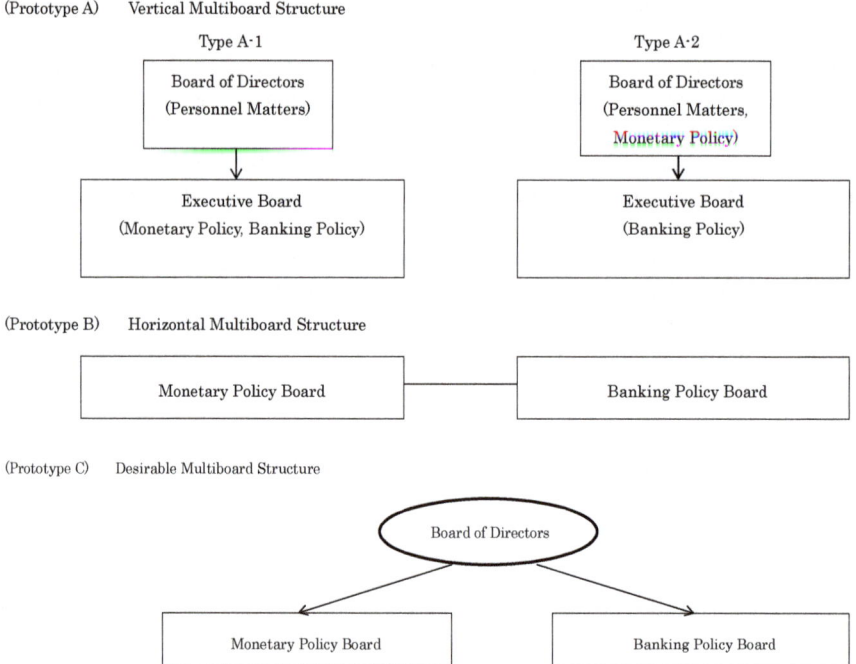

Fig. 2.3 Types of multiboard structure

and decides on the appointment of central bank executives and basic central bank management strategy. The lower board is equivalent to 'executive board' and executes monetary policy and banking services. This type is in line with the purpose of integrating public governance and corporate governance. Therefore, as will be discussed in Chap. 3, Sect. 3.3.4, only upper board members are appointed by the legislature/government and, in turn, the upper board appoints lower board members that execute actual policy and operations. This contributes to reducing influence from the legislature/government and strengthens central bank independence. Examples here are the FRS of the US (explained in Sect. 2.4.2.1 of this chapter) and the Swiss National Bank (SNB; see Chap. 3, Fig. 3.3).

Prototype B
This is a multiboard structure where boards are established for each central bank function: 'monetary policy board' and 'banking board' (the banking area includes prudential policy board, payment system board, etc.). This type places importance on the relationship between monetary policy and banking function. If monetary policy is considered public governance and the banking function as corporate governance, this type may fulfill the purpose of integrating public and corporate governance within the organization. Examples here are the Board of the Bank of England (BOE; explained in Sect. 2.4.2.2 of this chapter).

Prototype C
This type merges prototype A and B and can be termed a 'three-board system.' That is, while the monetary policy board and banking board are separated, there is an upper board, the 'board of directors,' that presides over them and decides basic central bank management strategy and appoints board members.

This seems like an ideal board structure that places importance on central bank independence and the relationship between monetary policy and banking, but does not exist in reality.

2.4.1.3 Advantages of a Multiboard Structure

There are various thoughts regarding which board structure is suitable for a private firm. For example, Turnbull (2000) states that a "unitary board" (different from how it is called in BIS, 2009) does not differentiate between the board of directors and the executive board which thus results in a conflict of interest within that board. Therefore, he believes that a multiboard is superior in terms of corporate governance. There are four major benefits in adopting a multiboard structure to a central bank:

Integration of Public Governance and Corporate Governance
As discussed, central bank governance structure has two features and there is a need to integrate both within one central bank organization. To this end, a multiboard structure is useful. For example, the central bank could establish two boards, and have one assume authority and responsibility for public governance and the other, corporate governance.

The board that is responsible for the central bank's public governance will make important decisions on central bank services as public goods. Therefore, it is appropriate that the board members be the general public or its representatives rather than someone who is an expert on actual central bank operations.

As for the board responsible for the central bank's corporate governance, it will decide important aspects of central bank services as club goods. Therefore, its members should be experts on specific central bank operations and club members. That is, the board should consist of main service users and representatives of member banks.

How much authority and responsibility should be allocated to each board and how to decide respective members varies according to each central bank's institutional environment. But, compared to a single board structure, a multiboard structure is at least clearly a structure that incorporates the two features of central bank governance. In this sense, a multiboard structure is more efficient than a single board structure.

Enhancing the Banking Function of the Central Bank

As will be studied more deeply in Chap. 4, when we adopt a single board governance structure, board members are likely to focus on central bank services that are purely public goods, mainly regarding monetary policy. On the other hand, banking functions of a central bank such as lending, deposit taking, and payment (in some cases prudential policy) may not attract adequate attention. One of the reasons is because the government, financial markets, the mass media, and the general public are very interested in monetary policy and the board members are likely to lean in the same direction. Another reason is that within a single board structure, monetary policy becomes the center of discussion and, therefore, it is quite likely that board members consist mainly of experts on macroeconomic policy.

As a result, in a single board structure, there will be no platform to seriously discuss issues regarding banking services. Board members may lack interest in or only have poor understanding of club good services that should be provided by the central bank (e.g., interbank payment services) and, therefore, may well delegate them to bank staff. There will be no safeguard under such a central bank governance structure and transaction costs will likely be high for the principal users (member private banks) of central bank club good services.

On the other hand, under a multiboard structure, while single board is responsible for monetary policy decisions, the other is responsible for services related to club goods. Therefore, authority and responsibility can be dispersed. In this way, a multiboard structure allows the board in charge of services related to club goods to make decisions with the necessary expertise and dedication.

This type of multiboard structure may not necessarily be based directly on the difference between club goods and public goods, but can secure the feature of corporate governance while encompassing the public governance feature within the central bank governance structure (e.g., the board structure of the FRS in the US, as will be mentioned under Sect. 2.4.2.1).

Adequate Distance and Adjustment Between Monetary Policy and Prudential Policy

As will be explained in Chap. 5, Sect. 5.4.1, if the central bank is also responsible for prudential policy, there is a risk of a trade-off against monetary policy as well as the concentration of power. Also, the expertise required differs between monetary policy and prudential policy. While it is important to gather experts for each policy, adopting a multiboard structure is likely to mitigate such issues by adequately adjusting the trade-off between policies. For example, the BOE established two boards, one for monetary policy (Monetary Policy Committee) and another for prudential policy (Financial Stability Committee), and thus it is endeavoring to manage both policies adequately (see Sect. 2.4.2.2).

Securing Central Bank Independence

It is considered essential that central bank governance structure include a mechanism that secures independence from any particular group, especially the government. In this sense, a multiboard structure can be useful in securing central bank independence. Specifically, we could establish a governance structure where a government agent can participate on one board (let us call this the 'upper board') but not on the other (the 'lower board'). Additionally, if the upper board's power could be limited to the appointment of lower board members and approval of the budget and/or statement of accounts, and the lower board can make decisions on monetary policy, government influence over the central bank would become indirect and thus we could enhance central bank independence (for example, the board structure of the SNB <see Chap. 3, Fig. 3.3>).

2.4.2 Examples of a Central Bank Multiboard Structure

Board structure has an important meaning in central bank organizational governance. Most central banks in the world adopt a multiboard governance structure. In this connection, let us introduce the multiboard structure adopted by the Federal Reserve System (United States) which is an interesting example of integrating public and corporate governance. Also, we look at the board structure of the BOE (United Kingdom), a close example of prototype C in Fig. 2.3, and additionally the single board structure of the BOJ, which is a rare example.

Putting integration of public and corporate governance aside, Chap. 3, Sect. 3.3 will introduce the multiboard structure of the SNB from the perspective of maintaining central bank independence. And, as an example of establishing separate boards for various central bank functions, the Reserve Bank of Australia (RBA) places emphasis on enhancing its banking functions, especially payment services and established "Payment System Board" separated from "Reserve Bank Board."

2.4.2.1   Governance Structure of the Federal Reserve System (US)

The FRS consists of the Board of Governors of the FRS (the Board) in Washington D.C., and Federal Reserve Banks (FRBs) of 12 districts in the US. According to McCrackin (1994), the FRS is an amalgam of public and private elements, and, since its establishment, is well aware of the commercial bank-like nature of district FRBs and the governmental nature of the Board of Governors in Washington.

As shown in Fig. 2.4, the FRS clearly integrates the two features of central bank governance structure. District FRBs are quasi-independent entities that are well versed in regional financial needs (McCrackin, 1994) and therefore a considerable degree of corporate governance attaches to them as is the case in private companies. On the other hand, public governance is very evident with the Board. Seven governors, including the Chair, are appointed by the President and confirmed by the Senate. The Federal Open Market Committee (FOMC) that decides important monetary policy matters is a mixture of the two. All board members participate in the FOMC and the president of the FRB of New York and presidents of four other FRBs have voting rights on a rotating basis (President of FRB NY has always voting right). Important banking service issues concerning the FRS overall are decided at the Conference of Presidents in which Board governors also participate.

Even the governance structure of each district FRB is designed so that both public and corporate governance are integrated. FRS (2016, p. 12, Fig. 2.3) states as follows:

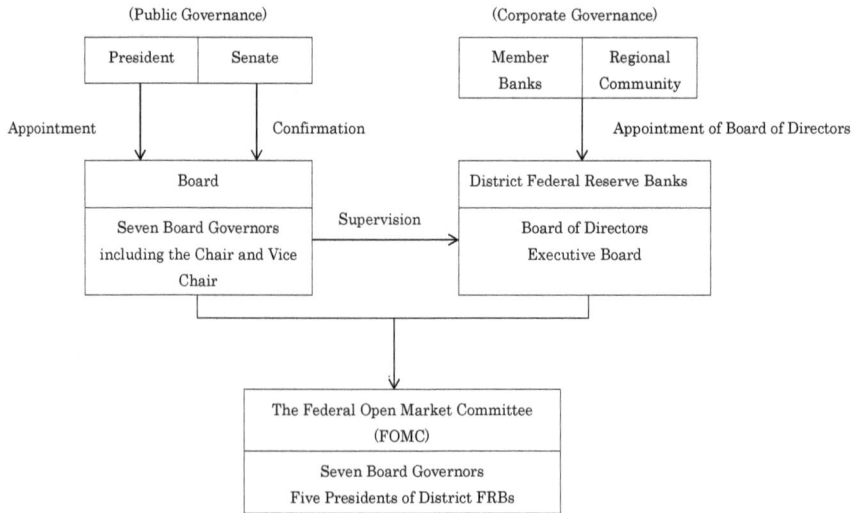

Fig. 2.4 Governance structure of Federal Reserve System

Federal Reserve member banks elect three Class A directors (represent District member banks) and three Class B directors (represent the public). Federal Reserve Board of Governors appoints three Class C directors (represent the public). Reserve Bank presidents are nominated by Class B and C directors and approved by the Board of Governors.[12]

Class B and C directors represent public governance, and representatives of the member commercial banks reflect corporate governance. The Executive Board consisting of a president and vice president have the authority and responsibility over execution of district FRB banking services.

The fact that each FRB's board of directors consists of directors appointed by the Board of Governors, representatives of member commercial banks, and the public implies that it is an adequate governance structure based on Williamson's theory on corporate governance (Sect. 2.2.1.2) suggesting that stakeholders can economize transaction costs by becoming members of the board of directors.

2.4.2.2 Governance Structure of the Bank of England (UK)

The governance structure of the BOE is depicted in Fig. 2.5. Senior officials such as the governor and vice governor are appointed by the government (Her Majesty's Treasury; to be precise, members of the Court of Directors are appointed by the Crown based on advice from the government), and therefore public governance is predominantly stronger than corporate governance. In 2013, when the department responsible for micro prudential policy was transferred from the Financial Services Authority (FSA) to the BOE, a Financial Policy Committee (FPC) was newly established in addition to the already existing Monetary Policy Committee (MPC) within the Bank. In this way, BOE adopted a function-oriented multiboard governance structure (see Fig. 2.5).

As the upper board, the Court of Directors is responsible for determining the Bank's objectives and strategy and is also superior to other committees that supervise the day-to-day management of the Bank (i.e., subcommittees of the Court). However, the MPC is not considered a lower board vis-à-vis the Court of Directors. In this regard, MPC and FPC are not in parallel but are structured so that the public governance aspect of monetary policy and corporate governance aspect of the banking function are separated.

Moreover, the Prudential Regulation Authority (PRA) was created by the Financial Services Act of 2012 as a subsidiary of the BOE responsible for prudential regulation and supervision of financial institutions. Significant PRA decisions are made by its Board (not depicted in Fig. 2.5), comprising the Governor of the BOE, the Deputy Governor for Financial Stability, the Chief Executive Officer of the PRA (and Deputy Governor of the BOE for Prudential Regulation), and independent nonexecutive members. Therefore, there are four boards including the Board of the PRA.

---

[12]The Dodd-Frank Act of 2010 changed that Class A directors would no longer vote for Reserve Bank presidents.

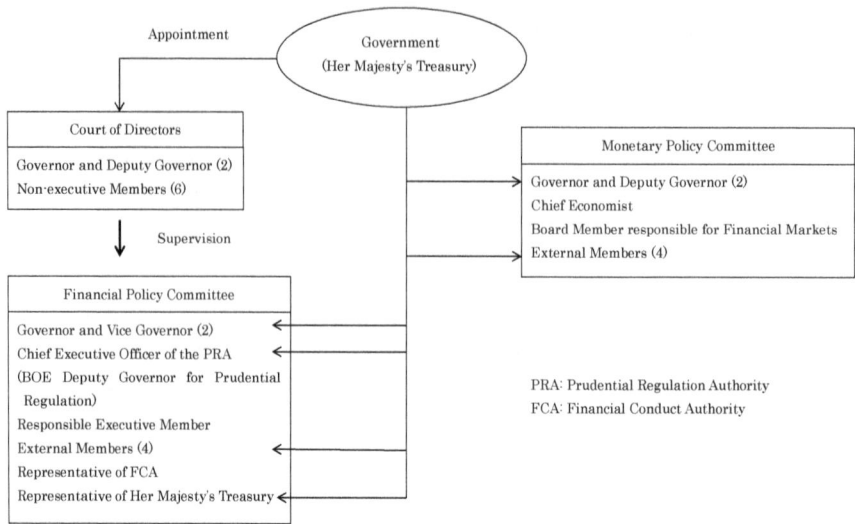

Fig. 2.5 Governance structure of the Bank of England

2.4.2.3 Board Structure of the Bank of Japan (Japan)

Under the new BOJ Act (effective 1998), BOJ's governance structure has a single board structure, the imperfect multiboard structure under the former BOJ Act being abolished. The BOJ Act of 1942 adopted a single board system with only an Executive Board but, when revised in 1949, a Policy Board was established in addition to the Executive Meeting, thus realizing a multiboard structure. Later, the new BOJ Act (Article 16) that came into effect in 1998 stipulated that the Bank adopt a single board system with just a Policy Board:

> Board members shall consist of six Members of the Policy Board, the Bank of Japan's Governor and two Deputy Governors. In this case, the Governor and the Deputy Governors shall perform their duties as Board members independently of each other.

The reason why the 'quasi-multiboard structure' was abolished was based on the understanding that decision-making by the Executive Board was given priority over the Policy Board, undermining the transparency of the policy making process. Generally speaking, the authority and responsibility of each board needs to be clear in a multiboard structure or else the coordination costs between the boards may surpass the mitigation effect of transaction costs. And, if the appointment process of members is unclear, one of the boards may in fact hamper the other board's function to avoid such coordination costs. The Policy Board under the old BOJ Act was considered to be in this situation.

The first problem concerning the BOJ's single board structure is that while the BOJ is responsible for monetary policy and prudential policy, responsibility within the Board is not separated. As mentioned in Sect. 2.4.1.3, it is difficult to maintain adequate distance and adjustment between monetary policy and prudential policy.

The second problem is that in addition to being a single board structure, the two features of public governance and corporate governance are not clearly integrated. From the BOJ Act (1997), Article 23:

> The Governor and the Deputy Governors shall be appointed by the Cabinet, subject to the consent of the House of Representatives and the House of Councillors. The Member of the Policy Board shall be appointed by the Cabinet, subject to the consent of the House of Representatives and the House of Councillors, from among persons with relevant knowledge and experience including experts on the economy or finance.

The appointment of Board members is based solely on the judgment of the Cabinet and the two Houses and thus only reflects public governance. No feature of corporate governance in appointing the Governor, Deputy Governors, and Members of the Policy Board reflecting the intention of private banks is incorporated in the BOJ's governance structure. Contrary to Williamson's explanation in his corporate governance theory, a safeguard for member private banks, which are major stakeholders, does not exist. In this regard, the BOJ's governance structure burdens member private banks with high transaction costs, and there is a possibility that this will become a significant problem when using the BOJ's payment services (see Chap. 7, Sect. 7.4.3).

2.5 Role of Capital Stock

When we look at the ownership aspect of central bank governance structure, all major central banks have 'capital stock,' just like private firms, and stockholders do exist. However, the rights of central bank stockholders are strictly limited in various ways and therefore they cannot be regarded as owners like those of private companies. This section will look at specific facts regarding the capital stock of the major central banks of the US, Europe, and Japan. Then, Williamson's theory will be applied to central bank capital stock and, following discussion of the need for such and the purpose, we conclude that his theory cannot explain either the rationale or function. Based on organizational governance, we will explain the meaning of a central bank's capital stock as a symbol of central bank independence.

2.5.1 Identifying Matters Related to Central Bank Capital Stock

We will first examine the fact that central bank stockholders cannot be considered owners and then observe features of major central banks' capital stock and ratio of capital stock to total assets.

2.5.1.1 Relationship Between Central Bank Capital Stock and Ownership

The central bank differs from the government which is a mere spending body, and is termed a 'balance-sheet agent' (which holds both assets and liabilities). A central bank balance sheet also shows 'net assets' which is the balance between assets and liabilities. Net assets of a central bank include 'provisions' and 'reserves' as well as 'capital stock' invested by the stockholders just like private companies, i.e., a stock company. A central bank's overall net assets are called 'capital'[13] but this section will discuss narrowly-defined capital that is subscribed by stockholders, and not 'net worth' that is broadly-defined capital including provisions and reserves. Narrowly-defined capital may simply be called 'stock' to differentiate from broadly-defined capital, 'net worth' (stock here means capital stock). Also, the owners of stock are subscribers and are sometimes called 'stockholders.'

These subscribers (stockholders) of the central bank cannot be considered as owners of the central bank like would be the case for private firms. This is due to the fact that central bank capital stock is extremely small compared to its net assets and that subscribers' rights are limited in various ways. From a legal point of view, for example, the Companies Act cannot be applied to the BOJ, and therefore rights of stockholders of companies as stipulated under the Act are not given to those of the BOJ.

Nevertheless, it is mistakenly regarded that capital stock does represent central bank ownership. For example, when BOE shares came to be held by HM Treasury in 1946, it was called nationalization of the BOE (explained under Sect. 2.5.2.3). And, as district FRB stock is held by respective member banks, district FRBs are sometimes termed "privately-owned Federal Reserve Banks" (Mullins, 1993). And, as will be mentioned (Sect. 2.5.3.2), when discussion was held to revise the BOJ Act in 1960, the idea to abolish private subscription to the Bank's capital stock was interpreted as 'nationalization' of the BOJ. Such view is based on a misperception merely considering that central bank stockholders are the same as those of private firms without carefully analyzing the features of central bank capital stock.

2.5.1.2 Capital Stock of Major Central Banks

Looking at the major central banks in the US and Europe as well as Japan, all have capital stock on their balance sheets. And, as shown in Table 2.1, the amount is negligible in comparison to overall assets. Moreover, type of stockholder and attaching rights are extremely limited compared to a private firm, and it is common across central banks that stockholders have no power regarding bank policy and management. However, the scope of limitation differs somewhat among central banks. We will look more closely at such differences in the following.

---

[13]For example, Milton and Sinclair (2011) also discuss the necessity of capital for a central bank and what they mean by 'capital' is 'net worth' that includes provisions and reserves.

Table 2.1 Major central banks' capital stock (figures from respective central bank's annual report)

	Capital stock (A)	Overall assets (B)	Capital adequacy ratio (A/B) (%)
Bank of Japan (billion yen)	0.10	139,457	0.00000072
Federal Reserve Bank of New York (billion dollars)	8.68	1,630	0.0053
Bank of England (billion pounds)	0.02	315	0.000063
ECB (billion euros)	10.76	2,733	0.0039
Deutsche Bundesbank (billion euros)	2.50	837	0.0030
Banque de France (billion euros)	1.00	709	0.0014
Banca d'Italia (billion euros)	0.0002	532	0.00000038

Note As of end-December 2011 except the Bank of Japan (as of end-March 2012).
With respect to FRS, the figures are from FRB of New York.

Bank of Japan (Japan)

The amount of the BOJ's stated capital stock is ¥100 million to be contributed to by both the government (¥55 million) and non-governmental persons (¥45 million). The BOJ issues 'investment securities' for capital stock contribution and holders may transfer or pledge them, but have no power regarding policy or management of the Bank. Should the BOJ be dissolved, residual assets in excess of paid-up capital (¥100 million) shall belong to the national treasury.

Federal Reserve System (US)

As mentioned under Sect. 2.4.2.1, the FRS consists of the Board (Washington D.C.) and 12 district FRBs covering the US. The Board in Washington D.C. only has a headquarter function and does not conduct any banking operations such as deposit taking, lending, and payment services, nor does it own any kind of capital. On the other hand, respective district FRBs conduct banking operations and have capital stock in their net worth in addition to assets and liabilities such as deposits and loans (therefore, each district FRB is a balance-sheet agent).

Among the major central banks, the capital stock of district FRBs (issued capital stock) is most similar to the capital stock of private firms. Not only is all issued capital stock of an FRB owned by member private banks (i.e., member banks of the FRB concerned), but also such member banks have the right to select directors to an FRB's Board of Directors (see Sect. 2.4.2.1). The FRS (2016, p. 6) explains as follows:

> The 12 regional Federal Reserve Banks issue shares of stock to member banks. Owning Reserve Bank stock is, however, quite different from owning stock in a private company.

The Reserve Banks are not operated for profit, and ownership of a certain amount of stock is, by law, a condition of membership in the System. The stock may not be sold, traded, or pledged as security for a loan, and dividends are, by law, paid to member banks at a maximum rate of 6 percent, determined in part by each member bank's total assets.

Bank of England (UK)

The BOE does issue stock but since 1946 all stock is owned by HM Treasury. BOE's Annual Report and Accounts 2017–18 (p. 115) explains as follows:

The entire capital comprising £14,553,000 of bank stock is held by the Treasury Solicitor on behalf of HM Treasury. The Bank regards its shareholder's funds as the capital it uses to support its normal operations.

European System of Central Banks

The capital stock of the European Central Bank (ECB) comes from the national central banks (NCBs) of all European System of Central Banks (ESCB) members and amounted to €10,825 million as of 1 January 2019. NCB shares of this capital are calculated using a formula which reflects a respective country's share of the total population and GDP of the ESCB. These two determinants have equal weighting. The ECB adjusts the shares every five years and whenever a new country joins the ESCB.

The largest contribution to the ECB's capital is from the Deutsche Bundesbank (18.4% of total) and the smallest is from the Central Bank of Malta (0.07% of total). The net profit of the ECB is distributed to its shareholders in proportion to their paid-up shares (the distribution may not exceed 80% of net profit), though contribution share has no direct relationship with policy and management of the ECB.

The Deutsche Bundesbank itself is established with capital stock amounting to €2.5 billion, all of which is owned by the Federal Republic of Germany. The second largest contributor after the Deutsche Bundesbank is the Banque de France (14.2% of total) which is established with capital stock of €1.0 billion and, likewise, all is owned by the government.

2.5.2 Application of Williamson's Theory to Capital Stock

This section will apply Williamson's theory on TCE to a central bank's capital stock and discuss its features. While Williamson's theory clarifies various features of central bank capital stock, it cannot explain either the rationale or function.

2.5.2.1 Application of Williamson's Corporate Governance Theory to Capital Stock

Williamson's corporate governance theory will be applied to explain that: the amount of central bank capital stock is low compared to the total assets and therefore stockholders do not need a safeguard, stockholders' rights are extremely limited legally and they are not regarded as owners, and central bank stakeholders are not limited to stockholders and a wide range of stakeholders participate in the governance structure of a central bank.

Amount of Central Bank Capital Stock and Necessity of a Safeguard
As mentioned in Sect. 2.5.1.2, the capital stock of major central banks is negligible compared to their total assets. From the perspective of Williamson's corporate governance theory, the degree of stake held by stockholders is relatively low compared to degree held by stakeholders who are not stockholders such as the public, legislative body/government, and private banks that utilize central banking services ('customer' as in Williamson's theory). Thus, even though stockholders cannot take part in a central bank's governance structure as a safeguard, transaction costs would not be so large that they would refuse subscription.

This is in stark contrast to private firms. The ratio of capital stock to net assets of private firms is far larger than that of central banks meaning that the stake held by subscribers is large. Therefore, in order to reduce transaction costs, a safeguard is necessary and stockholders are allowed to participate in shareholders' meetings and on the board of directors as owners.

Restriction of Subscribers' Rights and Ownership
Against the background of the above economic reasons, a central bank's subscribers' rights are also restricted legally compared to those of the stockholders of private firms. Therefore, a safeguard is not necessary for central bank stockholders in the first place, and, even if they feel the necessity, they do not have the owner's right to create a safeguard within the central bank governance structure like those of private firms do.

Scope of Stakeholders and their Participation in Central Bank Governance
Williamson's corporate governance theory suggests that all stakeholders, whether they are stockholders or not, should participate in corporate governance, and this corresponds with the central bank governance structure. In a central bank, all major stakeholders (or their representatives) take part in the central bank governance structure regardless of subscription. So, central bank stockholders are not the one and only stakeholders of central bank governance structure.

Actually, even if the government is not a stockholder, it still participates in central bank governance as the public's (who are a stakeholder) representative (this reflects the 'public governance' feature of central bank governance structure). Also, the same could be said for member banks (this reflects the 'corporate governance' feature of central bank governance structure).

In the case of the ECB, in view of the fact that its stakeholders are limited to member countries' governments and central banks, respective governments take part in the ECB's governance structure by appointing members of the Executive Board through the European Council (EC), and central banks take part as members of the ECB's Governing Council.

2.5.2.2   Application of Williamson's Corporate Finance Theory to Capital Stock

This section will consider whether Williamson's corporate finance theory can be applied to a central bank's capital stock. In conclusion, the theory cannot explain either the rationale or functions of central bank capital stock.

Transaction Specificity and Capital Stock of Central Banks
The theory regarding the relationship between transaction specificity and corporate finance cannot be applied to central bank capital stock. That is, central bank capital stock is not limited to purchasing assets with transaction specificity such as equipment (for example, the BOE clearly states that it uses capital to support its normal operations as mentioned under Sect. 2.5.1.2). In addition, the amount of central bank capital is negligible compared to its net assets and meaningless as a funding instrument.

Pecking Order Theory of Finance and Central Bank Capital Stock
Also, Williamson's pecking order theory of finance cannot basically be applied to central bank capital stock. Central banks have banknote issuance, deposits, retained earnings, and capital stock listed in the main accounts on the right side of their balance sheets, but currently none can be considered funding instruments. Central banks do not conduct operations such as issuing banknotes, and collecting deposits, for the purpose of purchasing certain assets. Therefore, there are no priorities among accounts such as banknote issuance, deposits, and capital stock and so this theory cannot explain the rationale behind a central bank's capital stock and functions.

2.5.2.3   Historical Background to Central Bank Capital Stock

As we have seen so far, Williamson's theory on TCE cannot explain the rationale and functions behind a central bank's capital stock. Nevertheless, historically, a central bank in its initial stage took the form of a stock company and was a private bank implying that it was once an organization to which we could apply Williamson's theory.

Let's look at the history of the BOE, one of the oldest central banks in the world. The BOE was established in 1694 as a joint stock company by 120 stockholders. Based on Hirayama (2006), if we look at its capital stock from the perspective of corporate finance, capital stock was £1.78 million against £3.3 million in net assets (53% as of 10 November 1696) which shows the importance of capital stock as a funding instrument. For reference, funding instruments other than capital were: (a) sealed bank bills (£0.89 million), (b) banknotes (£0.76 million), and (c) borrowing from Holland (£0.3 million). The use of capital is not limited, but most of the assets are loans to the government (£2.98 million) without any collateral and therefore an asset with high transaction specificity. Therefore, stockholders were major stakeholders and, in line with Williamson's theory, were at the center of the Bank's corporate governance as a safeguard. Later, in 1946, the BOE was nationalized by having all its stock be held by HM Treasury, but the fact that it is a stock company remains unchanged, even to this day.

2.5.3 Central Bank Capital Stock from the Perspective of Organizational Culture Theory

According to TCE, there is no actual meaning to central bank capital stock. Therefore, during the course of central bank history, it could have been abolished. Especially with respect to the FRS (established in 1913) and the RBA (established 1959), established relatively recently, they could have done so with no capital stock.

Nevertheless, almost all central banks of the world have capital stock. The reason is the fact that it has a symbolic meaning that cannot be explained by TCE.[14] 'Symbolic' does not mean that it has no significance. Rather, based on organizational culture theory that emphasizes the importance of symbol in an organization, capital stock as a symbol plays an important role in expressing the peculiarity of central bank organization. Specifically, capital stock is a symbol of central bank independence, suggesting that the central bank is not part of the government but an independent organization. If all or part of the capital stock is owned privately, capital stock clearly evidences the fact that the central bank is an independent organization, but even if all is owned by the government, it still acts as a symbol of central bank independence that tells a historical story that the central bank was once established as a private organization. The above will be explained further based on cultural sociology and organizational symbolism that are included in organizational culture theory.

2.5.3.1 Explanation Based on Cultural Sociology

Tognato (2012) published a book entitled *Central Bank Independence: Cultural Codes and Symbolic Performance* and clarified how a central bank's symbolic performance when monetary affairs come to the fore could influence discussion on central bank independence. His research is based on an idea from cultural sociology's 'Edinburgh school' (otherwise known as Strong Program Theory)[15] which believes

---

[14]TCE cannot explain the meaning of central bank capital stock but this does not mean that no economic theory can explain it. For example, 'signaling theory' can, to a certain extent, explain the significance of central bank capital stock. However, this theory uses somewhat meaningful information for a signal that aims to overcome asymmetric information. To the contrary, the function of symbol does not necessarily assume asymmetric information and signs and codes that have no meaning are used as symbols. Considering that central bank capital stock no longer has any significance as 'capital', it may be more adequate to apply symbol theory rather than signaling theory.

[15]Edinburgh-based school of thought, the 'Edinburgh school' (or Strong Program Theory) is one of the schools based on sociology that research the social background of science. It was founded by David Bloor of Edinburgh University in the UK (in his book published in 1976). This school proposes

that the discovery of scientific knowledge is influenced by the cultural background of a society in which the scientist exists.

This suggests that the degree of public support for the idea (scientific knowledge) that central bank independence contributes to macroeconomic stability (low inflation, price stability) depends on how stable the culture surrounding the central bank is (stability culture). Stability culture includes attitudes towards inflation as well as central bank symbolic performance regarding monetary affairs. For example, in Germany, the Bundesbank has, in the past, appealed to the public in the form of a 'morality play'[16] when it was in conflict with politicians and the government. This morality play is symbolic performance by the Bundesbank. Such a play can exist because there is a stability culture in German society where there is an understanding that hampering central bank independence is seen as an act of swaying the foundation of German society and violating the "sacred center of the society" (Tognato, ibid.).

This research does not directly explain the symbolic significance central bank capital stock has for central bank independence. However, it does capture head on the influence of a central bank's symbolic performance on its independence, and if we replace its symbolic performance with its capital stock, it would illustrate the symbolic significance of capital stock.

2.5.3.2 Explanation Based on Organizational Symbolism

'Organizational symbolism' is a theory not tailored toward central banks like Tognato's theory, but about economic management discussing the role of symbolism in an organization. We will give an outline of this theory and then apply it to central bank capital stock, clarifying that capital stock has a symbolic meaning for central bank independence.

Outline of Organizational Symbolism

Sakashita (2002) states that "organizational symbolism is basically interested in various symbolic actions within an organization" and "as symbolism is an act of using and expressing symbol, the concept of symbol for organizational symbolism is thus extremely important" (translated from Japanese). Having said this, he adds that symbols can be categorized as:

- Verbal (such as myths, legends, tales),
- Active (such as rituals and rites of passage),
- Materialistic (such as status symbols, products, and company logos).

And, according to Takahashi (2006), "Organizational symbolism focuses on understanding the patterns of symbolic performance that creates and maintains the

---

that since scientific knowledge is also affected by the social environment, it is not necessarily objective. Therefore, it suggests that both 'true' (rational) and 'false' (irrational) scientific theories require explanation using the same types of cause. This is why it is called the Strong Program.

[16] 'Morality play' can be interpreted as 'moral lesson' and is an allegorical play popular in Europe during the 15th and 16th centuries. The characters personify abstract qualities or concepts (as virtues, vices, or death) and try to prompt a protagonist to choose a Godly life over one of evil.

organization's meaning" (translated from Japanese). Moreover, Sakashita (2002) gives the following three functions of symbol in an organization:

- **Descriptive functions**: A function where a symbol expresses an organization's reality. For example, a company's logo symbolically expresses its organizational and operational characteristics.
- **Energy control functions**: A function to control organizational energy by inspiring organizational members or relaxing their tensions.
- **Maintenance of system functions**: A function to protect and maintain systems from change by showing the basis for harmony, order, and stability, or by announcing in advance "acceptable pattern of change."

Among the symbols, 'tale,' one of the verbal symbols, is said to enhance behavioral commitment by reminding members of the organization's philosophy and principles, creating confidence, and promoting traditional values. Sakashita (2002, p. 96) explains the relation between symbolism and organizational culture (discussed in Chap. 4) as follows:

> Symbolic actions such as using and expressing verbal, active, and materialistic symbols are 'symbolism' and, if the meaning of a symbol is shared through such symbolism, the shared meaning and symbol that mediated it comprise the 'organizational culture' (translated from Japanese).

Application to a Central Bank

In line with the above theory on organizational symbolism, capital stock of a central bank can fit in with all the three categories of a symbol. In the first category, central bank capital stock is 'verbal' in the form of a 'tale.' Central bank capital stock announces the fact that the central bank evolved from being a private bank with capital stock. According to the theory of organizational symbolism, this 'tale' reminds everyone of the values and principles of a central bank, and creates confidence and promotes traditional values. That is, capital stock reminds staff of a central bank's private banking origins and that it is an organization with values independent from those of the government.

As for the second category, the 'action' to raise capital stock reminds people of a private firm and clearly shows that it is an independent organization, though the act itself does not have any meaning. In a private firm, such investment action is an important act to decide the basis of ownership, a governance structure. And, as mentioned in Sect. 2.4.2.1, in the case of FRS's governance structure, member banks participate as stockholders to a certain extent. Though required to do so legally, making an investment (though small) could be considered as a symbolic act to safeguard the stake of member banks.

With regard to the third category, although central bank capital stock is not purely 'materialistic', it functions like a company's logo and illustrates that a central bank is an organization similar to a private organization. The logo of a central bank, 'capital stock,' symbolically expresses that a central bank has common organizational and operational characteristics like those of private organizations. In this regard too, central bank capital stock plays the role of a symbol showing that the central bank concerned is indeed an organization independent of the government just like any private organization is.

Moreover, the theory of organizational symbolism recognizes that as a system maintenance function, a symbol has the function of protecting and maintaining the system from changes. If we apply this to a central bank, capital stock, its symbol, plays the role of protecting central bank independence. This could be realized by announcing an "acceptable pattern of change" when the "harmony, stability and order" (Sakashita, 2002, translated from Japanese) that central bank independence represents are threatened.

As such, according to the theory of organizational symbolism, central bank capital stock is effective in maintaining central bank independence and cannot be considered simply as a relic of the past. Therefore, abolishing capital stock means to lose the symbol of central bank independence. Of course, nationalizing a central bank by having the government own all its capital stock also affects central bank independence.

This corresponds with the argument for abolishing the capital stock of the BOJ. In 1960, at the time when the BOJ Act was being revised, the Bank proposed abolishing its capital stock in an effort to oppose the idea of 'nationalizing' the Bank through full government ownership of capital stock that had the objective of weakening its independence. The government's argument in 'nationalizing' the Bank reflects the fact that the global standard concerning central bank independence had yet to be established at that time, and, moreover, attention was only paid to a central bank's public governance with not much understanding of a central bank's corporate governance feature. To the contrary, when the BOJ Act was revised again in 1997, not much discussion was held on nationalization through the retirement of privately invested capital stock, and much less on abolishing capital stock. This implies that since 1960, a consensus had been built to strengthen central bank independence.

2.6 Conclusion

Based on the theory of club goods, central bank services have two types of functions, those classified as public goods such as the issuance of banknotes and monetary policy implementation, and those classified as club goods such as payment services. As a result, central banks have two organizational features—as a public organization to provide public goods, and as a private organization to provide club goods. Of the two, public governance will be discussed more deeply in Chap. 3 and corporate governance in Chap. 7, Sect. 7.4.3.

To effectively integrate these two features of governance structure, it would be appropriate to adopt a multiboard structure for a central bank's organizational governance. As a matter of fact, the FRS of the US and the BOE of the UK adopt a multiboard structure. On the other hand, the BOJ adopts a single board structure as stipulated under the BOJ Act, which is a rare example. Looking at this from Williamson's theory, no safeguard for the BOJ's stakeholders (i.e., member private banks) is incorporated in the BOJ's governance structure and, therefore, they need to shoulder considerable transaction costs when making transactions with the BOJ.

Governance structure not only incorporates the above aspect of organizational governance, but also the aspect of who owns the organization, the ownership. All major central banks have capital stock just like private firms which have stockholders. However, the rights of central bank stockholders are restricted in various ways and they therefore cannot be regarded as a central bank's owners like they would for private firms. And Williamson's theory cannot explain the raison d'être of central bank capital stock. However, if we apply the recent theory of organizational culture that emphasizes the importance of symbolism, it becomes clear that central bank capital stock is significant as a symbol of central bank independence to prove that a central bank is not part of the government but an independent organization.

In this chapter, how we should design the board structure is only discussed from the perspective of integrating features of governance structure. Chap. 4, Sect. 4.4 will discuss the subject from the perspective of balancing monetary policy and the banking function within a central bank, and Chap. 5, Sect. 5.4 will discuss it from the viewpoint of the relationship between prudential policy and monetary policy. Moreover, Chap. 7, Sect. 7.4 will take up the discussion from the viewpoint of central bank governance over central bank payment systems. Any organizational governance issue of a central bank also includes discussion on how an organization should be managed in addition to that on designing board structure, which will be taken up in Chap. 4, Sect. 4.4.

Chapter 3
Public Governance of Central Banks

3.1 Overview

As discussed in Chap. 2, Sect. 2.3, the governance structure of central banks has two aspects: corporate governance and public governance. This chapter analyzes the latter in depth using the theoretical frameworks provided by new institutional economics. In this chapter, 'public governance'—a term now widely used in the literature on public organization[1]—is understood to be an institutional framework, where the general public governs the central bank by and through the legislative and executive bodies in a country.

The central bank, being an organization with a public mandate, belongs to the government in a broad sense, as do the legislative, executive, and judicial branches. It acts in interplay with such other governmental bodies within a country's governance structure. The relationship between a central bank and the legislative and executive branches has long been an issue for lively debate. While a central bank needs operational independence to discharge its mandate efficiently, at the same time it should be subject to public governance in a representative democracy since it is an organization with a public mandate. Debate has centered on how to structure the relationships between the central bank, the legislature/politicians, and the executive branch (the cabinet/government head) and ministries, and how to strike the right mix of independence and accountability in order to ensure that a central bank performs its functions to best effect.

These are public governance issues which we attempt to analyze from a new perspective, namely by applying several relevant theories on governance, each of which has seen significant development and application in the past few decades: transaction cost economics (TCE), agency theory, and public choice theory. These theories have

---

[1] For example, Bevir (2007).

This chapter is based on *BIS Working Papers*, No. 299, "Public governance of central banks: an approach from new institutional economics," by Y. Oritani, March 2010.

© Springer Nature Singapore Pte Ltd. 2019
Y. Oritani, *The Japanese Central Banking System Compared with Its European and American Counterparts*, https://doi.org/10.1007/978-981-13-9001-2_3

several common features: they broadly come under the new institutional economics umbrella, which extends economic analysis to the understanding of the various institutions in the economy and society; they are based on rational choice by economic agents which maximize self-interest; they have voters, elected representatives, and bureaucrats at the core of their analytical models, along with other typical economic agents; their interest is in positive, empirical questions that seek to understand how things work rather than normative questions as to how they should be.

Section 3.2 considers and applies two theories based on TCE: Williamson's theory of 'governance as probity' and Moe's theory that scrutinizes the nature of autonomy in public bureaucracy. Governance as probity provides an answer to the question as to why a central bank needs to be a public organization similar to other government organizations where profit and efficiency maximization are not their objectives. Here, this chapter goes beyond public governance in the narrow sense of the relationship between a central bank and the legislative and executive branches to examine the internal organizational structure of a central bank from the public governance perspective.

While Williamson describes foreign affairs as "sovereign transactions," we consider central banking as a sovereign transaction. Central banking needs 'governance as probity' in order to avoid "probity hazard." It can achieve this through very low-powered incentives, career staff with employment security, extensive administrative controls, and appointment of the leadership of the agency by the president (here, Williamson is referring to the US president). Such a public organization solution, however, may come at the cost of some inefficiency.

Moe's theory of public bureaucracy extends TCE to analysis of the political process. Moe's theory argues that political parties and politicians in an "uncertain" political situation, where changes in majority control can and do occur, may want to install autonomy (independence) at the central bank in order to reduce to a minimum the cost of policy swings at the central bank as the majority party changes. Using Moe's theory, we try to ascertain whether central bank independence from politics is justified not only on the grounds of better central banking but on that of a better political process. Insights are obtained into the situation in Japan, where changes in the majority party are very rare. Given this state of affairs, the theory predicts that the political tendency to reinforce central bank independence may not be as strong in Japan as in countries where changes in the majority party are less infrequent.

Section 3.3 applies agency theory to the issues associated with public governance of a central bank, mainly those related to central bank independence and accountability. With regard to central bank independence, we examine why some theories, based on the congressional dominance hypothesis, argue that central banks are strongly influenced by the legislature/politicians or the executive branch in spite of their formal independence—an important characteristic of a central bank, similar to that of an independent agency in the government.

We emphasize a central bank's multiple principals (vis-à-vis both the heads of the executive and legislative branches). While this can cause inefficiency within a central bank, this chapter shows that it may be instrumental in preventing central bank policies from becoming biased. We also address an interesting legal discussion in Japan that occurred when the Bank of Japan (BOJ) Act was amended. The major issue was whether it was constitutional for the BOJ to conduct some functions that could be conceived as an exercise of executive power.

Section 3.3 also examines whether a multiboard system—following Fama and Jensen—is a more effective way of governance to ensure central bank independence than a single board system. Fama and Jensen's theory considers a multiboard system at private corporations as a mechanism for shareholders to cope with agency problems arising from the separation between ownership and management. We show that a multiboard system may be beneficial for similar reasons in the central banking context, in that it can ensure independence by allowing the government to appoint only upper board members.

With respect to central bank accountability, we analyze what aspects are important for central banks, based on the work of Jackson which regards accountability as a principal's tool for monitoring its agent in a principal–agent setting. Following Jackson's approach, we distinguish several types of accountability: political, legal, financial, and efficiency. We argue that accountability with respect to efficiency is not important for a central bank because of the significant difficulties in measuring such efficiency, or more fundamentally, in defining it.

Section 3.4 revisits the fundamental question of why a central bank needs to be independent from the legislative and executive branches in a representative democracy, from the perspective of public choice theory. Benefiting from studies that critically scrutinize majority rule in the decision-making process in a representative democracy, it shows that the public interest is not always correctly represented and conveyed to the central bank. The literature suggests that in such circumstances a central bank finds itself susceptible to political pressure from politicians maximizing votes and seeking short-term gains. It is thus necessary to ensure central bank independence to guard against such pressure.

3.2 Application of Transaction Cost Economics

This section applies TCE to the public governance of a central bank. First, Williamson's governance as probity hypothesis is applied to central banks and clarifies why they should be considered public organizations similar to bureaucratic organizations that do not pursue profit or efficiency maximization. Next, Boylan's theory that central bank independence is necessary to reduce to a minimum the potential for, and hence the costs of, policy swings—a theory based on Moe's autonomy of bureaucracy hypothesis—is introduced.

3.2.1 Application of Williamson's Governance as Probity Hypothesis

Williamson (1999) directly applied TCE to public sector transactions and proposed a new category of governance structure, governance as probity,[2] in addition to the original three categories (market, hierarchical, hybrid). This new governance structure is structured to mitigate probity hazard, one of the transaction costs in public sector transactions that Williamson considers the most important. It is held that such a governance structure can be realized in public agents but not in private organizations. After explaining Williamson's governance as probity theory, public governance of a central bank is examined by applying the above theory.

3.2.1.1 Importance of Probity in Sovereign Transaction

According to Williamson, public agents constitute a "puzzle" for economics since they continue to exist despite being regarded as "a haven for inefficiency." Therefore, he believes it necessary to look into "public sector transactions" based on the fundamental question of why private organizations cannot substitute for public agents.

Williamson first divides public sector transactions into six: procurement, redistributional, regulatory, sovereign, judicial, and infrastructure. "Sovereign transactions" are an extreme case among the six, being uniquely conducted by the public sector. "Examples of sovereign tasks include foreign affairs, the military, foreign intelligence, managing the money supply, and, possibly, the judiciary," but Williamson mainly analyzes foreign affairs.

In line with the analytical procedure of TCE, the transaction costs of public sector transactions—especially sovereign transactions—are scrutinized. Such transaction costs are essentially "contractual hazards." Having pointed out "asset specificity" and "probity hazard" as two important contractual hazards in sovereign transactions, Williamson regards probity hazard to be more important. With respect to asset specificity, while physical assets are negligible (since they are hardly used in sovereign transactions), human assets that undergo non-transferable training are necessary. Thus, contractual hazards based on human asset specificity, specifically the "hold-up problem,"[3] cannot be neglected. Nevertheless, since the hold-up problem is not unique to sovereign transactions, "what really distinguishes the foreign affairs transaction…is the hazard of probity," and so the latter is examined in more depth. It should be noted that the "hazard of operating cost excesses" that poses a serious threat in private sector transactions is not considered a big issue.

For Williamson, "probity" is the same as the "loyalty and rectitude" or "high standard of integrity" with which a foreign affairs transaction (for example) is dis-

---

[2]Williamson (1999) used "governance as integrity" but, considering the content of his paper, 'governance as probity' (used frequently hereafter) seems more appropriate.

[3]Refer to Klein (2004) for details of the hold-up problem.

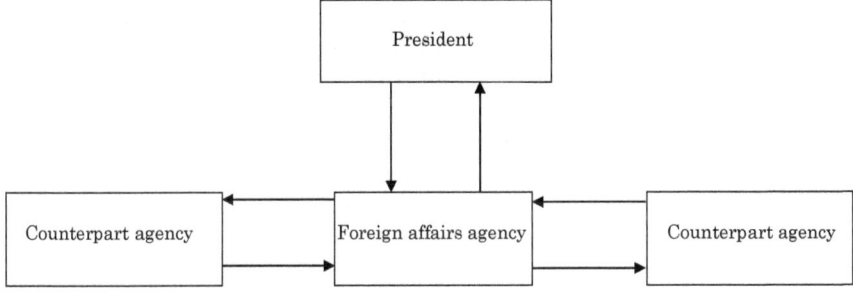

Fig. 3.1 Probity considerations (Williamson, 1999)

charged.[4] Here probity means an honesty that has a deep relationship with trustworthiness, and that if a person has probity, others will trust his words and have faith in his judgment. Moreover, "professional excellence" at the service of the organization and "fidelity to self-defining principles" are also considered to be included in probity. Williamson explains that transactions that require probity are extremely long term, self-renewing and ongoing, and require "loyalty to leadership and to the mission" and "process integrity."

With these definitions as a premise, the probity of foreign affairs transactions is shown to consist of three aspects as portrayed in Fig. 3.1: vertical, horizontal, and internal. Probity under each aspect and the probity hazard that may arise are explained as follows.

First, "the vertical aspect" of probity concerns relations between the foreign affairs agency and the president (Williamson is referring to the US president; same hereafter in Sect. 3.2.1), who is primarily responsible for the administration of foreign affairs. Williamson points out that probity is involved when considering responses to the following questions: "Does the president have confidence in the information and assessments that are provided by the foreign affairs agency?" "Does the agency comply with directives in a timely and efficacious way?" "Is the agency sufficiently responsive to the president?"[5] "Is the agency perceived to be adventurous?" "Does the agency have an abiding respect for the mission?" The probity hazard here is the risk of breaking such relationships between the president and the agency.

Second, the "horizontal aspect" with regard to the probity of the foreign affairs agency concerns the relationship with "counterpart agency[ies]" which are the foreign affairs agencies of countries with which it negotiates. Probity in this respect includes "accurate communication" and "authority" although the former may inten-

---

[4] According to *Webster's Third New International Dictionary*, 'probity' is defined as honest, upright, virtuous; uncompromising adherence to the highest principles and ideals; unimpeachable integrity. Shirakawa (2018a, b) points out the importance of probity for the central bank.

[5] "Responsiveness" is a concept used in the theory of public administration to show how swiftly and wholeheartedly bureaucrats respond to requests from the public and politicians. It is considered to be in a trade-off relationship with the concept of "neutrality" which shows to what extent bureaucrats give neutral suggestions and analysis without having to fawn on politicians.

tionally be made vague in some cases. Should counterpart agencies perceive that the agency lacks authority, probity hazard arises, thereby hampering effective negotiation. The reason why this probity hazard arises stems from two aspects: probity hazard in relation to the president and that in relation to the internal organization.

Third, the probity of the internal organization refers to the integrity of officers and staff of the foreign affairs agency and accordingly encompasses a broad concept that includes professional ability and process integrity. Probity hazard in this regard is considered to cause probity hazard in both vertical and horizontal aspects.

3.2.1.2   Governance of Sovereign Transactions

Williamson thinks public agents have a more "adequate" governance structure than private organizations in maintaining the necessary probity for sovereign transactions and reducing transaction costs to a minimum (i.e., mitigating probity hazards). 'Adequate' is not in the sense of reducing financial costs to a minimum, of course, but whether a transaction's objective could be achieved or not.

Based on practical analysis of the US Department of State, the public agent that actually conducts foreign affairs in the US, Williamson identifies four attributes of a governance structure that are essential for maintaining probity and adequately countering probity hazard:

- Very low-powered pecuniary incentives.
- Career staff with employment security.
- Extensive administrative controls and procedures.
- Appointment and termination of agency officers by the president and legislature.

Williamson calls a governance structure with the above attributes 'governance as probity' and argues that public agents are best suited for realizing such an arrangement. Inappropriate as it may seem in light of efficiency, it is difficult for private organizations to realize the above governance structure. In summary, public agents are considered the "best feasible governance response" against probity hazard affecting sovereign transactions.

Since these attributes are correlated with one another, Williamson does not explain them separately. His explanation is summarized as follows.

Very Low-powered Incentives
The first attribute of a governance structure that prevents probity hazard is that the organization's incentive scheme should be "low-powered" and would not contain any high-powered incentives designed to maximize profit and efficiency.[6] Specifically, (a) "lest pressure to realize operating cost savings arises at the systems level, unexpected

---

[6]Moe (1990b) introduced the concept of "inefficiency by design" whereby public agent inefficiency was deliberately intended by parliament and voters as a means to counter political uncertainty. Moe explains that if a public agent is efficient, unwanted policy may then be efficiently carried out with a change in political power. Therefore, by intentionally introducing complex administrative procedures, public agents are made inefficient.

budgets will not accrue to the agency but will be returned to the central Treasury"; (b) "payments contingent on realized cost savings will not be made to individuals who discover and implement cost savings; neither will such savings be used to improve on-the-job consumption of amenities"; (c) "compensation in such an agency will be flat and also resource deployment will be restricted"; and (d) the organization "has little risk of bankruptcy and has a reliable budgetary base in the face of economic adversity."

High-powered incentive schemes would undermine the probity of the overall organization. High-powered incentives increase probity hazard, and since probity hazard cannot be prevented by imposing a penalty, it is necessary to use a low-powered incentive scheme. By making the incentive scheme low-powered, "adventurousness" and "unwanted enterprise" can be restrained. A low-powered incentive scheme is also necessary for employment security.

Career Staff with Employment Security
Generous employment terms, such as job security, is a second attribute of governance as probity. This would nurture "career staff" within the organization and strengthen loyalty towards the organization and "vocational commitment." At the same time, such an approach is expected to overcome staff reluctance to specialize.

Based on employment security, strong value is placed on "skills in negotiation, cultural sophistication and good manners." Deep knowledge and "integrity to the mission" is similarly highly valued within an organization. Additionally, "caution, an aversion to bold language or action, a desire for consensus," the importance of accuracy prevailing throughout the organization, that "seniors should be consulted (vertical coordination)" when responding to non-routine events, and that any discontent should be expressed via "administrative due process," are also vitally important traits. In order to promote staff specialization, "specialized training will be used to inculcate the distinctive values and practices of the foreign affairs organization."

As a result, staff are endowed with high "social conditioning" and career staff participate in foreign affairs on a long-term basis. Although doors are open to outside employment, career staff mostly look inward for "career moves" and a "specialized internal labor market" develops within the organization. Therefore, it is highly likely that foreign affairs leadership comes from promotions from amongst the career staff.

Extensive Administrative Controls and Procedures
When employment is secured under the above low-powered incentive scheme, it may induce some staff to "shirk," causing the organization to be inefficient. Therefore, governance to limit "egregious shirking" through detailed administrative controls such as "bureaucratic rules, regulations, and standard operating procedures" becomes the third attribute. While admitting its effect against shirking, Williamson states that "the main purpose of administrative controls is to promote probity."

Examples given of such administrative controls are "respect for protocol," "stipulated obligation," "jurisdictional ordering by official rules and regulations," and clearly established "hierarchical authority." Moreover, in light of due respect for probity, even the slightest breach of secrecy will be treated as an inexcusable breach of contract.

Appointment and Termination of Agency Officials by President and Legislature
Fourth, it is necessary to have a governance structure whereby an agency chief is
appointed by the president and approved by the legislature. This is necessary for
the foreign affairs agency to gain the confidence of both domestic and overseas
parties. The foreign affairs organization must exhibit adequate "responsiveness" to
the president, and, on the other hand, authority given by the president will enhance
probity when negotiating with counterpart agencies.

Williamson considers approval by the legislature of presidential appointments is
good governance practice. In a division of powers system, the agency chief's probity
towards the mission can be strengthened through the hearings and approval process of
the legislature. The president will have a stronger incentive to choose a candidate who
inspires confidence, rather than choosing on the basis of personal likes and dislikes.
Williamson also points out that, "since the legislature can reach an understanding
with the agency chief as to his policy and plans through the process, deviations from
the expressed policy and plans can be made the subject of hearings."

However, agency officers should not always be passive vis-à-vis the president and
the legislature, but may need to collide with short-term political interests in order
to protect probity towards the mission. Since a trade-off exists between short-term
political interests and the long-term interests of the state, Williamson suggests that
"mission safeguards" should be introduced when designing governance structures.

3.2.1.3 Replication by a Private Organization

Private Organization and Four Attributes of Governance
An organization incorporating the above governance structure is of course considered
to be a public organization, but Williamson intentionally raises the question: Can a
private organization replicate such governance? By proving that it cannot, Williamson
emphasizes the importance of the probity of the public organization.[7]

Williamson argues that if a private organization took on responsibility for foreign affairs, it would end in failure. Since a private organization attaches greater
importance to cost control and profits, probity would be sacrificed. A private organization tends to appropriate the net income resulting from cost savings stemming
from reforms. But such savings should go to the Treasury—and the very low-powered
incentive in a public agency is part of this mechanism and reinforces the commitment of career staff in a public institution. By contrast, a strong incentive scheme is
one of the main features of a private organization, but this would loosen administrative controls, weaken the responsiveness of the agency to the president, and erode
the employment security of career staff. That is, if a private organization were to
take responsibility for foreign affairs, trade-offs would exist between foreign policy

---

[7]Moreover, Williamson discussed governance structure where a "regulatory agency" that is neither a
public agent nor a private organization assigns foreign affairs to a private organization and supervises
the organization, and reached the conclusion that a public agent was the most appropriate for
sovereign tasks.

efficacy and net income. Against such a background, to safeguard the interests of the state, the state would not fully delegate authority concerning foreign affairs to a private organization. Accordingly, counterpart agents in other nation states would not regard a private organization as the clear representative of the State and would frequently request review, change, or complete renegotiation.

Incomplete Contract and Adaptive Coordination
Williamson believes that this is because a contract to entrust foreign affairs transactions to a private organization cannot but be very incomplete. How could a private firm reconcile the contract to shoulder responsibility for foreign affairs with the demands of responding to an unanticipated event? How should a competitive bid be carried out? It would be very difficult, if not impossible, to write a contract that specified in advance what the firm should do in each case, since neither governments nor private organizations can accurately forecast all future contingencies.

As such, Williamson believes that "adaptive coordination" (adaptive and sequential decision-making) is the only feasible way to counter contingencies not covered in a contract and be able to play a negotiation game rich in countermove strategies. Williamson's theory of adaptive coordination places importance on probity during the "adaptive process," and accordingly differs from the theory of Hart, Shleifer, and Vishny (1997) that emphasizes human asset specificity. Hart et al. consider that human asset specificity will lead to the hold-up problem and for this reason there are transactions that cannot be entrusted to private organizations. While Williamson admits that the hold-up problem is one of the reasons that some transactions cannot be entrusted to the private sector, it is only part of the adaptive process. He considers that probity hazards that affect the overall adaptive process are the more significant impediment.[8]

3.2.1.4 Application to Central Bank Governance

Williamson's theory applies to central banks—and Williamson himself considered the management of the money supply as an example of a sovereign transaction.

Features of Central Bank Transactions
The first step is to examine the features of central bank transactions. Though features of central bank transactions have been discussed in Chap. 2, Sect. 2.3.1 by differentiating between public sector goods and club goods, this chapter will reinvestigate them in line with Williamson's typology of public sector transactions.

Central bank transactions are similar to foreign affairs transactions in that they are made not in pursuit of private profit but for the benefit of the country. However,

---

[8] According to Williamson, "adaptive process" entails eight steps: (a) the occasion to adapt needs to be disclosed, after which (b) alternative adaptations are identified, (c) the ramifications of each are worked out, (d) the best adaptation is decided, (e) the chosen adaptation is communicated and accepted by the agency, (f) the adaptation is implemented, (g) follow-up assessments are made, and (h) adaptive, sequential adjustments are made thereafter," and Williamson criticizes that of these eight steps, Hart et al. (1997) consider only steps (a), (d), and (e).

while foreign affairs transactions are limited to sovereign transactions, central bank transactions involve not only sovereign transactions (management of the money supply) but also transactions providing infrastructure. The central bank provides three types of services: (a) management of the money supply (monetary policy, market operations); (b) payment and settlement services; and (c) maintenance of financial system stability.

First, it seems appropriate to classify management of the money supply under sovereign transactions as suggested by Williamson. However, monetary policy is normally, in advanced countries, conducted through market operations. And, market operations are carried out as part of banking operations centering on financial transactions (sales of securities and fund loans) in the financial markets between a central bank and private financial institutions. This differs greatly from foreign affairs transactions.

Second, payment and settlement services, unlike foreign affairs transactions, should be classified under "infrastructure" according to Williamson's types of public sector transactions. The payment and settlement services of a central bank comprise the issuance and circulation of banknotes and interbank settlement services, both of which are considered transactions that provide infrastructure.[9] However, the provision of payment and settlement services entails the characteristics of a sovereign transaction and cannot be considered as the simple provision of infrastructure. This is because, as described in Chaps. 1 and 7, interbank settlement services accompany credit extension by a central bank to participants in payment and settlement systems. And this credit extension has the feature of a sovereign transaction just like monetary policy and the maintenance of financial system stability.

Third, services related to the maintenance of financial system stability through central bank transactions seem to have a strong similarity to sovereign transactions as is the case with monetary policy. Also, central bank loans to private financial institutions to maintain financial system stability are similar to monetary policy in the sense that sovereign transactions are made in the form of financial transactions with private financial institutions. And, while the supervision and regulation of private financial institutions by a central bank have the aspect of sovereign transactions, they also have the feature of transactions accompanying the provision of infrastructure considering that they are implemented to monitor participants of payment and settlement systems as part of the provision of payment and settlement services.

As such, central bank transactions consist of varying degrees of sovereign transactions: (a) high-degree sovereign transactions (monetary policy); (b) low-degree sovereign transactions (payment and settlement services); and (c) medium-degree transactions (maintenance of financial system stability). All central bank transac-

---

[9]Among public sector transactions, Williamson (1999, p. 321) explains "infrastructure" as follows: "The administration of police, fire, roads, parks, prisons, education, etc. is mainly a matter for state and local government. These transactions will not be considered here but are gist for the study of comparative economic organization and are increasingly coming under scrutiny." And, having the construction of prisons in mind, Williamson considers that although the possibility of probity hazard in providing infrastructure is less than for foreign affairs transactions, the possibility of contractual hazard with regard to asset specificity and cost savings is higher.

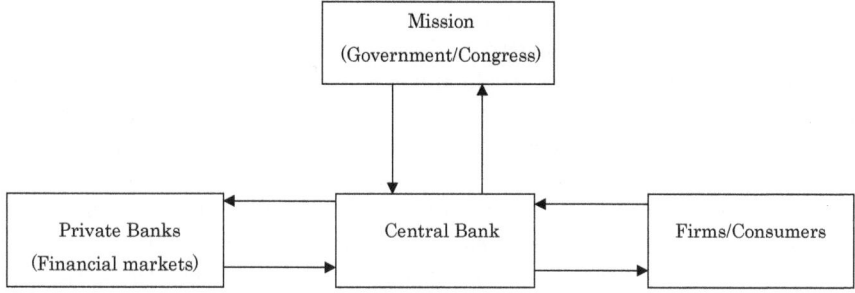

Fig. 3.2 Probity structure of central bank transactions

tions share, albeit to a different degree, the common feature of being a sovereign transaction. Therefore, we will consider central bank transactions comparing with foreign affairs transactions focusing on their common feature of being sovereign transactions.

While foreign affairs transactions are conducted using relatively stable skills such as foreign affairs negotiation tactics, central bank transactions are conducted through banking operations that are easily influenced by changes in information technology (IT) and financial transaction techniques. Therefore, it is necessary to change and renew the skills and facilities/services related to central bank transactions in accordance with changes and progress in IT and financial transaction techniques. Such a difference in transaction features should be taken into consideration when applying Williamson's discussion on foreign affairs transactions to central bank transactions.

Probity Structure of Central Bank Transactions

Based on the features of central bank transactions as mentioned above, probity and probity hazards relating to central bank transactions in line with the three aspects of probity in Williamson's foreign affairs transactions are shown in Fig. 3.2.

In Fig. 3.2, what clearly differs from foreign affairs transactions in Fig. 3.1 with regard to the vertical aspect is that the central bank does not have a direct relationship with the president (executive branch) and enjoys a considerable degree of independence from both the executive and the legislative branches. As such, the "mission of the central bank" will take the position of president in foreign affairs transactions. In this respect, central bank probity will be "abiding respect for the central bank mission" such as price stability and the stability of financial systems, in line with Williamson's "abiding respect for the mission." The mission will not be self-determined, but typically defined by the legislature (often in consultation with the central bank). While a central bank enjoys independence from the executive and legislative branches, it nevertheless has regular indirect contact, which means that probity with respect to responsiveness such as "whether reliable information is provided" to the executive and legislative branches will become an issue, albeit less than with foreign affairs transactions.

Therefore, probity hazards in this respect would be, for example, being disloyal to the mission, not providing information faithfully to the executive and legislative branches, and the lack of a relationship of trust with the executive and legislative branches. Such hazards would undermine the basic attributes necessary for conducting central bank transactions and would also greatly affect the second aspect which will be explained in the next paragraph. As for probity regarding responsiveness, this is deeply related to the 'accountability' of public agents, including the central bank.

Looking at the horizontal aspect, while there are overseas central banks and international organizations that are equivalent of overseas foreign affairs organizations in the case of foreign affairs transactions, counterparties of central bank transactions are basically domestic financial institutions and the general public. Therefore, the direct counterparties of monetary policy and market operations are the participants in financial markets, and indirect counterparties include firms and the general public. As is the case with foreign affairs transactions, probity is required on the part of a central bank in dealing with such counterparties with some intended and necessary reserve or discretion. As for the counterparties of payment and settlement services, they are financial institutions that have current deposit accounts with the central bank in the case of interbank settlement services, and the general public that uses cash in the case of small-value settlement services such as banknotes. The direct counterparties of transactions concerning the maintenance of financial system stability are private financial institutions, although firms and the general public are also included indirectly.

Probity hazard in this respect consists in the words and actions of the officials and staff of a central bank that undermine so-called 'market confidence' or weaken 'policy credibility.' Market participants will deem that the central bank does not have the appropriate authority if central bankers lose the confidence of the market and also if they lack probity vis-à-vis their mission or if the relationship of trust with the executive and legislative branches is lost. In this sense, what Williamson pointed out with respect to foreign affairs transactions also holds true for a central bank. The same could also be applied to central bank transactions such as payment and settlement services and maintenance of financial system stability.

With respect to the third probity aspect, the internal aspect of a central bank, this is basically the same as probity regarding the internal aspect of a foreign affairs agency. Specifically, probity refers to the integrity of central bank officials and staff toward the mission, their professional ability and adequacy of the process. The fact that probity hazard in this respect will bring about probity hazard in the first and second aspects is also the same.

Table 3.1 summarizes the features of central bank transactions and probity structure in comparison with foreign affairs transactions.

Attributes of Central Bank Governance
Based on the above features of central bank transactions and probity structure, when we consider the attributes of governance structure that would maintain the probity necessary for central bank transactions and mitigate probity hazards, the four attributes proposed by Williamson can be applied almost perfectly to central bank transactions as well. It is impossible for private organizations (e.g., private banks) that pursue efficiency and net profit to fulfill such attributes. Central bank transactions

Table 3.1 Comparison of transaction features and probity structure

	Relationship with Executive and Legislative Branches	Relationship with Counterparties	Relationship with Internal Organization
Foreign Affairs Agency	Responsiveness alone	Negotiations on foreign affairs	• Stable necessary skills • Low necessity for innovation
Central Bank	Responsiveness and autonomy	• Financial transactions • Bank supervision, regulation	• Evolving necessary skills • High necessity of innovation

are best conducted by a public organization with a low incentive scheme, specifically a central bank, even if efficiency is sacrificed.[10] The governance of foreign affairs transactions, central bank transactions and private bank transactions is compared for each attribute in Table 3.2.

Very Low Incentive Scheme

If a strong incentive scheme were to apply to central bank transactions in order to achieve efficiency and profit, it would conflict with the intrinsic purpose of central bank transactions and would cause probity hazard. The maintenance of price stability requires the forgoing of opportunities to maximize revenue by expanding monetary issuance. As final supplier of liquidity to the monetary system, a central bank could use its monopoly power to extract rents from financial institutions.

Even if a contract with an objective aim is introduced so that the intrinsic purpose of central bank transactions is not hampered by the pursuit of efficiency and profits, it would be impossible to write one that could cover all unexpected situations which might arise, as Williamson pointed out. Therefore, it would be impossible to delegate central bank transactions to a private organization and successfully counter probity hazard through the terms of a contract intended to cover all levels of the adaptive process in all situations.

For example, if a private bank implemented monetary policy and market operations, it would use the information gained from such implementation to obtain profits from investments and fund raising in the markets causing 'ultimate insider trading.' Even if the private bank specialized in monetary policy and market operations, it would face the problem of how such transaction costs are calculated and how information leakage should be prevented (such issues are related not only to a strong incentive scheme but also to employment security and management control which will be discussed later).

---

[10]This explanation also illuminates the raison d'être of a central bank. Chap. 1, Sect. 1.4 explained the raison d'être of a central bank through transaction costs incurred by competition among private banks in a world where a central bank does not exist.

Table 3.2 Comparison of governance features

	Incentive scheme	Staff	Management scheme	Appointment of officers
Foreign affairs transactions	• Very low incentive scheme • Efficiency neglected • No adventurousness	• High degree of employment security • Mainly career staff	• Detailed administrative control • Clear hierarchical structure	• Direct appointment by government, the legislature
Central bank transactions	• Relatively low incentive • A certain level of efficiency needed • A certain level of adventurousness accepted	• Intermediate level of employment security • Mixture of career staff and mid-career people	• Intermediate level of administrative control • Intermediate level of hierarchical structure	• Indirect appointment by government, the legislature
Private bank transactions	• Strong incentive scheme • Efficiency strongly pursued • Regards adventurousness as entrepreneurship	• Low employment security • Low perception of career staff	• Low administrative control • Flexible hierarchical structure	• Independent from government, the legislature

Note According to BIS (2009), 80% of governors are appointed by the head of state, and nearly 25% by the government or Minister of Finance (see Fig. 19, p. 70).

Also with regard to payment and settlement services, a strong incentive scheme focusing on cost savings might undermine the security and quality of such services. For example, with regard to the maintenance of financial system stability, a strong incentive scheme whereby the compensation of bank examiners is based on simple indicators, such as the number and importance of suggestions made during on-site examination, may involve the risk of creating probity hazard similar to other central bank transactions.

As mentioned above, Williamson also identifies "adventurousness" as a probity hazard and considers the role of a low incentive scheme in restraining such adventurousness. Its application to central bank transactions provides a valuable insight. Since central bank transactions are implemented using state-of-the-art financial transaction techniques and skills, especially IT, constant innovation is necessary in line with the progress of IT and financial transaction techniques (innovation is more important than in foreign affairs transactions). In this regard, central bank governance requires an incentive scheme with strong but "not adventurous" characteristics that allow for innovation.

Career Staff with Employment Security
Employment security, which Williamson pointed out as a useful governance attribute of a foreign affairs agency, could also be applied to a central bank. While an increasing number of firms in Japan are adopting salary schemes based on short-term performance, these cannot be fully applied to a central bank since they would increase the possibility of the central bank encountering probity hazard. In addition, central bankers have to confront infrequent events, and their policies take effect only after long time lags. Employment security in such circumstances facilitates the employment of staff with a good institutional memory and longer time horizons.

Extensive Administrative Controls and Procedures
The "extensive administrative controls and procedures" pointed out by Williamson can be applied to a central bank almost in their entirety. When the various administrative controls described by Williamson are applied to a central bank, it is notable that insider trading regulations must be strictly adhered to by bank executives and staff. Such strict compliance is necessary since central bank transactions are implemented through financial transactions with private financial institutions and decisions on monetary control directly influence interest rates and various financial assets, all of which provide rent-extraction opportunities. The exceptionally high standards required of central bankers mean that the press and politicians will often criticize senior officials for actions that even hint of a conflict of interest.

An example of the exceptionally high standards required of central bankers in this regard is provided by the experience of the former Governor of the BOJ, Toshihiko Fukui. In June 2006 the Cabinet and the media criticized the then Governor for investing in the Murakami Fund and cancelling the contract only after he had been Governor for over two years. Such criticism seems to be inevitable (see Sect. 3.3.4.2).

A trade-off is also seen between the "clearly defined hierarchical authority" that Williamson considers a governance attribute of foreign affairs transactions and the necessity of innovation in central bank transactions. Excessively rigid hierarchical authority may carry the risk of slowing innovation in central bank transactions. But if central bank officials become too flexible or act in an ad hoc way, authority and responsibility would become ill-defined and might invite probity hazard.

Appointment and Termination of Agency Officers by President and Legislature
The appointment of central bank executives differs somewhat from that pointed out by Williamson and this is a notable feature of the governance of a central bank. Governors are more often appointed by the head of government via a process that involves checks and balances than by the government directly. And strong protections against being fired by the current government are built in. Although central bank transactions have the characteristic of sovereign transactions, independence from the government so as to maintain focus on the mission is of paramount importance compared to foreign affairs transactions.

This is consistent with Williamson's view that "lest the integrity of the state be seriously compromised, mission safeguards need to be introduced into the design" in appointing officers of a foreign affairs agency. The same can be said for a central bank. A central bank conducts monetary policy to realize its mission of price stability and, since this may conflict with the government's objective of shrinking the fiscal deficit, mission safeguard is also necessary for a central bank. Appointment procedures, restrictions on dismissal and central bank independence more generally are such safeguards. Central bank independence is the main distinctive feature of the public governance aspect of a central bank, and will be discussed in detail throughout this chapter.

3.2.2 Application of Moe's Theory on the Autonomy of a Bureaucratic Organization

Positive political theory (PPT) applies economics—including TCE—to political science. While notable research includes that by Epstein and O'Halloran (1999), a series of studies by Moe seem to be the most valid when considering public governance of a central bank. Moe's theory not only applied TCE to the political process, but also provided a justification for the autonomy of bureaucratic organizations based on TCE. Moe's theory is briefly summarized below and then applied to central bank governance.

3.2.2.1 Moe's Theory on the Autonomy of Bureaucratic Organizations

According to Moe (1990a), the theory of public bureaucracy that was initiated by the pioneering work of Niskanen (1971) can be roughly divided into "bureaucratic politics," which analyzes the behavior of bureaucratic organizations in the political process such as their relation with the legislature, and "bureaucratic organization," which analyzes the internal organization of public bureaucracy.[11] In both, bureaucrats are not assumed to be just an entity that executes requests from voters and the legislature passively and efficiently. Rather, the theory is based on the assumption that, just like other economic entities, bureaucrats also act to maximize their self-interest.

Moe (1991) surveyed existing research on the interrelationship between political science and organizational economics, concluding that in order to integrate the two, organizational economics should be applied after identifying the essential features of the political process. Moe (1984) had earlier proposed applying TCE to the political process and in Moe (1990a, b) pointed out the importance of bureaucratic organization in the political process. In particular, how the autonomy of bureaucratic

---

[11] The aforementioned theory by Williamson can be considered as one of the theories on public bureaucracy. However, his theory cannot be categorized according to Moe's dichotomy since it has features of both sides.

organizations emerged was clarified. An outline of Moe's theory on the autonomy of bureaucratic organizations is as follows.

When private firms and bureaucratic organizations are compared, bureaucratic organizations are similar to private firms in that they have a mission, resources, and strategy. However, while private firms are guaranteed property rights, the right to exercise "public authority"—the equivalent of property rights—is not guaranteed to the political actors. This is because, in a democratic state, public authority can be transferred from one party to another based on elections, etc. Such transfer risk of public authority is called "political uncertainty." All political actors, including bureaucratic organizations, face such political uncertainty, and on this point greatly differ from private firms. Today's policy decisions can be overturned in the future, should public authority be transferred to today's opposition parties.

Both bureaucrats and politicians have an incentive to incorporate autonomy for bureaucratic organizations into the institutional framework to mitigate such uncertainty. First, bureaucrats seek autonomy in order to neutralize, as much as possible, the impact of "political disruption"—that is, a favorable political power suddenly turning hostile because of a regime change. Motivating the case for autonomy involves seeking strong professionalism and promoting operational experience. Such technical and operational expertise becomes all the more significant for achieving autonomy as time passes, which could be explained by the concept of "transaction specificity"[12] in TCE. For example, even if a bureaucratic organization does not have any special technical and operational expertise at the time of its establishment, such expertise will accumulate as the organization continues operations. Accumulated expertise cannot be readily duplicated by alternative agents (a hold-up problem caused by mutual interdependence as in TCE).

Second, the legislature and voters (interest groups) also have a tendency to favor extending a certain level of autonomy to bureaucratic organizations as a countermeasure against political uncertainty. By insulating bureaucratic organizations from the legislature, even if there is a change in regime the new power cannot easily implement a bold and unfavorable policy through such autonomous bureaucratic organizations.[13]

---

[12] Looking at "transaction specificity" from the asset side, it is called "transaction-specific asset" and the feature of such an asset is called "asset specificity" (see footnote 3, Chap. 2). Refer to Williamson (1985) for details.

[13] Kanemoto (1991) takes the police as an example and states that: "For politicians in power, autonomy of the police may not be desirable, but considering that they may not stay in power in the future, it may be desirable to continue to maintain such autonomy" (translated from Japanese).

3.2.2.2   Application to Central Bank Governance

Central banks can readily be seen as bureaucratic organizations—although some aspects of corporate governance apply, public governance aspects dominate.[14] Applying Moe's theory, central bank autonomy might also be seen as a countermeasure against political uncertainty.

From the perspective of central bank executives and staff as bureaucrats, the consistency of monetary policy cannot be maintained if major changes are forced on monetary policy whenever there is a shift in political power. Should swings in political power affect not only monetary policy but also staff management, it would be difficult to implement highly professional central bank operations based on banking operations. Long since established, the professionalism of central bankers is deeply embedded in the organization and this serves as a strong foundation for the autonomy of a central bank, as explained in the concept of transaction specificity in TCE. And politicians and voters may also benefit from the stability that results from giving autonomy to a central bank, since it then becomes impossible to pursue a policy that is completely opposite to the one pursued by the previous political administration.

Applying Moe's theory to an examination of the political background to central bank reforms in Chile in 1989 and Mexico in 1993, Boylan (2001) concluded that central bank autonomy was an "insulation strategy" to insulate the central bank from changes in political power. According to Boylan, central bank reform in both countries was: "by making the central bank autonomous, control over monetary policy is effectively removed from the hands of politicians,"…"where authoritarian elites fear the populism that may be endemic to new democracies and know that a change of regime is imminent, they can be expected to create an autonomous central bank to lock in a commitment to price stability over the long haul."

The revision of the BOJ Act in 1998 was implemented to enhance independence of the BOJ, although the major objective seeming to have been to curtail the power of the Ministry of Finance (bearing in mind the criticism leveled against it during the so-called "bubble economy" in the latter half of the 1980s that led to financial system turmoil in the 1990s). This cannot be regarded as consistent with Moe's theory and the suggestions made by Boylan, since changes in the political regime in Japan are very rare. Thus, the motivation to enhance central bank autonomy as a counter to political uncertainty may not be as strong in Japan as in the US and Europe, where changes in political power are more frequent. Indeed, independence under the new BOJ Act was not as comprehensive as in the US and European countries (e.g., the expense budget is subject to approval by the Ministry of Finance, government representatives attend monetary policy board meetings, the government has the right to request postponing a vote on proposals regarding monetary policy matters, etc.). Even under such conditions, statements undermining the BOJ's independence are frequently heard from politicians (see Sect. 3.3.3.2).

---

[14]Many studies have applied organization theory to the central bank assuming it is a bureaucratic organization (e.g., papers given in Mayer 1990, and Toma and Toma 1986).

Thus, while Moe's theory provides insights into the reasons for central bank independence, it is not a complete explanation. There are differences between a central bank and other bureaucratic organizations. Two significant ones stand out. First, as noted in Chap. 2, Sect. 2.3.2, in addition to a public governance concept, a corporate governance concept can be applied to a central bank. Therefore, a central bank has the characteristic that it cannot easily or should not be affected by public governance (influence from politicians and the government). Second, central bank independence is required for purely economic reasons regardless of political factors. Such a necessity comes from the fact that banknotes issued by a central bank are money in a fiat currency system. In other words, under the gold standard, the quantitative constraint of a natural resource, gold, restrained the money supply so that price stability was maintained. In a fiat currency system, however, it is the independence of a central bank that is expected to restrain the money supply and hence inflation.

In regard to the above two points, Boylan (ibid) terms the grounds for the argument on central bank independence by Cukierman (1992) and Maxfield (1997) "credibility literature" and emphasizes that her treatment of the economic effect of central bank independence differs from theirs. While "credibility literature" stresses that central bank independence enhances credibility of a central bank and brings about price and foreign exchange stability, Boylan considers central bank independence necessary to minimize political transaction cost in the political process and that the economic effect is not its direct objective. In this sense, she argues that central bank independence in her theory is based on "institutionalism" in political science.

3.3 Application of Agency Theory

In this section, agency theory will be applied to the public governance issues of a central bank. First, after introducing agency theory in general, we will observe what kind of principal–agent relationship exists between a public agent and legislature/politicians when the theory is applied to the political process. Then, the central bank's principal–agent relationship will be compared with that of government ministries and its features considered. Also, the congressional dominance hypothesis that asserts the superiority of the legislature over public agents is introduced and the possibility of sanctions and threats the central bank would receive from the legislature/politicians based on the hypothesis is considered. Then, by applying the multiboard theory advocated by Fama and Jensen, we review mechanisms to lessen the possibility of sanctions and threats to the central bank from the legislature and executive branch through the appointment of senior central bankers. Moreover, central bank accountability is proposed as a principal's monitoring measure over an agent in agency theory.

3.3.1 Agency Theory and the Political Process

3.3.1.1 What Is Agency Theory?

Agency theory, or principal–agent theory, analyzes the relationship between the employing organization and staff as a relationship between 'principal' and 'agent.' There are numerous relationships that can be considered principal–agent relationships in our social system as seen in that between doctor (= agent) and patient (= principal), and solicitor (= agent) and client (= principal). Such relationships, where a certain entity relies on another, came about since the division of labor generally enhances productivity. As Hayek (1945, p. 524) put it:

> If we can agree that the economic problem of society is mainly one of rapid adaptation to changes in the particular circumstances of time and place, it would seem to follow that the ultimate decisions must be left to the people who are familiar with these circumstances, who know directly of the relevant changes and of the resources immediately available to meet them. We cannot expect that this problem will be solved by first communicating all this knowledge to a central board which, after integrating all knowledge, issues its orders.

That is, such relationships are created when it is deemed efficient to use professionals as agents rather than principals doing everything themselves. As such, the principal–agent relationship creates efficiency, but has costs or risks. Such costs are called 'agency costs' or 'agency problems.' They arise when the agent acts not on behalf of a principal's benefit alone, but also for its own benefit.

Agency theory and TCE have many points in common. For example, the principal–agent relationship in agency theory is equivalent to the transaction relationship in TCE, and agency cost to transaction cost. And, the incentive system to counter the agency problem in agency theory has the same function as governance structure in TCE. However, while agency theory pays attention to the difference in the concerned parties' position (principal or agent) and places importance on the prior design of a contract to mitigate agency problems, TCE takes the stance that it is impossible to design a perfect contract that prevents opportunism due to transaction specificity that arises after the contract. Therefore, TCE pursues governance structure that reduces transaction costs in the whole transaction process to a minimum.

3.3.1.2 Application to the Political Process

The political process is a structure where voters, the legislature, and the executive branch make policy decisions through interaction. Numerous studies in the field of political economy have recently applied agency theory to the political process. For example, Stevens (1993) believes it significant to apply agency theory to the political process for the following three reasons.

First, laws (including constitutions) envisage hierarchical relationships in the political process and, in this regard, the application of agency theory is in line with the spirit of the law. Since voters select cabinet members through election, they can be considered as a legislature's principal, and the legislature the agent of the voters. Moreover, with regard to authority relationships within the government, in the case of a parliamentary system, the prime minister is selected by the legislature and he/she in turn appoints cabinet members and executives of public agencies. The cabinet and public agencies jointly constitute the executive body. Here, the legislature is the principal, and the executive body (cabinet and public agencies) is considered an agent. Within the executive body, the cabinet is the principal and public agencies the cabinet's agent. In the case of a presidential system, the president is directly elected by the voters and although the legislature has the role of checking the activities of the executive body including the president, it is not the president's principal.[15]

Second, the respective parties of the political process hold different information, both quantitatively and qualitatively. For example, politicians have less professional knowledge than bureaucrats. Agency theory is suitable for analyzing the behavior of such parties with differing information since the main objective of agency theory is to study how an efficient incentive system can be structured between parties with differing information as in the relationship between a doctor and a patient. The governance structure of the political process, that is, public governance, can be regarded as such an incentive system

Third, agency problems evidently arise in all relationships in the political process. For example, voters sometimes feel that the legislature is not necessarily keeping its promise or the legislature criticizes public agencies for not acting in line with their intentions (this point will be closely looked at from the perspective of accountability in Sect. 3.3.5).

3.3.2 Features of the Principal–Agent Relationship of a Central Bank

Agency theory can be applied to central banks, as to other government institutions. However, the principal–agent relationship of a central bank can be characterized as having multiple principals and having the feature of an independent agency, which will be explained below and the implications for public governance studied.

3.3.2.1 Multiple Principals of a Central Bank

In major countries, the central bank's direct principals often include the legislature, as well as the head of the executive body (president or prime minister). This places the central bank in a different position than the executive branches of the government. No senior central banker (such as governor) is elected (or recommended, nominated,

---

[15]Palmer (1995) and Moe and Caldwell (1994) made a comparative analysis of presidential and parliamentary systems based on agency theory.

appointed, approved, etc.) by a national referendum. Therefore, although the general public is the ultimate principal of a central bank, it is not the direct principal.

In major developed countries, the governor of a central bank (or Chairman of the FRB in the US) is appointed by the head of the executive body, president, or cabinet (prime minister), and, in this respect, the principal of the central bank is the head of the executive body. At the same time, there are countries where not only the executive body, but also the legislature is involved in electing senior central bankers. In this case, the legislature also becomes the principal. The US Congress is involved in the selection process in the form of approving the Chairman and Governors of the Federal Reserve Board appointed by the President. In the case of the BOJ, members of the Policy Board are appointed by the Cabinet and approved by the Diet. Also, with respect to the European Central Bank (ECB), ECB executives, such as the President, are determined through consultation among member nations' government representatives and the European Parliament based on a recommendation from ECB's General Council. In this regard, the ECB has multiple principals such as the General Council, the member nations, and the European Parliament.[16]

Dixit (1996) calls such relationships with several principals "multiple principals" and compares the situation with a single principal. Dixit argues that the existence of multiple principals weakens an agent's incentives, which is a source of inefficiency in public agencies with multiple principals. If applied to a central bank, there would be little incentive to follow the monetary policy line proposed by one specific principal. Since the executive body and the legislature may have different opinions concerning central bank policy, the existence of multiple principals may even be useful in preventing a central bank from pursuing a biased policy. And, as explained in Sect. 3.2.1.2, according to Williamson (1999) the necessity of congressional approval of executives appointed by a president has the benefit of reinforcing the probity of the executives vis-à-vis the mission.

3.3.2.2 Independent Agencies

What Is an Independent Agency?
The nature of the principal–agent relationship in the political process is not homogeneous. Independent agencies exist in the US and Japan (and elsewhere); these differ from government ministries in their structural proximity to the executive, and thus in the executive's ability to command and control. Central banks in both the US and Japan have some features of independent agencies. Ito (1982, p. 493) describes the independent agency as follows (translated from Japanese)[17]:

---

[16]See Sect. 8.1 of BIS (2009) for details of cross-country practices.

[17]An independent agency is an organizational concept of US federal government and Japan's central government. It is an agency that exists outside federal executive departments and is not part of a fourth branch of government. Instead, it exercises executive functions outside of any executive department.

The so-called independent agency system was developed in the US from the end of the 19th century to the beginning of the 20th century with a view to introducing legal economic restrictions in line with the development of advanced capitalism. Such agencies have a quasi-legislative power to enact regulations and also quasi-judicial powers to settle disputes in addition to dealing with administrative affairs. After World War II and reflecting the desire of the General Headquarters of the Allied Forces, many independent agencies were established in Japan to eliminate bureaucracy-led executive branches in the government, lessen concentration of power in the Cabinet, and better convey the public will to the administrative authorities.

Specific examples of independent agencies are the Interstate Commerce Commission in the US and the Fair Trade Commission in Japan. While both US and Japanese independent agencies are independent from the President (Cabinet), they are subject to public governance by the legislature. The degree of independence is not total, just greater than for other government ministries. That is, the President (Cabinet) cannot intervene in an independent agency's budget or operations but can appoint agency heads. In this regard, independent agencies can be considered to be endowed with "independence within government."

The Central Bank as an Independent Agency

Most central banks are not pure independent agencies,[18] but many have key features of independent agencies because of the following characteristics:

Decision-Making

In many cases, decisions regarding the operations and policies of a central bank do not need to be authorized by the executive branch if due process is observed. However, changes to decision-making procedures and high-level policy strategies need, in general, to be authorized by the government.

Staff Matters

As mentioned, the legislature is involved in the selection of senior central bankers. Also, the terms of senior central bankers are often longer than those in government ministries and strict criteria must be observed in dismissing them during their term of office. Looking at the terms of office of central bank governors and executives, for example, in the case of the US Federal Reserve System, it is 14 years (but for the Chairman, four years), the President and executives of the ECB eight years, and the BOJ Governor five years. Most central banks have strict criteria for dismissing senior central bankers and the appointor cannot dismiss them at will. This differs from the dismissal of senior civil servants in government ministries.

Accounting

With regard to procedures to decide the budget of major central banks, some operations of the BOJ and the Bank of England (BOE) need approval from the budgetary authority. But other central banks decide their budgets independently. As for financial statements, the BOJ needs to obtain approval from the Minister of Finance, and the Bank of Canada has to submit financial statements to the national legislature via the

---

[18] The Board of Governors of the Federal Reserve System in the US is regarded as a pure independent agency.

Minister of Finance (the BOE needs to obtain approval for some operations from the Treasury). However, other central banks do not need to obtain approval from either their financial authority or legislature and their autonomy is duly observed.

Constitutional Doubts about Independent Agencies and the BOJ Act

Constitutional doubts have been raised both in the US, the birthplace of the independent agency, and in Japan. The US Constitution stipulates that "The executive power shall be vested in a President of the United States of America." (Article II, Section 1) and the Constitution of Japan (Article 65) says that the executive authority belongs to the Cabinet.

In the process of discussing revision of the BOJ Act and during actual revision in 1997, there were arguments regarding the considerable independence of the central bank despite it having to fulfill various administrative obligations pursuant to Article 65 of the Constitution. Japan's Cabinet Legislation Bureau issued an opinion that, in order to secure the constitutionality of the BOJ's independence, the executive branch of the government would have to take control of the 'budgetary authority' and 'appointive authority.' Based on this opinion, under the new BOJ Act, a budget for expenses (limited to those specified by a Cabinet order as not hampering currency and monetary control) needs to be authorized by the Minister of Finance, and executives (Governor, Deputy Governors, Policy Board members) appointed by the Cabinet, subject to approval of the House of Representatives and the House of Councilors.

However, the Study Group on the Central Bank from the Perspective of Public Law (there is no official name in English; chaired by Professor Hiroshi Shiono of Tokyo University) discussed, in detail, the constitutionality of both the independent agency and the new BOJ Act. It reached the conclusion that the Cabinet Legislation Bureau's opinion was wrong. The Study Group considered that "although the Cabinet Legislation Bureau mentioned budgetary authority and appointive authority as a basis for the constitutionality of the BOJ Act, if true, then even the Supreme Court can be said to be under the control of the Cabinet." As for appointive authority, the Study Group said that "the Cabinet's control over the appointive authority of the BOJ is not a condition for securing constitutionality." Rather, it concluded that "considering that the policy and operations of the BOJ are entrusted to it by the nation, involvement of the Cabinet and the Diet in the staff matters of the BOJ should be perceived from the perspective that the public should select the person that bears ultimate responsibility for what they entrust." And as for budgetary authority, the Study Group reached a consensus that "the Cabinet need not have budgetary authority over the BOJ in order to prove that the Bank is under the authority of the Cabinet subject to the Constitution" (translated from Japanese).

3.3.3 Congressional Dominance Hypothesis and a Central Bank

As mentioned in Sect. 3.3.1.2, according to the law, the legislature acts as an agent of voters and principal of the executive branch (including independent agencies). There is heated discussion as to what extent this principle is actually the case, especially as regards the relationship between the legislature and the executive branch ('the executive branch' in this section refers to public agencies such as general government ministries). In this discussion, the view that considers that the legislature controls the executive branch in line with the law is called the 'congressional dominance hypothesis.' According to this hypothesis, the legislature, as the principal, can in various ways sanction the executive branch, the agent, in place of monitoring. This hypothesis will be applied to the central bank, pointing out the strong influence of the legislature and politicians on a central bank, with due attention to the threat posed through the authority to appoint senior central bankers.

3.3.3.1 What is the Congressional Dominance Hypothesis?

Major research on the congressional dominance hypothesis based on the agency theory has been conducted by Weingast (1994) and Weingast and Moran (1993). In this research, the authors believe it mistaken to conclude that the legislature does not closely monitor the executive branch in the US political process, even though protagonists of such a view point to "(a) the lack of oversight hearings, (b) the infrequency of congressional investigations and policy resolutions, (c) the perfunctory nature of confirmation hearings of agency heads, (d) the lack of ostensible congressional attention to or knowledge about the ongoing operation and policy consequences of agency choice, and (e) the superficiality of annual appropriations hearings" (Weingast and Moran, ibid).

Yet Weingast (1994) believes that this point of view is mistaken. Because politicians, as principals, have the power to sanction the executive branch, the executive branch has an incentive to be sensitive to politicians' intentions. Based on the US political system, Weingast lists measures that politicians can use against the executive branch as sanctions "that substitute for direct, continuous surveillance of regulatory administration: (a) approval of budgets; (b) the use of a veto against appointment of officials; (c) and policy interference."

3.3.3.2 Application of Congressional Dominance Hypothesis to a Central Bank

As noted, a central bank commonly enjoys greater independence than government ministries and has features of independent agencies. Several observers have, however, noted that central banks can still be influenced by the political forces from which they are formally independent. This section considers the potential for informal influence through the lens of the congressional dominance hypothesis. It goes on to discuss political business cycle theory and associated research, which provides some empirical backing for the existence of such an influence.

Influence of Legislature and Politicians on a Central Bank

Using the lens of the congressional dominance hypothesis to examine the potential for political influence on the central bank—over and above that formally provided for in the relevant legislation—this section evaluates several specific mechanisms for influence. The first set involves mechanisms that various theorists argue are in fact not supportive of the congressional dominance hypothesis. The second set relates to the possibility of political sanction/threat to a central bank. And the third involves the possibility of cooperative action between the legislature, politicians, and the bureaucracy.

Counter Observations Given by Those Opposing the Hypothesis

Those opposing the congressional dominance hypothesis provided five arguments as to why the hypothesis is wrong in asserting the political domination of independent agents. The relationship between the legislature and a central bank can be examined under five corresponding headings.

- **Lack of oversight hearings**:
  In fact, many central banks regularly take part in public hearings in the legislature. For example, the BOJ Act (Article 54) stipulates that in addition to biannual explanations to the Diet of a written report on the Bank's business operations, the Governor (or representative) shall also attend Diet (including committee) sessions when requested.
- **Infrequency of congressional investigations and policy resolutions**:
  According to BIS (2009), only 15% of central banks face no legislative reviews, and just under half have regularly scheduled reviews (more than a quarter of these being more than annually), and half face reviews "on special request."[19]
- **The perfunctory nature of confirmation hearings of agency heads**:
  It depends on the country. In some cases, effective confirmation hearings may not be easy. In many cases, however, the legislature and politicians do intervene in the selection process.
- **Lack of knowledge about ongoing operations and the policy consequences of agency choices**:
  Since monetary policy is easy to understand superficially, even politicians without expert knowledge can give their judgments and, as a matter of fact, they do so quite frequently.
- **Superficiality of annual appropriation hearings**:
  Although as a matter of routine, the central bank will take care to avoid provoking the legislature or the public by lax spending decisions. Many central banks do not need to discuss their budget with the legislature.

---

[19]Table 17 of BIS (2009).

Possibility of a Central Bank Being Sanctioned/Threatened by the Legislature/Politicians

A second potential channel of influence is the threat of sanction of the central bank by the legislature and politicians. There are various forms of sanction/threat, both formal and informal. Major sanctions are as follows:

- **Use of legislative power**:
  Current central bank legislation guaranteeing independence, unless the relevant legislation is deeply embedded (for example in a constitution), can usually be changed. For example, according to Willett and Keen (1990, p. 17): "The institutional independence of the Federal Reserve from political pressures is far from complete....The current institutional arrangements are legislative provisions, not constitutional provisions. Such legislation is not lightly changed, but the possibility is not so remote that Fed officials have felt free to ignore signals coming from Congress and the executive branch. Ironically, in order to maintain the Fed's independence, Fed officials often have bowed to political pressure."
- **Exercise of appointive authority**:
  In many countries, the possibility of reappointment gives politicians implicit influence. Even in countries where it is not, incumbents' concerns about the future composition of the governing body might lead them to avoid policies that directly challenge politicians' views.
- **Budgetary authority**:
  No central bank in developed nations has to obtain budget confirmation from the legislature. However, the legislature can question a central bank's financial statements as well as budget, and the way they question may pose a threat to the central bank as will be explained below.
- **Questions in the legislature**:
  The central bank governor and executives can be summoned to testify before the legislature and, in the case of Japan, depending on the content and how questions are presented, such events could become a sanction/threat to the governor and executives who are called on to respond. This involves a form of 'reputation risk' for the central bank governor and executives. Since monetary policy is implemented under uncertainty, and assessing the appropriateness of policy is difficult even well after the event, how their judgment is evaluated is of concern to the central bank governor and executives.

Cooperative Action Among the Legislature, Cabinet, and the Bureaucracy

The central bank may conflict with officials (the Ministry of Finance) on the financing of a fiscal deficit. If the Minister disagrees with the Bank concerning financing of the fiscal deficit, he/she can impose a sanction or threaten to use his/her authority. If the Minister of Finance disagrees with the central bank on this issue, the ministry will have several ways of putting pressure on the central bank.[20] Concerning financing of the fiscal deficit, he/she can impose a sanction or threaten to use his/her authority.

---

[20]For instance, the central bank's budget is subject to Minister of Finance veto in several countries (see BIS, 2009).

Especially in Japan where a political power shift rarely occurs, the relationships between the ruling party, the cabinet, and the bureaucracy have traditionally been close. They are thus more likely to cooperate in pressuring the central bank. Where the opposition party has little influence, the bureaucracy will tend to act in accordance with the ruling party's wishes.

Abe Administration and the Bank of Japan
In Japan, the 'congressional dominance hypothesis' was proved correct by the second Abe administration in a typical and dramatic fashion. Let us examine this from the political aspect and how the BOJ reacted.

- **Political pressure by the Abe administration**:
  In 2012, Shinzo Abe became President of the Liberal Democratic Party and won a landslide victory in the lower house election, taking power from the Democratic Party of Japan and becoming prime minister. During the election campaign, Abe's platform included an economic stimulus package based on the so-called 'three arrows,' which came to be termed 'Abenomics.' The first arrow was large-scale monetary easing, the second the expansion of fiscal stimulus, and the third, structural reform.
  Prime Minister Abe requested the BOJ to acknowledge inflation targeting of 2%. He made it clear that the BOJ Act should be revised if then Governor Masaaki Shirakawa refused to do so (use of legislative power).
  In March the following year, when Governor Shirakawa's term of office expired (and also that of two deputy governors), Prime Minister Abe appointed Haruhiko Kuroda as Governor and Kikuo Iwata as Deputy Governor, both of whom were in favor of Abenomics (exercise of appointive authority).
- **Response of the BOJ**:
  Governor Shirakawa only acknowledged inflation targeting of 2% but Governor Kuroda clearly stated at the press conference when he took office that the Bank would achieve its 2% inflation target in two years (the target is yet to be attained even though more than seven years have passed, and, in 2018, the Bank finally omitted the timeframe within which it would be achieved).
  At the same press conference, he stated that the target of monetary policy would change from interest rates to the quantity of base money which would be doubled in two years. Increasing the quantity of base money meant that the purchase of government bonds had to be increased. For this purpose, the Bank abolished the rule that the balance of government bonds held by it should not exceed banknotes issued. This operation was not only in line with the Abe administration's policy but was also welcomed by the Ministry of Finance (cooperative action among the legislature, cabinet, and the bureaucracy).

Political Business Cycle Theory

Although the congressional dominance hypothesis can be applied to relationships involving the central bank, there is no direct research as to any effect on monetary policy. Political business cycle theory (a branch of public choice theory, as will be explained later) does, however, indirectly capture the influence of politicians/bureaucrats on monetary policy in related empirical research.

Political business cycle theory was first advocated by Nordhaus (1975) who argued that the business cycle in the US was correlated with the electoral cycle. The evidence for this was that in the year before a presidential election year, the US government adopts an expansionary policy to increase spending but then pursues a contractionary policy after the election to prevent inflation.

For such a policy to succeed electorally, a trade-off needs to exist between the unemployment rate and the inflation rate, at least in the short term (short-term downward sloping Phillips curve). In the 1970s, when the political business cycle theory was advocated, a short-term downward sloping Phillips curve was generally accepted, and may have been in the minds of those determining economic policy. More recently, most macroeconomists doubt that there is a stable—or at least exploitable—relationship between the unemployment rate and the inflation rate. Accordingly, more modern researchers are skeptical about the political business cycle (e.g., Beck, 1982). Mueller (1989) summed up such views, writing that "although there exists clear evidence that some governments in some countries at some point in time have behaved as the political business cycle model predicts, the evidence is not strong enough to warrant the conclusion that this type of behavior is a general characteristic of democratically elected governments."

There is also research on a more direct relationship between politics and monetary policy. Beck (1987) tested whether the federal funds rate (policy rate controlled by the FRS) tended to be lower during US election (presidential and congressional elections) years than normal years. No such evidence was found. Willett and Keen (1990), however, using a different methodology, did find an election cycle in Treasury bill rates (interest rates fluctuate closely related with the federal funds rate).

Chang (2003) also shows that the appointment of the Fed Chairman and members of the Board of Governors is an important avenue of political influence. This econometric analysis examined both voting on monetary policy (using data from the Fed's voting records) and the opinions expressed on monetary policy in presidential and senatorial statements.

3.3.4   Multiboard System of a Central Bank Based on Agency Theory

In Chap. 2, Sect. 2.4.1, we analyzed the features of central bank services and came to the conclusion that a 'multiboard,' which consists of one board from the perspective of public governance and another from corporate governance, is desirable. Using Fama and Jensen's agency theory, we argue that a multiboard is indeed desirable to secure central bank independence even from the perspective of public governance alone. With regard to the appointment of senior central bankers, the involvement of the legislature and the executive branch should be limited to that of the upper board, which should in turn be responsible for appointing the lower board.

3.3.4.1   Fama and Jensen's Multiboard Theory

According to Fama and Jensen (1983a, b), "complex organizations" have "decision hierarchies": "decision management" and "decision control." Such decision hierarchies help to mitigate the agency problems arising from the separation of ownership and control.

Fama and Jensen hold that a multiboard scheme consisting of a Board of Directors and an Executive Board help to prevent management (= the agent) from acting contrary to the interests of the shareholders. The Board of Directors makes decisions on the employment and compensation of members of the Executive Board. The Board of Directors also monitors and ratifies important decisions made by such staff. Fama and Jensen consider that if management is divided into controller (Board of Directors = upper board) and manager (Executive Board = lower board), a mutual monitoring system would result as the two boards would informally monitor each other,[21] in addition to formal checking via the upper board controlling the lower board.[22]

Under a multiboard scheme, the principal–agent relationship overlaps at various levels from shareholders to the Board of Directors and the Executive Board. This is called a "multi-level principal–agent relationship." Such overlapping relationships may be desirable since, as pointed out by Hayek (1945), decentralized decision-making is more efficient than concentrated (authoritarian) decision-making.

3.3.4.2   Application of Multiboard Theory to a Central Bank

Fama and Jensen also believe that the superiority of the multiboard scheme applies also to non-profit organizations and large professional partnerships. In the following paragraphs, their discussion will be applied to central banks in relation to their public governance. This reviews the potential role for a multiboard structure where further safeguards for independent central bank decision-making from political influence are desired.

Governance Structures of Central Banks in Major Developed Countries
First, looking at the governance structure of major central banks, all but the BOJ adopt a multiboard scheme as shown in Table 3.3.[23] The multiboard scheme adopted

---

[21] Stevens (1993) also pointed out mutual monitoring of agents as one measure to counter the agency problem (see Sect. 3.3.5.1).

[22] Also, Turnbull (2000) further argued that a multiboard scheme was more desirable than a unitary board scheme since corruption of power and restricted information feedback to shareholders occur under the latter scheme. Williamson (2008) explained the importance of a Board of Directors even if it does not always exercise vigilant monitoring of the Executive Board.

[23] Until enactment of the new BOJ Act in 1998, the BOJ had Executive Meetings in addition to Policy Board Meetings. This could be regarded as a multiboard scheme, but, under the new Act, a

Table 3.3 Two-tier principal-agent relationships of major central banks in developed nations

	Upper board	Lower board
Bank of Japan	Policy Board	None
Federal Reserve System	Federal Reserve Board, Federal Open Market Committee	(Conference of Presidents)
Federal Reserve Banks	Board of Directors	Executive Meeting
Swiss National Bank	Bank Council	Governing Board
European Central Bank	Governing Council	Executive Board
Bank of England	Court of Directors	(Monetary Policy Committee, Financial Stability Committee)
Bank of Canada	Board of Directors	Executive Committee

Note See also Table 8 in BIS (2009). The bodies shown in parenthesis may not be considered lower boards in the normal sense.

by central banks traces a hierarchical relationship between the two boards. Both the nature and degree of hierarchy differ among central banks. It is also very complex, containing both formal and informal elements. Summary comparisons across different central banks, therefore, necessarily entail some oversimplification. This should be kept in mind in the paragraphs that follow.

A two-tiered principal–agent relationship is formed within each central bank. The hierarchical relationship can be seen from the fact that the upper board is involved in, and makes decisions on, the appointment of lower board members, not to mention its power to decide the baseline of central bank management. Therefore, the distance between the legislative/executive branches and lower board of a central bank is greater than that of general government ministries.

Adoption of a multiboard scheme has often been a legacy of history—that many central banks began as private banks. In addition, central banking requires specialized professional knowledge. A decision to adopt such a scheme may have been made as it would be better to leave the direct conduct of business operations to the agent (lower board) with professional skills rather than the principal (upper board). Therefore, the intention of the multiboard scheme in Fama and Jensen's theory, which is to mitigate the agency problem by separating the internal organization into monitoring and execution, may apply less to a central bank than to a private corporation.

The same may also be seen in how top management and members are decided with respect to the two boards. Excluding the Swiss National Bank (SNB) and the US Federal Reserve Banks, the same person heads both the upper and lower boards. Moreover, there have been cases of overlapping members. Hence, the two boards are not in a genuine hierarchical relationship.[24]

---

single board scheme was adopted. However, the BOJ is less of an outlier when a wider sample is taken: about one-third of BIS member central banks do not have a supervisory board (see Table 8 in BIS, 2009).

[24]For example, in the case of the ECB, the President heads the Executive Board, the lower board, as well as the Governing Council consisting of member central bank governors and members of the

Considering that monetary policy is a central bank function, it is quite natural to separate the board for implementing monetary policy from that for monitoring according to Fama and Jensen. The upper board should confine its responsibility to the monitoring of the lower board and in this sense overseeing the operations of the central bank. However, the lower board, the internal board of the central bank, should take responsibility for conducting monetary policy.

Problems Stemming from Direct Involvement of the Executive/Legislative Branches in Appointing Senior Central Bank Officials

Strong public governance characteristics with respect to monetary policy are reflected in the way the executive branch and legislature are involved in the appointment of senior central bankers. In most countries, the executive branch and the legislature are directly involved in the selection of board members that are responsible for monetary policy. In the exceptional case of Switzerland, the executive branch and the legislature are only involved in the selection of upper board members, and delegate to the upper board the selection of the lower board members who decide monetary policy.

Direct appointments might give rise to a problem from the standpoint of central bank independence. As mentioned earlier, according to the congressional dominance hypothesis, the legislature, politicians, and the executive branch could exert pressure (such as threats/sanctions) on a central bank through various channels, one of which is through involvement in the appointment of executives. Good public governance of central banks suggests that the executive branch (the agent of the legislature and politicians that are in turn the agent of the general public) be closely involved in the appointment of senior central bankers. However, since central bank (public) governance arrangements are also intended to provide central bank independence, it would be inconsistent if the legislature, politicians, and the executive branch were to use appointive authority to pressure a central bank on specific decisions. In order to safeguard against such pressures, appointment and dismissal arrangements in many countries incorporate a system to secure the status of executives.

Multiboard System of the Swiss National Bank

As noted earlier, the SNB provides an example of a multiboard structure. This case provides a useful example for discussing some of the public governance issues introduced above. After describing the SNB arrangement, two issues are discussed: the continuing relevance of the specifics of the appointment mechanism and accountability.

The SNB's governance structure is shown in Fig. 3.3. The Swiss federal government appoints six members of the Bank Council (the upper board), including the president and vice-president (chair and vice-chair). Shareholders choose five members. At the same time, members of the Governing Board (the lower board that has

---

Executive Board. Moreover, the Governing Council has the authority to decide monetary policy and from these facts it is apparent that emphasis is placed on monetary policy. As for the US Federal Reserve Banks, members of the two boards are completely separated, but this may be due to the fact that the banks do not directly have the authority to make decisions on monetary policy.

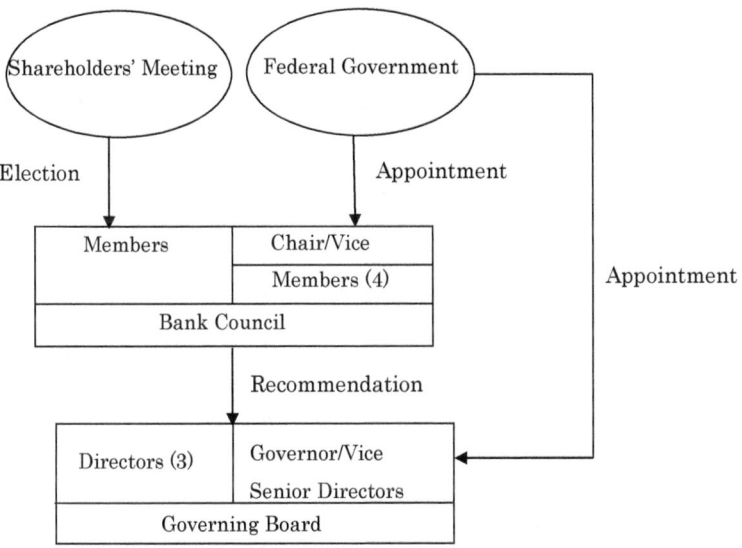

Fig. 3.3   Multiboard system of the Swiss National Bank

authority to implement monetary policy) are appointed by the Swiss federal government but on the recommendation of the Bank Council. Thus the government does
not have unilateral discretion over the appointment of Governing Board members.
The Governor of the SNB does not concurrently hold the posts of Chair of both the
Bank Council and the Governing Board, and there are no overlapping members.

The appointive authority of the Swiss government with respect to the upper board
is restricted by the ability of shareholders to elect five members—a significant proportion of the total, though not the majority. In contrast, the Swiss government retains
some influence over lower board appointments, by virtue of the double veto arrangement used to select Governing Board members, and by virtue of the fact that the
government selects which of the three prime Governing Board members will be
chair and which vice-chair. In addition to structure, appointment details matter.

It is a misperception that a multiboard scheme undermines the ultimate accountability to the executive and legislative branches. A two-tiered structure may aid
accountability—while guarding against congressional dominance-type effects—by
allowing close monitoring by the upper board of executive decision-making. The
upper board may be influenced by political pressures, but does not directly represent
political interests; and by virtue of appointment and dismissal safeguards, it may
have greater loyalty to the mission.

Table 3.4 Governor Fukui and the Murakami Fund

Oct 1999	Investment made in two investment funds within the Murakami Fund (10 million yen)
Feb 2001	Fixed return of 2.43 million yen upon dissolution of the above funds
Apr 2001	Investment again made in two investment funds within the Murakami Fund (10 million yen)
Mar 2003	Fukui took office as Governor of the Bank of Japan
Dec 2005	Net profit of 5.62 million yen, and valuation profit of 6.69 million yen at this point
Jan 2006	Takafumi Horie, CEO of Livedoor, arrested
Feb 2006	Fukui notified cancellation of the contract to Murakami Fund
Jun 2006	Yoshiaki Murakami, President of the Murakami Fund, arrested
Jun 2006	Investment in the Murakami Fund disclosed by Fukui in a statement in the Diet
Jan 2007	Returned all invested funds (total of around 22 million yen)

An Opposite Case in Japan

In Japan, board members and governors are protected from dismissal, except in tightly specified circumstances under the single board system.[25] This is in order to protect them from pressure from the legislature and executive branch with respect to their policy decisions. In June 2006, BOJ Governor Toshihiko Fukui became embroiled in a scandal over his investments in the Murakami Fund (see Table 3.4). The government defended the Governor against charges of impropriety and strong criticism from the opposition party. Press reports later speculated that a subsequent policy decision had reflected a sense of obligation to the government, notwithstanding the Governor's legal protections against dismissal (see the *Asahi Shimbun* article below). It may be noted that had the Governor been appointed by an upper-level board, and answerable to that board for his conduct, the government may have been able to remain insulated from the case, and speculation about indirect involvement in policy making may not have arisen.

Pressure from the legislature and executive branch seemed to have arisen in a reverse direction from that envisaged under the framework to secure the Bank's independence. With regard to the appointive authority of executives, considerations

---

[25]Under the BOJ Act (Article 25), executives (excluding Executive Directors) cannot be dismissed against their will during their term of office except in the following cases: (a) an officer has received a ruling of commencement of bankruptcy proceedings, (b) an officer has received punishment under this Act, (c) an officer has been sentenced to imprisonment without labor or a heavier punishment, (d) an officer has been deemed incapable of carrying out his/her duties due to mental or physical reasons.

such as security of status[26] were made so that the government would not be able to dismiss any executives they happened to dislike. However, in this case, to the contrary, the then Cabinet would be held responsible for appointing Governor Fukui if he were to resign, and was said to have been facing a difficult situation. In this regard, while there had been strong criticism from the general public and the opposition party that Governor Fukui should resign for acting contrary to probity, then Prime Minister Koizumi and the Cabinet defended him. Of course, security of status[27] prevented the Cabinet from removing the Governor from his post in the first place, but if there had been a higher board that made judgment from a neutral standpoint regardless of political judgment under the multiboard system, and if Governor Fukui had not been dismissed based on such higher-board's decision, the trustworthiness of Governor Fukui would not have been brought into question.

> The BOJ decided not to hike the interest rate at the last minute. Although there had not been solid evidence to support the recovery of personal consumption, the decision cannot but be considered as an outcome of political considerations under obvious pressure from the government that threatened to revise the BOJ Act. There was undoubtedly a desire to avoid friction with the government and the ruling party concerning appointment of the next Governor and members of the Policy Board. And there was probably also a feeling of indebtedness over the Murakami Fund issue. If the above decision made politicians believe they could control monetary policy by exhibiting a strong-willed stance and the general public to think that 'the Bank of Japan is soft on politicians after all,' then the BOJ lost something very significant (*Asahi Shimbun*, 19 January 2007, "Failed dialogue with the markets" by Yasuyuki Nishii, member of editorial board, translated from Japanese).

3.3.5 Agency Problem of a Central Bank and Accountability

Devices needed to counter the agency problem should be built into the principal–agent relationship. The following section will first introduce some fundamental ideas on this and then look at various countermeasures actually employed in the central bank case. Second, a general view on accountability, which is considered to be the most important measure taken by public agents against the agency problem, will be introduced and applied to central banks.

---

[26]Refer to footnote 25.

[27]The Cabinet may not be able to dismiss the Governor, but if he were to be punished for violating the BOJ Act, then it would fall under Article 25 whereby an officer being punished under this Act would not enjoy security of status. In this case the Act includes the internal regulations of the Bank. Therefore, whether Governor Fukui violated internal regulations or not became a focal point but the Cabinet deemed that he did not (internal regulations were revised after this incident). The Cabinet's intention to protect Governor Fukui is thus evidenced by such judgment.

3.3.5.1 Measures to Counter the Agency Problem and Central Banks

Measures to Counter the Agency Problem

Among the numerous studies of the design of an incentive structure to counter the agency problem is Kiewiet and McCubbins (1991). They propose four mechanisms to overcome agency costs:

Screening and Selection

Agents should be selected carefully taking into consideration the agent's previous performance and reputation.

Contract Design

Contracts should be designed as clearly as possible so as to limit the potential for an agency problem to arise.

Monitoring and Reporting

An agent's activities should be monitored, with the agent being required to submit adequate reports.

Institutional Checks

Multiple agents should check one another.

Central Bank Measures to Counter the Agency Problem

In this section, Kiewiet and McCubbin's four categories are used to examine the countermeasures built into the institutional frameworks of central banks.

Screening and Selection

Since multiple central banks do not exist in a single country, there is no alternative. However, cautious screening when selecting senior central bankers is possible. Since the abilities required of senior central bankers cannot be gauged by simple indicators and are, therefore, difficult to grasp, it is highly likely that indirect information such as a candidate's previous performance and reputation will be looked at, as is the case in selecting agents in many professional vocations.

Contract Design

Generally, making the contract with an agent as explicit as possible reduces the agency problem. Studies that have applied this idea to monetary policy show that it is desirable for an explicit contract regarding monetary policy to be drawn up between the central bank and the government (for example, Walsh, 1995)[28]. The Reserve Bank of New Zealand provides an example: there the central bank enters into an agreement with the government as regards the inflation rate (discussed further below).

---

[28]Walsh (1995) regarded the central bank as the government's agent, and, based on agency theory, discussed what sort of incentive should be incorporated to draft the most appropriate contract to eliminate inflation bias. He considered it was most appropriate to link senior central bankers' compensation and the inflation rate. In order to ensure flexibility vis-à-vis new situations that might arise after signing of a contract, the inflation rate used should not be a simple one, but one that can reflect changes.

As mentioned by Williamson (1985), however, it is difficult to devise a perfect contract in advance. For central bank policy activities, evaluation based on specific indicators such as an inflation rate provides only partial information on degree of efforts made by the agent (a central bank). It is therefore difficult to create a clean incentive structure. The Reserve Bank of New Zealand example does not contain any pecuniary incentive structure, although the law provides the potential for the governor to be dismissed for failing to meet contracted policy targets.

Monitoring and Reporting

It is common practice for the executive and legislative branches to monitor central bank activities and require reports to be submitted. For example, the central bank governor explains bank activities as well as submits annual reports to the legislature. Central bank accountability involves such reporting requirements.

Institutional Checks

Basically, there is no alternative central bank within a single country, and therefore institutional checks cannot function. However, legislatures may delegate some monitoring tasks to other specialized public organizations (in the case of Japan, the Board of Audit). Such arrangements may be considered examples of institutional checks.

Further, as discussed in Sect. 3.3.4.2, a multiboard structure can provide for a system of institutional checks within the central bank organization. In New Zealand, for example, the role of the Board of Directors is explicitly to monitor the performance of the Governor, on behalf of the Minister of Finance.

Agreement between the Reserve Bank of New Zealand and the Government

The Reserve Bank of New Zealand Act that was revised in 1989 stipulates that an agreement should be made between the Bank Governor and the Minister of Finance concerning monetary policy. Namely, Sect. 9, Article 1 of the Act stipulates that "The Minister shall, before appointing or reappointing, any person as Governor, fix, in agreement with that person, policy targets for the carrying out by the Bank of its primary function during that person's term of office, or next term of office, as Governor." The agreement based on this Act is called the "policy targets agreement" and, in the first agreement made in March 1990, a document stating that the annual inflation rate of CPI should be lowered to within the range of 0–2% by the end of December 1992, was signed by the Governor and the Minister of Finance.

The reason why such an agreement is made between the Governor and the Minister of Finance is that the Minister is regarded as the principal and the Governor, the agent. The Governor is appointed by the Minister based on the recommendation by the Bank's Board of Directors. The agreement also recognizes the possibility of failing to achieve the required target due to unforeseen events, and possibility of the target being changed. Successive agreements have provided that the Governor must explain both the reasons for missing the target and the steps planned to return to target. According to Walsh (1995), in the process of revising the central bank act in 1989, financial incentives such as giving a bonus to the Bank's executives for achieving the target were discussed, but, in the end, such an incentive scheme was not included.

3.3.5.2   Accountability as a Measure Against the Agency Problem

Kiewiet and McCubbins (1991) emphasized the monitoring and reporting requirement of agent activities as one measure to counter the agency problem. Formal requirements to account for their actions are often imposed on public agents. The section below introduces Jackson's (1982) study on the accountability of public agents which will be applied to central banks.

Accountability of Public Agents

Various Facets of Accountability
Jackson's *The Political Economy of Bureaucracy* (chapter entitled "Accountability and Control of Bureaucracy") explains that there are a number of facets to the concept of accountability, of which the major ones are as follows[29]:

- **Political accountability**:
  This is the most common and basic facet of accountability—the accountability of responsible people (for example, ministers and chief executives of public agents) for the overall activities of their respective organizations to the legislature and the general public.
- **Legal accountability**:
  Accountability concerning whether activities are lawful or not.
- **Financial accountability**:
  Accountability concerning whether public agents are using resources as designated by the legislature. Specifically, submitting financial reports to the legislature.
- **Efficiency accountability**:
  A requirement for solid reasoning for the cost incurred, and for whether the most efficient measure has been taken to achieve the objective.

Necessity of Accountability
Being agents of the general public and/or the legislature, it is quite natural that public organizations should be accountable to the general public and the legislature. From such a perspective, Jackson points out the following three objectives for accountability:

- Making public agents responsive to the needs and demands of the electorate, especially in a changing environment.
- Ensuring that decisions are 'fair', i.e., that they conform to the general climate of ethical opinion.
- Monitoring and evaluating the performance of the bureaucracy with a view to providing value for money.

---

[29]Besides the study by Jackson introduced in this chapter, Lupia and McCubbins (1994) analyzes the mechanism of the legislature formulating a public agent's accountability as a system using game theory.

Jackson (ibid, p. 225) indicates that the last objective is becoming more important, with efficiency accountability becoming increasingly valued. This follows, in Jackson's view, from a premise of modern institutional economics that bureaucrats are self-interested, and that such self-interest "can come into conflict with 'the public interest.'" This presumes that the self-interest of bureaucrats can make a bureaucratic organization inefficient. This contrasts sharply with the probity perspective of Williamson (see Sect. 3.2), who argues that low-powered incentives and limited attention to efficiency of resource utilization are elements of effective governance for public organizations undertaking sovereign transactions.

From Jackson's perspective, the accountability and independence of public agents are subject to a trade-off: "the control of these dispersed agents of government does, however, have to be balanced against the effectiveness and efficiency which comes from their autonomy."

Application to Central Banks

Difference between a Central Bank and General Government Ministries
When applying the above discussion on accountability to a central bank as a public institution, it is first necessary to pay attention to the difference between a central bank and other public agents.

First, central banks are also subject to corporate governance requirements, as argued in Chap. 2, Sect. 2.3.2. The legislature may be the principal of the central bank, but accountability may need to be broader than simply reporting to the legislature. This point forms the foundation for the following second and third points.

Second, as indicated by Jackson, it may be necessary to strike a balance between accountability and the autonomy (independence) of a central bank. Requirements to render an over-detailed account may infringe on central bank independence, undermining the intrinsic objective of accountability.

Third, it is necessary to take into consideration the influence that information released by a central bank will have on financial markets. Since a central bank pursues its public objectives through participating in financial markets, prior leakage of its course of action could generate market speculation that could cause market turmoil, making it more difficult for the central bank to achieve its initial objectives. For example, assessing the likelihood of such problems may influence the timing of the release of minutes and announcement of interest rate projections.

To Whom Is a Central Bank Accountable?
Ultimately, the principal of a central bank is the general public. Indeed, it may be argued that the central bank is accountable not to the legislature, but to the general public. However, in a representative democratic system, the central bank is not a direct agent of the general public, but is formally an agent of the legislature or the executive branch. This goes to the heart of the problem of multiple principals. The formal principal (e.g., a government at the end of its mandate) may have incentives that lead it to misrepresent the interests of the ultimate principal (e.g., the public). The formation of a mission statement that reflects the interests of the ultimate principals, and structuring governance and incentives to focus on achievement of that mission, can help in this regard.

Jackson's Four Facets of Accountability

Of Jackson's four facets of accountability, three clearly apply. Monetary policy actions are clearly subject to public accountability. Central bank governors provide testimony to the legislature, and take part in ministerial level meetings to explain their actions. These are examples of political accountability. Legal accountability is obviously necessary and, as for financial accountability, most central banks submit financial reports to the legislature.

With regard to efficiency accountability, the earlier discussion noted a tension between different views on its place in central bank accountability. Williamson's (1999) perspective was that it would distract from probity but Jackson suggested that it is becoming increasingly relevant. It should be noted that it is extremely difficult to measure central bank efficiency. Even the concept of monetary policy efficiency is a difficult one. Nevertheless, there is an example where "budget maximization by bureaucrats" (Niskanen, 1971) is simply applied to the monetary policy of a central bank. Toma (1982) argues that the FRS adopts a budget maximization policy and therefore has a tendency to raise interest rates on its holding assets.[30] Others (e.g., Munger and Roberts, 1990) counterargue that such a simple model cannot explain the behavior of the FRS. The complexity of the issue and diverse opinion suggest that more studies are needed. Views on appropriate central bank accountability may need modification.

3.4 Application of Public Choice Theory

In this section, public choice theory will be deployed to underpin the argument for central bank independence from the legislature and executive branch of government. Public choice theory is an aspect of public economics, which applies economics to the analysis of the political process and government behavior. This theory regards government (in a broad context including the legislature) as an assembly of many individuals with different interests and objectives; therefore it is mistaken to treat government as a single individual or to presume that it has a clearly defined objective. Such a perspective enables public choice theory to propose a mechanism behind inconsistent behavior on the part of governments.

Also, the theory holds that just as the private sector carries the risk of market failure, the public sector may see government failure (political failure). This is because, even in a democratic system, political decision-making (collective decision-making) behavior faces intrinsically difficult issues when aggregating the preferences of individuals to determine public sector behavior.

Below, two aspects of public choice theory—so-called 'cycle theory' under majority rule and the vote-maximizing behavior hypothesis—will be discussed, in connection with public governance of a central bank.

---

[30]Toma and Toma (1986) and Mayer (1990) include many analytical papers on monetary policy of the FRS from the perspective of public choice theory.

3.4.1   Cycle Theory Under Majority Rule and Central Banks

Following Arrow's (1951) impossibility theorem, it became clear that majority voting will not in general lead to consistent collective decisions. Decisions might not necessarily reflect voter wishes; in some circumstances a "cycle" of better options might be generated, resulting in an imperfect decision or a stalemate. Nevertheless, collective decision-making based on majority voting remains the dominant practice in democracies. Theorists explain this paradox using the concept of structure-induced equilibrium. The section below applies these theories to the situation of central banks, and proposes that their independence plays a role in achieving structure-induced equilibrium in collective decision-making.

3.4.1.1   Emergence of the Cycle Theory and Structure-Induced Equilibrium

The Impossibility Theorem and Cycle Theory
Arrow's (ibid) impossibility theorem demonstrated that it was generally impossible to come up with a voting procedure that satisfied various rational criteria such as the consistency and transitivity of choices. This insight was a key building block for theories that explain the potential for government failure within democratic systems.

The impossibility theorem has been specifically applied to majority rule. Various names have been given to this theory such as 'cycle theory,' 'paradox of voting,' 'chaos theory,' and 'instability theory.' Stevens (1993) explains the theory as follows. Let us assume that, in Fig. 3.4, three politicians have to decide the subsidies to be given to industry X and industry Y. Point A shows the combination of subsidies to respective industries preferred by politician A. The greater the distance from point A, the more undesirable it will be for politician A. Similarly, the sums of subsidies to the two industries preferred by politicians B and C are shown as points B and C respectively. When a decision is to be made by majority vote in such a situation, all sorts of results may arise and the outcome would remain unsettled. That is, if the point is within area A/B, seeing that the point is in a more desirable area than the initial value, politicians A and B will vote for this area and become the majority. Similarly, when the point is in area B/C, politicians B and C will vote for this area and, as for area A/C, politicians A and C will become the majority. Since all three areas have the possibility of becoming a majority, decisions cannot be made, thereby causing a "cyclical problem" (or "preference stalemate"). This example shows that majority rule in a democratic system may not necessarily bring about a result reflecting the voters' wishes. This is called "government failure."

Structure-Induced Equilibrium
Despite the theoretical possibility that no one policy option outranks all others (in terms of majority preferences), policy decisions are still routinely made in democ-

Fig. 3.4 Cyclical theory of
majority rule

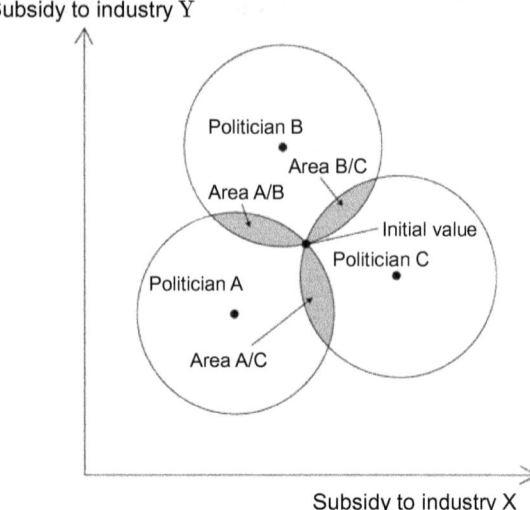

racies with majority voting systems. To explain this, Shepsle and Weingast (1981) introduced the concept of "structure-induced equilibrium."[31]

According to this concept, in a situation where more than two policy options exist, and thus there is a potential for a preference stalemate, the order of presenting the alternatives matters. By deciding which plan to be shown first, the result could be controlled in a way that does not apparently produce a preference stalemate. Thus, equilibrium can be attained if an institution is constructed to decide how to submit policy proposals. As pointed out by Ordeshook (1990), there are various such institutions, of which a committee system of the legislature is an example.[32]

In his theory, majority rule functions as a successful collective decision-making procedure only when there is a well-defined institution such as a committee that creates an appropriate set of constraints on the set of options. Such institutions will endogenously arise in order to make majority rule function effectively. In this regard, Ordeshook (ibid) noted that this "new institutionalism" in political economy not only provides key insights into the part played by legislative committees, regulatory agencies, budgetary procedures, agendas, voting rules, etc., but also provides a synthesis of several intellectual traditions (including those already discussed in this chapter).

---

[31] Other procedures include "logrolling" among politicians to make up a majority group or attain equilibrium through "agenda control."

[32] For example, in Fig. 3.4, let us assume that politician A or B (or both) are the ranking members of the committee and are able to play a leading role in forming an opinion, and that the committee has the authority to submit an alternative policy to the plenary session. In this case, an alternative policy in area A/B will be submitted to the plenary session and will in fact be approved.

Fig. 3.5 Cyclical theory and policy choices faced by the central bank

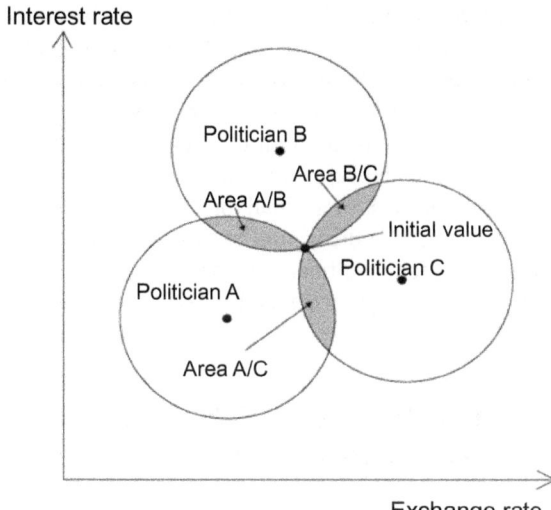

3.4.1.2 Application to a Central Bank

Application of the Cycle Theory

Decisions related to central bank activities are made collectively and the possibility of a policy stalemate cyclical problem arises. For the sake of argument, let us suppose that the subjects for decision are the desirable levels for the interest rate and foreign exchange rate. Decision-making is illustrated in Fig. 3.5. In this figure, similar to Fig. 3.4, three politicians make decisions according to majority rule with regard to a two-dimensional issue. In this case, for the same reason discussed in Fig. 3.4, no combination of desirable levels of interest rate and foreign exchange rate achieves equilibrium and the cyclical problem ensues.

This occurs because decision-making is considered two dimensional, assuming there is no definite correlation between the level of interest rate and foreign exchange rate. Since economic variables are correlated with one another and if such relationships are known, the multi-dimensional decision-making problem could be reduced to a one-dimensional issue. Once reduced to one dimension, the 'median voter theorem'[33] can be applied and the cyclical problem would not emerge.

In practice, of course, the links between the interest rate and the exchange rate are too complex for the interest rate/exchange rate choice to be reduced to a single dimension. This complexity itself creates the need for an expert institution (e.g., a central bank) to assess alternative policy options.

---

[33]The "median voter theorem" states that a majority rule voting system will select the outcome most preferred by the "median voter." "Median voter" is the voter with an equal number of votes on either side.

Equilibrium Attained by the Central Bank System

As described above, a preference stalemate may emerge with respect to monetary policy if it is decided by a majority in the legislature. Nowadays, such decision-making is usually delegated to the central bank. By playing a similar role as a committee in the structure-induced equilibrium theory, the central bank is preventing a stalemate.

Nevertheless, unlike a committee in the legislature, policy decided by a central bank will, in most cases, be final. In a few countries, the legislature formally reserves the right to override the central bank's decision in extremis. Not utilizing this right is tantamount to a continuing endorsement of the process by which the decision is taken—even if the government does not agree with all monetary policy decisions.

3.4.2 Vote-Maximizing Behavior Hypothesis and Countermeasures

Another theory that explains government failure is the vote-maximizing behavior hypothesis of politicians. This section explains the hypothesis and introduces the concepts of 'constitutional restriction' and 'public agent as a commitment' as devices that provide countermeasures. Central bank independence turns out to be one such countermeasure.

3.4.2.1 Vote-Maximizing Behavior Hypothesis

The vote-maximizing behavior hypothesis ascribes utility-maximization motivated behavior to politicians. The theory was first introduced by Downs (1957) and developed by Buchanan and Tullock (1962). According to this hypothesis, "parties formulate policies in order to win elections, rather than win elections in order to formulate policies" (Downs, ibid). Ideally, politicians should act to maximize the welfare of society, but, it is argued, their behavior can be better explained by assuming that they act to maximize their number of votes. That is, the hypothesis considers that politicians are not perfect agents for voters but have their own incentives.

Breton (1974) developed this line of thinking, noting that not only politicians but also bureaucrats are involved in the supply of public goods, where the amount supplied is decided by negotiation between them (see Fig. 3.6). There are only voters on the demand side for public goods. Participation of voters in political activities provides a feedback mechanism from the demand side to the supply side.

Such political activities range widely from voting to taking part in pressure groups. However, such participation incurs costs. Voters might not therefore participate in political activities despite their discontent with the supply of public goods if the cost incurred exceeds the degree of discontent.

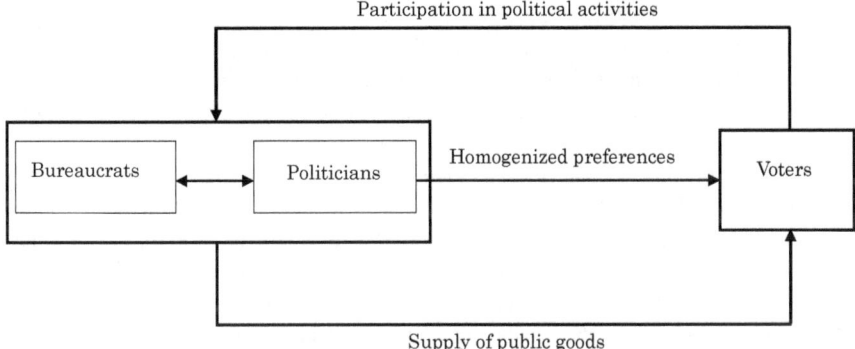

Fig. 3.6   Breton model (Simplified Diagram based on Breton, 1974)

According to the Breton model, the factors behind possible divergence between voter preferences and the actual supply of public goods are as follows:

- Voters do not show their preference for a politician's individual policy but comprehensively judge the policy package proposed by the politician. Therefore, some policies that are not supported by voters may be implemented.
- Public goods are not traded in the market. The free rider problem makes it hard to measure voter demand for public goods.
- Since voters do not take part in political activities, if costs incurred exceed their degree of discontent, their discontent would not be fully communicated to politicians.
- A politician may be able to ignore the preference of voters whose vote is not needed to win an election.

With respect to Breton's argument, it should be underlined that in a representative democracy the actual supply of public goods might not satisfy voter expectations. Of the many studies about specific policy outcomes, the research on fiscal deficits by Buchanan and Wagner (1977) has a significant bearing on the public governance of a central bank. They argued that it is almost inevitable that political parties in pursuit of vote maximization willingly neglect fiscal discipline in order to win voters. Democracy has the inclination, almost inevitably, to see fiscal deficits increase. This has an implication for the governance of the money creation process, which will be discussed below.

3.4.2.2   Measures Against Vote-Maximization Behavior

Constitutional Restriction
To counter government failure where government policy is inclined to pursue short-term interests based on vote-maximization behavior, public choice theorists advocate

an approach called 'constitutional restriction.' 'Constitution' here refers to not only a codified constitution, but also any basic rule that cannot be easily changed. Kanemoto (1991) notes that "when making common and long-standing rules, the general public will make a choice based on a wider perspective rather than be influenced by short-term interests."

Levacic (1990) has named this approach "constitutional political economy" and calls Buchanan and others that advocate it "constitutionalists." According to Levacic, the theory can be summarized as follows: "Constitutionalists are keen to establish pre-commitment rules which will prevent the zero and negative sum political games caused by government from being used for securing redistributive transfers."

Buchanan (1991) gives the reason why such rules can help achieve a consensus that produces superior longer-term outcomes. The first is: "The individual who recognizes his/her own possible 'weakness of will' in future periods may choose to impose upon himself/herself binding constraints that will effectively prevent his/her situational responses, as those responses might be dictated by in-period utility maximization." The second reason is: "Individuals may do so because they do not 'trust' fellow members to refrain from 'temptation,' and because they recognize that, in majoritarian settings, they cannot effectively forestall undesired political choices."

Public Agents as Commitment

As another measure to counter government failure accompanying vote-maximization behavior, Kanemoto (1991) cites the autonomy of public agents and calls this "public agents as commitment." Autonomous public agents may have longer horizons than politicians facing periodic reelection, and may thereby reduce policy volatility. In Kanemoto's view, in some situations (e.g., the delivery of police and prosecution services) this may be a reasonable return for the risks associated with self-interested public agents acting in their own, rather than the public's interest.

Independent public agencies can be considered as such commitment devices. This explanation of the raison d'être for independent agencies shares many features with Moe's theory, explained earlier (Sect. 3.2.2 on the autonomy of bureaucratic organizations).

3.4.2.3 Application to Central Banks

Underlying Problems for Central Banks

Buchanan and Wagner (1977) applied their analysis of the relationship between the vote-maximization behavior hypothesis and the fiscal deficit to central banks in a chapter entitled "Budget Deficits Financed by Money Creation."

They began their discussion by "dropping the independence and wisdom assumptions and replacing these by the plausible hypothesis that monetary authorities are, like elected politicians, subjected to both direct and indirect political pressures." Under such an assumption, "[public] demand will take the form of pressures brought to bear on elected politicians for expansion in the levels of budgetary outlay" and budget deficits would be financed by money creation. They pointed out the underlying fact that "there will be an inflationary bias when governments are allowed to create deficits and to finance these with currency is very elementary common sense." Against such a background, since "among all forms of extracting resources, inflation is perhaps the most indirect, and it is the one that probably requires the highest degree of sophisticated understanding on the part of the individual,"..."elected politicians approve programs of public spending; they impose taxes. If they are not required to balance projected spending with revenues, they will not, because the voting public does not hold them directly responsible for the inflation that their actions necessarily produce." That is, Buchanan and Wagner claim that the risk of bringing about inflation by financing budget deficits through money creation is built into a democratic system.

Price stability, which is a service offered by the central bank, can be viewed as a public good. The free rider problem attaching to public goods applies equally to price stability, and creates the familiar problem of undersupply (i.e., price instability).

In Fig. 3.7, it is assumed that there are two citizens, A and B. The figure shows the respective marginal valuation (marginal utility) that A and B give for the provided service, i.e., price stability, overall marginal valuation which is the sum of that of A and B, and also marginal costs to provide such a service. If the two citizens reveal their true marginal valuations, and, summed up as they are in the political process, the supply of this service can be determined at level S. However, considering that the service is assumed to be a public good, it has the feature of 'non-rivalness' and 'non-exclusion.' Then there is the strong likelihood that the two citizens do not reveal their true marginal valuation honestly. For example, even if A only gave a low valuation than actual valuation in order not to bear the cost, if B gave a high valuation, and the service is supplied based on the latter valuation, A can also enjoy the benefit as a free rider. On the premise of such free rider valuation, should policy be determined by politicians who pursue vote-maximization behavior, there would be an undersupply of the service, i.e., price stability, compared with demand. Deviation of voter demand for public goods and actual supply caused by the free rider problem of public goods is also incorporated into the Breton model.

Central Bank Countermeasures
A central bank could take several countermeasures against government failure. First, Friedman's k-percent rule is well known as a constitutional restriction measure. Here, the money supply being increased by a central bank by a constant percentage rate (k-percent) every year is stipulated in the constitution or law.[34] Other examples such as the policy targets agreement of the Reserve Bank of New Zealand—more generally, the clarification of central bank objectives in central bank acts is considered to be a form of constitutional restriction. There are differences of view on the practicality

---

[34]Friedman (1986, pp. 30–31) proposes: "Set a target path of several years ahead of a single aggregate....The Federal Reserve Governors submit their resignations at the end of year in which the growth of a specified monetary aggregate has departed from the advance target by more than a designated amount." However, he himself says: "Unfortunately, I do not really think that's feasible."

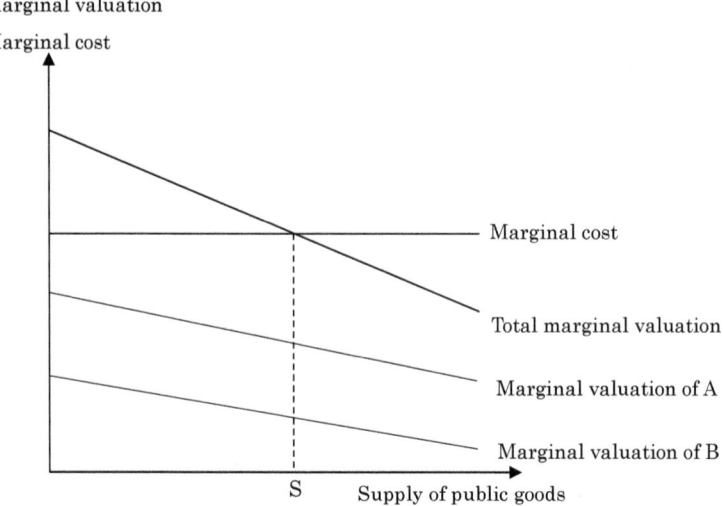

Fig. 3.7 Free rider problem

of such constitutional restrictions on monetary policy. Many agree that rules such as the k-percent rule are overly rigid, and might hamper the flexibility of monetary policy. Greater clarity of policy objectives in law provides less of a constraint, and may be more realistic.[35]

Second, discussion on public agents as a commitment behavior has clear relevance for understanding why central bank independence may be desirable. For example, looking at the relationship between the budget deficit and inflation, Buchanan and Wagner (ibid) state that "when we assume that there does, in fact, exist a monetary authority, an idealized FRB or central bank, that is totally and completely immune from the pressures of democratic politics, there need be no direct linkage between debt-financed deficits and inflation because of the control powers of the monetary authority."

Such thinking applies not only to the macro policy of a central bank, but also to its banking operations and supervisory function. In this case, since the banking operations and supervisory function of a central bank are based on individual transactions, pressure from the legislature may well come from individual politicians concerning a specific transaction (or activity) of the central bank. In order to prevent such pressure, central bank independence can be considered effective as is the case with central bank macro policy.

---

[35]The so-called 'inflation targeting' of monetary policy may be regarded as a variant of the k-percent rule and, for a similar reason, may not be a realistic measure, excluding cases in small economies.

3.5 Conclusion

This chapter has applied new institutional economics to various issues of public governance such as central bank independence and accountability. New institutional economics—specifically, three disciplines of economics: TCE, agency theory, and public choice theory—extends economic analysis to the understanding of the various institutions in the economy and society. The approach provides a common theoretical framework for discussing central banking system issues, at least with respect to relevant public governance issues. The main findings of this chapter, drawing on such theories, are as follows:

First, when Williamson's theory of 'governance as probity' based on TCE was applied, it was apparent that probity is very important for central bank transactions. A central bank organization needs 'governance as probity,' such as a low-power incentive scheme and employment protection, in order to mitigate probity hazard. Such governance attributes cannot be provided by private organizations (such as private banks) that pursue efficiency and profit maximization. Therefore, central bank transactions should be conducted by a public organization even if efficiency is sacrificed.

Applying Moe's related theory on the autonomy of public bureaucracy, central bank autonomy can be seen as a device to reduce to a minimum the potential for and the cost of policy swings that could otherwise be present when central bank policies are determined by the majority political party. In this light, it can be argued that in Japan, where a change in majority is very rare, the political tendency to reinforce central bank independence may not be as strong as in the US and Europe, where a change in majority is more frequent.

Second, considering a central bank's principal–agent relationships from the perspective of agency theory, a central bank may have multiple principals (such as the executive branch and the legislature). This may cause some inefficiency. On the other hand, multiple principals may reduce the risk of the central bank taking monetary policy decisions to suit particular political interests. Another approach to limiting the influence of potentially biased principals is to give the central bank independent agency status. The constitutionality of this became a big issue when the BOJ Act was revised. Research discussed in this chapter suggests that the revision was consistent with the Constitution.

The congressional dominance hypothesis suggests that a political principal can still greatly influence the decisions of an independent agency, through actual or threatened sanctions. The authority of the legislature and/or executive branch to appoint central bank executives may create such a channel for influence. Some evidence of a 'political business cycle' in monetary policy provides suggestive corroboration of the existence of political influence over monetary policy decisions. A potential countermeasure would be for central banks to use a multiboard structure, along the lines that Fama and Jensen suggest for private firms. Private firms divide authority into monitoring and execution—with the former assigned to the board of directors and the latter to the executive board—as a mechanism for shareholders to counter agency problems arising from the separation of ownership and control. In both cases, the appointive power of the principal can be restricted to appointments to the upper board, which in turn appoints the executive board. In the case of the central bank, this would diminish the degree of potential leverage of political principals over monetary policy decisions taken by the executive board. It was noted that such a separation of appointive authority is rare.

Third, public choice theory concepts were used to provide another strand of reasoning for central bank independence from the legislative and executive branches in a democratic system. Essentially, central bank independence, coupled with a clear specification of objectives in the relevant legislation, can guard against a diversion of monetary policy away from serving long-term public interests towards serving short-term political interests.

The various theories under new institutional economics used in this chapter share a common perspective in that they all start from the viewpoint that the behavior of the relevant political and bureaucratic actors is likely to be based on self-interest. Nevertheless, they are not necessarily consistent in every detail. Accordingly, they were applied to the problem of the public governance of central banks separately, with mostly consistent but somewhat different insights being obtained. However, new institutional economics is as yet only legal theory. Should new institutional economics become more developed empirically, it could well yield further insights into the public governance of central banks.

Chapter 4
Governance of Monetary Policy

4.1 Overview

Monetary policy is currently well-established as an intrinsic function of a central bank. However, from a historical perspective, it is a relatively new addition to a central bank's traditional banking functions such as the provider of payment systems and lender of last resort (LLR). Compared to such traditional functions, monetary policy places emphasis on a macro consideration of finance and the economy overall. And, since monetary policy has a macroeconomic influence on the national economy, it attracts more attention from the public and legislature compared to other central bank functions.

Due to this characteristic of monetary policy, various questions are likely to arise for a central bank in simultaneously conducting monetary policy along with its traditional functions. To begin with, there is the ownership of monetary policy that poses the question of whether a central bank should really own monetary policy. And, based on the fact that currently a central bank is the owner of monetary policy, there is also the question of organizational governance that raises concern as to what sort of consideration should be given to its internal organizational aspect since a central bank also performs other central bank functions. Such ownership and organizational governance issues regarding monetary policy are the same as those that exist in terms of the governance of organizations such as corporations. The objective of this section is to examine the governance of monetary policy. The subject is diverse, but with regard to ownership we will focus on the organizational integration of the monetary policy body with the market operation and foreign exchange policy bodies. As for organizational governance, we will discuss the design and management of a board system (decision-making body of a central bank) to resolve and ease various problems that arise in managing monetary policy.

In considering the above, three theories from organizational economics (transaction cost economics <TCE>, agency theory, and the theory of organizational culture) will be applied. First, with regard to TCE, the theory of organizational boundaries will be applied to the ownership of monetary policy from the perspective of the

© Springer Nature Singapore Pte Ltd. 2019

Y. Oritani, *The Japanese Central Banking System Compared with Its European and American Counterparts*, https://doi.org/10.1007/978-981-13-9001-2_4

make-or-buy problem between the monetary policy body and those responsible for traditional banking functions. Second, multitask agency theory from agency theory is applied to discuss the organizational governance issue that arises when a central bank conducts monetary policy. The question is mainly considered from the perspective of the incentive problem that emerges from a central bank commissioned with multi-functions as well as from how it could be solved. Third, concerning the theory of organizational culture, not only organizational economics, but also the theory of organizational culture based on management theory is applied to discuss both central bank ownership and organizational governance. Specifically, organizational culture of a central bank is, similar to standard corporate culture, composed of a two-tiered structure, that is, a common culture across all sectors and the different subculture of each sector. As for the latter, there are significant differences between the monetary policy sector and traditional banking sectors. Therefore, from the perspective that there might be a conflict of organizational cultures between such subcultures, this chapter will look into the issues surrounding the integration of monetary policy and banking functions, and also the introduction of a multiboard structure as a solution.

4.2   Issue Identification

This section first defines monetary policy and then points out that monetary policy invention by a central bank considerably lags invention in terms of other central bank functions. At the same time, the experience of the Bank of England (the BOE) will be cited to see what issues underlie the governance aspect of monetary policy. Then, monetary policy governance will be clarified from the two aspects of ownership and organizational governance.

4.2.1   What is Monetary Policy?

Before we consider what governance actually is in terms of monetary policy, we first need to define monetary policy. Monetary policy can be defined through considering its basic goal, operational targets, and instruments to achieve such goal and targets.

4.2.1.1   Definition by Goal, Targets, and Instruments

The basic goal of monetary policy is, since it is public policy, clearly stipulated in law (central bank law) as a result of legislative deliberations and can be summed up as "a common understanding around the world that the goal of monetary policy is to realize continuous economic growth through price stability" (Shirakawa, 2008a, translated from Japanese). However, the goal of monetary policy has historically been evolving around the globe, and, according to Shirakawa (ibid.), Japan saw periods where maintenance of a fixed exchange rate regime, full employment, and economic growth were variously focused on as goals.

In any case, monetary policy is public policy, the basic goal of which is to realize macroeconomic stability and growth, and can be differentiated conceptually from prudential policy the objective of which is to maintain financial system stability. However, in actuality, as is evident following the recent global financial crises, such differentiation is not necessarily clear and blurring of the above two objectives may occur.

Next, according to Shirakawa (ibid.), a specific target is set based on the goal. Examples of specific targets include interbank short-term interest rates and the official discount rate. Others include money supply targeting adopted by the US and European countries in the 1970s which sets money supply as the interim target of monetary policy, and inflation targeting which targets the inflation rate.

As instruments to achieve the above basic goals and specific targets, there are both indirect and direct instruments. While indirect instruments try to achieve the goals and targets through open market operations, direct instruments utilize some form of public authority to achieve them in a compulsory manner. A specific example of indirect instruments is, most commonly, interest rate intervention through market measures such as open market operations. On the other hand, examples of direct instruments are change in the reserve requirement based on a reserve requirement system, regulations on interest rates linked to the official discount rate, and window guidance on the amount of private bank lending to customers.

4.2.1.2 Unconventional Monetary Policy

Since the recent global financial crises, monetary policy pursued under the zero-interest rate constraint to attain macroeconomic stability has been termed unconventional monetary policy. Shirakawa (2011a, p. 8) wrote on specific examples as follows:

> One example is the increase in the government bond purchases decided by the Federal Reserve in the autumn of 2010, which aimed at absorbing interest risks in the private sector and lowering long-term interest rates. Another example is the comprehensive monetary easing decided on by the Bank of Japan (BOJ) in the autumn of 2010, which includes various unconventional measures. The measure is quite exceptional in that eligible assets for monetary policy operations were expanded to include not only government bonds but also CP, corporate bonds, exchange-traded funds (ETFs), and real estate investment trusts (REITs). The BOJ's purchases aim at stimulating economic activity through a reduction in various risk premiums, as there is little room for a decline in short-term interest rates.

Shirakawa (ibid., p. 12) pointed out the negative aspect of such unconventional monetary policy:

> "It cannot be ruled out that central banks eventually incur losses through these measures," and "the more policy measure become involved in the micro-allocation of resources and capital, the more these measures have the flavor of quasi-fiscal policy."

4.2.2 Period When Monetary Policy was Conceived

Understanding how monetary policy came to be conceived and how it subsequently evolved gives us a clue as to the governance issues that relate to monetary policy and how to tackle them theoretically. Below, we discuss the period when monetary policy was conceived and the period when other functions of a central bank were born. Shirakawa (ibid., p. 13) says that the invention of monetary policy is an innovation of monetary management and believes the inception period coincides with when the monetary system changed from the gold standard to a managed fiat currency system as follows:

> The third major innovation I would like to mention, although it may sound somewhat strange, is the 'invention of monetary policy.' While I will touch later on the issue of how to define monetary policy, for the time being I will use the term in the conventional sense of 'policy that aims at actively influencing the inflation rate or the economic growth rate by controlling the level of short-term interest rates.' Under the gold standard, the quantity of money was constrained by gold holdings and thus the central bank could not influence the price level and economic activity in an active manner. In this sense, central banks had limited room to deploy monetary policy. In fact, monetary policy was not discussed in Bagehot's book. Monetary policy worthy of the name started only with the transition to a fiat money system. Nowadays, appropriate monetary policy conduct has become one of the key tools contributing to macroeconomic stability.

As above, if we accept that monetary policy was conceived when the monetary system changed to that of a fiat money system, then the timing would be around the middle of the 20th century in various countries. If we compare this with when banknotes were issued and interbank settlement services provided, monetary policy was introduced at a considerably later stage. For example, the BOE began banknote issuance at the same time as it was established in 1694, and became the sole issuer in 1844 (Bank Charter Act of 1844). Also, private banks opened deposit accounts with the BOE and bilateral settlement among private banks using these accounts commenced around the latter half of the 18th century and beginning of the 19th century (Fujita, 1987). Net positions in the London clearing house began to be settled multilaterally using private banks' deposit accounts at the BOE from 1854 (Kanai, 1989).

Next, monetary policy invention also considerably lags prudential policy. Taking the BOE as an example, the LLR function in times of economic recession was provided as early as the mid-19th century and, at the same time, the BOE, as LLR, began regulating and supervising private banks.[1]

The above indicates that monetary policy was conceived and developed around banking functions such as the prudential function and LLR function. Therefore, when the Federal Reserve System (FRS) and the BOJ were established (taking the BOE as an example) as central banks with a monetary policy function from the outset, albeit

---

[1]Goodhart (1988) explains that the BOE's regulatory and supervisory authority emerged from the role of "club president" of a club established by the banking community to gain trust from depositors (see Chap. 1, Sect. 1.6.3).

under the constraint of the gold standard currency system, they were based on the assumption that they would have banking functions such as payment function and LLR function.

4.2.3 Governance Issues of Monetary Policy

Based on the definition and historical background of monetary policy, the governance of monetary policy will be considered from two aspects: ownership and organizational governance. The reason why ownership is included in governance is that who is the owner and how such entity is structured greatly affect governance. On the other hand, organizational governance deals with the decision-making structure on the premise of specific ownership.

4.2.3.1 Ownership of Monetary Policy

Generally speaking, monetary policy is regarded as an intrinsic function of a central bank. However, as previously noted (Sect. 4.2.1.1), the basic goal of monetary policy is legally stipulated and, as for specific targets, there arises the question of whether the central bank should be the entity to decide and manage such. Moreover, with regard to recent unconventional monetary policy and exchange rate policy, there is also the question of whether the central bank should be making the decisions and effecting implementation. These issues revolve on the ownership of monetary policy. Details of the respective issues are as follows:

Separating Monetary Policy from a Central Bank
There is discussion as to whether it is adequate to separate several or all monetary policy components such as basic goals, specific targets, and instruments from a central bank. This is similar to the discussion on central bank independence. However, while discussion of independence examines to what extent a central bank can make decisions independently of the government or the legislature, the ownership issue raised in this chapter involves a wider aspect of separation from a central bank. Namely, not only the division of roles with the government but also, in an extreme case, it includes the outsourcing of monetary policy decision-making to a private think tank.

As to the basic goal of monetary policy, "Currently, the central bank in any country has the goal of monetary policy stipulated in law and, in this sense, there is no central bank with 'independence of goal'" (Shirakawa, 2008a, translated from Japanese). That is, the decision-making right regarding the basic goals of monetary policy is separated from the central bank and thus the bank does not have ownership. On the other hand, "with respect to specific targets, the situation differs in each country." That is, if the central bank owns the decision-making right regarding specific targets of monetary policy, then it is considered independent and has ownership of monetary policy. The issue of whether monetary policy should be separated from a central bank boils down to whether the central bank has the right to make decisions regarding specific targets of monetary policy.

Next, monetary policy instruments, especially managing indirect instruments through market operations (monetary operations), are considered to be an intrinsic function of a central bank and there are no instances where a central bank does not have ownership. This is because a central bank has a special fund raising instrument (i.e., the issuance of banknotes) and functions as a kind of bank.[2] As for direct instruments, a central bank does not need to have ownership, but since direct instruments are closely related to market operations, such ownership is rarely separated from the central bank.

Moreover, monetary policy decision-making in the sense that the bank decides specific goals of monetary policy, and implements market operations based on such decisions, is managed by different parts of the central bank organization. For example, in the FRS, monetary policy decision-making is conducted by the Federal Open Market Committee (FOMC) of the Board of Governors (the Federal Reserve Board) in Washington, D.C., while the Federal Reserve Bank of New York implements actual daily market operations based on decisions made. And, at the European System of Central Banks (ESCB), the European Central Bank (ECB) in Frankfurt decides monetary policy and national central banks conduct actual market operations. Such division of labor between monetary policy decision-making and implementation of market operations within the central bank organization is not considered as the separation of monetary policy from the central bank.

Ownership of Exchange Rate Policy

Ownership of exchange rate policy as to who should manage it needs to be considered when discussing the ownership of monetary policy. That is, although exchange rate policy is not monetary policy, the two are closely linked. For example, it is said that 'price stability is the stability of a currency's internal value, and exchange rate stability is stability of the currency's external value.' Looking at the history of the BOE, monetary policy developed through exchange rate policy as a consequence of the country's gold reserves being kept by the BOE.

Exchange rate policy in a broad sense includes decisions about the exchange rate system such as whether to adopt a fixed exchange rate or flexible exchange rate system.[3] However, since the decision-making right here undoubtedly belongs to the government, an ownership question arises as to what extent a central bank can judge whether the country's exchange rate is appropriate and in certain cases has the power to intervene in the exchange rate market (e.g., timing, amount and intervention technique, negotiations with foreign authorities) given that a flexible exchange rate system is adopted.

---

[2]Goodhart (2010, p. 9) notes that "Lord Cobbold, former Governor of the BOE, is reputed once to have said, 'A central bank is a bank, not a study group.' I take this to mean that the essence of central banking lies in its power to create liquidity, by manipulating its own balance sheet."

[3]Refer to Shirakawa (2008a) for definition of exchange rate policy system and current situation in various countries.

Ownership of foreign exchange rate policy differs among countries as do specific targets of monetary policy. According to the Bank for International Settlements (BIS, 2009, Table 2), Japan and Norway are the only two countries out of 29 surveyed that have absolutely no authority over exchange rate policy. And, in the US, the Department of the Treasury and FRS divide ownership between them and the ECB has total ownership of exchange rate policy. In the UK, ownership of exchange rate policy was transferred from the BOE to the Chancellor of the Exchequer under the BOE Act 1946, but the power to intervene in the exchange rate market was partly delegated to the BOE under the BOE Act 1998.

Ownership of Unconventional Monetary Policy

The aforementioned unconventional monetary policy (Sect. 4.2.1.2) can entail risks for central banks (to incur losses) and, by intervening in resource and fund allocation in the microeconomy can be considered to "have the nature of quasi-fiscal policy," though "in a democratic society fiscal policy is, and should be, decided by the legislature" (Shirakawa, 2011a). Therefore, unconventional monetary policy raises the question of whether it is proper for central banks to implement it.

Having said this, although it is called 'unconventional,' it has the same function as the LLR function for central banks (especially with a market liquidity provisioning function). Considering that monetary policy developed gradually from the LLR function as we have seen in the history of the BOE, it is not necessarily 'unconventional.' To support banks, the LLR function of the BOE allows the purchase of risk assets and as such losses may be incurred, similar to unconventional monetary policy. And, since it is a credit extension to the bank being supported, the BOE is intervening in credit allocation at the microeconomic level.

Ownership of Prudential Policy

Various discussions have been heard on the appropriateness of the central bank simultaneously undertaking the role of implementing prudential policy (such as private bank supervision) as well as that of conducting monetary policy. In response to the recent global financial crises, various legal revisions to enhance the role of central banks regarding prudential policy have been made in the US and European countries (see Chap. 5). Goodhart (2010, p. 9) states:

> The question is often asked whether a central bank that sets interest rates should also manage financial stability. This question is put the wrong way around; it should be whether a central bank that manages both liquidity and financial stability should also be given the task of setting interest rates.

4.2.3.2 Organizational Governance of Monetary Policy

In addition to the above question of ownership, the governance of monetary policy also involves the organizational governance of a central bank which manages monetary policy based on the premise that a central bank conducts monetary policy.

This organizational governance aspect of monetary policy is considered in detail by Shirakawa (2008a) under "Decision-making by a Committee (Chap. 6)" and by BIS (2009) under "Decision-making structure (Chap. 4)" of overall central bank functions. The following two issues are specifically considered:

Designing a Committee (Board) System

First, monetary policy is not decided solely by the central bank governor but "in most cases, a framework where a committee makes the decision is adopted" (Shirakawa, ibid.). This said 'committee' is the broadly defined committee as discussed in Chap. 2, Sect. 2.4, namely, the 'board.' A board is the decision-making body at management level. According to Nicholl (2009), the board exists in a central bank because the central bank has characteristics of a private sector corporation. "Indeed, there is no single answer to what the term 'board' means in a central bank. In some central banks, the board is a mix of non-executive and executive members and chaired by a non-executive member. In some, it is the same mix but chaired by the governor. In others, the term is applied to the senior group of executives." Moreover, the board may either be endowed with the actual implementation function or not, in the latter case only overseeing the lower board.

According to BIS, there are three types of board: policy board, management board, and supervisory board. Some central banks have boards for each respective function and there are central banks with only single board (e.g., the BOJ).[4] Also, from the perspective of monetary policy decision-making, Shirakawa (ibid.) gives two types of board system—one where the same board (committee) makes decisions on monetary policy and other policies (e.g., the BOJ) and the other where a board (committee) specializing only in monetary policy decision-making is established (e.g., the BOE).

Shirakawa (ibid.) says that how a board system is designed, such as number of necessary boards and how authority is shared among such boards (in a multi-board structure), will affect the way monetary policy is implemented and how policy decisions are made. Specifically, in the case of a single board system, while (a) information and skills obtained from managing banking supervision and payment systems will help in considering monetary policy, (b) it may become difficult to have sufficient discussion on monetary policy due to lack of sophisticated professional knowledge.

Moreover, the design of a board system not only affects monetary policy but poses an important question regarding the organizational governance of the central bank overall. As will be mentioned later (Sect. 4.4.2.2), monetary policy attracts a high degree of interest from the markets and politicians. This may result in differing

---

[4]If there is only one board, it is called a 'single-board system' and if multiboards exist, it is called a 'multiboard structure' (within which, if there are two, a 'two-board system'). The Reserve Bank of Australia (RBA) and the Bank of Thailand (BOT) have multiboards, one for each function. The RBA adopts a two-board system, comprised of the Reserve Bank Board as the supreme decision-making body of monetary policy, and Payment System Board as the supreme decision-making board for payment systems (the RBA does not have the prudential policy function). The BOT has a Monetary Policy Committee, Financial Institutions Policy Committee, and Payment System Committee for its main three functions.

incentives between officials making monetary policy and those in other banking areas. And, also, a difference in organizational culture can be seen between the monetary policy arena and other banking areas (Sect. 4.5.2.2).

Management of the Board
Shirakawa (2008a) discusses the number of committee members, appointment of committee members, and also agenda to be considered. BIS (2009) discusses issues such as "What determines whether decision-making is by voting or by consensus?"…"When is it valuable to bring in outsiders to sit on boards?"…"Is there an optimal size for a board?"

As regards the appointment of board members, there arises the question of the professional background of members, and diversification. Even if a central bank does not adopt a multiboard structure, by diversifying members, it could, to a certain extent, expect the effect of a multiboard structure.

4.3 Approach from Transaction Cost Economics

This section will apply TCE to study the ownership of monetary policy that is included in the governance issues mentioned in the previous section. Among Coase-Williamson type theories of TCE, there is the phenomenon of organizational boundary issue that examine the pros and cons of organizational integration from the perspective of minimizing transaction costs.[5] Considering the ownership of monetary policy to be an element of a central bank's organizational boundary we apply this concept to discuss the organizational integration of the monetary policy body and its related four functions/policy areas (market operations, exchange rate policy, unconventional monetary policy, and prudential policy)[6] as well as implications for the organizational governance of monetary policy (designing and managing a board system).

---

[5]Refer to Williamson (1975, 1985) and Douma and Schreuder (2002).

[6]Looking only from the perspective of TCE, monetary policy and fiscal policy both relate to macroeconomic policy and the pertinent policy bodies should be integrated. But, since there is a fundamental difference in their public governance, integration is inefficient and will not be discussed in this book. In fiscal policy, tax revenues are distributed under a national budget based on the right to collect tax, and therefore fiscal policy decisions should be made through the direct political process. On the other hand, if monetary policy is placed under direct political influence it would be contrary to its basic goal of price stability, and therefore monetary policy should be independent from any political process. However, should a central bank incur losses from unconventional monetary policy, exchange rate policy, or prudential policy, the amount paid to the national treasury would be reduced, thus indirectly increasing the taxpayer burden. As such, those policies that may incur losses are considered 'quasi-fiscal policy' and discussion on whether a central bank should manage them from the perspective of public governance is ongoing.

4.3.1   Integration of Monetary Policy and Market Operation Bodies

Monetary policy is conducted using price stability as its specific target. To achieve such targets, central banks in developed countries control interest rates in short-term money markets and the amount of reserves at the central bank through financial market transactions. This instrument of monetary policy is called 'market operations' (also 'monetary operations'). It is natural for a central bank to conduct such market operations since it issues banknotes, has a balance sheet, operates payment systems, and is in possession of the necessary tools/authority to conduct market operations not to mention the historical imperative. Therefore, it is unthinkable that other organizations could fulfill the role of undertaking market operations.[7]

Based on the fact that market operations are implemented by a central bank, monetary policy and market operations are in an interdependent relationship and both utilize common production factors[8] that bring about economies of scope according to TCE. Therefore, on the premise that a central bank conducts market operations, the interdependent relationship between market operations and monetary policy gives a theoretical foundation for the monetary policy body being integrated within a central bank which is the market operation body, and that the policy should be conducted by the central bank. The relationship between market operations and monetary policy will be discussed in detail below.

4.3.1.1   Interdependence Between Monetary Policy and Market Operations

First, looking from the aspect of vertical integration contained in the theory of organizational boundaries, the necessity to integrate monetary policy and market operations depends on the transaction cost of information, which is determined by to what extent 'information' (goods and services produced by each) is interdependent (Table 4.1). This is a make-or-buy question regarding necessary information and transaction costs pertaining to a long-term contract.

Interdependence between the monetary policy body[9] and market operation body can be illustrated as in Fig. 4.1. Looking at such interdependence in Table 4.1,

---

[7]Even if it is technically possible to outsource market operations to a private bank (regardless of the relationship between market operations and banknote issuance, management of payment systems), as Williamson (1999) clarified, the probity of involving a private organization, whose objective is to pursue profit, arises (see Chap. 3, Sect. 3.2.1).

[8]Teece (1994) explicated that integration of organizations with common production factors could enjoy economies of scope stemming from production cost reduction and transaction cost reduction unless the integration increases internal transaction cost beyond the production and transaction costs reduction. We can categorize common production factors into four aspects: (a) indivisible tangible assets, (b) technical know-how, (c) organizational know-how, and (d) brand name.

[9]Not only the board but also the research arm supporting its decision-making will be included under the monetary policy body.

Table 4.1 Determinant of transaction cost and governance mechanism (Partly altered based on Kikusawa 2006 and Douma and Schreuder 2002)

		Asset Specificity (Interdependency)		
		Low for both entities	High for both entities	High for one and low for the other
Uncertainty (including complexity)	High	Dependent on frequency	Organizational integration	Organizational integration
	Low	Spot contract	Long-term contract	Organizational integration

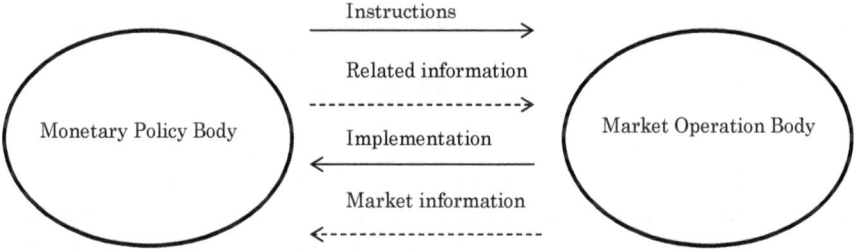

Fig. 4.1 Interdependence between monetary policy and market operations

the relationship can be either 'high for both entities' or 'high for one and low for the other.' We could say that their relationship is 'high for both entities' since if a central bank cannot implement market operations as an instrument of monetary policy, it cannot achieve the goal of monetary policy. Moreover, while various bits of information are necessary to come to monetary policy decisions, monetary policy depends on market operations to obtain information on financial markets through the implementation of such operations. On the other hand, market operations also depend on monetary policy since they cannot function as an instrument if the monetary policy body does not give a 'directive' on how to implement market operations.

As such, considering that interdependence between the monetary policy body and market operations body is 'high for both entities,' whether organizational integration is necessary or if just a long-term contract will suffice depends on the degree of uncertainty including complexity of transactions as shown in Table 4.1.[10] If both bodies are public entities, then uncertainty such as the possibility of financial default is low. However, the complexity of transactions is considerable. That is, while instruction given by the monetary policy is relatively simple, understanding the related background information would not be that easy.

And vice versa, information given to the monetary policy body by the market operation body, such as the extent to which instruction is implemented, as well as

---

[10]In a case where interdependence is 'high for both entities,' a long-term contract that does not necessitate organizational integration can be possible. Since both organizations are very dependent on each other, should one party not comply with the contract, then the other party can force it to perform the contractual obligations.

financial market-related information are also sophisticated and complex. Therefore, if the monetary policy and market operation bodies are to be completely separate entities that make transactions under a long-term contract, transaction costs will be high and therefore inefficient. In particular, transaction costs may become high in such cases where the market operation body does not faithfully implement the instruction given by the monetary policy body or where the market operation body does not present the latter with accurate implementation progress or financial market information. Therefore, in this case organizational integration of the two bodies (i.e., the central bank that implements market operations will become the monetary policy body) will reduce transaction costs.

Next, let us take a look at a case where interdependence between the monetary policy and market operation bodies is 'high for one and low for the other.' Such a case exists since, although a central bank (a market operation body) cannot implement market operations without an instruction from the monetary policy body, it would not have any particular problem in not implementing market operations for the specific purpose of monetary policy. In this case, the central bank is not dependent on the monetary policy body, rather the monetary policy body that needs to have market operations implemented is unilaterally dependent on a central bank that could implement such operations. Moreover, the monetary policy body needs to obtain necessary information on financial markets from the central bank in order to consider monetary policy and, in this respect too, is dependent on the market operation body. If the two bodies are in such a relationship, regardless of the degree of uncertainty including transaction complexity, organizational integration of the two (i.e., the central bank becomes the monetary policy body) can reduce transaction costs.

4.3.1.2   Common Production Factors of Monetary Policy and Market Operations

We will apply horizontal integration from the concept of organizational boundaries to the integration issue regarding the monetary policy and market operation bodies.[11] This idea considers the economic advantage of horizontal integration (diversification) to be to lower production costs by utilizing economies of scope based on common production factors, rather than to save on transaction costs in the case of high interdependency as above. However, even though production costs may be reduced technically, whether the overall cost could be lowered taking transaction costs into consideration awaits analysis of transaction costs incurred on the specific content of common production factors.

Therefore, when we judge whether integration of the monetary policy and market operation bodies is efficient or not based on horizontal integration, the starting

---

[11]The same organizational relationship is observed from both vertical and horizontal integration since service production taken up in this chapter is not necessarily clear as in the case of material production. Therefore, the two services could be seen either as a vertical relationship or diversification of services.

point will be to consider whether common production factors exist. And, if common production factors do exist, then the transaction costs (bureaucracy costs) incurred when those common production factors are used in the integrated organization as well as the transaction costs that arise when 'usage rights' of the common production factors are leased to outside organizations (long-term contract) should be compared. Organizational integration is considered necessary if transaction costs of a long-term contract are high.

Specifically, whether or not common production factors exist between the monetary policy body and market operation body in four aspects (indivisible tangible assets, brand name, technical know-how, organizational know-how) as well as associated transaction costs are outlined below. In conclusion, common production factors that could be utilized through organizational integration did not exist for indivisible tangible assets and brand name, but did for technical know-how and organizational know-how. And thus for technical know-how and organizational know-how, should we opt for economies of scope, it is essential that the two bodies be integrated.

Indivisible Tangible Assets

Indivisible tangible assets include a database[12] that could be jointly used by the monetary policy and market operation bodies. This database cannot be sold or purchased in the market but attached usage rights can be leased based on a long-term contract. In this case, organizational integration is unnecessary in order to utilize this common production factor's economies of scope.

Technical Know-How

Monetary policy judgment and implementation of market operations may need different know-how but at the same time share common know-how in some aspects. Such common know-how includes that regarding market operations and knowledge of financial market mechanisms. Though market operations are only an instrument for the monetary policy body, know-how of both market operations and financial market mechanisms is crucial for determining appropriate monetary policy.

Such know-how is developed and accumulated in the form of human resources. By hiring or seconding (long-term leasing of human resources) staff trained in the market operation body to the monetary policy body (market transactions), such know-how could be utilized without organizational integration. Nevertheless, organizational integration will enable much smoother (and with less transaction costs) utilization of staff.

Organizational Know-How

Important organizational know-how inherent to the monetary policy body is in the form of the independence given to a central bank. On the other hand, the market operation body also needs to sustain neutrality and fairness in its transactions, and therefore the two have many aspects in common. This common production factor was given to a central bank by law and it is thus impossible to enter into a long-term

---

[12]Here, 'database' refers to a system that can retrieve information ranging from macro financial/economic data to various other data regarding financial statements of individual banks that is accumulated in the form of paper or as data on a computer.

leasing contract let alone sell or purchase it. Therefore, economies of scope with respect to this common production factor can only be utilized by changing the legal system to allow both bodies to categorically have it, or have a body holding this production factor to function both as the monetary policy body and market operation body (i.e., organizational integration).

Brand Name
For the monetary policy and market operation bodies brand name equates to credibility, confidence, and integrity, which are difficult to transfer via a long-term leasing contract. Since both bodies are public entities, their integrity is on a par and, as such, there is no need for transfer in the first place.

4.3.2 Integration of Monetary Policy and Exchange Rate Policy Bodies

The historical development of monetary policy that emerged as a result of maintaining gold reserves at the BOE implies that both the monetary policy and exchange rate policy body should undoubtedly be integrated. However, there are cases where they are separate, as in Japan, and discussion of the question of the ownership of exchange rate policy in relation to monetary policy continues. This issue will be discussed applying the theory of organizational boundaries based on TCE.

4.3.2.1 Two-Tiered Interdependence

The interdependent relationship between monetary policy and exchange rate policy is two-tiered as shown in Fig. 4.2 (interdependence between the two policies, and that between two implementation instruments for the two policies). At the policy level, monetary policy affects exchange rates and, at the same time, exchange rate policy affects monetary policy through exchange rate fluctuation that impacts financial and economic conditions. Therefore, monetary policy-related information is important in making exchange rate policy decisions, and, similarly, exchange rate policy-related information is important in making monetary policy decisions. In this regard, monetary policy and exchange rate policy are interdependent.

Next, at the instrument level, market operations, the implementation instrument of monetary policy, affect the foreign exchange market through change in the demand and supply of funds in the money markets. At the same time, foreign exchange market intervention, the implementation instrument of exchange rate policy, affects the conduct of market operations through the demand and supply of funds in both domestic and overseas money markets. In this regard, market operation-related information is important for deciding exchange rate policy and, in turn, foreign exchange intervention-related information is important for deciding monetary policy. In this sense, market operations and foreign exchange intervention are interdependent.

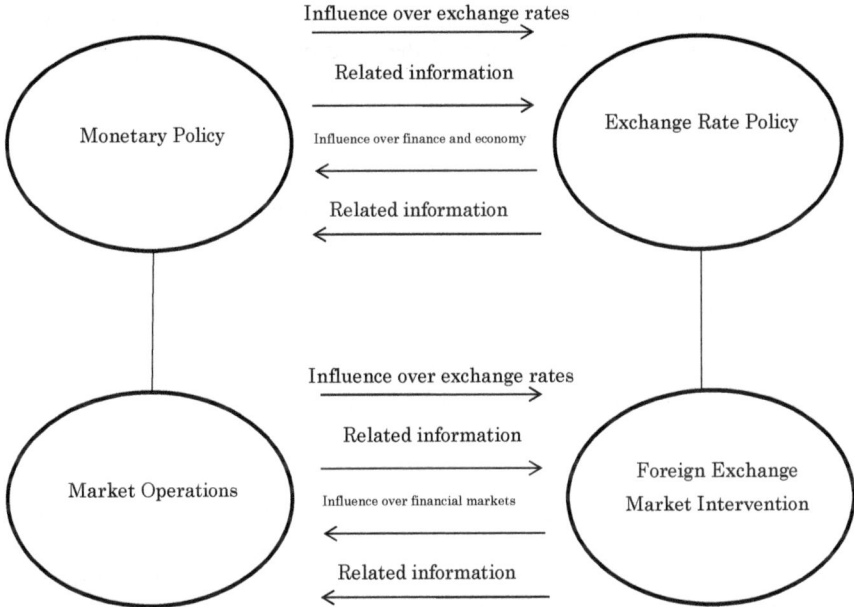

Fig. 4.2 Interdependence between monetary policy and foreign exchange rate policy

If we examine their relationship in line with Table 4.1, interdependence is 'high for both entities' at all levels. Therefore, whether organizational integration is necessary or whether a long-term leasing contract will suffice depends on the degree of uncertainty. Considering that the monetary policy and exchange rate policy bodies are public entities, uncertainty such as default does not exist. However, transaction complexity is considerably high. That is, as previously mentioned (Sect. 4.3.1.1), related information regarding the instruction given to the market operation body as regards monetary policy is extremely complex. As for exchange rate policy, information itself is highly complex and, moreover, mostly confidential, which will pose further complexity for outsiders. When we look at monetary policy and market operations as one package and exchange rate policy and foreign exchange intervention as another, monetary policy and exchange rate policy are interdependent through highly complex transactions combined with the complexity of information to/from market operations and foreign exchange intervention. As a result, the monetary policy and exchange rate policy bodies are better able to save on transaction costs if they integrate rather than operate as separate bodies under a long-term contract. In other words, a central bank should act both as the monetary policy body and exchange rate policy body.

The relationship between exchange rate policy and foreign exchange intervention is similar to that between monetary policy and market operations and, therefore, from the transaction cost standpoint, it would be efficient to integrate the two into one. In the case of Japan, the Minister of Finance makes decisions on exchange rate policy and foreign exchange intervention, while the BOJ does not have any power over exchange rate policy and acts only as the agent of the Minister of Finance to conduct operations related to foreign exchange intervention. This does not have any rationality in light of TCE.

4.3.2.2   Common Production Factors Between Monetary Policy and Exchange Rate Policy

We will apply horizontal integration based on TCE to consider four common production factors between the monetary policy and market operation bodies and also look at transaction costs. In conclusion, common production factors exist in all areas except indivisible tangible assets and so the two bodies need to be integrated to enjoy economies of scope.

Indivisible Tangible Assets
A database that could jointly be used in monetary policy and exchange rate policy exists. While it cannot be sold or purchased in the market, usage rights could be leased under a long-term contract. In this case, organizational integration is unnecessary to utilize economies of scope stemming from common production factors.

Technical Know-How
Judgment relating to both monetary policy and exchange rate policy requires common technical know-how related to the macro financial economy. Normally, a central bank has a research department to mainly support monetary policy management and which holds accumulated technical know-how regarding macro financial and economic analyses. This is a common production factor that would also be useful in managing exchange rate policy. When we look at monetary policy and market operations as one package and exchange rate policy and foreign exchange intervention as another, technical know-how regarding market operations and technical know-how regarding foreign exchange intervention have many aspects in common and thus share even more common know-how.

Such know-how is developed and accumulated in the form of human resources. By hiring or seconding (long-term leasing of human resources) staff trained at the monetary policy body (market transactions) to the exchange rate policy body, such know-how could be utilized without organizational integration. Nevertheless, organizational integration will enable smooth (and with less transaction costs) utilization of staff.

Organizational Know-How
The stability of currency value has domestic and international aspects. The domestic aspect is price stability which is the goal of monetary policy while the international aspect is the stability of the foreign exchange rate which is the goal of exchange rate policy. Therefore, organizational know-how for maintaining the independence of monetary policy so as to avoid political pressure and intervention in the value of the currency can also be beneficial for exchange rate policy. Hence, as was the case

with the monetary policy and market operation bodies, economies of scope stemming from common production factors should be utilized by having an organization with such common production factors function both in the field of monetary policy and exchange rate policy (i.e., organizational integration).

Brand Name
From the standpoint of stabilizing both domestic and international aspects of currency value, both the monetary policy body and exchange rate policy body have a common production factor equivalent of brand name, namely credibility and public confidence in them. Like the same reason for integrating the monetary policy and market operation bodies, if we wish to utilize the credibility and confidence that attaches to the monetary policy body in the pursuit of economies of scope, then the two need to be integrated.

4.3.3 Integration of Monetary Policy and Unconventional Monetary Policy Bodies

Unconventional monetary policy is regarded as quasi-fiscal policy (Sect. 4.2.1.2) and since fiscal policy should be decided by the government in a democratic society, there is the question of who should be responsible for unconventional monetary policy. TCE will be applied to discuss whether a central bank, in addition to undertaking its traditional monetary policy function, should also undertake unconventional monetary policy. We study the subject by looking at interdependency and common production factors between the two policies, and not from risk inherent in unconventional monetary policy (discussion on such risk appears in Sect. 4.3.5.2).

4.3.3.1 Interdependence Between Traditional and Unconventional Monetary Policy

Traditional monetary policy (hereafter monetary policy) and unconventional monetary policy have, as shown in Fig. 4.3, a strong relationship on two levels—interdependence between their policies and common implementation instruments.

At the policy level, monetary policy affects unconventional monetary policy through macro financial and economic conditions, and at the same time unconventional monetary policy affects monetary policy through changes in microeconomic market conditions such as price changes in purchased assets. Therefore, information related to monetary policy is important in deciding unconventional monetary policy and vice versa. In this regard, monetary policy and unconventional monetary policy are dependent on one another.

Looking at the relationship according to Table 4.1, interdependence is 'high for both entities' at all levels. Therefore, the degree of uncertainty including complexity decides whether organizational integration is necessary or whether a long-term

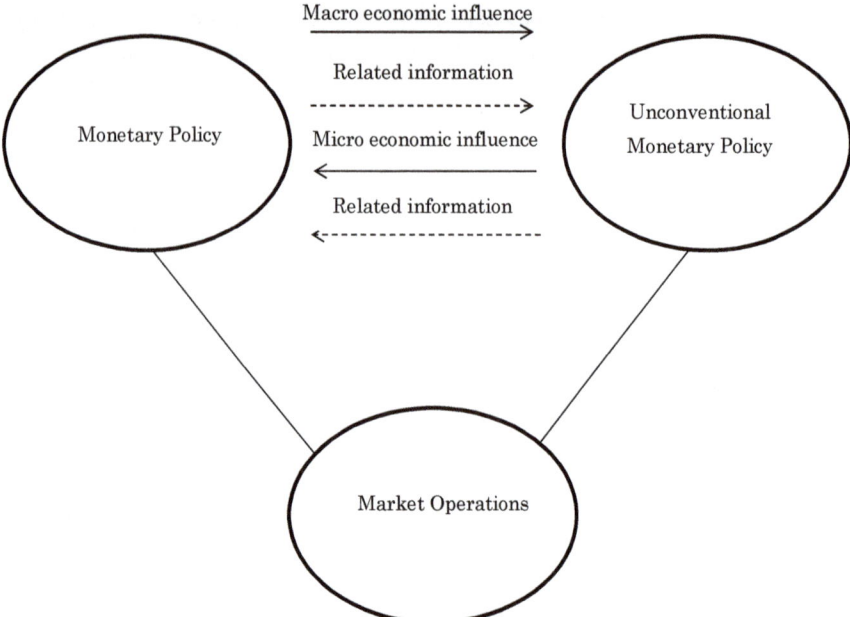

Fig. 4.3 Interdependence between traditional monetary policy and unconventional monetary policy

contract will suffice. Both the information from the monetary policy body and from unconventional monetary policy body is extremely complex as mentioned earlier (Sect. 4.3.1.1). Therefore, both conventional and unconventional monetary policy bodies can save on transaction costs if they are integrated (a central bank managing both) rather than managed as separate entities based on a long-term contract.

Next, with regard to their instruments, it is rational and efficient for both policies to utilize the market operation function of a central bank. This is because both policies commonly make transactions utilizing a central bank's banking function (in this regard, the market operation function of the central bank can be considered as a common production factor of both conventional and unconventional monetary policies according to horizontal integration, Sect. 4.3.3.2). As monetary policy and market operations are indivisible, so are unconventional monetary policy and market operations. As such, in addition to policy level interdependence, it makes sense for the central bank to manage both policies from the aspect of instruments as well.

4.3.3.2   Common Production Factors of Monetary Policy and Unconventional Monetary Policy

Horizontal integration based on TCE is applied to see what types of common production factors lie between monetary policy and unconventional monetary policy as

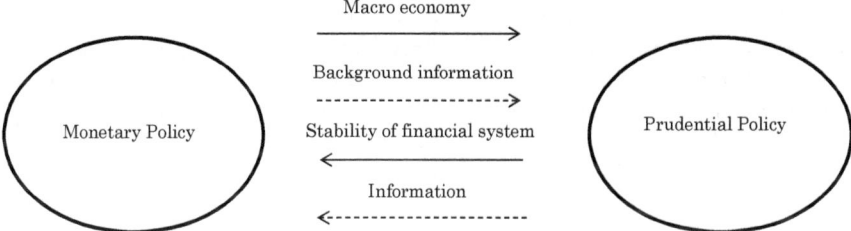

Fig. 4.4 Interdependence between monetary policy and prudential policy bodies

well as the transaction costs. They have the same, or more, similarity as in the case of common production factors for monetary policy and market operations, and it would be difficult to make a long-term leasing contract. Therefore, organizational integration of the monetary policy and unconventional monetary policy bodies is necessary in order to pursue economies of scope utilizing their common production factors.

4.3.4   Integration of Monetary Policy and Prudential Policy Bodies

Integration of monetary policy and prudential policy bodies is discussed in Chap. 5, Sect. 5.4.1, mainly focusing on conflict of interest. The chapter will suggest that there is no conflict of interest between the two and that if there were to be a problem it would be a trade-off issue which could be efficiently solved by internalizing within the central bank (monetary policy body). On the premise that the prudential policy body is a central bank, this section will discuss how it would affect ownership of monetary policy. We will apply TCE to consider such organizational integration of the monetary policy and prudential policy bodies.

4.3.4.1   Interdependence Between Monetary Policy and Prudential Policy Bodies

Looking at the interdependent relationship between the monetary policy and prudential policy bodies, as shown in Fig. 4.4, the monetary policy body affects the prudential policy body through macroeconomic conditions and, at the same time, provides monetary policy-related information. On the other hand, the prudential policy body affects monetary policy through financial stability and provides information on financial and economic conditions gained through prudential policy. Information on micro financial and economic trends gained through financial regulation and supervision play an especially important role in making and deciding monetary policy.

In line with Table 4.1, such interdependence is 'high for both entities' at all levels. Therefore, the degree of uncertainty including complexity decides whether organizational integration is necessary or a long-term leasing contract will suffice. Needless to say, transaction costs can be reduced if both bodies are integrated (the central bank manages both prudential policy and monetary policy) rather than managed by separate bodies under a long-term contract.

4.3.4.2   Common Production Factors of Monetary Policy and Prudential Policy Bodies

In Chap. 5, Sect. 5.3.1.3, horizontal integration based on TCE will be applied to see what common production factors lie between monetary policy and prudential policy as well as the transaction costs. In brief, it was found that they share common production factors in every respect, including indivisible assets such as database, and it became clear that transaction costs become high in the case of a long-term leasing contract. Therefore, organizational integration of monetary and prudential policy bodies is necessary in order to pursue economies of scope that utilize their common production factors.

4.3.5   Implications of the Arguments

In the previous sections, TCE was applied to mainly consider ownership issues and it was concluded that functions and policies related to monetary policy would be more efficiently managed if they were integrated. In the following sections, we will discuss characteristics of the approach from TCE and then point out problems found in integrating functions and policies of monetary policy when considering ownership. Then, from the viewpoint of organizational governance, we will consider design and management of a central bank board system.

4.3.5.1   Characteristics of the Approach from Transaction Cost Economics

The ownership of monetary policy that was discussed earlier in this chapter is similar to the discussion on central bank independence. The independence issue discusses to what degree a central bank can (or should) independently decide the goal of monetary policy, especially targets and instruments. Similarly, ownership also discusses whether a central bank should decide the monetary policy goal.

However, the approach the two discussions take greatly differs. The independence discussion mainly centers on perspectives in light of political economy and little attention is paid to efficiency, only touching upon relevance between degree of independence and macroeconomic performance. On the other hand, the aforementioned discussion on ownership takes an approach to determine whether the services to decide the monetary policy goal should be provided by a sole organization along with other services such as market operation, exchange rate policy, and prudential policy, in light of efficiency in terms of production costs and transaction costs.

As a result of taking the latter approach, the ownership discussion considered two perspectives that were not taken up in the independence discussion. One of them is that the discussion was able to shed light on efficiency of the central bank in conducting monetary policy taking into consideration the interdependence between monetary policy and other central bank functions, such as market operations, as well as economies of scope. The other is, assuming that the central bank has ownership of monetary policy, that organizational governance (e.g., design and management of a board system) in a central bank's monetary policy body was determined in a consistent manner along with ownership based on TCE. As described in Chap. 2, Sect. 2.3, the governance issue in a broad sense has two aspects, ownership and organizational governance, and hence it is important to consider them in a consistent manner.

4.3.5.2 Implications for Ownership

With regard to the ownership of monetary policy, it became apparent that monetary policy and related functions and policies would be efficiently managed under an integrated entity since interdependence and common production factors existed between them and economies of scope could be pursued through integration. Specifically, (a) the market operation body conducts monetary policy, (b) the monetary policy body conducts exchange rate policy, (c) the monetary policy and prudential policy bodies should be integrated, and (d) the monetary policy body conducts unconventional monetary policy. However, it should be noted that such integration may involve the following problems, which may be solved or mitigated by how the organization is governed, and it is thus important to consider this along with implications for organizational governance.

Bureaucracy Cost Issue
TCE often points out an increase in transaction costs accompanying expansion of scope and scale of an organization, which also needs to be considered in integrating organizations related to monetary policy. Specifically, transaction costs in the internal organization called 'bureaucracy costs' may increase, 'economies of specialization' may disappear, and 'conflict of organization cultures' (Sect. 4.5.2.2) may arise. To tackle these problems, organizational governance of a central bank, especially the design and management of a board system, needs to be considered.

Problems Associated with Integrating Exchange Rate Policy
If a central bank is involved in both monetary policy and exchange rate policy, two problems may arise. One is the possibility that stability of the currency (goal of monetary policy) and foreign exchange rate (goal of exchange rate policy) may conflict when deciding macroeconomic policy. For example, in a situation where a central

bank needs to act in the direction of tight monetary policy from the perspective of price stability, some senior officials may be against the idea from the perspective of international competitiveness since tight monetary policy invites a hike in exchange rates. Such conflict of interest is the reason behind the argument for keeping the monetary policy body and exchange rate policy body separate. However, as mentioned (Sect. 4.3.2.1), since monetary policy and exchange rate policy are very interdependent and have common production factors that bring about economies of scope, it would be better to integrate the two bodies and coordinate such underlying conflict of interest within the integrated organization, i.e., so-called 'internalization,' rather than effect coordination as different bodies since it would lower coordination cost. Nevertheless, even if coordination cost is minimized through internalization, in order to achieve stability of both the value of the currency and the exchange rate, it is necessary to prioritize the goals of macroeconomic policy.

Another aspect with regard to problems accompanying integration of exchange rate policy is that since there is risk of the devaluation of foreign currency assets purchased through foreign exchange intervention, exchange rate policy has a feature of 'quasi-fiscal policy.' Therefore, there is an argument that it is inappropriate for a central bank to become the responsible body for exchange rate policy that carries the risk of incurring losses. Such discussion should be made from the perspective of risk to central bank assets rather than from a transaction cost perspective as in the case of discussion concerning the quasi-fiscal policy feature that unconventional monetary policy has (see the following section).

Problems Associated with Integrating Unconventional Monetary Policy
From a transaction cost perspective, it is efficient for a central bank to manage unconventional monetary policy as well as monetary policy. However, a central bank is also inevitably exposed to the risk of incurring losses from the devaluation of assets purchased through unconventional monetary policy. Looking back at the history of the BOE, the same kind of policy was adopted to maintain financial system stability and is not necessarily 'unconventional.' In addition, even looking from the perspective of a central bank's seigniorage and public governance, there seems to be no fundamental problem.

With respect to seigniorage, it is reasonable to cover the loss incurred from devaluation of central bank assets through unconventional monetary policy by seigniorage. Central bank seigniorage was initially a by-product of a central bank's monopoly over currency issuance in order to prevent financial system turmoil due to inflation. To utilize seigniorage in order to prevent financial system turmoil, such as financial crisis, is the same as preventing financial system turmoil caused by inflation and we could say that seigniorage is similar to 'earmarked tax' (see Chap. 6, Sect. 6.3.3). Next, with respect to the public governance perspective of a central bank, governance is structured so that government and the legislative body can influence the central bank through the appointment of senior officials (such as the governor), the budget process, and accounts. Therefore, even if the central bank uses seigniorage to purchase risk assets for unconventional monetary policy, it is not contrary to democratic principles. Moreover, whether the above ideas could be applied to devaluation of foreign currency assets purchased through the above exchange rate policy depends on whether stability of the exchange rate might invite financial system turmoil. Pursuing what Shirakawa (2008a) said "We should not focus on the fluctuation itself but need to judge in accordance with whether such fluctuation affects the price stability or long-term growth," foreign exchange intervention should be limited to cases where there is a threat of grave influence on one's economy (for example, emergence of financial system turmoil) and there appears to be no serious problem in using seigniorage, and not public funds, to cover losses incurred by such intervention.

4.3.5.3 Implications for Organizational Governance

The organizational integration of entities responsible for functions and policies related to monetary policy is efficient from a transaction cost perspective, but is also accompanied by an increase in bureaucracy costs reflecting enlarged scope and scale of organization. Considering a central bank's organizational governance issue, namely designing and managing board systems, will lead to finding countermeasures to issues related to the integration of ownership above. Based on TCE, three countermeasures listed below can be considered with regard to designing and managing board systems.

Multiboard System
It is desirable that a central bank establish a 'banking board' that makes decisions on prudential policy and policies related to payment systems including the issuance and management of banknotes and currency, separate from the 'monetary policy board' that makes decisions on monetary policy.[13] Such a multiboard structure is useful in avoiding an increase in bureaucracy cost that arises when a central bank integrates the monetary policy function with its traditional functions such as prudential policy and policies related to payment systems. By adopting a multiboard structure, the central bank can establish an 'organization within an organization' for each board and thus prevent increases in internal organizational transaction costs (bureaucracy cost) accompanying the expansion of organizational scope.

However, it is also desirable that the same board make decisions on monetary policy and exchange rate policy (of course including unconventional monetary policy). As aforementioned (Sects. 4.3.2.1 and 4.3.3.1), these two policies enjoy substantial interdependence and economies of scope through a common production factor (macroeconomic research). Moreover, since two policies may face trade-offs, it is better to have the same board deal with such in order to hold down coordination costs.

---

[13] See Fig. 4.8. The banking board can be divided further into the 'prudential policy board' that makes decisions on macro and micro prudential policies and the 'payment system board' that deals with payment systems.

Leadership by a Governor and Establishment of a Supervisory Board

Even if multiboards are established within a central bank, the central bank governor needs to oversee such boards, or some of the board members including the deputy should participate in the various boards. From the outset, the objective of a central bank in undertaking multiple functions and policies under TCE was to effectively diminish transaction costs since such functions and policies are very interdependent and share common production factors. Thus, it is necessary to share and coordinate information among the boards in order to minimize transaction costs stemming from transactions among them. This could be achieved to some extent at a staff level, but it is more important that information is shared and coordinated at the paramount level.

When considering the design and management of a central bank's board system, we need to strike a balance between segregation and integration in accordance with degree of interdependence and common production factors. In the case of monetary policy and exchange rate policy, interdependence and common production factors are very strong and, therefore, it is desirable to integrate them in the same board. On the other hand, with regard to monetary policy and banking policy such as prudential policy and payment system policy, the degree of interdependence is low and therefore it is desirable to have separate boards (but not so segregated that they become completely separate bodies outside the central bank).

Also, in place of the governor, a supervisory board can be established to overview each board and enhance coordination and sharing of information among them. But, as discussed in Chap. 3, Sect. 3.3, if such a supervisory board is specialized only in appointing members of the respective boards, then actual coordination and information sharing among the boards will be in the hands of the governor and other members.[14]

Diversification of Board Members

Even if a multiboard structure is not adopted (e.g., the BOJ), the same effect can be achieved to a certain extent by appointing members with diversified backgrounds and expertise. For example, members' backgrounds should not be concentrated in the field of macro monetary policy so, by introducing specialists in the fields of prudential policy and payment systems as members, it is possible to attain the same kind of effect as a multiboard structure. This is because these specialist members are expected to play the role of a representative of each board under the multiboard structure.

---

[14]As noted in Chap. 3, Sect. 3.3.4, a supervisory board might not be established with the objective of coordination and information sharing among the boards. Rather it might be established for the purpose of reflecting the will of the public and legislature with respect to appointment of central bank officials and making policy decisions. And, a multiboard structure is adopted in order to segregate policy making and policy implementation.

4.4 Approach from Agency Theory

This section will mainly take up organizational governance from among the monetary policy governance issues discussed in the previous section by applying multitask agency theory based on principal-agent theory. We explained that, from the transaction cost perspective, it would be problematic to separate monetary policy from the central bank. In this section, assuming that a central bank has ownership of monetary policy, we will discuss problems related to organizational governance that arises from having multiple functions. The countermeasures will also be discussed.

First, multitask agency theory will be outlined which will then be applied to multi-functions of the central bank. In applying the theory, to clarify the possibility of providing 'non-intentional high compensation' to the monetary policy area, we point out that an incentive mechanism called the 'Hawthorne effect' may affect central bank activities.

4.4.1 Outline of Multitask Agency Theory

A multitask agency problem was formally defined by Holmstrom and Milgrom (1991) based on principal-agent theory. As shown in Fig. 4.5, when an agent is given multitasks by a principal, if there is a task that offers comparatively higher compensation, other tasks with less compensation will not attract much attention or effort.

Such a problem arises in the case where it is difficult to monitor or measure the performance of the task (activity). Milgrom and Roberts (1992, p. 228) define it as follows, calling it the "equal compensation principle."

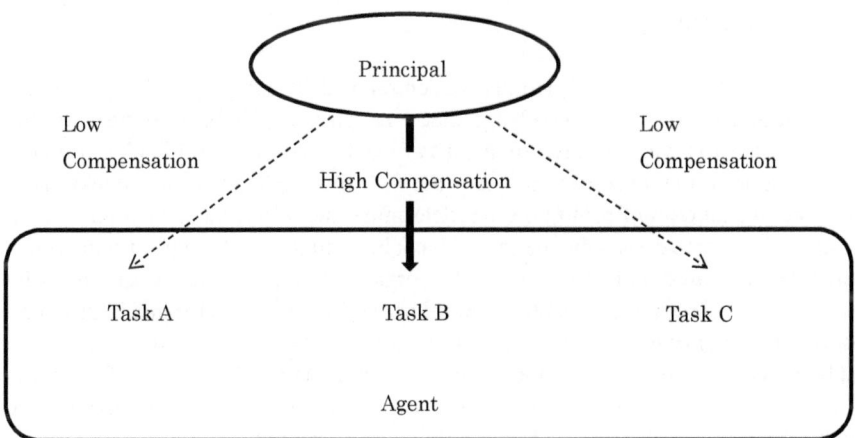

Fig. 4.5 Multitask agency problem

If an employee's allocation of time or attention between two different activities cannot be monitored by the employer, then either the marginal rate of return to the employee from time or attention spent in each of the two activities must be equal, or the activities with the lower marginal rate of return receive no time or attention.

That is, when a certain activity receives especially high compensation (called "incentive compensation"), even if it is difficult to measure the performance of all the activities, the agent will have the incentive to devote more efforts to that activity and neglect the others.

Based on the equal compensation principle, as a measure to prevent the emergence of a multitask agency problem, efforts should be made to accurately measure the performance of each activity. But, when it is difficult to measure performance accurately despite efforts, no incentive initiative should be given to the activity concerned. All activities should be given equal compensation as suggested by the equal compensation principle.

4.4.2   Multitask Agency Problem in a Central Bank

Multitask agency theory assumes that a worker has multiple tasks. In the same way, by assuming that an organization has multiple missions, the theory can be applied to organizational governance regarding a central bank's multiple functions. There is significant interdependence between monetary policy conducted by a central bank and prudential policy and the payment system function, but which can nevertheless be distinguished from them. As such, there are different units within a central bank organization which are equivalent to multitasks in multitask agency theory.

4.4.2.1   Necessity of Equal Compensation for Respective Areas Within a Central Bank

When considering multitask functions of a central bank by applying multitask agency theory, it is necessary to acknowledge that it is extremely difficult to measure the performance of services offered by a central bank. First, a central bank's primary goal is not profit maximization as is the case for private companies and banks, and, therefore, the amount of profit does not determine the performance of central bank services. Second, there is only one central bank in a country, and its performance thus cannot be compared with the same kind of organization domestically and the only way would be to compare with other central banks but which are located in different institutional environments. Third, central bank services are an intrinsically macro public service in the sense that they affect the whole national economy. Therefore, although central bank functions are similar to government activities (some of which can be measurable), they are more macroeconomic oriented.

When it is difficult to measure performance, the equal compensation principle of multitask agency theory suggests that all tasks should be given equal compensation and no specific task should be given higher compensation. Therefore, in the case of a central bank that has multiple immeasurable functions (tasks), favorable incentive compensation should not be given to monetary policy alone but should be equally distributed among other functions and policies such as prudential policy and the payment system function. Otherwise, there is a risk that a central bank will allocate more time and labor to monetary policy and neglect prudential policy and other functions.

4.4.2.2 Hawthorne Effect in Monetary Policy

Although equal compensation is necessary for each central bank department that provides services that are difficult to measure, there is a factor within central banks that opposes this principle. This is well known in business management as the Hawthorne effect. Through this effect, unintentional high compensation is given to the monetary policy area which may give rise to a multitask agency problem.

Hawthorne Effect
The Hawthorne effect is a form of influence on worker productivity through a response to the fact that workers know that they are being studied. This effect was found and named after experiments at the Hawthorne Works (a Western Electric factory in the US). This experiment was conducted between 1924 and 1932 to see if its workers would become more productive in higher or lower levels of light. Productivity initially improved with a higher level of light, but even with a lower level of light it was found that productivity remained higher than that before the experiment. It was suggested that the productivity gain occurred due to the impact of the motivational effect on the workers as a result of the interest being shown in them. This experiment showed that attention to a specific worker provides the same level of incentive as compensation.

Attention to Monetary Policy
The same kind of phenomenon like the Hawthorne effect can be observed with a central bank's monetary policy as shown in Fig. 4.6. Because monetary policy is of considerable interest to the general public it receives more attention from politicians and the mass media compared to other central bank functions such as prudential policy and the payment system function. The reason behind such attention is that (a) monetary policy is easier to understand compared with other central bank functions, (b) the general public feels the effect of monetary policy, (c) as a result of increased marketable financial assets owned by investors in developed countries, investors have become sensitive to monetary policy that influences financial markets through stock prices and exchange rates, and (d) with the development of financial markets, the speed and degree of the influence of monetary policy over financial markets has increased.

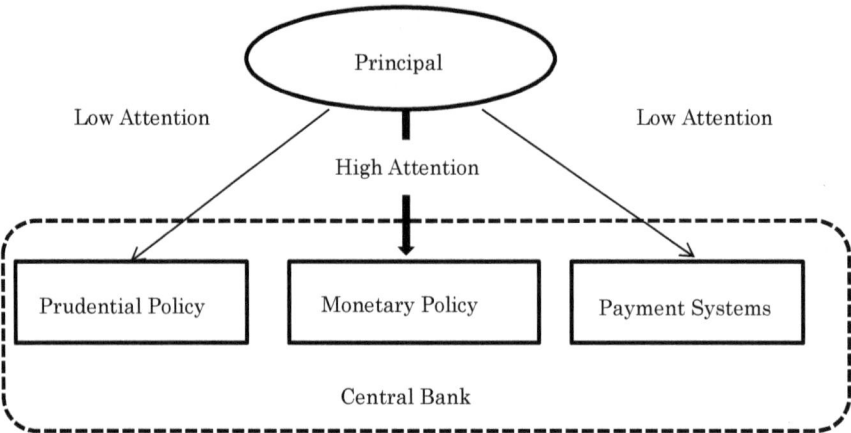

Fig. 4.6 Hawthorne effect on central bank

Such great interest in monetary policy from the mass media is highly likely to be regarded as 'unintentional high compensation' by management and staff in the monetary policy area within the central bank organization, just like the workers monitored during the Hawthorne experiment. However, it is difficult to determine whether the monetary policy area of a central bank that has been given unintentional high compensation achieved higher performance than other areas. This fact differs from the Hawthorne experiment where an increase in productivity was objectively confirmed.

Negative Sides of Hawthorne Effect on the Central Bank
Since high interest in monetary policy gives high compensation to the monetary policy area compared to other areas such as prudential policy and the payment system, it is contrary to the equal compensation principle of multitask agency theory. As a result, while a central bank puts considerable effort into monetary policy, there is a possibility that it will make light of prudential policy and the payment system function. Even when they are neglected, since it is difficult to measure their performance, it is in turn difficult for the central bank's principal, namely the public and legislature, to determine to what extent the bank made efforts in the respective areas.

On the other hand, one cannot deny the possibility that considerable attention towards monetary policy could be regarded as 'pain' instead of compensation. However, attention to monetary policy is focused on how it is conducted and not what it has achieved. Since its performance cannot be evaluated objectively, it is likely that the attention will be regarded more as compensation than as a pain.

4.4.2.3 Prevention of Multitask Agency Problem

When multitask agency theory is applied to central bank activities, there is a likelihood that a multitask agency problem will materialize since the incentive mechanism of the Hawthorne effect (as a consequence of the considerable attention from the public and legislature) exists in central bank activities. A preventive measure to lessen attention from the public and legislature to weaken the Hawthorne effect is not realistic. As considered under TCE, it is also inappropriate to separate monetary policy from a central bank to annul the multitask agency problem.

Adoption of Multiboard Structure
As mentioned in Sect. 4.2.3.2, many central banks adopt a multiboard structure. There are various reasons why central banks adopt a multiboard structure, one of which is to avoid the multitask agency problem. For example, the Bank of Thailand (BOT) has separate boards for monetary policy, prudential policy, and payment systems. In such a case, responsibilities for each function can be clearly defined and decentralized at board member level. This would prevent problems that could occur under a single-board system where most central bank managements concentrate their attention on monetary policy that attracts attention from the public and legislature. And even at staff level, staff could secure attention from senior officials through having a separate line of reporting for each function, thus easing the Hawthorne effect. It is also necessary to have at least someone (e.g., a governor) or board to preside over all boards in order to secure the 'unity of responsibility' principle[15] and to share necessary information among the boards based on their interdependence.

Diversification of Board Members
Similar to the approach from TCE (Sect. 4.3.5.3), even if a multiboard structure is not adopted (as in the case of the BOJ), the multitask agency problem could be solved to a certain extent by diversifying board members.

Consideration to Staff Matters
It is necessary to adopt a careful staff policy where staff of monetary policy affected by the Hawthorne effect would not be favored when promoting or transferring staff within the central bank. It is likely that staff department might mistake high attention to a job well done. By being careful, the negative side of the Hawthorne effect could be mitigated while bringing about the equal compensation principle.

Enhancing Performance and Monitoring of Each Area
While it is difficult to measure the performance of central bank functions, it is important to grasp how the performance of each area is determined and to enhance its monitoring. For example, with regard to prudential policy, multiple entities that are involved in prudential policy could be compared. And for payment systems, final

---

[15]Milgrom and Roberts (1992, p. 410) call this "the unity of responsibility" principle and state that "When the success of a project or operation depends on the coordinated execution of several separate tasks in a way that makes it difficult to assess performance separately in each, then it is usually best to make a single individual responsible for all the related tasks."

users and private banks could be included to consider a central bank's payment system governance as they may improve the quality of determining and monitoring performance (see Chap. 7, Sect. 7.4.3).

4.5 Approach from the Theory of Organizational Culture

This section will consider the governance of monetary policy based on the theory of organizational culture. This theory developed mainly in the field of management theory but has recently been discussed actively in economics, becoming one of the major theories of organizational economics. Applying it to the governance of monetary policy may deviate somewhat from discussion of pure economic efficiency, but is beneficial in studying the ownership structure and organizational governance of monetary policy.

The theory will be outlined both in the field of management and economics. Then it will be applied to a central bank concluding that the organizational culture of a central bank is a two-tiered structure composed of common organizational culture and subcultures specific to each sector. As for subcultures, we will point out that the monetary policy sector and the banking function sector differing considerably may give rise to a conflict of organizational cultures. Based on these analyses, we will then discuss the benefit of managing both monetary policy and the banking function within the central bank as an implication of the monetary policy governance study. In addition, while strengthening both the common organizational culture and subcultures, the designing and managing of a central bank board system is considered as a measure to prevent conflict among the subcultures.

The theory of organizational culture also uses TCE mentioned in Sect. 4.3. Such TCE will be termed 'Williamson's theory of organizational culture' and applied to monetary policy governance.

4.5.1 Outline of the Theory of Organizational Culture

The theory of organizational culture first became popular in the field of management in the 1980s which later influenced various models in the field of economics. We will outline the theory of organizational culture in the two fields, but will focus on the theory of organizational culture by Williamson and Kreps for economics. And, since the objective is to apply the theory to monetary policy governance, the outline will consist of three aspects:

- Definition and function of an organizational culture.
- The formation process of organizational culture.
- Conflict of organizational cultures.

4.5.1.1   Theory of Organizational Culture in the Field of Management

The theory of organizational culture in the field of management has been studied extensively including its relations with management strategy and leadership, but we will focus only on theories that would be beneficial in considering organizational governance with respect to monetary policy. As it is difficult to take up a specific theory like that for the field of economics, various theories will be covered.

Definition of Organizational Culture
In the first place, as the concept of 'culture' is vague and has wide meaning, there is no definite definition of 'organizational culture.'[16] Wikipedia explains as follows:

> Organizational culture also known as corporate culture is the collective behavior of people that are part of an organization. It is also formed by the organization values, visions, norms, working language, systems, and symbols, including beliefs and habits.

Function of an Organizational Culture
According to Wikipedia,

> a healthy and robust organizational culture may provide various benefits, including the following:

- Competitive edge derived from innovation and customer service,
- Consistent, efficient employee performance,
- Team cohesiveness,
- High employee morale,
- Strong company alignment towards goal achievement.

However, while there are benefits, there are downsides called 'negative functions' where too strong an organizational culture may homogenize value and thinking habits of an organization and weaken its adaptability to environmental change and inhibit innovation.

Formation of Organizational Culture
There is no formal model regarding the formation process in the theory of organizational culture in management, but Schein (2000, pp. 24–25) emphasized the evolutional factors of organizational culture as follows:

> The direction of that evolution will be a product of several forces: (a) technical and physical changes in the external environment, (b) changes in the internal dynamics of the social system, and historical circumstances that are fortuitous or serendipitous.

Schein (ibid., p. 25) also stressed daily interaction among members within the same organization in the formation process.

---

[16]A concept similar to 'organizational culture' is 'corporate culture,' which is often used in the context of corporate strategy, but here, organizational culture and corporate culture are considered the same. Akerlof and Kranton (2010) included 'identity' in the utility function and by doing so discussed it in the framework of economics. They defined 'identity' as an activity that brings about gain through acting in line with the norms and ideals of a specific group.

At the same time, we can study the day-to-day interactions of the members of an organization with each other and with members of other organization to determine how given cultural assumptions are reinforced and confirmed or challenged and disconfirmed. We can analyze the impacts or these perceptual interactive events in order to understand how cultures evolve and change.

Existence of Subcultures and its Conflicts

The theory of organizational culture in terms of management points out not only common organizational culture but also the existence of subcultures within respective parts of an organization. For example, according to a multi-paradigm approach suggested by Meyerson and Martin (1987) and Martin (1992), an organizational culture can be divided into three paradigms, namely "integration paradigm," "differentiation paradigm," and "fragmentation paradigm." The differentiation paradigm points out the importance of subcultures within an organization and the possibility of conflict among them.

Conflicts within organizational culture have similar aspects to negative functions in the sense that they have a negative effect on the organization. However, while such conflicts are based upon the assumption that a hierarchical structure (such as subcultures) exists within an organizational structure (or the existence of different organizational cultures within a single organization brought about by the merger of two organizations), negative functions are not.

4.5.1.2   Theory of Organizational Culture in Economics

Hermalin (2001) who surveyed organizational culture theory in terms of economics wrote "with a few exceptions, economists have ignored the issue of corporate culture in their studies of firms and other organizations,"…"most non-economists would question whether economists know anything about culture." However, one of the "few exceptions" is that the Kreps model brought about formal models of organizational culture using game theory. In the section below, the theory as it pertains to economics will be discussed focusing on the Williamson model and Kreps model.

The Williamson Model

Williamson provided the concept of "atmosphere" which is very similar to organizational culture in his book of 1975. In his later papers, he unfolds his theory on organizational culture referring to the Kreps model. Williamson's economic theory of organizational culture proposed in his books and papers will be introduced below.

Definition and Function of Organizational Culture

Williamson's theory of organizational culture is discussed mainly in Williamson (1996). The section entitled "corporate culture" in Chap. 10 of the book explains organizational culture as a kind of "embeddedness" that determines transaction costs of an organization and governance structure. And he also emphasizes the importance of "atmosphere" introduced in his book (Williamson, 1975), a similar concept to embeddedness. As for the concept of "atmosphere," Williamson (1996, p. 270) wrote as follows:

A colleague noted that the economics of atmosphere plays a larger role in *Markets and Hierarchies* (Williamson, 1975) than in *The Economic Institutions of Capitalism* (Williamson, 1985) and asked about the de-emphasis. I replied that I thought atmosphere at least as important to an understanding of economic organization in 1985 as I had in 1975. Not having made more headway, however, I had little to add.

According to Williamson (1975), atmosphere affects all factors that cause transaction costs and eventually influences governance structure. This is because transaction costs change according to the atmosphere of where the transaction is made in addition to the nature of the transaction. For example, under a cooperative atmosphere, the major cause of transaction costs, "opportunism," will be suppressed, allowing the cost to diminish. Therefore, atmosphere within an organization will change the amount of transaction costs within that organization, thus influencing the governance structure of the organization.

As a specific example of such atmosphere, Williamson (1996, p. 269) points out "focal point" and "informal organization" from the Kreps model. With regard to an informal organization, he states as follows:

Informal organization contributes to the viability of formal organization in three significant respects: One of the indispensable functions of informal organizations in formal organizations is that of communication. Another function is that of maintaining the cohesiveness in formal organizations through regulating the willingness to serve and the stability of objective authority. A third function is the maintenance of the feeling of personal integrity, of self-respect, and independent choice.

Concerning the communication function, Williamson (1975) says that trading atmosphere within an organization is "more satisfying" than that in the market. He points out "language" as one of the benefits of trading internally. 'Language' here is a communication function explained by Williamson (1996) and therefore is organizational culture.

Formation of Organizational Culture
With regard to the formation of corporate culture, Williamson (ibid.) notes "Corporate culture displays both spontaneous and intentional features and works mainly within particular organizations." "Spontaneous features" means "intertemporal process transformation," and "intentional features" the strategic introduction of organizational culture by the leaders.

For the former, Williamson details the transformation of transactions, especially with the passage of time. First, Williamson (ibid.) introduces "repeated game" over the long term of the Kreps model to stress the spontaneous feature of organizational culture. Then, using "transaction specific asset," a core idea of his model, he explains the spontaneous feature of organizational culture. "Transaction" here means the various "interactions" among members of the organization and between departments within the organization. By repeating such transactions (= interactions) over the long term, each member and respective departments will accumulate specific assets, in this case "capabilities," to lessen transaction costs and make transactions more efficient (as mentioned under Sect. 4.5.1.1, Schein, 2000, also points out the same concept). Williamson (ibid., p. 228) points out organizational culture and communication codes as examples of the specific capabilities:

> If the benefits of capabilities vary with the attributes of transactions, which arguably they do, then the cost effective thing to do is to shape culture, develop communication codes, and manage routines in a deliberative (transaction specific) way.

Conflict of Organizational Culture

Williamson's economic theory of organizational culture basically considers 'corporation' as one unit bearing in mind the common organizational culture of the corporation. However, content of the theory can also be applied to subcultures intrinsic to various departments within the organization. That is, the formation of transaction specific assets that hold great importance in the formation process of organizational culture depends on the nature of transactions (including frequency). When comparing the nature of transactions within an organization to outside organizations, transactions within the organization have more similarity and frequency is higher. However, when we consider transactions among the various departments within the same organization, transactions within a certain department have greater similarity and more frequency than those in other departments. Therefore, when we compare organizations, while common organizational culture will be formed within an organization, within various departments differing organizational culture (subcultures) will be formed. In this regard, conflict of organizational culture not only occurs between organizations, but also between departments within the same organization (conflict of subcultures).

When we look at organizational integration (boundary of firms) from the perspective of organizational culture conflicts, we need to pay attention to the role of language played in organizational culture. According to Williamson's economic theory of organizational culture, language in the broad sense is considered to play an important role. As the nature of a transaction reflects the content of function, language, which is organizational culture (= transaction specific assets that are formed based on the characteristic of a transaction), is influenced by degree of similarity of functional content. Even within the same organization, conflict of subcultures between the marketing department and accounting department may emerge due to their different functions, resulting in the fact that "they don't understand our language." In an extreme case, there may be a possibility where sectors from different organizations with similar functions may share a common "language" rather than with other departments in the same organization.

As such, when a conflict among subcultures is intense in various organizational cultures such as language, and interdependency among the various departments within an organization is not strong, then it may be appropriate to outsource the department concerned to a professional organization that specializes in such functions. In other words, whether or not outsourcing should be utilized can be decided by comparing transaction costs incurred by conflict of organizational cultures within the same organization and transaction costs accompanying transactions with other organizations (the same logic used in Kreps' theory of the boundary of firms).

Economic Theory of Organizational Culture by Kreps

As above, Williamson (ibid.) points out the concept of "focal point" by Kreps (1990) as a specific example of an organizational culture and at the same time introduces "repeated game" that lasts over a long time period as regards the spontaneous nature of organizational culture. Also, Hermalin (2001) first takes up Kreps' theory in his book where he surveyed the few exceptions among economists that neglected the issue of corporate culture.

Definition and Function of Organizational Culture

Kreps' theory considers corporate culture as the "focal point," a concept from game theory, and applies it to the actual organization to define it. "Focal point" in game theory is the rule of choice from outside the model in selecting a certain equilibrium from among multiple equilibria (best solution) that exist in a game. Examples of focal point in the actual organization (organizational culture) are implicit rules, norms, conventions, etc. Instruments to communicate such implicit rules (i.e., language), cohesiveness, and identity applied to organizational behavior are also considered to be included in the concept.

The function of organizational culture is to reduce coordination costs by providing guidance in a situation where an organization faces unforeseen contingencies such as multiple equilibria. According to the incomplete contract theory, setting a formal rule to maintain cooperation in every unforeseen event would be too costly (eventually infeasible). Rather, it is much more efficient to use implicit rules (organizational culture) to maintain a cooperative relationship.

Formation of Organizational Culture

Like Williamson's theory, Kreps' theory considers that organizational culture is formed as a result of pursuing economic efficiency. Therefore, the abovementioned function of organizational culture could also explain the formation mechanism of organizational culture. As Williamson (ibid.) emphasized the point made in Kreps' theory, repeated games over a long time explicitly explain the spontaneous nature of organizational culture.

According to Kreps' theory, time (history) spent in an organization plays an important role in two ways. First, in a situation where prisoner's dilemma prevents attaining best equilibrium in a one-time game, time plays an important role in the process of repeating the game that eventually enables such equilibrium to be attained. Second, time plays a key role in forming the focal point which will be useful should there be multiple equilibria.

With regard to the roles time plays in organizational culture, Young (1996, 1998) enhanced Kreps' model and proposed an adaptive learning approach from the perspective of adapting the organization to a new situation. That is, an organizational habit (= organizational culture) will be formed if the players of a game are limited, rational, and can adapt to their past experiences. Significant experiences of success and/or failure remain in the organizational memory and the content of organizational culture is thought to change in order to integrate such memories.

Conflict of Organizational Culture
Based on Kreps' theory, and similar to Williamson's, conflict of organizational culture occurs when subcultures that are formed for different sectors within the same organization conflict with one another. The reason why such conflict occurs is because repeated games that create organizational culture are more frequent and last for a long time within the same sector compared to repeated games that take place over several sectors. Another reason is that when Young's theory is considered, "past experience" that organizational culture absorbs differs among sectors. Since there is a possibility that organizational cultures in different sectors may conflict, we could also consider the boundary issue of an organization from Kreps' theory, in addition to Williamson's theory above.

4.5.2 Application of Theory of Organizational Culture to a Central Bank

Organizational culture of a central bank differs somewhat from that of private companies in that it is not affected by the founder or its leader[17] but also has much in common. Therefore, the theory of organizational culture that developed in the area of management and economics by studying organizational cultures of private companies may also be useful in considering governance issues of monetary policy. In what follows, the theory of organizational culture will be applied to look at the features of a central bank's common organizational culture and its subcultures. Then we will consider its implication for monetary policy governance. Specifically, two implications will be considered: that for ownership governance of monetary policy and that for organizational culture of organizational governance. Assuming that a central bank has ownership of monetary policy management, organizational governance includes the design and management of a central bank board system, which is another aspect of monetary policy governance.

4.5.2.1   Features of Common Organizational Culture of a Central Bank

Organizational culture of a central bank is similar to that of large organizations with a two-tiered structure of common organizational culture and subculture for each sector. Of the two-tiered structure, the common organizational culture of a central bank is

---

[17]The organizational culture of a central bank is less affected by its founders than private companies since a central bank is not founded by a specific individual. It is also less affected by its leader since a central bank is publicly governed through the legislature (see Chaps. 2 and 3).

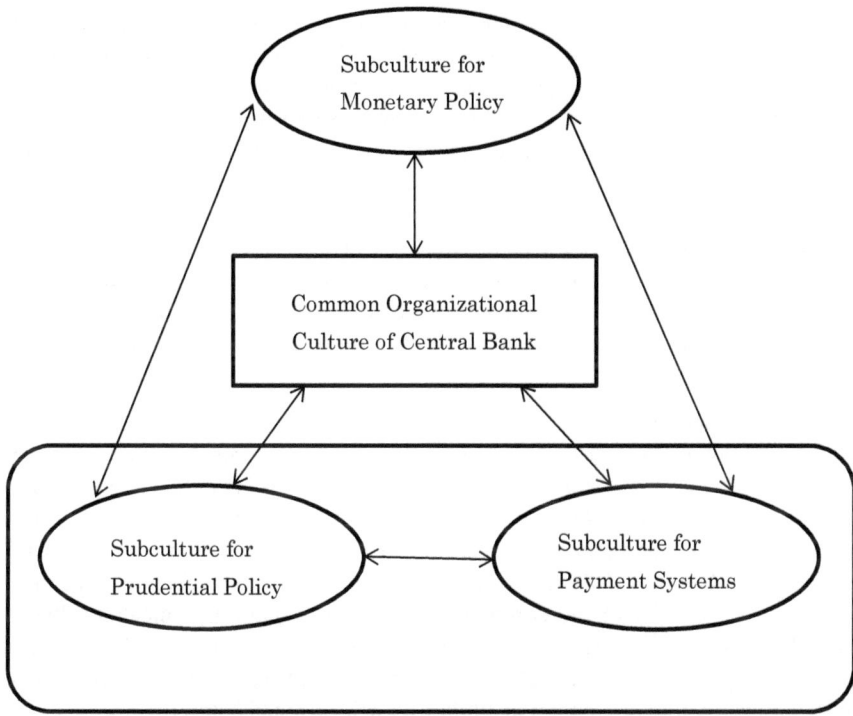

Subcultures for Banking Sector

Fig. 4.7 Structure of organizational culture in central banks

similar to that of a private organization. As shown in Fig. 4.7, there are roughly four types of organizational culture—all being formed based on central bank functions, purpose, and mission, and are useful in the efficient implementation of functions and purposes of a central bank.

Respect for Research and Banking Activities
The organizational culture of a central bank that respects research and banking activities can be regarded as forming part of the informal behavioral rules and norms of a central bank. Shirakawa (2008b) points out that "the role of organizational culture that respects research and banking activities is important….Such feature is common to major central banks and therefore, by having a common organizational culture that respects fundamental and theoretical research, it plays an important role in smooth communication and exchange of information among central banks." As for the reason why an organizational culture that emphasizes research was formulated, Shirakawa (ibid.) points out the content and objective of central banking, i.e., "projection and policy analysis of the macroeconomy."

On the other hand, organizational culture that respects banking activities stems from the fact that a central bank is a type of bank that provides banking services, i.e., deposit and lending, payment and settlement. Central banks own and manage vaults, distribute banknotes and coins, as well as take part in monetary transactions in the markets. Therefore, organizational culture that emphasizes reliable administrative work and accurate record taking was firmly established. Moreover, organizational cultures that are created from developing and managing IT systems to provide payment services are also important. Such culture will be useful in implementing banking activities of a central bank accurately and efficiently. There is also an organizational culture that was formulated through central bank credit extension in a broad sense, which is equivalent to the culture in private banks formulated through lending services. Such culture developed from the central bank's risk evaluation of these counterparties and is related to organizational culture concerning a central bank's prudential policy.

Respect for Independence
The organizational culture of respect for central bank independence falls under the 'value principle' of central banking. Although, a central bank is a public organization, its organizational culture places emphasis on independence from the government, the legislature, and politicians. This is related to the organization's mission and goal stated by Schein (1999) and is formulated from the basic goals of a central bank such as 'stability of the currency value.' Also, 'neutrality,' meaning that a central bank will not take sides with a specific corporation or profit-seeking entity, is also organizational culture that stems from a central bank's goals (this is also organizational culture of a public institution as will be noted below).

Being stipulated in central bank legislation, this organizational culture of independence and neutrality is also official but is insufficient to maintain behavioral norms that are very specific. Therefore, the unofficial rules permeating among central bankers in the form of organizational culture will play the role of enhancing the effectiveness of the official rules. As stated in Sect. 4.3, central bank independence as organizational know-how is a common production factor that brings about economies of scope to various functions of a central bank. Such central bank independence includes both official and unofficial rules.

Organizational Culture from Being a Public Institution
A central bank's organizational culture is that of a public institution, formulated from the bank's nature as a public institution. Regarding "probity" of the central bank mission, Shirakawa (2011b, p. 15) states as below. The importance of probity to the mission of public institutions is also explained by Williamson (1996) using TCE and is applied to the central bank in Chap. 3, Sect. 3.2.1.

> Probity attaching to the organization's mission creates culture that is necessary in achieving such mission. The Bank of Japan has its own unique organizational culture. Such organizational culture is formulated naturally when the Bank tries to pursue its mission. One of the features of the Bank's organizational culture is a culture in which we feel pleasure and pride in realizing public benefit. The culture where we feel pleasure and pride in achieving the public mission of economic and financial stability is the greatest feature of the Bank's organizational culture (translated from Japanese).

Hawthorne Effect in Monetary Policy and Identity of a Central Bank
The identity of a central bank is also formed and strengthened by the Hawthorne effect over monetary policy as aforementioned in Sect. 4.4.2.2, and becomes common organizational culture. That is, considerable attention towards monetary policy from the legislature and the public will not only enhance the identity of the monetary policy sector but also that of the overall central bank (common organizational culture). The Hawthorne effect has such a positive effect as well as the aforementioned negative effect mentioned in Sect. 4.4.2.2.

Also, according to Akerlof and Kranton (2010), identity is said to have "externality" in that utility of a member will affect the utility of other members in the same group. Based on this theory, officials and staff of the monetary policy sector that are the object of attention from the legislature and the public will see increased utility through the Hawthorne effect, which in turn will positively affect members of other sectors, thereby formulating the identity of the central bank overall (common organizational culture).

4.5.2.2 Subculture of a Central Bank

A central bank has various subcultures in respective sectors as shown in Fig. 4.7 apart from common organizational culture as mentioned above. We will look at the features of subcultures in major sectors of a central bank and then discuss the possibility of conflict of organizational culture between subcultures of the monetary policy sector and those of the banking sector.

Features of Subcultures in Major Sectors
Let us look at the features of subcultures in three major sectors of a central bank (Fig. 4.7). While there are differences, relatively speaking, organizational cultures of the prudential policy sector and the payment system sector are alike. On the other hand, organizational culture of the monetary policy sector differs considerably from them. Based on the theories of Williamson and Kreps, this is due to the fact that transactions among the organizational members, an important factor in formulating organizational culture, are more frequent within the sector rather than with other sectors. Another reason could be that since the mission of each respective sector differs, it leads to differences in their work experience. Let us look at this more specifically with respect to major central bank sectors in the following.

Subculture of the Monetary Policy Sector
The feature of the monetary policy sector's organizational culture is that, it places emphasis on the macro perspective concerning the overall financial and economic arena. Such a macro perspective plays an important role not only in research on monetary and economic conditions and basic decision-making with respect to monetary policy, but also in financial transactions with private bank counterparties as part of its market operations in the sense that such individual financial transactions are made to achieve macroeconomic effects. Such a perspective differs from financial transactions under micro prudential policy that are made with a view to supporting

individual banks (of course, maintaining stability of the overall financial system is in the background of achieving the soundness of individual banks).

Second, with emphasis on the macro perspective, macro monetary economics is often used as a tool in the monetary policy sector, and often the language used as its organizational culture is based on vocabulary found in macro monetary economics.

Third, as aforementioned (Sect. 4.4.2.2), since monetary policy influences the overall economy from a macro perspective, it attracts attention from politicians and the public, and therefore the monetary policy sector has an organizational culture that takes heed of the intention of politics and public views more than other central bank sectors.

Fourth, if we differentiate monetary policy from market operations and look at monetary policy alone, its decisions are not really directly related to banking functions. Therefore, its organizational culture differs considerably from that formulated from banking functions.

Subculture of the Payment System Sector
A characteristic of organizational culture of the payment system sector is that it has many similarities with that formulated from banking operations in private banks. Specifically, first, the organizational culture stemming from the distribution management of cash, bills, and checks, use of vaults, and management of paper-based payment systems, is similar. Such organizational culture emphasizes accuracy and strictness in terms of individual and daily functions. The formation process of such organizational culture at the central bank can also be found in the historical background where the central bank emerged from private banks.

Second, this organizational culture is formulated through designing and managing IT-based payment systems and is nurtured through transactions in the workplace where many software engineers jointly conduct IT operations. In this sector, computer engineering is used as a basic tool, and the language used is often IT vocabulary. Such organizational culture is similar to that of the IT sector of private banks.

Third, this is a culture deriving from the fact that a central bank operates payment and settlement systems. That is, whether paper-based or computer-based, it entails systemic risk where a problem occurring at one of the members will affect other members. Also, as the central bank provides liquidity to members of payment systems as needed, it checks and monitors members. Such organizational culture is similar to the subculture of prudential policy which will be mentioned below.

Subculture of Prudential Policy
Like organizational culture in the payment system area, prudential policy organizational culture has many aspects in common with that formulated from the banking operations of private banks. In particular, micro prudential policy such as regulation, supervision, and on-site examination, is implemented based on the knowledge of private banks held by the prudential policy body. Therefore, its organizational culture is similar to that of private banks. For example, asset classification of private banks executed at the time of on-site examination is to check their lending activities and, therefore, the common language in this sector will be that pertaining to

the perception of 'credit risks,' as well as technical terms and knowledge regarding bookkeeping/accounting used for the financial analysis of corporations. And, not only 'credit risks,' but terms used in overall risk management (e.g., 'operational risks') are also common language.

Nevertheless, prudential policy of a central bank differs from private banks in that it does not pursue private profits but aims at securing stability of the overall financial system. Therefore, its organizational culture places emphasis on safety and integrity rather than efficiency. Also, the role of prudential policy is not like that of the payment and settlement system, where systems are developed and managed, but only to monitor and evaluate private banks. Hence, organizational culture in this sector places importance on 'critical thinking' and, in this sense, differs from the cultures of both private banks and the payment system area of a central bank. Moreover, with regard to macro prudential policy, it places emphasis on the macro perspective just like the monetary policy sector, and as such differs from the aforementioned sectors.

Function of Subcultures and Possibility of Conflict
As above, it can be pointed out that a central bank also has common organizational culture as well as subcultures in respective sectors. While these subcultures can be useful in efficiently achieving the objectives and missions of each respective sector, the possibility of conflict between them is not precluded. Subcultures of a central bank are in place to reduce coordination costs through a reduction in transaction costs among members and therefore increase the efficiency of respective sectors, as introduced in Williamson's theory (Sect. 4.5.1.2). This is attained as organizational culture prescribes rules, principles, and norms for each respective sector and at the same time provides necessary language to smoothen communication among members within each sector.

However, such central bank subcultures may, when negotiating with other sectors, conflict with one another and bring about negative effects. In particular, the organizational culture of monetary policy has many differing aspects from the banking function sector, and so the possibility of conflict is high. In this case, various inefficiencies such as different non-official rules, principles, and norms as well as language barrier, will occur. As a result problems may arise in the following three aspects.

Conflict with Organizational Culture of the Banking Sector from Perspective of Monetary Policy Sector
The macro-based organizational culture of monetary policy will conflict with the micro-based organizational culture of the banking sector which may have adverse effects in achieving the sector's objective and mission. For example, in order to develop and manage IT-based payment systems, it is imperative to have a knowledge and understanding of the culture of the IT sector. However, should staff immersed in the monetary policy sector's organizational culture be transferred to the IT sector, they may not be able to understand its language, specific rules, and norms, which will eventually hinder development and operation of IT systems.

Similarly, in prudential policy, knowledge of the functions of private banks, laws, accounting, as well as research and analysis of respective problems and making appropriate judgments, are imperative in dealing with various issues of respective private banks. Nevertheless, if a staff member who has only experienced the organizational culture of monetary policy (that places emphasis on the macro perspective) is transferred to be a senior official or staff member in the prudential policy sector, they would not be able to understand the language, rules, and norms, and may fail in dealing with the issues of private banks.

Conflict with Organizational Culture of Monetary Policy from Perspective of the Banking Sector

Contrary to the above, the organizational culture of the banking sector that places emphasis on micro perspectives may conflict with that of monetary policy and, as a result the objective and missions of monetary policy may not be executed adequately.

For example, it is difficult to implement monetary policy that needs to be based on appropriate macroeconomic analysis if emphasis is placed on the organizational culture of the payment system sector that focuses on accuracy and strictness. And, in implementing monetary policy, one needs to judge from a broad perspective that might even include making a political assessment. Against such background, if staff who only have a micro perspective based on the organizational culture of the banking sector are transferred to the monetary policy sector, they would not be able to understand the language, rules, and norms and may hinder appropriate economic analysis and implementation of monetary policy.

Conflict with the Organizational Culture of the Banking Sector from the Perspective of Senior Central Bank Officials

If most central bank board members have only experienced the macroeconomic-oriented organizational culture of monetary policy, the same problem as noted under "*Conflict with Organizational Culture of the Banking Sector from Perspective of Monetary Policy Sector*" may arise. Moreover, if the business administration section is under the influence of monetary policy organizational culture, and is either obedient to board members' intentions or cannot understand the organizational culture of the banking sector, this problem will become even more serious.

Since monetary policy is accompanied by the Hawthorne effect, it is not often that most central bank board members are only influenced by the organizational culture of monetary policy. Therefore, it is unlikely that conflict of organizational culture in the opposite direction to that noted above under the subtitle "*Conflict with organizational culture of monetary policy from perspective of the banking sector*" will occur. That is, it is difficult for board members to be solely influenced by the organizational culture of the banking sector while being closely observed by external sources regarding monetary policy.[18]

---

[18] However, as mentioned in Sect. 4.2.2, before monetary policy was considered as a central bank function, macro-perspective based organizational culture did not develop, and, therefore, activities with no regard for the macro perspective became a serious problem.

Such conflict of subcultures within a central bank is not considered as fierce as that seen in the merger and acquisition activities of private corporations. However, conflict of subcultures may occur daily even if there is no change in the central bank organization and system, and this would pose serious problems should there be a significant change in central bank organization and system. For example, if the monetary policy function were to be added to traditional central bank functions such as the banking function, and here we are reminded of the BOJ pre-World War II when supervisory authority over individual private banks was added to the monetary policy function, and more recently, authority to implement prudential policy was transferred from the United Kingdom's Financial Services Authority to the BOE. Also, such problems may arise even in the case where payment systems see a transition from being paper-based to IT-based.

4.5.2.3   Implications for Governance of Monetary Policy

Various features of central bank organizational culture discussed in the previous sections provide implications for the governance of monetary policy. Such implications will be considered from the two aspects of ownership and organizational governance. With regard to ownership, whether the central bank should implement monetary policy will be considered using the theory of organizational culture. And, on the premise that the central bank has ownership in managing monetary policy, implications of organizational culture for organizational governance such as designing and managing a central bank board system will be discussed.

Implications for Ownership of Monetary Policy
The current situation of central bank organizational culture is very meaningful in considering adequate ownership of monetary policy. Should the common organizational culture within the central bank increase and the possibility of conflict among subcultures diminish, it would become desirable to merge monetary policy with other banking functions (if the contrary, it might be desirable to detach monetary policy from the central bank).

According to the theory of organizational boundaries based on the theory of organizational culture by Williamson and Kreps, if organizational culture is shared, transaction costs will not increase even if organizational boundaries are broadened (Williamson). This is because tacit agreement (= organizational culture) brings about efficiency (Kreps). The shared organizational culture plays a similar role as the common production factors that realize economies of scope. However, on the other hand, conflict between the subculture of the monetary policy sector and that of the banking sector will bring about inefficiency in achieving central bank objectives and missions. Therefore, if the possibility of conflict is high, then it is desirable to detach the monetary policy sector from the central bank.

Common central bank organizational culture and the subcultures of respective sectors are independent of each other to a certain degree. It is not a relationship where the stronger common organizational culture is, the less possibility there is of conflict among subcultures. Should conflicts arise among subcultures, if there is a strong enough common organizational culture that could overcome such conflicts, organizational unity can be maintained. In other words, as long as the efficiency of common organizational culture exceeds the inefficiency of conflicts among subcultures, then it is desirable to integrate monetary policy within the central bank.

Also, actual ownership of monetary policy should not only be decided solely from the aspect of organizational culture. Factors other than economic efficiency such as historical background should be considered. In addition, even when limiting to economic efficiency, ownership should be decided taking into consideration the interdependency of central bank functions based on TCE, economies of scope, and balance between multitask issues based on agency theory.

Implications for Organizational Governance of a Central Bank
As mentioned above, the desirable ownership model with respect to monetary policy differs depending on the organizational culture of a central bank. Moreover, organizational culture of a central bank changes in response to how its organization is governed. Based on the assumption that a central bank has ownership of monetary policy management, implications of organizational culture for central bank organizational governance, another aspect of monetary policy governance, will be discussed. Emphasis will be placed on the fact that by improving organizational governance of a central bank, common organizational culture will be strengthened and at the same time such improvement reduces the possibility of conflict among subcultures. Also, designing and operating a central bank board system and its relation to organizational culture will be discussed taking the current board system of the BOJ into consideration.

Necessity to Strengthen Organizational Culture in a Central Bank
As overviewed under Sect. 4.5.1, in a corporate organization both common organizational culture and subcultures play important roles and thus it is necessary to strengthen organizational culture in a direction beneficial to the organization.

The same can be said of a central bank. That is, if the central bank has ownership of monetary policy management, strengthening a central bank's common organizational culture will be beneficial in achieving central bank objectives and missions adequately by overcoming subculture conflicts between the monetary policy sector and other sectors. Also, while strengthening of subcultures in respective sectors of the central bank may increase the possibility of conflicts, it will be of benefit in increasing the efficiency of each sector's function.

Measures to strengthen central bank organizational culture include encouraging understanding of organizational culture through staff training programs, like in any corporation. Also, various activities to increase central bank identity play an important role. In addition, it is necessary to nurture core staff that can shoulder and be responsible for the common organizational culture of a central bank through strategic staff transfers.

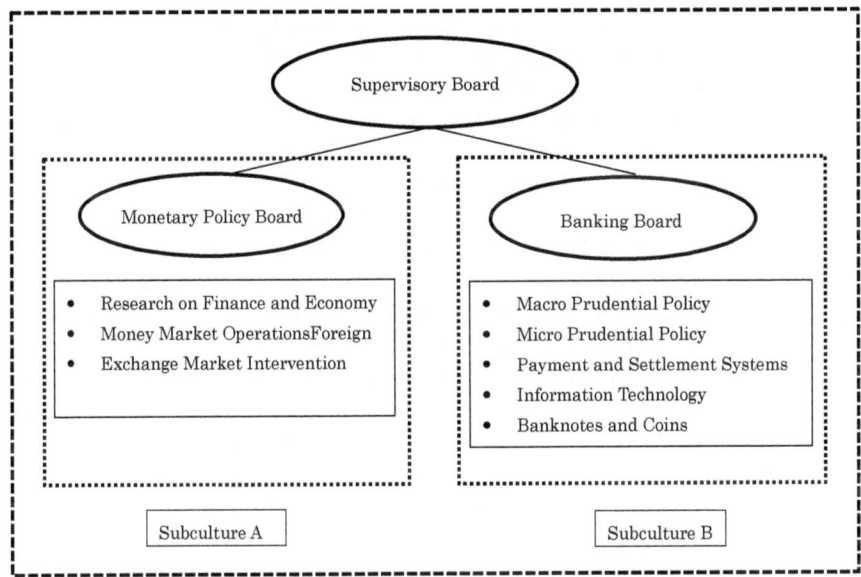

Common Organizational Culture

Fig. 4.8 Structure of a multiboard system and organizational culture

As noted in Sect. 4.5.2.1, the Hawthorne effect has significant influence in increasing central bank identity, and benefits a central bank in conducting monetary policy. Even officials and staff that have nothing to do with monetary policy, might see their awareness as central bankers enhanced because of public scrutiny.

Strengthening of Organizational Culture and Multiboard System
In addition to the above measures to strengthen organizational culture through organizational management, more basically, organizational culture can be strengthened by adopting a multiboard system as shown in Fig. 4.8 for the governance structure of a central bank. The Figure is just one example of a multiboard system, and, as mentioned in Sect. 4.3.5.3, in addition to the monetary policy board that makes decisions on monetary policy, a banking board that decides policies regarding such as prudential policy, payment systems, the issuance and management of banknotes and coins, will be established along with a supervisory board that supervises the two boards.

By adopting such a multiboard system, subcultures of the monetary policy and banking sectors could be strengthened and common organizational culture enhanced which would ease conflicts among subcultures. That is to say, a monetary policy board will bring together the economic research, market operation, foreign exchange departments, etc. that place emphasis on macroeconomic perspectives, and, by so doing, subcultures unique to monetary policy will be strengthened. Similarly, a banking board will coordinate prudential policy, payment system, computer system, banknote and coin departments to enhance subcultures unique to banking. And, by establishing a supervisory board to oversee the two boards, a central bank's common organizational culture will be enhanced and subcultures of monetary policy and banking boards have less possibility of conflict.

In order to equally strengthen subcultures and common organizational culture, members of the monetary policy and banking boards need to be experts in the respective fields. And, supervisory board members should include experts from both.[19] The central bank governor needs to head all the boards or at least head the monetary policy and banking boards to enhance common organizational culture.

And, even in cases where the above multiboard system is not adopted (e.g., the BOJ), diversity can be created by including experts of prudential policy and payment systems as board members besides experts on macro monetary policy which could enhance subcultures to a certain extent (same as the integration issue from TCE Sect. 4.3.5.3, and measures to tackle the multitask agency problem, Sect. 4.4.2.3). In this way, the common organizational culture can shift from being macro monetary policy-oriented to being a well-balanced culture based on central bank functions.

Single-Board System of the BOJ and its Organizational Culture
When we look at the current governance structure of the BOJ based on the relation between the above governance structure and organizational culture, we see it is appropriate for strengthening the common organizational culture but not for enhancing subcultures. That is, under the 1998 BOJ Act, the governance structure of the BOJ changed from a two-board system comprising a policy board and executive board to a single-board system with only a policy board as shown in Fig. 4.9. As a result, while common organizational culture can be created at a policy board level, subculture can only be shared within each department.[20]

And, since the governance structure does not allow coordination of monetary policy and banking at a board level, should the area of expertise and interest focus on monetary policy, common organizational culture of the overall BOJ will be similar to the subculture of the monetary policy sector and hence it would be difficult to strengthen the subculture of the banking sector. To the contrary, monetary policy subculture would be difficult to strengthen if common organizational culture matches the subculture of the banking sector. However, this is unlikely to happen considering the Hawthorne effect (Sect. 4.4.2.2).

---

[19] In this case, should the supervisory board consist only of experts from second-tier boards, it would just be a place for representatives with the respective board's interest. Therefore, members of the supervisory board should be composed of experts as well as individuals having a broad perspective.

[20] However, in 2005, in accordance with its internal rules, the BOJ established the Management Committee with a view to examining and managing bank-wide issues regarding the banking operations. The Deputy Governor is the chairman and executive directors its members. If we consider this committee as a board, then the BOJ can be said to have adopted a two-board system. The Management Committee fulfills the role of coordinating sectors related to banking functions and may be beneficial in strengthening subcultures of sectors related to banking functions.

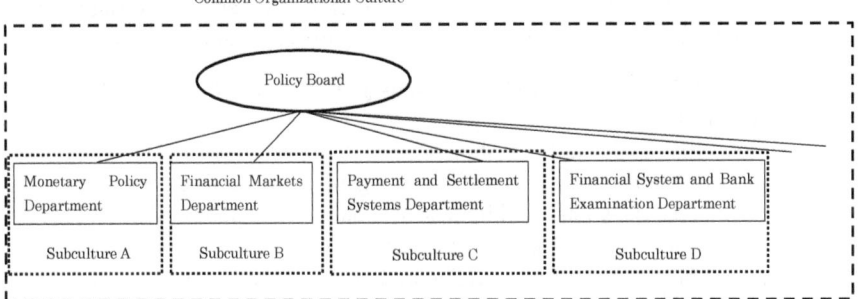

Fig. 4.9   Governance structure of the Bank of Japan and its organizational culture

Creating diversity among policy board members by including not only monetary policy experts but those from prudential policy and payment systems will, to a certain extent, strengthen the subcultures of various sectors. And the common organizational culture of the BOJ could shift from being a macro monetary policy biased culture to a well-balanced culture based on central bank functions.

4.6   Conclusion

When we apply organizational economics to the governance of monetary policy, with regard to ownership it is desirable for the central bank to manage monetary policy as well as integrate monetary policy-related policies and functions such as foreign exchange policy and prudential policy. When we apply the theory of organizational boundaries in TCE to the above issue, from a transaction cost perspective it is appropriate for a monetary policy body to integrate the following entities related to central bank functions and policies.

Monetary Policy and Market Operations Should be Integrated at a Central Bank

It is not appropriate to separate monetary policy from the central bank. As the central bank is basically implementing market operations, should they be segregated, transaction costs will increase between the monetary policy body and the central bank that implements market operations. Looking at interdependency and the common production factors between monetary policy and market operations, they should be integrated into the same organization (i.e., the central bank).

Monetary Policy and Foreign Exchange Policy Should be Integrated at a Central Bank

Provided that monetary policy is managed by the central bank, foreign exchange policy should also be managed by it. Monetary policy and foreign exchange policy are interdependent at two tiers (i.e., policy making and implementation, that is, financial market operations and foreign exchange market intervention) and, at the same time, by utilizing common production factors, economies of scope could be realized.

Conventional and Unconventional Monetary Policy Should be Integrated at a Central Bank

It is understood that a central bank should manage conventional monetary policy. However, unconventional monetary policy is regarded as quasi-fiscal policy and, therefore, there is the question of which entity should be the policy body for quasi-fiscal policy in a democratic society. But, based on TCE, since there is a strong interdependence between the two policies and common production factors exist, it would save transaction costs if the central bank manages both conventional and unconventional monetary policy.

Monetary Policy and Prudential Policy Should be Integrated at a Central Bank

If the central bank is the entity that manages prudential policy then this could be the reason for a central bank to manage monetary policy. That is to say, information on micro financial and economic conditions obtained through supervising private banks plays an important role in monetary policy planning and decision-making. Therefore, monetary policy and prudential policy are interdependent of one another and, at the same time, by utilizing common production factors such as independence from politics, economies of scope may be realized.

Also, in addition to the perspective from TCE, from the standpoint of the theory of organizational culture, it is desirable to integrate both traditional banking functions and the management of monetary policy at a central bank. The organizational culture of a central bank has a two-tiered structure composed of common organizational culture that includes the overall central bank identity and the subcultures that differ between respective sectors. And, in order to strengthen common organizational culture, it is beneficial to integrate monetary policy and traditional banking functions.

Nevertheless, the integration of monetary policy management and traditional banking functions may pose several problems for a central bank. First, from the perspective of TCE, as the scale and scope of organization increases, there is a possibility that 'bureaucracy costs,' which are a kind of transaction cost in the internal organization, will also increase. Second, looking from multitask agency theory, a central bank entrusted with multiple tasks should allocate equal compensation to all based on an equal compensation principle. However, compared to other traditional central bank functions, monetary policy attracts considerable attention from the public and legislature, which is special 'compensation' termed the Hawthorne effect. Therefore, it might transpire that a situation whereby a central bank makes significant efforts to manage monetary policy while paying less attention to the payment system and prudential policy might materialize. Third, according to the theory of organizational culture, the subcultures between the monetary policy sector and the traditional banking sector in a central bank differ greatly which may give rise to a conflict of organizational culture.

In response to these problems, it is desirable for a central bank to adopt a multiboard system based on all the above theories to solve and ease the issues accompanying monetary policy management and integration of related functions and policies.

First, from the perspective of TCE, a central bank could structure 'organizations within the organization' under respective boards, and thus prevent an increase of transaction costs in the internal organization (bureaucracy costs).

Second, from multitask agency theory, a possible problem under the single-board system where most board members concentrate on monetary policy that attracts attention from the public and legislature could be mitigated. And at the staff level, staff could secure the attention of their seniors by having their own communication channel to the board for respective functions which could ease the Hawthorne effect.

Third, from the perspective of organizational culture, a multiboard system where the central bank governor supervises all boards or there is a supervisory board, could strengthen respective subcultures of the monetary policy sector and the banking sector and at the same time enhance the common organizational culture which could in turn ease the conflict of organizational culture among the subcultures.

Moreover, even in the case where a multiboard system is not adopted (e.g., the BOJ), by appointing members with diverse expertise and background, the positive effects of a multiboard system could to a certain extent be enjoyed. Specifically, board members should not only comprise experts on monetary policy but also include those on prudential policy and payment systems. This could bring about a similar effect as a multiboard system, which is endorsed by all the theories applied in this chapter.

The above conclusion is liable to change in response to changes in the "institutional environment" (see Chap. 1, Sect. 1.3). In particular, transaction costs, the Hawthorne effect, and organizational culture, important factors in the respective theories, are influenced by the institutional environment such as financial transaction technology and people's way of thinking. Therefore, even if a central bank is to manage monetary policy on a continuing basis, it needs to take appropriate measures regarding its organizational governance in response to varying issues accompanying monetary policy management. Also, details of planning and managing a central bank board system are determined by the country's historical background and institutional environment such as its legal system.

Chapter 5
Ownership of Prudential Policy

5.1 Overview

The US and some European countries considered one of the causes of the global financial crisis of 2007–09 to be defects in the regulation and supervision of financial institutions, i.e., prudential policy, and there has been active discussion of best practice in this regard. And indeed, actual system reform has already been seen, sometimes in the form of legislation—the basic trend of such reform is an emphasis on macro prudential policy, reflecting wide recognition that one of the root causes of the financial crisis was defects in the macro prudential policy system. And, since macro prudential policy is deeply involved with a central bank's macro monetary policy, the trend of financial system reform has seen an emphasis on the role of a central bank in prudential policy.

The objective of this chapter is to theoretically discuss ownership of prudential policy against the background of discussion on structural reform of the prudential policy system. Of the various issues regarding ownership, two are taken up—whether prudential policy bodies should be integrated, and what role a central bank should play in an integrated prudential policy system.

These questions involve not only the intrinsic nature of what kind of system is optimal in terms of financial system efficiency and stability but also what might be described as a kind of 'turf war' among policy bodies (supervisors) such as a central bank and government agencies, thus inviting active discussion among scholars, prudential policy bodies (supervisors), and politicians. However, there are few analyses based on economic theories and even then the theories applied are limited to traditional microeconomics. Theoretical analysis based on fast developing organizational economics and new institutional economics is rarely seen.

Nevertheless, while this issue might be seen as a turf war among policy bodies, it is basically a discussion of relationships among organizations. Hence, by applying organizational economics, we might be able to realize an objective discussion that overcomes the position of each body concerned. This chapter thus applies not only traditional microeconomics but also Transaction Cost Economics (TCE), as well

© Springer Nature Singapore Pte Ltd. 2019
Y. Oritani, *The Japanese Central Banking System Compared with Its European and American Counterparts*, https://doi.org/10.1007/978-981-13-9001-2_5

as the Resource Based View (RBV) to theoretically discuss ownership of prudential policy. In this way, we clarify the theoretical background of why a central bank's role is important in a prudential policy system that places importance on macro prudential policy, and at the same time show that micro prudential policy such as the on-site examination of financial institutions is vital for macro prudential policy.

In this chapter,'regulation and supervision' and 'prudential policy' are basically used in the same context but 'regulation and supervision' can be used especially to emphasize the power of a policy body. Generally speaking, 'prudential policy' is used to mean the maintenance of financial system stability through the regulation and supervision of financial institutions and financial markets, and includes both macro and micro prudential policies.

We already mentioned in Chap. 1, Sect. 1.6.3 the intrinsic significance of a central bank in being responsible for the regulation and supervision of financial institutions through discussing the raison d'être of a central bank based on TCE. However, discussion in Chap. 1, Sect. 1.6.3 was limited to the regulation and supervision of banks (depository institutions) and did not take up integration with the regulatory and supervisory bodies of financial institutions other than banks.

5.2   Issue Identification

This section categorizes prudential policy from various perspectives to clarify to the extent possible what prudential policy is. Then, questions regarding ownership of prudential policy are considered.[1]

5.2.1   Categories of Prudential Policy

Prudential policy encompasses a wide variety of implementation instruments from which those that are necessary for this section's discussion are specifically examined and categorized from two perspectives—first, in the standard way, and then based on risk management theory.

5.2.1.1   Standard Categorization

A definition of prudential policy based on standard categorization is given in this section. In addition, examination and supervision are distinguished, especially on-

---

[1] 'Ownership' here means 'owner (policy body)' of prudential policy and does not mean 'owner' of a central bank as discussed in central bank governance structure in Chap. 2, Sect. 2.3. Nevertheless, similar to governance structure, there is an ownership aspect as well as organizational governance aspect of prudential policy, namely the decision-making body (e.g., design of a board system) to manage prudential policy.

site examination and other supervisory methods that become the starting point of our discussion regarding the importance of on-site examination in this chapter. However, it should be noted that this is a tentative categorization and there are many overlapping categories that cannot be distinguished decisively.

Distinction Between Framework Design and Policy Implementation
When we categorize prudential policy, there is a need to distinguish the fundamental framework design of a financial system from policy implementation under the framework shown in Fig. 5.1. In designing the fundamental framework, questions such as 'What sort of business should be allowed to be undertaken by what kind of financial institution?' are considered including discussion on 'an optimal policy body for prudential policy' which will be taken up later in this chapter. Of course, the distinction between framework design and policy implementation is not necessarily clear. Nevertheless, according to pro forma distinction, a fundamental framework usually takes the form of law(s) and, therefore, its design would involve the creation of bills concerning the financial system (the legislature is the actual body that enacts a law, but, in this chapter, it is not considered to be a policy body).

And in drafting bills that formulate the framework, the policy body in charge of its design does not draft bills by itself, but, as a matter of course, collects information from organizations that are in charge of policy implementation and seeks their views. Having said this, the entity holding the ultimate power and responsibility for drafting bills and submitting them to the legislature is called the 'framework design body' in this chapter.

Distinction Between Purpose and Instruments
As in Fig. 5.2, prudential policy can be categorized into purpose and instruments. The purpose of prudential policy can be roughly categorized into depositor/investor protection and the maintenance of financial system stability. Depositor/investor protection falls under consumer protection and, considering that deposits are a sort of investment in a wide sense, depositor protection can be included in investor protection. Nevertheless, if emphasis is placed on the function of deposits as a payment instrument, then deposits have a deep connection with the maintenance of payment system stability and thus might be difficult to distinguish from the latter objective. The objective of the maintenance of financial system stability is to prevent any disruption in the overall financial system and markets that would have adverse effects

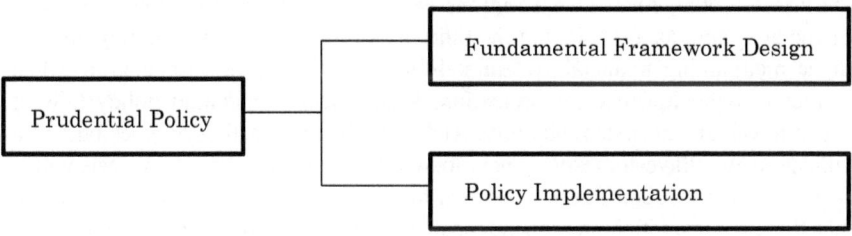

Fig. 5.1 Fundamental framework design and policy implementation

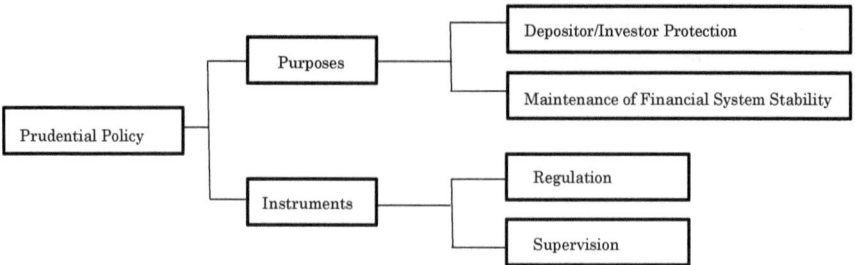

Fig. 5.2 Purposes and instruments of prudential policy

Table 5.1 Distinction between macro and micro prudential policy

	Depositor/Investor Protection	Maintenance of Financial System Stability
Micro Prudential Policy	Direct	Indirect
Macro Prudential Policy	Indirect	Direct

on economic activity. The policy objective is to prevent systemic failure of financial institutions which is similar to systemic risk management.

There are numerous measures to achieve these objectives and related categorization, but, in this chapter, discussion is based on categorization from two viewpoints: a distinction between macro and micro prudential policy as in Table 5.1, and distinction between regulation and supervision as in Fig. 5.2.

Distinction Between Macro and Micro Prudential Policy
In categorizing prudential policy, there is a distinction between macro and micro prudential policy. Macro prudential policy seeks to maintain financial system stability while micro prudential policy seeks to secure the safety and soundness of individual financial institutions. When we differentiate instruments of prudential policy into macro and micro and examine their relation with the objectives of prudential policy, micro prudential policy is a direct instrument for protection but an indirect one for the maintenance of financial system stability. That is, should a financial institution effect business contrary to the interests of depositor/investor protection and go insolvent as a result of losing creditworthiness, only if its failure systemically infected other financial institutions would such failure affect the stability of a financial system as a whole. On the other hand, macro prudential policy directly aims at maintaining financial system stability, but it is an indirect measure when it comes to depositor/investor protection. When macro prudential policy fails, it undermines financial system stability. And, if a financial institution goes bust as a result, depositors/investors would incur losses. Macro prudential policy deals with a financial system that comprises individual financial institutions as components, and hence there is substantial interdependence with whether micro prudential policy that

maintains the safety and soundness of individual financial institutions is properly implemented.

Distinction Between Regulation and Supervision
In categorizing the instruments of prudential policy, there is a difference between regulation and supervision. Regulation can be basically divided into 'organizational regulations' such as 'a bank must be a stock company,' and 'scope of business regulations' concerning the business of financial institutions. Moreover, 'conduct of business regulations' relates to the conduct of business within the scope admitted by scope of business regulations.

As for supervision, it is important to differentiate between 'narrowly-defined supervision' and 'widely-defined supervision.' Narrowly-defined supervision is 'narrow' in the sense that examiners do not examine on-site in contrast to widely-defined supervision that includes on-site examination where examiners actually visit financial institutions and carry out an examination. For example, analyzing data and reports submitted by financial institutions or conducting so called off-site monitoring where financial institution executives are summoned to explain business conditions fall under narrowly-defined supervision. Also, as part of supervision that is deeply related to regulation, there is the provision of licenses to financial institutions and issuance of cease and desist orders.

With regard to how regulation and supervision correspond to macro and micro prudential policy, as both target individual financial institutions, they form part of micro prudential policy. Nevertheless, when they are conducted aiming at the maintenance of financial system stability and not depositor/investor protection, they also contribute to macro prudential policy.

Considering the importance of information gained from on-site examination, whether the prudential policy body or other organization (and, if so, which?) conducts such examination is an extremely important distinction in drawing up best practice for prudential policy.

Distinction Between Regulation and Supervision of Prudential Policy and Conduct of Business
Here, regulation and supervision are not distinguished but focus is more on a difference of viewpoints when both are seen from an overall aspect. That is, regulation and supervision from a prudential viewpoint, and the same from a conduct of business aspect.

The former is a concept similar to general prudential policy that includes both macro and micro perspectives. The latter is regulation and supervision from the viewpoint of micro prudential policy, especially depositor/investor protection. This distinction is important in discussing the 'twin-peaks model' that separates the prudential regulatory and supervisory body from the conduct of business regulatory and supervisory body which will be mentioned in Sect. 5.3.2.3.

5.2.1.2   Categorization Based on Risk Management Theory

This section explains the three-step process of risk management based on risk management theory and categorizes prudential policy accordingly.

Three-Step Process of Risk Management
According to Morimiya (1985), the approach taken by risk management theory is to break down risk management into several processes and understand the whole as risk management. There are many processes but the following three are especially important when discussing risk management of the financial system.

- **Step1 Risk identification**:
  Process to identify risks—possible risks are identified, and, based on past experience and taking the current situation into consideration, their frequency and magnitude are evaluated.
- **Step2 Risk control**:
  Process to set up countermeasures so that identified risks will not materialize. Generally, this risk control is regarded as risk management. However, if we regard risk control as risk management, there is a possibility of neglecting Step1 'risk identification' and Step3 'risk finance.' Therefore, we need to understand that risk control is only one process in overall risk management.
- **Step3 Risk finance**:
  Process to cope with loss incurred from materialized risks that could not be suppressed completely in Steps1 and 2. Risk finance can be divided into two processes—'risk retention' where reserves are held within an organization and system to counter losses, and 'risk transfer' where losses are transferred to outside organizations and systems. By conducting risk finance effectively at this juncture, critical damage can be avoided even if risks materialize. Therefore, what we usually term 'crisis management' that occurs when risks materialize corresponds to this process (see Chap.6).

Instruments of Prudential Policy
Figure 5.3 shows instruments of prudential policy (mentioned in Sect. 5.2.1.1) which are categorized based on the three-step process of risk management. With regard to micro prudential policy, supervision, including on-site examination, is an instrument of risk identification, and regulation and supervision are instruments of risk control. As for risk finance, the crisis management of individual financial institutions such as the provision of liquidity and injection of capital based on LLR, deposit insurance, and prompt resolution[2] are the instruments.

As for macro prudential policy, it is necessary to analyze the macroeconomy and overall financial system to identify risk. To control risk, it is important to avoid a

---

[2]This crisis management for both macro and micro prudential policy is included in the risk finance stage. Therefore, the failure of the US monetary authorities in the global financial crisis of 2007–09 discussed in Chap. 6 is argument of the risk finance stage, the Step3 process, of prudential policy in a financial system. This chapter deals with the Step1 stage, risk identification, and the Step2 stage, risk control of prudential policy.

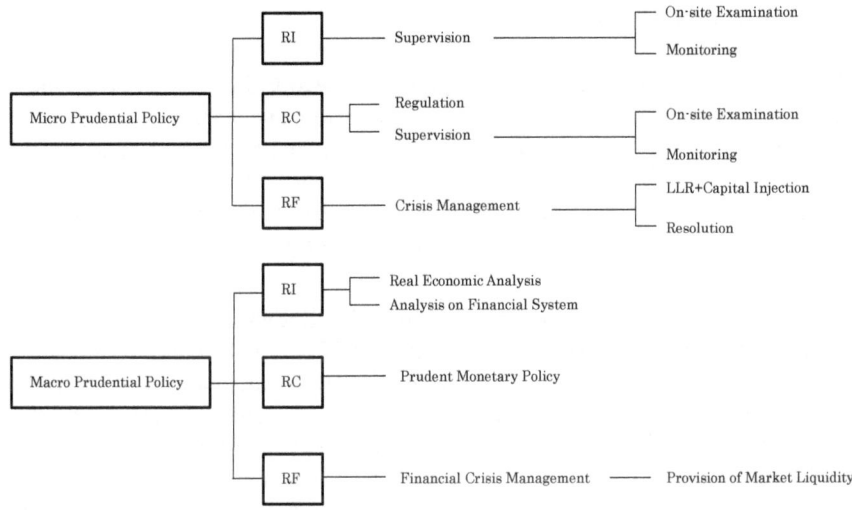

*RI: Risk Identification, RC: Risk Control, RF: Risk Finance

Fig. 5.3 Types of instruments based on risk management

speculative bubble by pursuing prudent monetary policy. And, market stabilization policy that provides market liquidity (i.e., the purchase of financial assets in the market) in the face of financial market turmoil functions as an instrument of risk finance.

We could also categorize regulation and supervision (i.e., micro prudential policy) between 'ex-ante measures' that prevent collapse of an individual financial institution and 'ex-post measures' that prevent a spillover effect to other financial institutions. Ex-ante measures are equivalent to risk identification and risk control in risk management theory and ex-post measures are the same as risk finance.

5.2.2 Ownership Issue of Prudential Policy

The following section explains ownership of prudential policy (i.e., which organization/policy body should be responsible for which policy) that is categorized and defined in Sect. 5.2.1. There are two major issues: one is the integration of policy bodies from the perspective of establishing a macro prudential policy framework and the other is the role of a central bank in prudential policy.

5.2.2.1 Integration of Policy Bodies

In light of establishing a macro prudential policy framework, the integration of policy bodies is discussed from two aspects: vertical integration and horizontal integration. Vertical integration refers to the integration of macro and micro prudential policy bodies, horizontal integration the integration of supervisors for respective financial industries such as banks, securities companies, and insurance companies. The section below discusses the above integration as well as concentration of power as a consequence. Moreover, discussion on the overlapping of supervisors is introduced.

Integration of Macro and Micro Prudential Policy Bodies
Having experienced the global financial crisis of 2007–09, the importance of macro prudential policy has become widely acknowledged and there are therefore calls to establish an entity responsible for macro prudential policy or to at least clarify which existing one is. For example, French et al. (2010) introduced a concept of "systemic regulator" and proposed that it should be responsible for macro prudential policy (*Squam Lake Group Report*[3]). And, in fact, such an entity has been newly established in the US and also at various levels in the European Union. In line with this, there is discussion as to whether the responsible body for macro prudential policy should be separated from, or integrated with, the micro prudential policy body.

Integration of Supervisors of Multiple Financial Industries
In addition to vertical integration of policy bodies from the perspective of establishing a macro prudential policy framework, the need to have a single policy body supervise multiple financial industries such as banks, securities companies, insurance companies, and non-bank financial institutions is also discussed. There are two aspects to this. One is the response bearing in mind the existence of conglomerates comprising different kinds of financial institutions and the other is the response to the increase in interdependence among various financial industries in the financial markets.

Response to Financial Industry Conglomerates
A typical conglomerate is as shown in Fig. 5.4—a financial group where a holding company holds various financial institutions such as a bank, securities company, insurance company, and non-bank as subsidiaries. Such conglomerates are increasing with the deregulation of financial services. The increase in conglomeration poses the issue that having different bodies supervise respective financial industries as shown in Fig. 5.5 may not have sufficient supervisory effectiveness (reasons are given in Sect. 5.3.2.1).

Response to Increase in Interdependence—Integration of Supervisors for Multiple Financial Industries
Even for individual financial institutions that do not belong to a financial group through a holding company like the above conglomerates, several from differing

---

[3] Squam Lake Group is a group of 15 of the world's leading economists including R. Rajan and R. Shiller who gathered at New Hampshire's Squam Lake in the US. Their goal was to map out a long-term plan for financial regulatory reform. The first meeting was held in the fall of 2008.

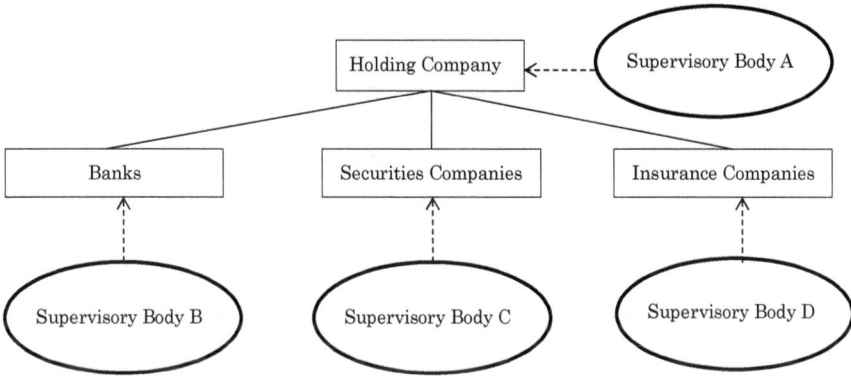

Fig. 5.4 Regulatory and supervisory framework of conglomerates

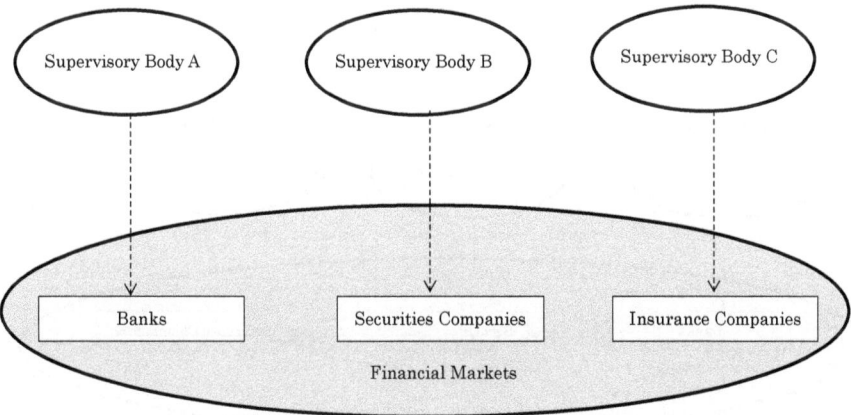

Fig. 5.5 Regulatory and supervisory framework for interdependent financial industries

financial industries have recently seen increasing interdependence within financial markets as shown in Fig. 5.5. For example, many financial products, including derivatives that caused the subprime loan crisis, are traded in financial markets where not only banks but various financial institutions participate. Therefore, in the global financial crisis of 2007–09, risk spilled over to other financial institutions through financial markets.

When integrating supervisory bodies, there are two modes of integration—the full integration mode that fully integrates the supervisory bodies of various financial institutions as shown in Fig. 5.6, and the indirect integration mode that maintains various supervisory bodies but newly establishes a "systemic regulator" (French et al., 2010) that governs them (indirect integration mode) as shown in Fig. 5.7.

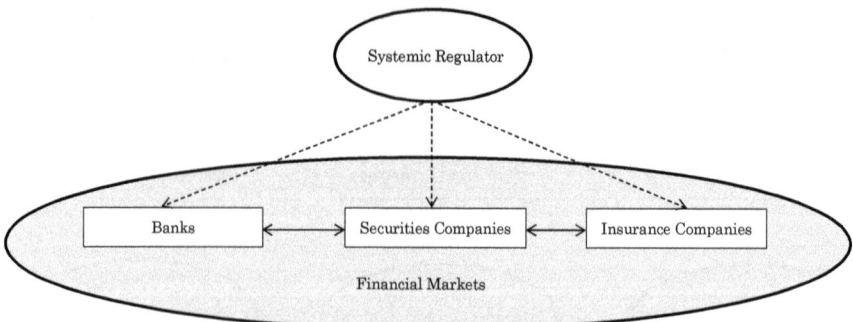

Fig. 5.6 Integrated regulatory and supervisory body for financial industries (full integration mode)

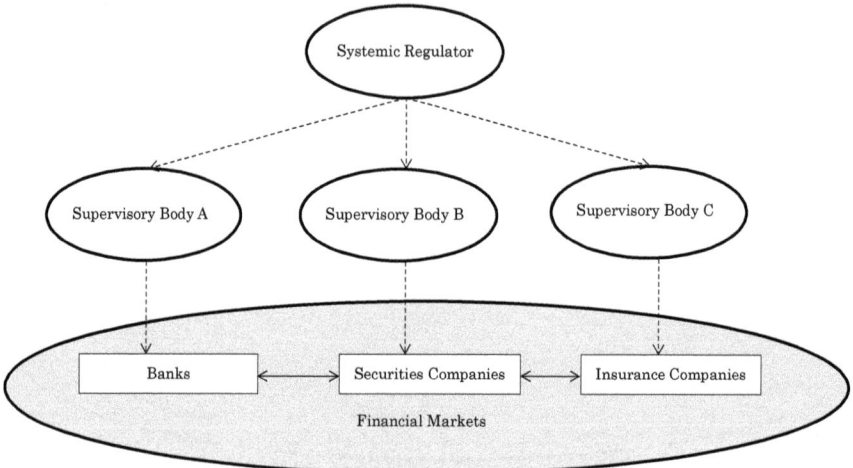

Fig. 5.7 Integrated regulatory and supervisory body for financial industries (indirect integration mode)

Concentration of Power Problem

The problem of the concentration of power in a single entity comes to the fore when prudential macro and micro policy bodies, as well as supervisors of various financial industries, are integrated. Some argue that adopting the twin-peaks regulatory and supervisory structure model proposed by Taylor (1995) could resolve or diminish the problem. For example, French et al. (2010) recommends the twin-peaks model suggesting that a "systemic regulator" should not be responsible for both the maintenance of financial system stability and the protection of depositors/investors.

As mentioned in Sect. 5.2.1.1, prudential policy has two different objectives: the maintenance of financial system stability and protection of consumers and depositors/investors. Therefore, having a separate supervisor for each objective could prevent the concentration of power. There could be other types of twin-peaks models such as separating the rule-making and supervisory functions.

Overlapping Supervisors

While the question of overlapping supervisors is similar to the issue discussed in the integration of supervisors of multiple financial industries, it is intrinsically different. The latter is a problem where differing policy bodies supervise respective financial industries (multiple policy bodies by type of financial industry) while the former is where a specific industry is supervised by multiple policy bodies (overlapping supervisors).

For example, both a central bank and government agency supervise banks in the US and in Japan. There are pros and cons to this supervisory framework. Greenspan (2007, p. 375) wrote:

> Sometimes several regulators are better than one. The solitary regulator becomes risk averse: he or she tries to guard against all imaginable negative outcomes, creating a crushing compliance burden. In the financial industries, where the Fed shares regulatory jurisdiction with the Comptroller of the Currency, the Securities and Exchange Commission, and other authorities, we tended to keep one another in check.

And, in the future, should supervisors of multiple financial industries be integrated, the issue becomes all the more crucial. That is, if supervisors are integrated, related policy bodies other than those integrated are excluded and would not be able to obtain necessary information. Also, there is a possibility of the concentration of power. As an effective countermeasure, the overlapping of supervisors could be considered useful, as will be mentioned later in Sect. 5.3.3.

5.2.2.2 Central Bank's Role in Prudential Policy

A central bank, since its inception, has traditionally played an important role in prudential policy through the use of LLR. For example, BIS (2009) noted as follows: "In the BIS survey of 2008, 90% of central banks considered that they had full or shared responsibility for financial stability policy and oversight of the financial system." Moreover, if policy bodies are integrated from the perspective of establishing a macro prudential policy system, it would be natural to integrate the function in a central bank. And, in this regard, the role of a central bank in prudential policy is discussed (for example, BIS, 2011). Specific discussion points include (a) whether a central bank should not be involved in prudential policy in the first place since there is a conflict of interest involving monetary policy, (b) the objective of central bank involvement, and (c) the scope of central bank involvement.

5.3 Theoretical Analysis of the Integration of Policy Bodies

Based on the ownership issue of prudential policy as discussed in Sect. 5.2.2, this section theoretically analyzes the integration of policy bodies.

5.3.1   Macro and Micro Integration

As mentioned in Sect. 5.2.2, as a lesson learned from the global financial crisis of 2007–09, the importance of macro prudential policy was recognized and thus related policy bodies were newly established separate from those pertaining to micro prudential policy. However, whether establishment of separate bodies for macro and micro prudential policies is the optimal ownership structure for prudential policy needs careful consideration. In the discussion below, we first show that macro and micro prudential policies are in an imperative interdependent relationship and then discuss the importance of on-site examination in micro prudential policy.

After drawing a conclusion based on RBV, the same issue is considered from TCE with the aim of reinforcing the conclusion.

5.3.1.1   Application of Knowledge Partitioning Theory to Macro-Micro Integration

We apply knowledge partitioning theory to consider the relationship between macro and micro prudential policy. This theory was proposed by Takeishi (2002) and pointed out the importance of integrating component-specific knowledge and architectural knowledge.

Knowledge Partitioning Theory

Knowledge partitioning theory falls under RBV as shown in Fig. 5.8. This theory is a collective term for theories that place importance on resources that an organization owns as a factor to decide boundaries of the firm and competitive strategy. Among the resources, theory that emphasizes knowledge is called knowledge-based theory.[4] Theory that focuses especially on knowledge creation and innovation and looks into the knowledge creating process is called knowledge management theory.

As shown in Fig. 5.8, knowledge partitioning theory can be explained as follows. In knowledge-based theory, Demsetz (1991) argues that efficient division of labor to create knowledge is to differentiate between "information to produce" and "information to use." And, while information to produce needs to be created within an organization (vertical integration), it is more efficient to purchase information to use from outside an organization. And Demsetz (ibid) says that this logic determines boundaries of the firm. Information to produce is equivalent to the acquisition of knowledge and requires in-depth knowledge. On the other hand, information to use does not necessitate such knowledge creation. Therefore, Demsetz (ibid) argues that it would be uneconomical, at least in the short term, if both types of information were to be created within an organization.

However, when Takeishi (ibid) conducted an empirical study on automakers' management of supplier involvement in product development in Japan based on

---

[4]Knowledge-based theory is also called resource-based theory, capability theory, and core competence theory (see Langlois and Robertson, 1995).

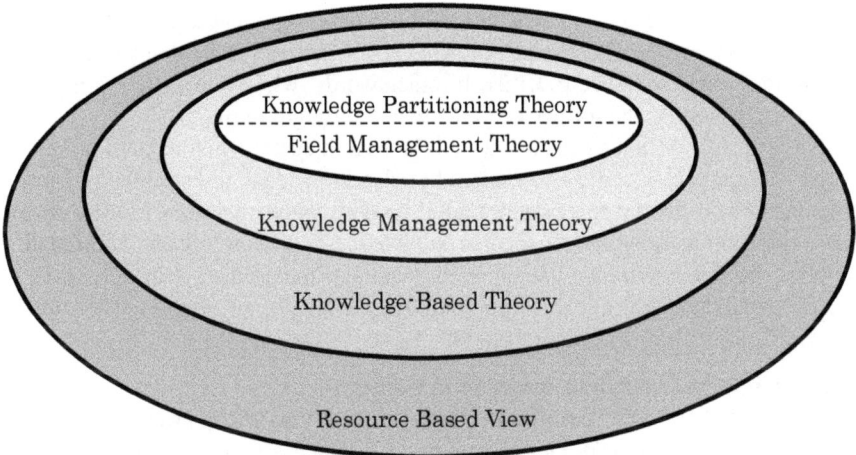

Fig. 5.8   Knowledge partitioning theory and field management theory

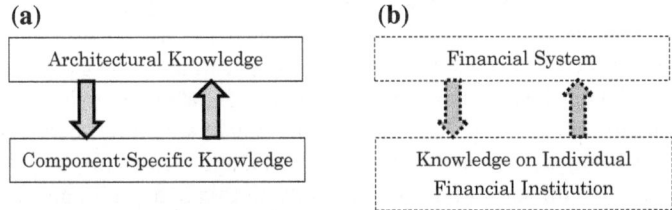

Fig. 5.9   (**a**) Architectural knowledge and component-specific knowledge (**b**) Knowledge on financial system and individual financial institution

the distinction between component-specific knowledge and architectural knowledge proposed by Henderson and Clark (1990), he found that Demsetz's argument was not valid and that effective knowledge partitioning demands overlap between the owners of component knowledge and those of architectural knowledge. According to Henderson and Clark (ibid), component knowledge is "knowledge about each of the core design concepts in parts of the system and the way in which they are implemented in a particular component," and architectural knowledge is "knowledge about the ways in which the components are integrated and linked together into a coherent whole."

Takeishi (ibid) argues that for architectural products that are composed of numerous parts, development of a new product (innovation) is not possible without deep knowledge of individual parts. Of course, vice versa, without manufacturing knowledge (architectural knowledge) to produce the final product, it is difficult to determine what product parts should be developed. As a result, as shown in Fig. 5.9(a), "some portion of architectural knowledge is intertwined with component-specific knowledge in the case of such integral products as the automobile" (Takeishi, ibid).

Takeishi (ibid) pointed out that the reason why component knowledge affects architectural knowledge is because knowledge for innovation is obtained through learning-by-doing (see Sect. 5.3.1.2). In other words, while knowledge is not the same as routine work, the former is often created through routine work.

Another reason is that since an automobile is an integrated architectural product, not only component-specific knowledge, but also knowledge to coordinate various components is important to develop a good product. Nevertheless, it is difficult to clearly differentiate component-specific knowledge and knowledge to coordinate. Therefore, he argues that for outstanding innovation to materialize, a certain overlapping of knowledge partitioning is important even though it may sacrifice short-term efficiency.

Application to Macro-Micro Integration Issue
When we apply knowledge partitioning theory to the ownership of prudential policy, we understand that micro prudential policy is indispensable for macro prudential policy, and, without macro prudential policy, micro prudential policy would just be meaningless carping criticism of financial institutions with no useful purpose.

This shows that the application of knowledge partitioning theory to prudential policy can be summed up in the following three analogies as shown in Fig. 5.9(b). First, component specific knowledge in knowledge partitioning theory is knowledge about individual financial institutions in terms of prudential policy and therefore corresponds to micro prudential policy. On the other hand, architectural knowledge is knowledge regarding the financial system as a whole and thus corresponds to macro prudential policy. In the same context, Takeishi's observation in his empirical study that problems within a certain component are likely to affect problems among various components under integrated architecture corresponds to a phenomenon where problems in a financial institution affect the overall financial system in the form of systemic risk.

The second analogy is that in the sense that innovation in knowledge partitioning theory means to find new knowledge, it corresponds to risk identification in prudential policy as well as to finding a measure to control such risk in risk management theory (Sect. 5.2.1.2). Specifically, innovation in component specific knowledge corresponds to risk identification and risk control of an individual financial institution (micro prudential policy), and innovation in architectural knowledge corresponds to risk identification and risk control concerning the overall financial system (macro prudential policy).

The third analogy is that risk identification and risk control in prudential policy correspond to the development of a new product in automobile manufacturing. Prudential policy not only looks at the state of financial institutions and system passively but also identifies new risks and works to find a new measure(s) to control such new risks. Thus, innovation is an absolute necessity. While there is some reluctance to think of knowledge about financial institutions and the financial system in the same light as knowledge regarding physical products such as automobiles, considering that the overall framework is made up of components in both cases, they are similar.

When we consider that the above three analogies hold true, the argument of knowledge partitioning theory that the outsourcing of components will erode not only component specific knowledge but also architectural knowledge implies that micro prudential policy is essential for macro prudential policy.

On the other hand, the fact that architectural knowledge influences component specific knowledge suggests that macro prudential policy (knowledge of the financial system) influences micro prudential policy (knowledge of an individual financial institution). This speaks for itself in the case of physical products such as automobiles and therefore knowledge partitioning theory does not strongly argue on this point. But for prudential policy, considering that macro prudential policy sets policy directions for micro prudential policy, this is extremely important. The direction of macro prudential policy influences every activity of micro prudential policy such as the viewpoint of on-site examiners. Therefore, we can say that macro and micro prudential policies are in an interdependent relationship.

5.3.1.2 Application of Field Management Theory to Macro-Micro Integration Issue

As above, interaction between macro and micro prudential policies is important and integration of these policies is necessary. With this in mind, we consider the importance of on-site examination in micro prudential policy. For this purpose we apply field management theory. The theory is explained below in comparison with situated learning theory. Then it is applied to on-site examination in order to evidence its importance.

Field Management Theory
The concept of the 'field' (shared space, "*Ba*" in Japanese) was originally proposed by Japanese philosopher Kitaro Nishida and further developed by Hiroshi Shimizu based on the complexity theory. Nonaka and Konno (1998) have adapted it for the purpose of elaborating a knowledge creation process. Field management theory is part of resource based view theory, knowledge management theory, and knowledge-based theory, just like knowledge partitioning theory as shown in Fig. 5.8.

On the other hand, situated learning theory, which is based on cognitive psychology, is a type of learning theory developed by Lave and Wenger (1991). However, both share the following three aspects:

Emphasis on Learning-by-Doing
For knowledge creation activities (innovation), it is important not only to receive knowledge, but also to learn it through actual experience. In this regard, emphasis is placed on learning-by-doing.[5]

---

[5]"Learning-by-doing" is a concept originally used by Arrow (1962) and Lucas (1988) in economic growth theory and currently regarded important in RBV. Learning includes creating new knowledge (innovation) in addition to simply absorbing new knowledge.

Both theories place emphasis on the importance of 'doing' in knowledge creation. For field management theory, this is a real activity within the shared space, and for situated learning theory, group work by a group called "community of practice."

Emphasis on Field (Ba)
For knowledge creation activities, it is important to know the field (situation) where the activities take place as it influences the degree of knowledge creation and effect of learning. Field (situation) not only influences the members sharing the space but it is also considered that members can influence the field. Therefore, field and members are considered to influence one another.

According to Nonaka and Konno (ibid), field (situation) is a platform of place that can be a physical place (office, distributed business space), virtual space, human relationship sharing a specific purpose, or, mental space shared by such human relationships (common experiences, thoughts, dreams).

Emphasis on Group Work
The community of practice group in situated learning theory considers that group work by members is effective in learning, which includes knowledge creation. Field management theory also considers that people in the same space are the equivalent of autonomous elements in a complex system as in complexity theory and that atmosphere of the shared space emerges through interaction during group work.

Applying Field Management Theory to On-site Examination
When we apply the above field management theory (situated learning theory) to on-site examination in micro prudential policy, its importance becomes apparent. The starting point of micro prudential policy is to identify risks by collecting information on the activities of individual financial institutions, and such risk identification is what field management theory calls knowledge creation activity, a type of innovation. It is a creative activity since one cannot identify risks just by dealing with routine work mechanically. For knowledge creation (innovation) like risk identification, off-site examination alone is insufficient since it is distant from a financial institution's actual location and reality. Field (situation), that is in this case on-site examination, is important.

The actual practice of on-site examination varies in detail depending on the examining body, financial institution being examined, and purpose of examination. Nevertheless, the basic procedures of all examining bodies share common features. With such common procedures in mind, let us consider the importance of on-site examination in micro prudential policy from the perspective of three aspects shared by field management theory and situated learning theory as explained under Field Management Theory.

Emphasis on Learning-by-Doing and On-site Examination
On-site examination is an act (doing) of examining the scene, equipment etc., and actual business conduct by an examiner and can be considered learning-by-doing. The fields checked include offices, vaults, and paper and electronic documents.

The act of listening to a financial institution's explanation during on-site examination is learning-by-doing. Unlike off-site monitoring that takes place at an examiner's office away from that of the actual financial institution being examined, on-site examination allows the examiner to interview numerous executives and staff while observing the actual scene, equipment, etc. In this respect, on-site examiners experience learning-by-doing to understand the actual situation of a financial institution.

Emphasis on Field (Situation) and On-site Examination
Field, as in field management theory is not restricted to physical space but, nevertheless, physical space is considered to be a typical field. Therefore, visiting the physical space of a financial institution in on-site examination can heighten the chance of risk identification as it is a type of knowledge creation (innovation) in field management theory which is valuable for micro prudential policy.

Group Work and On-site Examination
Field, as in field management theory includes not only physical space but also human relationships that share a specific purpose. And, group work based on human relationships is considered important in knowledge creation. It may sound strange that in on-site examination the examining team and financial institution being examined share the same objective, but in actuality a financial institution also finds it useful to know its risk accurately and thus it is likely that both share the objective to some extent. Therefore, in the field of on-site examination, creating an atmosphere of group work by both parties may lead to creation of knowledge (innovation) which is to identify new risk.

Such a group work relationship with the examined financial institution is further strengthened if the examiner is experienced in banking business. Therefore, as mentioned in Chap. 1, Sect. 1.6.3, a central bank examining team, members of which themselves are involved in banking, is more likely to conduct effective group work and possibly identify new risks than an examining body that is not engaged in banking.

5.3.1.3 Macro and Micro Prudential Policy and Transaction Cost Economics

So far we have dealt with integration of macro and micro prudential policy by applying knowledge-based theory (from diversification theory of the organization) such as knowledge partitioning theory and field management theory. To reinforce the conclusion drawn from knowledge-based theory, TCE is applied in the next section and explains that macro and micro prudential policy bodies should be integrated as they are in an imperative interdependent relationship.

Caution in Applying Knowledge-Based Theory
When we theoretically consider ownership of prudential policy, it is appropriate to apply TCE, although thus far we have applied knowledge-based theory from diversification theory of the organization. This was to underscore that both macro and micro prudential policies are knowledge creation and one type of innovation.

TCE considers a transaction as a unit of analysis and discusses boundaries of an organization from the perspective of an optimum governance mechanism that minimizes the transaction cost of an economic entity that may take opportunistic behavior. On the other hand, the unit of analysis for knowledge-based theory is not a transaction but resources held by an organization, especially knowledge, with which it analyzes diversification. Therefore, this theory is suitable in considering the relationship between knowledge creation (innovation) and boundaries (ownership) of an organization.

While knowledge-based theory is suitable for considering the knowledge creation aspect of prudential policy, it is too short-sighted to draw a conclusion on the integration of macro and micro prudential policies. For example, based on knowledge partitioning theory from knowledge-based theory, we explained that macro and micro prudential policy bodies should be integrated since they are in an interdependent relationship. However, TCE does not conclude that they should be integrated just because they are interdependent. TCE argues that the degree of transaction specificity (asset specificity) and increase in bureaucracy cost that accompanies boundary expansion of the organization need to be taken into consideration. In other words, knowledge partitioning theory suggests that component-specific knowledge is necessary for creating architectural knowledge since by combining the two would reduce production cost that accompanies creation of architectural knowledge. However, TCE holds that reduction of production cost alone should not be the focus of attention and that transaction cost to combine architectural knowledge and component-specific knowledge should also be considered.

Let us say that architectural knowledge and component-specific knowledge can only be combined within the same person. No matter how much production cost can be reduced by finding the right combination, transaction cost to combine a person with architectural knowledge and one with component-specific knowledge would be infinite. For example, if the above two types of knowledge are combined within a single person as in the case of an automobile manufacturing company, for an engineer not to lose architectural knowledge due to deterioration of component-specific knowledge, various arrangements are made to acquire and maintain component-specific knowledge. For example, transferring staff between the component section and architectural section, providing multiple-track type career paths, and offering various training programs.

Also, for prudential policy, a combination of macro and micro knowledge within the same person can heighten the possibility of knowledge creation. Therefore, there need to be similar arrangements like those provided in an automobile manufacturing company, i.e., rotating the same staff between macro and micro prudential policy bodies.

What is more important in the case of prudential policy is that knowledge creation does not necessarily need to occur within the same person. While the possibility of knowledge creation (reduction in production costs) may be lower than when combined in a single person, this could be achieved by having a person with macro knowledge cooperate with one with micro knowledge. Pursuing the above line of thought, cooperation (e.g., to identify risk) between micro and macro prudential policy bodies based on a contract can also have the result of bringing about a reduction in production costs without having to integrate the bodies. In this case, similar consideration to the discussion on the effectiveness of a memorandum of understanding (MOU) as will be explained in the next section is necessary, implying that it would be too hasty to draw a conclusion to immediately implement organizational integration just because micro and macro prudential policy bodies are in an interdependent relationship.

And, with regard to the importance of on-site examination in micro prudential policy, the same consideration from the above perspective needs to be made based on field management theory. In many cases on-site examiners and off-site examiners are different staff, and there are cases where an examining body does not conduct on-site examination but outsources it to another organization. From the perspective of TCE, we can point out that in this case an MOU between the supervisory body and examining body that conducts on-site examination is not sufficiently effective. And even from the perspective of field management theory, we can point out that just by reading reports from the on-site examiner, it is almost impossible for an off-site examiner to 'share the field,' which is a requisite in knowledge creation.

Explanation from Viewpoint of TCE
Thus far, knowledge-based theory has been applied to the integration of macro and micro prudential policy bodies, and its conclusion could be further reinforced by applying TCE. In the following, vertical integration theory and horizontal integration theory from TCE are applied separately to the same issue.

Vertical Integration Theory
According to vertical integration theory, the need for macro and micro prudential bodies to integrate depends on the transaction cost of information, i.e., the goods and services produced by each body. Interdependence between information held by macro and micro prudential bodies based on Chap. 4, Table 4.1 determines transaction cost. This is the make-or-buy decision pertaining to information that is necessary for prudential policy, and involves the effectiveness of an MOU.

For instance, if information produced by a micro prudential policy body is a requisite for macro prudential policy and not necessarily so vice versa, integration is necessary regardless of the degree of complexity and uncertainty of transaction. As the macro prudential policy body is unilaterally dependent on information provided by the micro prudential policy body, without the governance mechanism gained from integration, transaction cost becomes high in the sense that macro prudential policy cannot be implemented should the micro prudential policy body not provide information. 'Provide information' here includes risk identification by two supervisory bodies (that have differing perspectives based on their role expectation) regarding each other.

And if both macro and micro prudential policy bodies require each other's information, there are cases where organizational integration is necessary or where an MOU would suffice, depending on the degree of uncertainty (especially complexity of transaction). This is because even without integration, one side could prevent opportunistic behavior on the part of the other by threatening to retaliate. However, looking at the uncertainty and complexity of transactions, since both macro and micro prudential policy bodies are public organizations, uncertainty such as sudden insolvency does not exist. Nevertheless, transaction content is extremely complex and therefore there seems to be a limit to the effectiveness of an MOU. Moreover, eagerness to implement an MOU is determined by whether the policy body acknowledges the necessity of the counterpart's information and not by whether the information is actually a requisite or not. When the policy body does not acknowledge the information's necessity, it may misperceive the relationship to be unilateral rather than bilateral interdependence, and with no fear of retaliation may well not provide necessary information. Organizational integration would be the only solution to prevent this.

This analytical result supports the views of Conservative Party Shadow Chancellor George Osborne in his party's white paper (presented 20 July 2009) on financial services regulation which stated that the ownership framework of prudential policy in the UK was the source of the Northern Rock Bank problem (2007–08). In the UK, the authority for micro prudential policy was transferred from the Bank of England (BOE) to the Financial Services Authority (FSA) in 1997, and the BOE became responsible only for macro prudential policy. Despite an MOU (a kind of long-term contract) between the FSA and BOE regarding information provision, it did not seem to function effectively in the Northern Rock Bank case. As such, the FSA's information (if it had it) regarding business conditions at Northern Rock Bank (information on micro prudential policy) did not seem to have reached the BOE, in charge of macro prudential policy, in a timely and appropriate manner. From the perspective of the FSA, it did not regard macro prudential policy information held by the BOE to be necessary for its micro prudential policy. Therefore, the relationship between the BOE and FSA was not regarded as bilateral interdependence but rather the BOE seemed to be unilaterally dependent on the FSA's micro prudential information. Of course, there are other possibilities such as that the FSA might not have appropriately identified risk regarding Northern Rock Bank's business conditions or that the BOE could not assess the provided information properly from a macro prudential policy perspective. In any case, the Northern Rock Bank case implies that in considering ownership of prudential policy, we need to carefully understand the incompleteness of an MOU as pointed out by TCE.

Application of Horizontal Integration Theory
The following applies horizontal integration theory to the integration of macro and micro prudential policy bodies and studies four important common production factors similar to Chap. 4, Sect. 4.3.1.2.

- **Indivisible tangible assets**:
  Among indivisible tangible assets, there are cases such as usage rights attaching to machinery equipment where they can be traded in the market or leased (rental, franchising). However, when transaction cost accompanying negotiation is high, then horizontal integration is effected within an organization.
  For example, the Bank of Japan (BOJ) has developed a database that includes the financial statements of financial institutions, and which is shared with the Financial Services Agency (established July 2000, following reorganization of the Financial Supervisory Agency). This example shows that among the common production

factors used in prudential policy, there are those that can be leased based on a long-term contract even though they cannot be traded in the market. Therefore, organizational integration is unnecessary to exploit economies of scope for such common production factors.

- **Technical know-how**:
  It is difficult to trade technical know-how in the market compared to physical assets. In a case where technical know-how is relatively easy to transfer, it can be leased like physical assets. When a transfer is extremely difficult and transaction cost accompanying contract negotiations is high, horizontal integration is effected in an organization.

  Technical know-how concerning micro prudential policy is tacit knowledge that is accumulated as a human resource through learning-by-doing. Similarly, technical know-how for macro prudential policy is also tacit knowledge that is developed and accumulated as a human resource and, therefore, is basically difficult to trade in the market or lease based on a long-term contract (although seconding staff can be arranged).

  As a result, macro and micro prudential policy bodies need to be integrated to utilize the economies of scope provided by common production factors.

- **Organizational know-how**:
  Organizational know-how is either embedded in the organization as a legal system or accumulated as tacit knowledge held by staff. In this case, heavy transaction costs would be incurred if it were traded or lent. Therefore, for organizational know-how, the only way to enjoy economies of scope is to integrate horizontally within an organization. Organizational know-how of a central bank includes (a) behavior pattern as a public organization, (b) independence, (c) organizational culture, and (d) ability to provide credit.

  Important organizational know-how regarding prudential policy includes independence given to a central bank and also the authority to approve/license given to regulatory and supervisory authorities. These assets are common production factors of macro and micro prudential policy bodies, but are legally given to a specific organization and are impossible to trade or lease under a long-term contract.

  Therefore, such assets should either be given to both macro and micro prudential policy bodies through reform of the legal framework (in this case the asset will not be a common production factor), or the specific organization that holds such assets needs to conduct both macro and micro prudential policy (that is, organizational integration) to enjoy the benefits of economies of scope.

- **Brand name**:
  If brand name is sold in the market, there is a risk that the buyer may provide goods and services of poor quality that do not come up to expectations that the brand name itself formerly elicited. It should at least be franchised, and even if this cannot maintain brand value, it should be horizontally integrated within an organization.

  Brand name attaching to a prudential policy entity can be regarded as credibility and trust enjoyed by bodies such as the central bank and government agencies. Both a central bank and government agencies are public organizations and, in this sense, there is not much difference in the level of credibility and trust. However, in terms of political independence, a central bank is more independent than government agencies (see Chap. 3).

Therefore, in order to use the independence from political interference held by a central bank as a common production factor for prudential policy, we need to integrate both macro and micro prudential policies at a central bank in order to pursue economies of scope.

5.3.2   Integration of Supervisors of Multiple Financial Industries

As mentioned under Sect. 5.2.2.1, the integration of prudential policy bodies includes, besides the integration of macro and micro prudential policies, the issue of whether multiple financial industries such as banks, securities companies, and insurance companies should be supervised by an integrated supervisory entity. Moreover, this question also entails response to the conglomeration of financial institutions and also the fact that financial markets are witnessing strengthening interdependence among various financial industries. The issues are respectively considered in the following discussion. Then, regarding overall integration (complete integration) where the aspect of macro and micro integration as well as integration of the supervisory authorities for multiple industries are both integrated, we point out that there is a downside, that is, an increase in bureaucracy cost accompanying the expansion of organization. In response to this disadvantage, we take up the twin-peaks model as well as a check and balance made possible by having an overlapping supervisory structure.

5.3.2.1   Supervisory Structure in Response to Conglomeration

When we theoretically consider a supervisory structure to accommodate the conglomeration of financial industries, we can apply theories used in the integration of macro and micro prudential policy bodies. The relationships between the holding company and affiliated financial institutions such as banks and securities companies can be grasped as macro and micro relationships within one financial group. Therefore, as shown in Fig. 5.4, the fact that the supervisor for a holding company and those for banks, securities companies, and insurance companies are all different is similar to the framework of macro and micro prudential bodies which are also different.

Looking at this issue from knowledge partitioning theory applied to the macro-micro integration issue, a holding company is the architectural product, and the affiliate financial institutions are its components. Or, the group as a whole is the product and a holding company and affiliate financial institutions are the components. In any case, to have different entities supervise a holding company and affiliate financial institutions is equivalent to developing a product without any knowledge of its components. And, from field management theory, it means supervising a holding company or group as a whole without conducting on-site examination of affiliate financial institutions. Like in the case of Northern Rock Bank, when we segregate macro and micro prudential policy bodies under such a supervisory structure as above it is difficult to identify and control risks attaching to conglomerates. Therefore, supervisory bodies should be integrated in response to the conglomeration of financial institutions.

5.3.2.2   Full Integration of Supervisors of Various Financial Industries

Putting aside the supervisory issue of financial groups such as conglomerates, here we theoretically examine the integration of supervisory bodies for various financial industries that are seeing strengthening interdependence in the financial markets. Mainly vertical integration theory and horizontal integration theory from TCE are applied. In addition, bureaucracy cost and economies of specialization are also looked into to clarify that while it is necessary to integrate prudential policy bodies, a full integration mode that concentrates supervisory authority on a single entity is problematic.

Interdependence and Vertical Integration Theory
As mentioned in Sect. 5.2.2.1, the financial markets are witnessing increasing interdependence among financial institutions from different financial industries. As a consequence, the business condition of any particular financial institution affects other financial institutions that have different supervisors. Therefore, the integration of supervisors is under discussion. Moreover, in relation to a central bank's LLR function, requests to act as LLR from financial institutions such as securities companies (investment banks) and insurance companies that are usually not subject to central bank supervision, have increased (discussed in Sect. 5.4 under role of a central bank). The main question is whether the supervisor (i.e., a central bank) can obtain (or share) necessary information from other supervisors. Interdependence among financial institutions can be seen as interdependence among supervisors concerning information sharing. And so, if necessary information is adequately provided under an MOU between supervisors, then organizational integration is unnecessary. If not, supervisors need to be integrated. Therefore, similar to the integration of macro and micro prudential policy bodies discussed in Sect. 5.3.1, the vertical integration theory of TCE can be applied. The integrated supervision of different financial industries thus boils down to the make-or-buy decision regarding necessary information held among the supervisory bodies and can be regarded as a question of the effectiveness of an MOU. Hence, we can theoretically analyze whether an MOU would suffice or whether organizational integration is necessary taking into account the nature of interdependence among supervisors.

Next, interdependence among supervisory bodies is discussed based on Chap. 4, Table 4.1. If two financial industries are on equal terms, interdependence among supervisory bodies is also equal suggesting that interdependence is high for both sides. Supervisors of these financial industries are both public organizations and hence uncertainty would be low. Therefore, an MOU is sufficient for obtaining necessary information (integration is unnecessary, necessary information is bought). Here, the fact that financial industries are on equal terms means that: (a) a specific financial industry is not particularly important for the financial system or for the national economy or (b) a specific financial industry is not unilaterally affected by another financial industry.

However, if interdependence between two industries is not equal, interdependence between supervisors is also not equal and the situation would be 'high on one side and low on the other.' In this case, an MOU is insufficient and organizational integration is a requisite (necessary information is made). In actuality, the supervisor of banks is not on equal terms with other industries' supervisors. The former is unilaterally dependent on supervisors of other industries (related to the role of a central bank in Sect. 5.4.2.1). Banks are the core of a monetary system and of paramount importance for the financial system and national economy. In addition, banks, as liquidity providers, are unilaterally affected by financial institutions from other industries. From this perspective, in order for a supervisor of banks to gain necessary information, an MOU is not effective and therefore supervisors of other financial industries need to be integrated with the supervisor of banks.

Application of Horizontal Integration Theory
Horizontal integration is applied to the integration of supervisors of various financial industries and four important aspects of common production factors are studied as in Chap. 4, Sect. 4.3.1.2.

Indivisible Tangible Assets
Indivisible tangible assets include a database of financial institutions. While trading is not an option, such tangible assets can be co-constructed among various supervisors based on an MOU or a supervisor that constructed a database could lease it to other supervisors. In this case, organizational integration is not necessary. For example, the financial database that the BOJ constructed and shares with the Financial Services Agency is limited to banks (including *shinkin* credit unions) but it would be possible to include securities companies, insurance companies, and, moreover, non-banks.

Technical Know-How
Each financial industry has unique technical know-how regarding regulation and supervision (Sect. 5.3.2.3) specific to itself, but, at the same time, being itself comprised of financial institutions, shares some common know-how. Such common know-how is likely to provide economies of scope across industries as a common production factor. The know-how is developed and accumulated in the form of human resources and, while seconding staff is possible, it basically cannot be traded or leased under a long-term contract.

Organizational Know-How
Organizational know-how is already legally embedded in the supervisory body and is difficult to transfer by entering into a long-term contract. This common know-how

can be embedded in all supervisory bodies by legal reform, but such is not a realistic option. Therefore, if know-how required by supervisors across various financial industries is important (e.g., regulation and supervision from a macro prudential policy perspective), supervisors need to be integrated.

Brand Name
This is credibility of, and trust in an organization which is difficult to transfer via a long-term leasing contract. For example, if supervisors of various industries require political independence, they need to be integrated in a central bank that has such independence.

5.3.2.3 Disadvantages of Full Integration and Measures to Overcome Them

As analyzed in Sects. 5.3.1 and 5.3.2, the integration of macro and micro aspects as well as of various industries has respective advantages and so integration in each aspect is desirable. However, there are negative sides to fully integrating both aspects in a single body, such as expansion of organization and the concentration of power. To mitigate this, measures such as adopting the twin-peaks model and an overlapping prudential policy framework become necessary.

Disadvantages of Full Integration
Generally recognized disadvantages that accompany the expansion of organization and scope of business may also hold true for a fully integrated prudential framework where prudential policy bodies are integrated from macro and micro aspects as well as across various financial industries. Examples are as follows:

Increase in Bureaucracy Cost
TCE holds that organizational integration is likely to increase bureaucracy cost (transaction cost of internal organization).

Loss of Economies of Specialization
Historically since Adam Smith, it has been pointed out that economies of specialization are likely to be lost through the integration of policy bodies. The degree of loss is considered to be larger for the integration of bodies across multiple financial industries than the integration of macro and micro policy bodies. This is because the former requires more concrete and specific knowledge of each industry than the latter. For example, if the supervisor for banking is to supervise insurance companies and non-bank financial institutions, the disadvantages may surface more visibly.

Conflict of Organizational Culture
Respective macro and micro prudential policy bodies as well as supervisory bodies for various financial industries have different organizational cultures (organizational culture was taken up in Chap. 4, Sect. 4.5). For example, a different organizational culture attaches to 'prudential supervisor' and 'business conduct supervisor.' Hence, when integrating organizations with different cultures, conflicts may arise, making internal coordination difficult and eliminating beneficial organizational culture.

Having said this, in the case of integrating macro and micro prudential bodies, the fusion of organizational culture may bring advantages to both policy bodies. The mix of organizational culture may give the micro prudential policy body an opportunity to acquire macro viewpoints and the macro prudential policy body the opportunity to emphasize micro viewpoints.

Concentration of Power
As pointed out in Sect. 5.2.2.1, full integration in a single organization poses the question of the concentration of power. Economically speaking, this issue is related to above mentioned "*Increase in Bureaucracy Cost*" and "*Loss of Economies of Specialization,*" but at the same time it has the disadvantage of losing the check and balance system of democracy from a political perspective.

Measures to Overcome Disadvantages
Measures to overcome the disadvantages of the above integration of policy bodies are the twin-peaks model and an overlapping supervisory structure.

Twin-Peaks Model
The twin-peaks model as mentioned in Sect. 5.2.2.1 does not separate macro and micro prudential policy but divides micro prudential policy into two, creating a separate policy body for micro prudential policy in charge of depositor/investor protection that is not so directly connected to maintenance of financial system stability. From the perspective of TCE, this ownership structure of prudential policy suppresses an increase in bureaucracy cost and can utilize interdependence between macro and micro prudential policy as well as share common production factors.

Moreover, another type of twin-peaks model can be considered. In line with how framework design and policy implementation were separated when prudential policy was categorized in Sect. 5.2.1, the organization in charge of framework design forms one peak. And, in line with how regulation is separated from supervision, the entity in charge of regulation is added to it. This is because framework design is similar to regulation—they are neither urgent nor discrete risk control, but rather risk control measures that are conducted from a basic standpoint after risk is identified. Therefore, they are prudential policy that can be, compared to risk identification, relatively distant from micro prudential policy. Considering from a viewpoint that places importance on on-site examination, when we differentiate regulation and supervision, as long as there is supervisory power, especially power to examine on-site, risk identification, the main objective of prudential policy, can be achieved even without regulatory power. The objective of regulation is not really to identify new risk in the field like on-site examination.

Having said this, the prudential policy body needs to have explicit authority to enforce a business improvement order on individual financial institutions with a view to reducing and eliminating risks that are found in the process of risk identification at the risk control stage (policy implementation). Regardless of whether this authority should be included in supervisory power or regulatory power (hereafter the authority is considered to be included in supervisory power), it is a requisite authority for the prudential supervisor in the twin-peaks model.

In relation to the role of a central bank in Sect. 5.4 of this chapter, reflecting the nature of a central bank, the following twin-peaks model is considered appropriate. That is, the central bank should take responsibility as prudential supervisor while the other organization takes the role of business conduct supervisor responsible for framework design and regulation.

Check and Balance Through Overlapping Framework
Another countermeasure to overcome the disadvantages of integrating policy bodies is an overlapping framework of policy bodies. This framework is adopted in the US and Japan. In Japan, banks and securities companies are supervised by both the Financial Services Agency and the BOJ. In the US, large national banks with a bank holding company are supervised by both the Office of the Comptroller of the Currency (OCC) and Federal Reserve System (FRS). And, since 2010, under a new system, all large financial institutions (including large investment banks <securities companies> and insurance companies) are additionally supervised by their respective supervisory bodies (by industry) as well as the FRS, creating a stronger overlapping supervisory framework.

5.3.3 Issue of Overlapping Supervisors

As mentioned in Sect. 5.2.2.1, integrating the supervisory bodies of various financial industries carries the risk of accompanying side effects. For example, other related policy bodies that are excluded may not be able to obtain necessary information and power may become concentrated in the integrated body. To cope with these side effects, we have the twin-peaks model and overlapping supervisory framework of policy bodies. The latter is actually adopted in Japan and the US. However, there is heated discussion regarding its effectiveness. Here, the 'regulators separation theory' is useful to consider this issue. Below we give a summary and main ideas which are then applied to prudential policy.

5.3.3.1 Regulators Separation Theory

The regulators separation theory belongs to agency theory (especially contract theory or incentive theory[6]) based on the model by Laffont and Martimort (2002), and developed by Ito (2002, 2003). It basically means that multiple regulators are involved in a financial industry and embraces issues such as "in considering regulation and supervision for the electric power industry...should the regulator responsible for pricing policy be separated from the regulator responsible for environmental pollution

---

[6]Contract theory or incentive theory focuses on contractual arrangements in various systems and organizations, and, based on formal micro economics, considers incentive issues arising from asymmetric information.

control or should they be integrated as a regulator responsible for the electric power industry?" (Ito, 2002, translated from Japanese).

Outline of Regulators Separation Theory

The basic framework of the theory in line with Ito (ibid) is that first, under the principal-agent relationship, the agent is considered not to behave as set forth in the contract with the principal due to asymmetric information and opportunistic behavior. To prevent this, a proper incentive design for the agent is necessary.

Second, the principal-agent relationship among the public, regulator, and regulated firm is considered two-tiered as shown in Fig. 5.10. In this regard, the regulator is considered an intermediary which acts as agent to the public (the legislature) that is the principal, and becomes the principal in relation to the regulated firm. Therefore, incentive design under this framework needs to consider the following two (incentive) problems.

Incentive Problem Between Regulator and Regulated Firm

The regulator shirks the task of providing the regulated firm a sufficient incentive for managerial efforts when designing its regulatory structure.

Incentive Problem Between the Public (the Legislature) and the Regulator

The regulator's purpose of regulation and supervision deviates from the maximization of social welfare. For example, the regulator succumbs to political pressure and effects regulation that does not pursue the maximization of social welfare.

Advantages of Regulator Separation

The formal model analysis based on the above framework clarified that the separation of regulator has both pros and cons. The analysis pointed out the following pros for

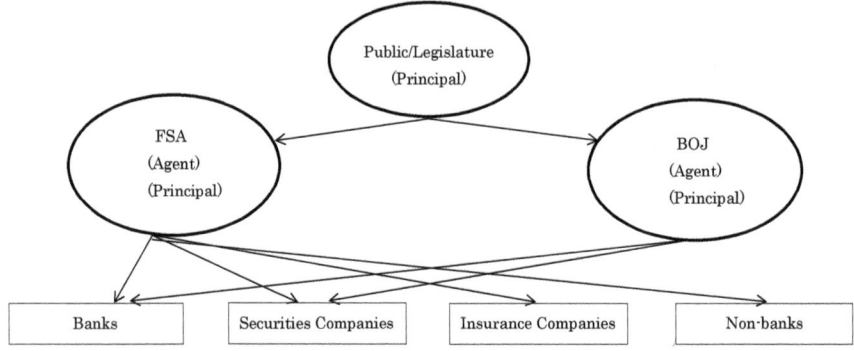

Fig. 5.10 Principal-agent relationship of prudential policy

the respective incentive problems listed above.

Solution to the Incentive Problem in the Relationship Between Regulators and Regulated Companies

- **Competition effect**:
  Regulators compete with each other to have regulated companies endeavor to comply with the regulation that they are responsible for. As a result, an incentive to make managerial efforts on the part of regulated companies may strengthen through competition among separate regulators.
- **Mutual check and balance effect**:
  When regulators are separated and each independently regulates the same company, they tend to strive harder so as not to be found wanting (by the other, which in a way is essentially a competitor) in their respective jobs. Therefore, as a result of such intensive scrutiny by two bodies a separated regulator system forces, so to speak, a greater imperative regarding managerial efforts on the part of the regulated company than would a single regulator. This can be seen as a check and balance effect stemming from there being separate regulators.[7]
- **Collusion prevention effect**:
  Regulators have an incentive to shirk collecting information on the regulated company and the company has an incentive to avoid providing accurate information. Therefore, in the case of a single regulator, there is risk of collusion between the two parties. However, competition as well as a check and balance among separate regulators have the effect of preventing such collusion between regulators and companies.

Solution to the Incentive Problem in the Relationship Between Regulators and the Public (the Legislature)

- **Benchmarking of regulatory performance**:
  The separation of regulators enables a comparison of each regulator's performance (benchmarking) and can provide them with an incentive to achieve their primary objectives.
- **Clarification of objective**:
  The separation of regulators reduces the scope of each regulator's duties which contributes to clarifying the objective. Therefore, quality of the incentive design also improves.
- **Solution of deadlock problem**:
  While each regulator has an incentive to select a status quo policy (the so-called deadlock problem), in facing contradictory information provided by another regulator, there is a possibility that they may have to rethink such policy.

---

[7]Tirole (1994) applied agency theory to the government sector and showed that the existence of checks and balances among government agencies provides society with more information.

Disadvantages of Regulator Separation
Above are advantages of regulator separation but the following disadvantages can also be pointed out. All disadvantages are found not in the relationship between regulators and regulated companies, but in the incentive problem between the public (the legislature) and regulators.

Imperfect Coordination Among Separated Regulators
In a separated regulator system, decision-making is made independently or under imperfect coordination and may likely be inefficient compared to a single regulator system.

Segmentation of Information
In a separated regulator system, incentive on the part of regulators to pay attention to information outside their own jurisdiction may be less strong, and information sharing among regulators can become difficult.

Localization of Purpose and Mission
Separated regulators are likely to pursue only their purpose and mission.

Situations When Advantages Would Exceed the Disadvantages
The separation of regulators has both pros and cons as discussed above, and, for pros to exceed cons, the following two situations (which are related to the severity of the incentive problems mentioned above) need to be the case:

The Regulatory Structure Designed by the Regulator is Seriously Inefficient
The regulator becomes too generous toward the regulated company and does not urge it to make sufficient managerial efforts.

The Regulator Itself Has a Serious Incentive Problem
This is because the objective of a single regulator is largely deviating from the maximization of social welfare. This means that the single regulator is not responding to a mandate from the public (the legislature) as principal. For example, perversion of the regulatory objective due to political pressure.

5.3.3.2 Application of Regulator Separation Theory

Regulator separation theory is, as evident from explanation in Sect. 5.3.3.1, adequate for discussing the overlapping of supervisors in prudential policy.[8] For example, the advantages and disadvantages of regulator separation correspond to the advantages and disadvantages of multiple regulators and supervisors supervising a specific financial institution. Let us again apply regulator separation theory to various issues of prudential policy.

---

[8]With regard to the application of the regulator separation theory to the integration of the prudential policy bodies of various industries, the same disadvantages exist, but not the advantages as the policy bodies for respective industries do not compete nor check one another like overlapping policy bodies do.

Reason Behind Why There Are Not Many Examples of Overlapping Supervisors

In the case of regulator separation in prudential policy (overlapping regulators and supervisors), when we consider whether the situation in various countries fulfills conditions for advantages to exceed disadvantages, it is extremely difficult to evaluate.[9] Therefore, there are no countries that clearly adopt regulator separation besides Japan and the US (Of course, simple accidents of history and/or politics may also play a part).

Political Pressure

Perversion of the regulatory objective due to political pressure has extremely high realistic validity considering the actual situation and possibility of perversion. Therefore, when supervisors are not overlapping and are integrated, there is a risk that the regulatory objective greatly deviates from maximizing social welfare.

Concentration of Power

Along with the twin-peaks model, having multiple regulators and supervisors is an effective measure to achieve a check and balance against the concentration of power arising from the integration of macro and micro prudential bodies and that of the policy bodies of various financial industries.

Preventing Collusion

There is a possibility that the regulator may act in collusion with regulated financial institutions even in prudential policy. For example, Goodhart and Schoenmaker (1993, p. 340) states as follows:

> Moreover, the regulatory authorities' concern with the 'health' of the banking system is only in some part due to the natural affinity ('capture') that may grow up between the regulated and the regulators.

Cost of Regulation and Supervision

Private financial institutions complain that overlapping supervision/examination increases cost. However, regulator separation theory does not deal with costs at all. This is because overlapping supervision/examination does not necessarily mean that costs multiply. By creating a ceiling on overall costs and have regulators coordinate cost sharing accordingly among them, a regulated organization may not have to shoulder any additional costs.

Even so, private financial institutions may still view costs stemming from there being overlapping regulators to be a problem. Assessing the situation, we can say that while separation and the overlapping of regulators have the advantage of increasing social welfare through competition and a check and balance effect as clarified in

---

[9]It is hard to quantitatively measure the costs and benefits of the regulation of government agencies. Tirole (1994) developed a model for the internal organization of government based on the premise that government agencies have a specificity of not having a measureable goal like a firm does in pursuing profit maximization.

regulator separation theory, private financial institutions see it as an unfavorable regulatory and supervisory structure since they are asked to adhere to strict managerial prudence.

5.4 Theoretical Analysis of a Central Bank's Role in Prudential Policy

Looking at the ownership of prudential policy, this section discusses a central bank's role based on economic theory. There are two aspects: conflict of interest between prudential policy and monetary policy, and purpose and rationale of central bank involvement in prudential policy. Each aspect is theoretically analyzed and any implication obtained given.

5.4.1 Theoretical Analysis of Conflict of Interest

As mentioned in Sect. 5.2.2.2, when a central bank becomes involved in prudential policy, conflict of interest may arise with monetary policy. Whether conflict of interest really exists between prudential policy and monetary policy is discussed based on agency theory below.

5.4.1.1 Distinction Between Conflict of Interest and Trade-off

Generally, agency theory is applied to theoretically approach conflict of interest. For example, Boatright (1992) says that the criterion for distinguishing between "narrow-sense conflict of interest" and "broad-sense conflict of interest" is whether two bodies have a principal-agent relationship or not and argues the importance of making such differentiation. According to Boatright, "narrow-sense conflict of interest" is, for example, a case where a counsel defends both plaintiff and defendant as shown in Fig. 5.11(a). That is, when a person (including a company) becomes an agent for multiple principals with conflict of interest. In this case, serious problems arise both morally and legally, undermining economic efficiency. On the other hand, "broad-sense conflict of interest" simply means conflict of interest or differing objectives, and is a generally used term. As shown in Fig. 5.11(b), this problem arises when an agent undertakes multiple tasks from a single principal. This is simply a case where trade-off exists among the multiple tasks and does not incur any problem either morally or legally and is not necessarily economically inefficient.

"Broad-sense conflict of interest" is analyzed in detail in multitask agency theory by Holmstrom and Milgrom (1991, 1994) and others (see Chap. 4, Sect. 4.4). Based on a formal model analysis, they analyzed the case where it would be adequate to

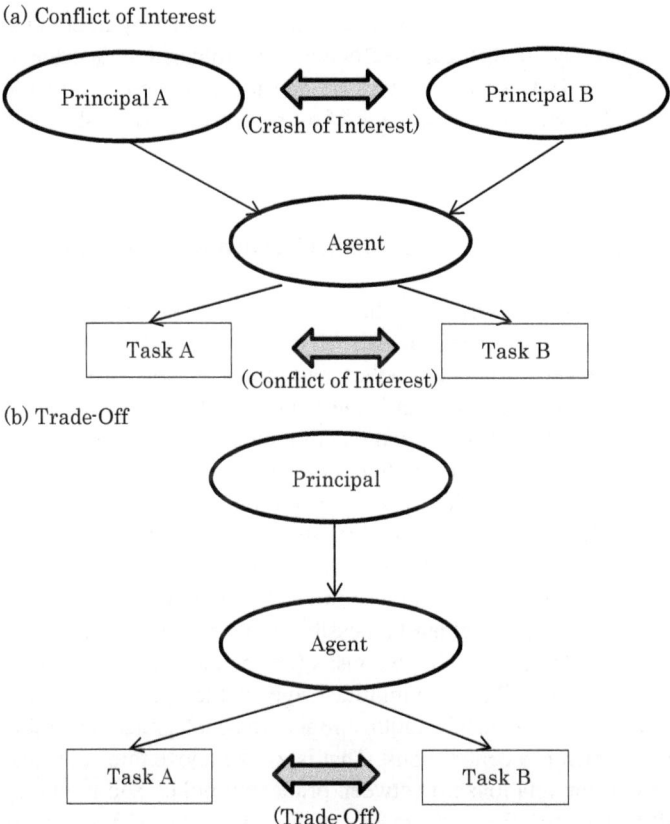

(a) Conflict of Interest

Principal A   (Crash of Interest)   Principal B

Agent

Task A   (Conflict of Interest)   Task B

(b) Trade-Off

Principal

Agent

Task A   (Trade-Off)   Task B

Fig. 5.11 Conflict of interest and trade-off

have a single agent take charge of multiple tasks and came to the following three conclusions:

- The more difficult it is to measure performance of productive activity, the greater the possibility of adopting integration.
- The more the value of assets fluctuates, the greater the possibility of adopting integration.
- The more important the activity for which it is difficult to design an incentive scheme, the greater the possibility of adopting integration.

It is both impossible and improper to internalize two tasks that are in a "narrow-sense conflict of interest" relationship into a single organization. However, on the other hand, it is possible and proper to internalize two tasks in a "broad-sense conflict of interest" relationship (trade-off relationship) into a single organization. Since one of the two tasks in a trade-off relationship can be considered to provide external diseconomy to the other, by internalizing both, external diseconomy can also be internalized, making efficient pricing possible. This implies that by internalizing tasks in a trade-off relationship, they can be efficiently coordinated in the same organization. And, based on TCE, such two tasks are considered to be in an interdependent relationship and transaction costs can therefore be saved by internalizing them into a single organization.

5.4.1.2   Distinguishing Conflict of Interest Related to a Central Bank

Based on Boatright's distinction, conflict of interest concerning central bank prudential policy cannot be regarded as "narrow-sense conflict of interest." Looking at the relationship between prudential policy and monetary policy, the principal that the central bank should obey as agent is the same in both policies as in Fig. 5.11(b) and the interest of prudential policy and that of monetary policy do not conflict. The principal of prudential policy is the public (or its representative, the legislative body) that uses the financial system. The principal of monetary policy is also the public (or its representative, the legislative body). Since the principal for both policies is the public (the legislative body), "narrow-sense conflict of interest" does not exist between central bank prudential policy and monetary policy.

On the other hand, there is at least a possibility of "broad-sense conflict of interest" that is a trade-off between the two tasks (i.e., prudential policy and monetary policy) as in Fig. 5.11(b). Based on multitask agency theory, such two policies in a "broad-sense conflict of interest" relationship should be integrated into a single agent (organization), which is a central bank. That is, of the above three conclusions, the first two apply to the relationship between prudential policy and monetary policy. It is difficult to measure the performance of the two policies' productive activity and also difficult to design an incentive scheme for them. Therefore, it will be more efficient to integrate both policies in a central bank and any trade-off can be solved through internalization.

With regard to internalizing prudential policy and monetary policy at a central bank, Wall and Eisenbeis (2000) clarified, based on agency theory, that trade-off can be more efficiently solved by having an integrated regulator and supervisor internalize conflict between different regulators and supervisors (see Sect. 5.4.2 for analysis based on TCE). Goodhart and Schoenmaker (1993, p. 343) also state the efficient solution of conflict through internalization as follows:

> It is, at least, possible to argue that where such conflicts really become important in an open, competitive, market-driven system, they (prudential policy and monetary policy <added by Oritani>) have, in order to obtain an efficient resolution, to be internalised within a single authority. Indeed, when there is separation, conflicts can occur not only because of differences of objectives, of information sets, or of preferences, but also as a result of simple administrative complications (a cock-up).

5.4.2 Purpose and Rationale Behind Central Bank Involvement in Prudential Policy

We have previously mentioned that there is discussion as to why a central bank should be involved in prudential policy and what superiority a central bank has in conducting prudential policy compared to other organizations. Vertical integration theory and horizontal integration theory from TCE are applied to this question in this section.

5.4.2.1 Application of Vertical Integration Theory

Vertical integration theory from TCE is used to discuss the purpose and rationale behind central bank involvement in prudential policy and, consequently, its significance. According to this theory as shown in Chap. 4, Table 4.1, the degree of interdependent relationship between providers of goods and services and trading counterparts determines the transaction cost of an MOU between the two sides and that of organizational integration. And, a governance mechanism with lesser transaction cost is adopted. In the section below, we clarify the purpose and rationale behind central bank involvement by comparing to what extent regulators and supervisors with differing objectives in prudential policy can reduce the transaction cost of information between transactions based on an MOU and organizational integration.

Additionally, discussion of central bank involvement has two aspects: one is the interdependent relationship between prudential policy and other central bank functions (such as monetary policy and payment function), and the other is the interdependent relationship within prudential policy. Both aspects are analyzed in sequence.

Interdependence Between Prudential Policy and Other Central Bank Functions (Monetary Policy, Payment Systems)
Interdependent relationships between prudential policy and other central bank functions can be seen in Fig. 5.12. Based on this figure, interdependence between prudential policy and monetary policy (see Chap. 4, Sect. 4.3.4) and that between prudential policy and payment system function are discussed separately, comparing transaction cost of an MOU and that of organizational integration.

First, macro prudential policy depends on monetary policy for information regarding the macroeconomic situation as well as how monetary policy influences the financial system. And, micro prudential policy depends on monetary policy for information regarding how monetary policy impacts the business conditions of individual financial institutions. On the other hand, monetary policy depends on macro prudential policy for useful information in deciding monetary policy, and micro prudential policy for information on individual financial institutions.

Second, looking at interdependence between prudential policy and market operations which is the implementation instrument of monetary policy (see Chap. 4, Sect. 4.3.4), macro prudential policy depends on the market operation body for information on degree of market stress. And, micro prudential policy depends on the

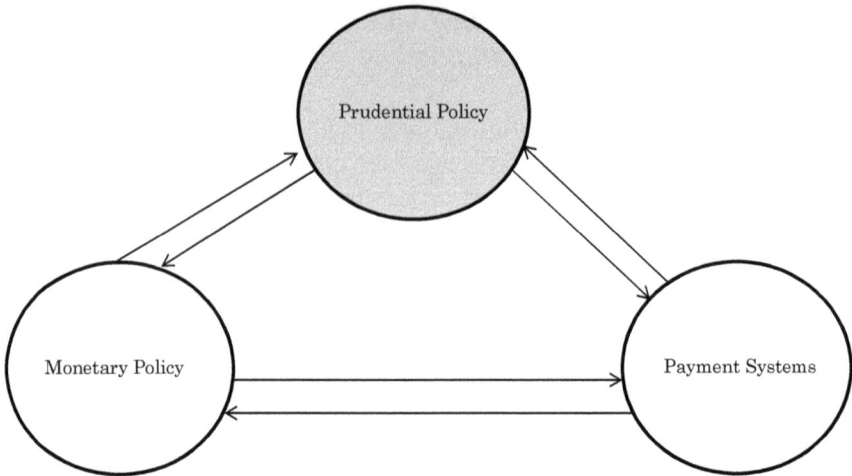

Fig. 5.12 Interdependent relationships between prudential policy and other central bank functions

market operation body for information regarding the behavior of individual financial institutions that the market operation body obtained through market transactions. Also, micro prudential policy relies on the market operation body for information about other financial institutions that are not transaction counterparts but which was nevertheless obtained through market transactions (peer monitoring). On the other hand, market operations depend on macro prudential policy for information regarding how the policy affects financial markets and on micro prudential policy for any useful information to select counterparts for market operations.

Third, with regard to the interdependent relationship between prudential policy and payment function, macro prudential policy depends on the payment function for information on how payment system integrity influences the financial system and also for information obtained through payment system oversight (see Chap. 7, Sect. 7.4.1). And, micro prudential policy depends on the payment system function for information on individual financial institutions obtained through operating payment systems. On the other hand, the payment system depends on macro prudential policy for information on how stability of the financial system influences payment systems. A payment system depends on micro prudential policy for information on payment system members obtained through supervision, which contributes to their screening and determining liquidity provision to members (see Chap. 7, Sect. 7.4.1).

Looking at the interdependence between prudential policy and monetary policy/payment system function based on Chap. 4, Table 4.1, it is "high for both sides." In this case, if uncertainty relating to a transaction including its complexity is low, it is possible to have a governance mechanism that utilizes an MOU to save transaction costs.

So, if we turn our attention to the uncertainty of transactions between a prudential policy body and monetary policy body, uncertainty such as insolvency is low since both are public organizations. However, the content of the transaction is extremely complex covering information necessary for prudential policy, monetary policy, and payment systems, and, in this respect, uncertainty is high. Therefore, an MOU between the two bodies does not function effectively and organizational integration is necessary. Another issue with an MOU is that if one side does not recognize that interdependence is high, an MOU does not function effectively. For example, until market-type systemic risk was brought to the forefront in light of the global financial crisis of 2007–09, macro prudential bodies did not adequately recognize that financial and economic business conditions as well as market information obtained through market operations were important for micro prudential policy bodies.

Interdependence Within Prudential Policy
The objective and rationale behind central bank involvement in prudential policy need to be discussed from the aspect of interdependence within prudential policy in addition to interdependent relationships between prudential policy and other central bank functions. Among interdependent relationships within prudential policy, a general case (not limited to central bank involvement) of integrating macro and micro prudential policy bodies was discussed in detail in Sect. 5.3.1.3 where vertical integration theory was applied. The findings can be applied to the case with central bank involvement without making any adjustment. However, it should be noted that in addition to macro and micro interdependent relationships, interdependence between LLR and prudential policy exists within prudential policy. And this relationship is precisely the most relevant reason and objective for central bank involvement in prudential policy.

The fact that a central bank makes a decision to provide liquidity to a certain financial institution in case of emergency based on micro information obtained through supervision and examination shows that micro information (upstream) and liquidity provision (downstream) are in a vertical chain relationship (Fig. 5.13) according to vertical integration theory (see Chap. 4, Sect. 4.3.4). This relationship is an interdependent relationship where the responsible body for LLR (central bank) is unilaterally dependent on supervision and examination as in Chap. 4, Table 4.1. In this case, an MOU between the LLR body (central bank) and supervisory and examining body is insufficient as a governance mechanism and organizational integration is necessary. In other words, an integrated entity (central bank) should conduct supervision and examination to collect necessary information on the business conditions of individual financial institutions and determine whether to make liquidity provision in time of emergency.

An MOU is insufficient in this case because the supervisory and examining body that is independent from a central bank may not make effort to obtain information that a central bank needs for determining whether or not to provide liquidity. Moreover, even if the body does have sufficient information, it may not provide the information to a central bank due to opportunistic behavior. The conclusion drawn from vertical integration theory is that it is difficult to come up with an MOU that prevents these risks.

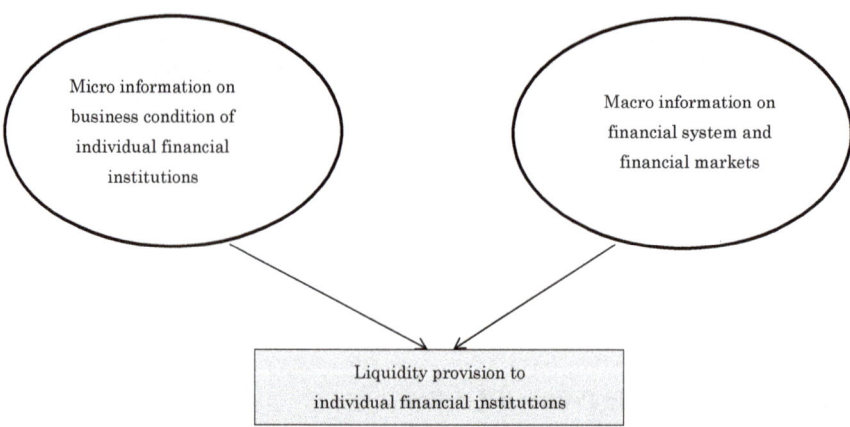

Fig. 5.13 Interdependence within prudential policy (between LLR function and supervision/examination)

And, in line with vertical integration theory, a regulator and supervisor independent from a central bank may not sufficiently understand what sort of information a central bank needs to determine liquidity provision (a bank run such as seen on Northern Rock Bank is highly likely to be the case). Necessary information could be specifically listed in an MOU. However, as apparent from analytical results of TCE, it is not easy to categorically say what would comprise necessary information before a financial institution faces a crisis, and, even if a central bank does succeed in compiling a list of information needed, regulators and supervisors could avoid the issue by interpreting the contract differently (incomplete contracts). And, information regarding the atmosphere of the actual site being examined is difficult to put on paper, which is one of the reasons why an MOU is insufficient.

Meanwhile, a decision to effect liquidity provision to a financial institution is not only based on the business conditions of the financial institution in question, but also takes into consideration the situation in the financial system and overall financial markets (macro information). Therefore, the entity that produces macro information and the entity conducting fund provision are in a vertical chain relationship and so an MOU as a mechanism to govern transactions related to their information provision is insufficient and organizational integration is necessary. In fact, a central bank that conducts liquidity provision as LLR is also an implementation body of monetary policy and therefore it can obtain necessary macro information within the organization as mentioned before.

Moreover, the above discussion on LLR function in the context of liquidity provision to individual financial institutions can also be applied to market liquidity provision in response to recent market-type systemic risk. In this case, as shown in Fig. 5.14, the entity that provides market liquidity and the entity that collects and obtains macro information are in a vertical chain relationship. Therefore, an MOU is insufficient and organizational integration is necessary. Also, since information

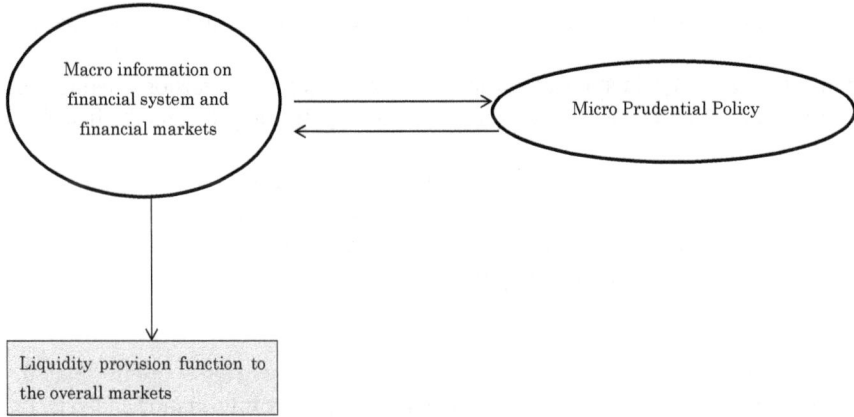

Fig. 5.14 Interdependence between provision function of market liquidity and prudential policy

obtained from micro prudential policy is required for analyzing macro information, if macro and micro prudential policies are integrated in a central bank, the entity that provides market liquidity and the entity that collects and obtains macro information should be integrated in a central bank.

5.4.2.2   Application of Horizontal Integration Theory

Horizontal integration theory that was used in the integration issue of macro and micro prudential policies in Sect. 5.3.1.3 is also applied to the objective and rationale for central bank involvement in prudential policy.

The following considers what common production factors as well as related transaction costs exist between prudential policy and other central bank functions. Similar to the macro and micro integration issue, four types of common production factors are discussed.

Common Production Factors Between Prudential Policy and Other Central Bank Functions (Monetary Policy, Payment Systems)
Similar to the case where vertical integration theory was applied in Sect. 5.4.2.1, common production factors between prudential policy and monetary policy as well as payment systems are respectively discussed.

Between Monetary Policy
Four common production factors and related transaction costs between monetary policy and prudential policy are as follows:

- **Indivisible tangible assets**:
   A database is an indivisible tangible asset between prudential policy and monetary policy (including market operations). An information database covering individual financial institutions as well as financial system that was constructed for prudential

policy can be used to make decisions on monetary policy and conduct market operations.

On the other hand, a database constructed for monetary policy decision-making and market operations can also be used for prudential policy to ascertain the financial system situation.

Such a common production factor can technically be leased based on an MOU similar to the database for macro and micro prudential policy in Sect. 5.3.1.3. However, information concerning monetary policy is highly confidential and so in fact it is difficult to lease. The only way to gain economies of scope is by utilizing common production factors through organizational integration.

- **Technical know-how**:

Prudential policy and monetary policy are interdependent in terms of information. This implies that they have common know-how regarding information analysis. In particular, common analytical ability with respect to the macroeconomy is required and accumulated via macro prudential policy and monetary policy.

And, to counter recent market-type systemic risk, technical know-how obtained by trading in financial markets for the purpose of market operations is becoming all the more important. That is, in the risk identification phase pertaining to the financial system and financial markets, the central bank's analytical know-how obtained through market transactions is becoming important. Additionally, in the risk finance phase, since a central bank is involved in market activity on a daily basis, it can make a transition smoothly from normalcy to crisis and provide liquidity to individual financial institutions or the overall financial market concerned. This common production factor can partly be leased on a long-term basis through seconding central bank staff, but basically it can only be utilized through organizational integration.

- **Organizational know-how**:

The most important common production factor between prudential policy and monetary policy is central bank independence, which is organizational know-how granted to monetary policy. Independence of monetary policy from politics is already institutionally established but independence of prudential policy is not completely so, although its importance has recently been emphasized.

Organizational know-how is something that is legally granted to a certain organization and is impossible to be leased under a long-term contract. Therefore, if we are to grant political independence to prudential policy, we could either utilize central bank independence as a common production factor, or legally grant political independence to a prudential policy body which would be a separate organization from a central bank.

However, it is constitutionally impossible to grant political independence to a prudential policy body that is established as part of the government's executive branch. Therefore, it is realistic to utilize central bank independence as a common production factor.

- **Brand name**:

Brand name for prudential policy is credibility of, and trust in, the prudential policy body as mentioned under Sect. 5.3.1.3, and the same can be said for monetary policy. Such a common production factor, credibility and trust, is difficult to lease under a long-term contract and can only be utilized through organizational integration.

There is a criticism that central bank involvement in prudential policy through organizational integration may undermine its reputation should it fail in financial crisis management, leading to loss of central bank credibility regarding monetary policy. However, on the other hand, by utilizing the credibility of, and trust in a central bank as a common production factor, it could enhance credibility of, and trust in both prudential policy and monetary policy.

Between Payment Systems

Four types of common production factors between prudential policy and a central bank's payment system function and related transaction costs are as follows:

- **Indivisible tangible assets**:
  A payment system operated by a central bank can obtain useful information for prudential policy such as members' financial conditions through monitoring their payment activities within the system. In this sense, a payment system is an indivisible tangible asset and is a common production factor between prudential policy and a central bank's payment system function.

  It is impossible to lease a payment system operated by a central bank to other prudential policy bodies under a long-term contract. The only way to secure economies of scope through utilizing this common production factor is organizational integration. Having said this, it is technically possible, to a certain extent, to lease only limited information useful for prudential policy gained through payment systems on a long-term contract (MOU). However, as discussed regarding the interdependent relationship between LLR function and supervisory function (Sect. 5.4.2.1), information provision may not necessarily be sufficient. And, in the first place, there is a fundamental question that if a central bank provides information gained through operating payment systems to other organizations, credibility of the payment system, which is an important foundation of credibility, and trust in a central bank, would be lost. This will be mentioned under 'brand name.'

- **Technical know-how**:
  As previously mentioned in Sect. 5.4.2.1, credit extension is a requisite in operating payment systems. While credit extension via the LLR function under prudential policy and that under payment systems are different in terms of objectives and measures, both share common technical know-how in the sense that they are credit extension to a financial institution. And, screening payment system participants means evaluating a financial institution's financial ability and administrative competency which necessitates common technical know-how (that prudential policy has) for evaluating the business conditions of financial institutions.

  This common production factor can be partly leased under a long-term contract through seconding staff, but basically it is difficult to utilize without organizational integration. And, an MOU related to information provision is technically possible, but does not necessarily guarantee sufficient information provision.

- **Organizational know-how**:
  Payment system organizational know-how comprises political independence and neutrality seen in the fair screening of participants, impartial credit extension, and payment system services. Such organizational know-how does not attract attention like that of monetary policy, and is simply basic payment system organizational know-how. Independence and neutrality are considered important in prudential policy and therefore organizational know-how is a significant common production factor. Organizational know-how can only be utilized through organizational integration.
- **Brand name**:
  Trust of the public, corporations, and financial institutions in the payment system function of a central bank, as well as its credibility, are just as important as such given to monetary policy. Therefore, the same argument as regarding the common production factor between monetary policy and prudential policy that stems from 'indivisible tangible assets' can be applied.

Common Production Factors Within Prudential Policy
As for the interdependent relationship between macro and micro prudential policy bodies, a general case was discussed in Sect. 5.3.1 and their common production factors in Sect. 5.3.1.3. The result also applies to the case where a central bank is involved in prudential policy and so this section focuses on common production factors between a central bank's LLR function and prudential policy.

Indivisible Tangible Assets
Various information technology (IT) systems of a central bank that are used for LLR are essential for the practical operation of prudential policy such as provision of fund liquidity and market liquidity. In this sense, these IT systems are indivisible tangible assets, and a common production factor between the LLR function and prudential policy. This is clear from the fact that no organization other than a central bank has any feasible instrument to provide fund liquidity or market liquidity as part of prudential policy implementation.

Technical Know-How
When a central bank provides liquidity to a financial institution as LLR, the decision is made based on micro information concerning the institution's business conditions in addition to macro information as shown in Fig. 5.14. Technical know-how concerned in coming to such a decision is similar to risk identification relating to business conditions carried out during supervision and examination of a financial institution. The only difference is that judgment to effect LLR is made in time of crisis when a problem financial institution faces bankruptcy while judgment on risk identification during supervision and examination is made during normal times. There is no intrinsic difference and therefore technical know-how can be considered a common production factor.

Similar to other technical know-how, this common production factor can partly be leased under a long-term contract in the form of seconding staff but basically can only be utilized through organizational integration. And, an MOU on information provision is technically possible to a certain extent but does not necessarily guarantee sufficient information provision.

Organizational Know-How

Liquidity provision by a central bank under its LLR function to an individual financial institution is especially likely to face pressure from politicians and many such examples have been reported throughout the world. Organizational know-how of a central bank to maintain independence in the face of such pressure can be considered a common production factor considering that independence is important for prudential policy as well.

Similar to central bank independence as organizational know-how, this common production factor can only be utilized by integrating the responsible body for prudential policy and the central bank LLR function.

Brand Name

Brand name related to a central bank's LLR is the credibility and trust a central bank enjoys. This credibility and trust are deeply related to central bank independence in the case of fund provision to individual financial institutions. A central bank has 'neutrality' in the sense that it neither gives preferential treatment nor discriminates against a specific financial institution. And this neutrality is the foundation of the credibility and trust a central bank can enjoy. Without credibility and trust, there is a risk that a central bank cannot effect liquidity provision to financial institutions appropriately due to criticism from the legislature and public. As for the provision of market liquidity, the credibility of, and trust in, a central bank is based on central bank independence as well as correctness of judgment (of course, this is also important for liquidity provision to individual financial institutions). The existence of this credibility and trust influences the effect of the LLR function via market perception. Such credibility and trust are also important for prudential policy and therefore can be considered a common production factor.

Similar to central bank independence as organizational know-how, this common production factor can only be utilized by integrating the responsible body for prudential policy and the central bank LLR function.

5.4.3 Implications for Central Bank Role in Prudential Policy

The results gained from applying vertical and horizontal integration theories have various implications for a central bank's role in prudential policy. This part discusses:

- a central bank's role in light of the relationship between LLR function and prudential policy,
- "piper logic" by Goodhart and Schoenmaker,
- the relationship between the importance of independence in prudential policy and a central bank's role.

5.4.3.1   Central Bank's Role in Light of Relationship Between LLR Function and Prudential Policy

The objective of central bank involvement in prudential policy is to be ready to fulfill the LLR function in time of crisis (financial crisis, bankruptcy of a financial institution) and also to utilize interdependence and the common production factor between monetary policy and prudential policy. At least, it is clear that the supervisory function (including on-site examination function) during normal times is a requisite for a central bank to fulfill its role as LLR in time of crisis. From this perspective we discuss the relationship between the LLR function and enlarging the scope of regulation and supervision to include organizations other than banks, and central bank prudential policy necessary for implementing LLR, based on the above theoretical results.

LLR   Function and Enlarging the Scope of Regulation and Supervision to Include Organizations Other than Banks
During the global financial crisis of 2007–09, central banks of the US and European countries provided liquidity mainly to banks but also to other financial institutions. This shows that in a situation where interdependence among various financial institutions through markets brings about market-type systemic risk, a central bank has no other choice but to provide liquidity to financial institutions other than banks as LLR.

Based on interdependence between the LLR function and other prudential policy, especially supervision and examination discussed in vertical integration theory, as well as economies of scope gained by utilizing a common production factor as in horizontal integration theory, it is a natural logical consequence that the scope of subject industries covered by a central bank's prudential policy should be expanded to include financial industries other than banks along with expanding the scope of subject industries covered by the LLR function. Whether such expansion of subject industries for LLR is the result of the trend toward the conglomeration of financial institutions centering on banks or not, it has the same logical consequence. Therefore, if regulators and supervisors of various industries are to be integrated in one organization, it is desirable that that organization is a central bank.

The reason why central banks had been providing liquidity to mainly banks is that within the two-tiered financial system, banks had the function to provide liquidity to all economic sectors and were in a pivotal position to stabilize a financial system. However, in the current situation where financial institutions other than banks can seriously impact financial stability, a central bank needs to expand its LLR function to include organizations other than banks and hence expand its supervisory function to include them as well.

The reform of supervisory systems in the US and European countries is in line with the above. This reform is implemented to counter market-type systemic risk coupled with consideration of the relationship between a central bank's LLR function and prudential policy. For example, with the euro crisis of 2009–10 as a turning point, the main reason why the authority for managing micro prudential policy (that oversaw systemically important financial institutions and financial institutions in trouble) was transferred to the ECB in December 2012 was because the public expected the ECB to function as LLR in time of crisis.

Central Bank Prudential Policy Necessary to Implement LLR Function

Based on the theoretical results under Sect. 5.4.2.1, if we differentiate regulation and supervision according to the twin-peaks model, a central bank only needs to have supervisory authority over financial institutions to carry out its role as LLR, meaning that it does not necessarily need regulatory authority to act as LLR. As is evident from theoretical consideration, information necessary for LLR is information regarding the business conditions, especially financial conditions, of financial institutions obtained through supervision, and is not information on whether each individual institution is in compliance with regulations. Moreover, design of the basic framework and content of regulation is not directly related to LLR. Common production factors between LLR and a regulatory body are technical know-how and organizational know-how regarding supervision but there is no common production factor that necessitates organizational integration. As long as a central bank can propose that the regulatory body includes necessary regulations, that would suffice.

Moreover, there are no interdependent relationships or common production factors that necessitate organizational integration between the regulatory body and monetary policy. And, while at a glance it seems that an interdependent relationship and common production factor exist between regulation and the payment system function, rules for payment systems are established as rules for peer groups and, since they differ from regulation for financial institutions in nature, they cannot be regarded as an interdependent relationship or common production factor that necessitate organizational integration (see Chap. 7, Sect. 7.4.1). As a result, according to the above theoretical results and based on the twin-peaks model that separates regulator and supervisor, the appropriate ownership of prudential policy is to grant only the supervisory/examining authority to a central bank from the perspective of prudence.

5.4.3.2 "Piper Logic" by Goodhart and Schoenmaker

Goodhart and Schoenmaker (1993) proposed "piper logic" where the provider of funds can have authority over prudential policy, thus, "he who plays the piper, calls the tune."[10] Their piper logic is considered to stretch the meaning of the relationship between LLR and prudential policy. Based on vertical integration and horizontal integration this stretched meaning is misleading for the following reasons.

First, interdependence between the entity which provides a large amount of risk money funded by taxpayers and that of prudential policy is considered relatively weak compared to interdependence between a central bank that provides the LLR function and prudential policy body. The different degree of interdependence reflects

---

[10]Goodhart and Schoenmaker (1993) argue, "Indeed, in view of the question of where the final responsibility will lie for supervision and regulation of the banking system will largely depend on the essentially mundane issue of who pays if, and when, things go wrong."

the urgency of the two fund provisions. Decisions whether to implement the LLR function of a central bank are often triggered by a liquidity shortage at either a troubled financial institution or in a financial market and therefore need to be urgently arrived at. A typical example would be when a liquidity shortage becomes apparent in the payment system. On the other hand, whether to provide a large amount of risk money funded by taxpayers is also an important decision, but its urgency is relatively weak compared to that made in implementing the LLR function. Risk money provision backed by taxpayers is considered a procedure that takes time to hear the opinions of interested parties and to conclude based on a consensus reached by the legislature. This procedure is taken not only because taxpayers' money is injected but also because a decision does not have to be made urgently.[11]

Second, if the fiscal authority of government that provides risk money becomes responsible for micro prudential policy including supervision and examination, there may be disadvantages such as an increase in bureaucracy cost due to organizational expansion and losing benefits gained from specialization. Let me give an analogy. Just because Japan's Ministry of Finance is responsible for making fiscal budget decisions concerning natural disasters, rather than seek assistance from the Ministry of Land, Infrastructure, Transport and Tourism, it itself retains experts on natural disasters, conducts related research and studies, and in time of crisis dispatches personnel to disaster sites and gathers information.

Third, from the perspective of a common production factor in horizontal integration theory, the Ministry of Finance does not share a common production factor with prudential policy. What is worse, being a component of government, it is impossible for the Ministry of Finance to realize political independence required for prudential policy.

Fourth, in accordance with the principle of separation of monetary policy from fiscal policy, it is highly likely that should the Ministry of Finance be involved in prudential policy, a narrow-sense conflict of interest would occur. This is because while the fiscal authority with fiscal deficits is the borrower of funds in relation to financial institutions and financial markets on the one hand, it is also required to supervise financial institutions and financial markets that are its lenders on the other hand.

And, though it has actually been seen, there is no clear relationship between the fact that in financial crises the payer of bailout money can be transferred from a central bank to the government and the fact that supervisory authority can be shifted from a central bank to the government. Indeed, in the global financial crisis of 2007–09, while a large amount of risk money funded by taxpayers was injected in the US and UK, to the contrary, regulatory and supervisory authority was transferred from the government to a central bank.

---

[11]The issue related to such procedure is discussed in Chap. 6 when we analyze the failure of the US authorities in its crisis management strategy in the face of the global financial crisis of 2007–09 and discuss the need for risk money provision by a central bank and accumulation of seigniorage for the purpose.

Therefore, instead of the fund provider becoming the prudential policy body as piper logic suggests, prudential policy (risk identification and risk control) during normal times should be left to an organization other than the Ministry of Finance such as a central bank. And, when a large amount of risk money funded by taxpayers needs to be injected in time of crisis (risk finance), it is preferable that the fiscal authority consult related parties including the central bank and request approval from the legislature.

5.4.3.3 Independence of Prudential Policy and Role of a Central Bank

As apparent from the discussion, among the common production factors between various functions of a central bank and prudential policy, organizational know-how of a central bank, that is political independence, is extremely important. With regard to the similarity between independence for prudential policy and central bank independence in monetary policy, Quintyn and Taylor (2007, p. 4) states, "The specific arguments in favor of regulatory and supervisory agency independence are very similar to those that have been used in support of central bank independence—in particular, the need for stable operating rules of the game and issues of time inconsistency." Therefore, Padoa-Schioppa (2007, p. 167) proposes utilizing central bank independence to secure political independence for prudential policy as follows:

> It is also widely accepted that supervisory duties should be carried out independently of political pressures in order to ensure that the quality of supervision is not compromised. Hence, one should not think that as central banks have been made more independent, governments should retain supervisory control over the financial industry. Actually, the high degree of operational independence of central banks could support an independent and reliable conduct of supervision as well.

5.5 Cases of Japan and the US

In this section we will take up cases in Japan and the U.S. to show that the theoretical analyses in Sects. 5.2, 5.3 and 5.4 are relevant to the real situation.

5.5.1 Japan's Case

Structure of Prudential Policy
The basic structure of Japan's prudential policy is an integrated overlapping one as shown in Fig. 5.15. The main features are: (a) all regulatory and supervisory authorities concerning financial institutions across financial industries are concentrated on the Financial Services Agency (FSA), (b) the FSA is the main entity for all prudential policies such as framework design of laws and regulations, granting of

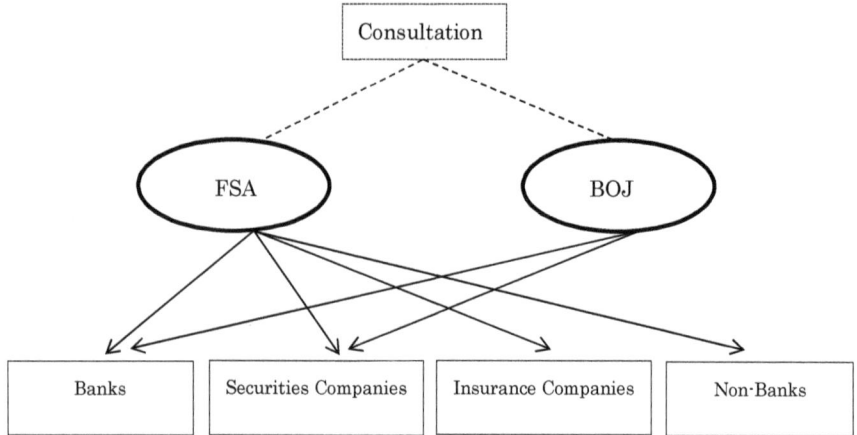

Fig. 5.15 Structure of Japanese prudential policy

licenses, supervision, and on-site examination (however, there are no explicit provisions for macro prudential policy), (c) the BOJ also has supervisory authority over
member banks (including credit unions) and securities companies (but no administrative authority to issue licenses) and therefore supervisory structure overlaps with
the FSA regarding banks and securities companies, and (d) consultation between the
FSA and the BOJ began from August 2009 (however it is neither formal nor on a
regular basis).

Lack of Political Independence
The distance between the FSA and politicians in Japan is the closest among the
developed countries as exemplified by creation of the office of "Minister of State
for Financial Services." Nishimura (2003) wrote "Various features emerged when
looking at the structure of financial supervisory organization in the developed countries. While distance between the organization and finance ministry differs among
countries, financial supervisory authority is held by a comparatively independent
specialist group and not headed by a politician, no minister in charge of financial
services exists" (translated from Japanese).

Therefore, cases where there appears to have been strong interference from politicians on financial regulations and supervision have often been seen in Japan. For
example, many suspect that the granting of a license to Incubator Bank of Japan
(2004) and examination after its start were influenced by the close relationship
between the bank's Chairman Takeshi Kimura and the then Minister of State for
Financial Services, Heizo Takenaka. Indeed, at a lower house budget committee
meeting (February 14, 2006), House of Representatives member Sumio Mabuchi
questioned the relationship in the granting of the bank's license. Later, in September
2010, the Incubator Bank of Japan (IBOJ) became the first institution to take advantage of the 'payoff' scheme in Japan. The FSA report (2011) by the Committee on the
Review of Administrative Actions (Chairman: Yoshiro Kusano) established by the

FSA also pointed out the "inappropriate granting of a license" although it could not clarify the relationship between Mr. Kimura and Minister Takenaka, and concluded that the FSA should not have granted a license to the IBOJ (As IBOJ did not open an account at the BOJ, the BOJ did not supervise the IBOJ).

Also, in September 2009, Shizuka Kamei became the Minister of State for Financial Services and in November announced a policy to increase liability on the part of banks when they extend loans. At the same time he took the initiative to pass the Small and Medium Enterprises Financing Facilitation Act. There are many views that, against such a background, banks had been encouraged at the time of FSA examination to bear more risks than they themselves felt adequate.

5.5.2 The US Case

Major reform of the prudential policy framework of the US was seen based on the Dodd-Frank Wall Street Reform and Consumer Protection Act (Dodd-Frank Act) of July 2010. In the previous framework, there was basically a separate prudential policy body for each financial industry as shown in Fig. 5.16 (financial holding companies were unilaterally inspected and supervised by the FRS). In the new framework, as shown in Fig. 5.17, prudential policy bodies of systemically important financial companies (SIFCs) are all integrated in the FRS. Also, the Financial Stability Oversight Council (FSOC) was newly established to oversee macro prudential policy.

FSOC is chaired by the Secretary of the Treasury and members include the FRS chairman, Comptroller of the Office of the Comptroller of the Currency (OCC), President of the Federal Deposit Insurance Corporation (FDIC), and Chairman of the Securities and Exchange Commission (SEC). The Council designates SIFCs from among various financial institutions. The Office of Financial Research (OFR) was newly established within the US Treasury to collect and analyze information for the FSOC. In the initial plan of the US Treasury in 2009, the FRS was to fulfill such functions without establishing any new institutions, but this was changed in the course of discussion in Congress.

In both previous and current frameworks, the US Treasury is responsible for designing the basic framework, and the prudential policy body discussed here is one that is responsible for regulations (the granting of licenses) and supervision (including on-site examination) other than design of the basic framework. The FRS continues to be responsible for consumer protection as it was in the previous framework, but the Bureau of Consumer Finance Protection (BCFP) was established within the FRS to enhance policy independence. As noted in Sect. 5.3.2.3, this is considered to be based on the idea of realizing a twin-peaks model. The initial plan by the US Treasury was to establish a Consumer Financial Protection Bureau (renamed the Bureau of Consumer Finance Protection in June 2018) to realize a genuine twin-peaks model by removing consumer protection authority from the FRS, but in the course of congressional discussion, the FRS remained responsible. As for investor

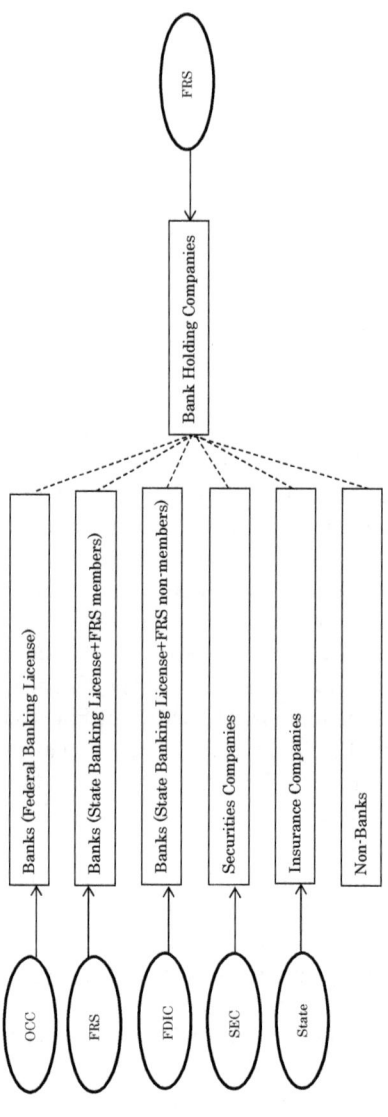

Fig. 5.16 Previous prudential policy framework of the US

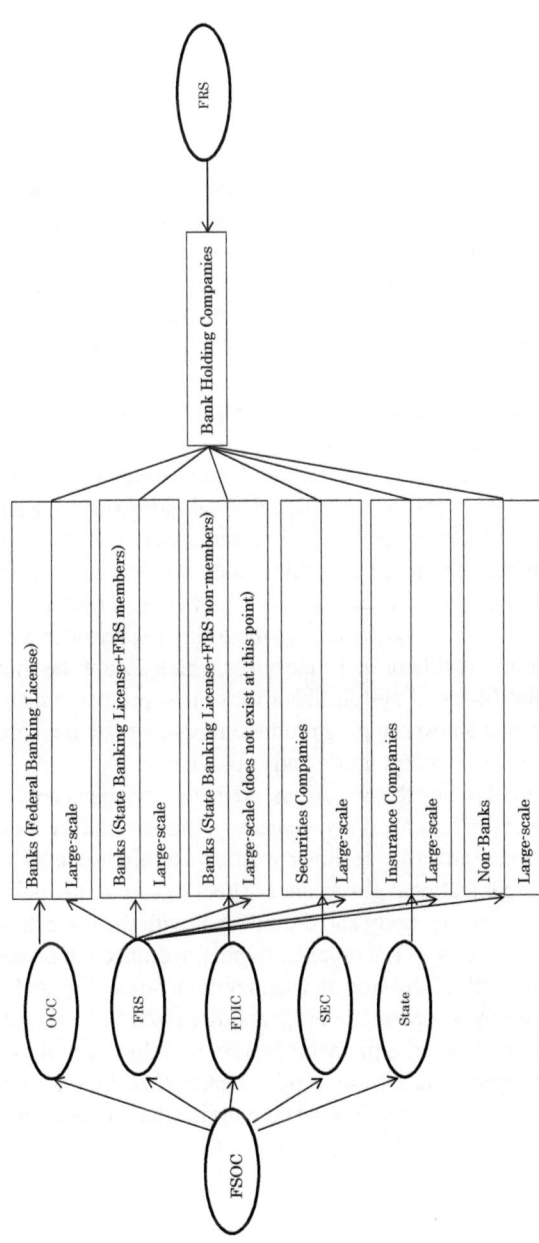

Fig. 5.17 New prudential policy framework of the US

protection, however, the SEC and Commodity Futures Trading Commission (CFTC) became responsible instead of the FRS and, in this sense, a twin-peaks model was realized.

5.6 Conclusion

This chapter discussed ownership of prudential policy focusing on the integration of policy bodies and the role of a central bank by applying economic theories. As a result, the preferable prudential framework based on various economic theories is to integrate various regulatory and supervisory bodies that oversee multiple industries and at the same time integrate macro and micro prudential policy bodies including on-site examination. For the latter, it became clear that the integrating body should be, if possible, a central bank. If the integrating body is not a central bank, a duplicate framework to include a central bank to supervise important financial institutions of a financial system such as banks, is desirable.

Having concluded that integration of macro and micro prudential aspects as well as integration of prudential bodies for multiple financial industries have advantages, and respective integration is desirable, it also became apparent that to further integrate these two aspects and create a sole policy body would cause an increase in bureaucracy costs due to organizational expansion and concentration of power. To challenge these issues, countermeasures such as the following are necessary: a twin-peaks model (that separates regulator and supervisor which secure the soundness of financial institutions and financial system from those that protect consumers such as depositors/investors) and an overlapping prudential policy system where multiple prudential policy bodies conduct regulation and supervision.

Ownership of prudential policy that we discussed in this chapter is only one aspect of the governance issue of prudential policy. Generally, the governance issue also has the aspect of organizational governance along with ownership aspect. This chapter only touched upon the organizational governance aspect by discussing political independence of the prudential policy body and did not deal with the issue head-on. The design of a board system, one aspect of organizational governance of prudential policy as in the Bank of England's discussion on whether monetary policy and prudential policy should be decided by a separate board, was discussed in Chaps. 2 and 4. If we distinguish normal times when a financial system is stable from times of crisis when a financial crisis occurs, discussion in this chapter is based on normal times. The role of a central bank in time of crisis is taken up in Chap. 6, Sect. 6.3.

Chapter 6
Role of Central Banks in Financial Crisis Management

6.1 Overview

This chapter will discuss the role of central banks in terms of financial crisis management based on the lessons learned from the failure of the US monetary authorities' financial crisis management strategy during the financial crisis of 2007–09. The role of central banks in prudential policy explained in the previous chapter is a role they fulfill during normal times, but this chapter will discuss their role in times of crisis.

Unrest in the US financial system began after the subprime loan problem materialized in August 2007. The disturbance spilled over to other countries and with the collapse of Lehman Brothers in September 2008 developed into the worst post-World War II financial crisis, a global financial crisis that basically originated in the US. With a view to investigating the fundamental causes of this financial crisis, considerable research has been underway focusing on such areas as the relationships among the real economy (the process of the emergence and collapse of the bubble), monetary policy and behavior of financial institutions, and issues related to the supervision and regulation of financial institutions.

This chapter does not focus on the fundamental causes of the financial crisis, but rather concentrates on the crisis management of the US authorities, in other words 'crisis management strategy' after the financial crisis intensified, and considers why the crisis worsened so dramatically. If adequate crisis management had been in place, though it might not have prevented the emergence of the crisis, the severity could have been contained to a minimum. From this perspective, we could say that the US authorities repeatedly made mistakes in their management of the financial crisis and indeed unnecessarily aggravated the situation from the onset of the crisis in August 2007 until the approval of the Emergency Economic Stabilization Act of 2008.

According to *Study of Failure* by Hatamura (2006), the process of inverse operation which tries to discover the failure mechanism from the result of failure is important. In order to theoretically effect inverse operation to ascertain why the financial crisis intensified, this chapter will apply behavioral new institutional economics proposed by Kikuzawa (2009, and his other works). Behavioral new institu-

© Springer Nature Singapore Pte Ltd. 2019   229
Y. Oritani, *The Japanese Central Banking System Compared with Its European and American Counterparts*, https://doi.org/10.1007/978-981-13-9001-2_6

tional economics is a theory that integrates theories of economics and strategy, and is sometimes called 'three-dimensional strategy.' One of its characteristics is that the world where behavior based on strategy occurs is based on Popper's (1972) "pluralistic world" where three worlds (the physical world, mental world, and intellectual world) interact with one another. Another characteristic is that each strategy in the respective three worlds is based on three different schools of economics (neoclassical economics, behavioral economics, and transaction cost economics <TCE>).

This chapter's failure analysis that applies such behavioral new institutional economics is, as is the case with all other failure analysis, based on hindsight. However, considering the immensity of the loss the world economy suffered from the global financial crisis that originated in the US, thorough failure analysis should be conducted and the lessons learned should be utilized to construct a system to prevent similar mistakes from happening again in the future. Notably, the financial crisis of 2007–09 was the most serious crisis since the Great Depression which gave additional momentum for the currency system to shift from the gold standard to a fiat money system. It would thus seem crucially incumbent upon us to clarify any institutional defect that prevented the system from making full use of the merits of a fiat money system in times of crisis, and to consider an alternative system.

As one candidate, in this chapter we consider a scheme where a central bank provides risk capital (injection of 'risk money'). From analysis of why the US monetary authorities failed in managing the financial crisis, we learned that the lender of last resort (LLR) function backed by eligible collateral proved insufficient, and that the public sector should have injected what would more or less have amounted to risk money to tackle such a crisis. The injection of money from the public purse plays a vital role in financial crisis management, but it is often 'too little, too late.' This is clearly because such injection needed approval from the legislature.

For a central bank to inject public money in a timely and appropriate manner without the consent of the legislature, a scheme where a central bank is able to provide risk money at its own discretion needs to be in place. Such risk money provision by a central bank must be accompanied by a mechanism to augment the risk-taking ability of a central bank or else confidence in the currency would be undermined. To enhance such risk-taking ability, the present system where seigniorage (to be explained in Sect. 6.3.3) is directly transferred to the national treasury should be dramatically changed. We need to create one whereby seigniorage is stored in a central bank.

Such a system would utilize seigniorage like an earmarked tax to maintain stability of the financial system. Buchanan's (1963) theory on earmarked tax in his public choice theory will be applied to explain that it is more efficient to utilize seigniorage as an earmarked tax rather than transfer it directly to the national treasury as in the case of general tax. Storing seigniorage in a central bank and using it to stabilize the financial system means that a central bank makes decisions regarding fiscal expenditure, igniting discussion on whether it is contrary to principles of democracy. We will point out that, as mentioned in Chap. 3, while a central bank is independent, it comes under public governance scrutiny from both the public and the legislature. Then, we will consider the issue by applying Congleton's (2005) public choice theory on consensus formation in times of crisis under representative democracy.

6.2 Study of the Failure of Financial Crisis Management by the US Authorities

In this section, the effects and process of the global financial crisis will be overviewed and the failure of financial crisis management by the US authorities studied based on behavioral new institutional economics.

6.2.1 Effects and Process of the US Originated Global Financial Crisis

The effects of the global financial crisis stemming from the US will be overviewed. Then, the crisis process will be divided into three periods to specify the period where crisis management strategy failed.

6.2.1.1 Effects of the Financial Crisis

The global financial crisis that originated in the US had a huge impact on the overall global economy, not to mention the US economy. Fed Chairman Bernanke (2009a, p. 4) gave the following view.

> Although concerted policy actions avoided much worse outcomes, the financial shocks of September and October nevertheless severely damaged the global economy — starkly illustrating the potential effects of financial stress on real economic activity. In the fourth quarter of 2008 and the first quarter of this year, global economic activity recorded its weakest performance in decades. In the US, real GDP plummeted at nearly a 6 percent average annual pace over those two quarters — an even sharper decline than had occurred in the 1981–82 recession. Economic activity contracted even more precipitously in many foreign economies, with real GDP dropping at double-digit annual rates in some cases. The crisis affected economic activity not only by pushing down asset prices and tightening credit conditions, but also by shattering household and business confidence around the world.

The plunge in the global economy stemming from the financial crisis may certainly be attributed to the bursting of a bubble, but, as will be mentioned in Sect. 6.3.1, it might have been avoided to a certain degree under a fiat money system. The reason why the global economy suffered such a large loss was because the US authorities could not efficiently utilize the merits of a fiat money system and failed in conjuring up adequate financial crisis management strategy. In short, the downturn in the global economy resulted not only from the bursting of the bubble, but also from the failure of financial crisis management strategy.

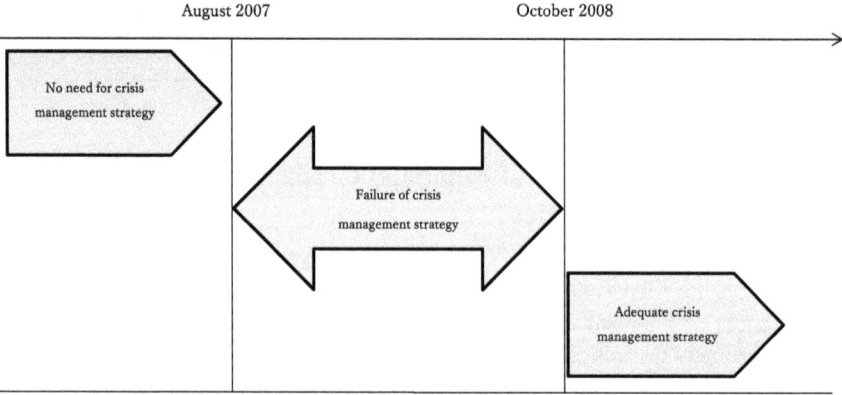

Fig. 6.1 Three periods of the financial crisis

6.2.1.2   Various Periods of the Financial Crisis

Looking at the crisis management strategy of the US authorities during the global financial crisis, the crisis can be divided into three periods and an outline of the respective periods as shown in Fig. 6.1.

Period That Did Not Need Crisis Management Strategy (Before the Onset of the Subprime Loan Problem <Until August 2007>)
Although there had been rumors about the subprime loan problem, it was yet to materialize, and therefore the economy was far from witnessing a financial crisis. Therefore, this is a period where financial crisis management strategy was not required. However, with regard to prudential policy in normal times, there were various problems. For example, securities companies (investment banks) and insurance companies were not subject to Federal Reserve System (FRS) regulatory oversight.

Period Where Crisis Management Strategy Failed (Materialization of the Crisis to Enactment of the Emergency Economic Stabilization Act of 2008 <August 2007–October 2008>)
This period begins on August 9, 2007, when the FRS and other major central banks effected emergency liquidity provision in the wake of BNP Pariba's decision to freeze its investment funds. Then, the failure of Lehman Brothers (the so-called 'Lehman Shock') occurred on September 15, 2008. The period ends on October 3, when the US Congress enacted the Emergency Economic Stabilization Act of 2008. The US authorities made numerous mistakes in their crisis management strategy in the face of heightening financial unrest during this period, which finally led to the ultimate mistake of letting Lehman Brothers fail.

Period Where Adequate Crisis Management Strategy was Adopted (From Enactment of the Emergency Economic Stabilization Act <October 2008 Onwards>)

The period begins from enactment of the Emergency Economic Stabilization Act when the US authorities implemented full-scale countermeasures against the financial crisis. Although the financial crisis deeply affected the real economy and a severe financial crisis ensued during the period, the US authorities' financial crisis management strategy was all in all adequate.

6.2.1.3   Objective of Analyzing the Failure of the US Authorities

As mentioned under Sect. 6.2.1.2, there are various reasons why the monetary authorities in respective countries could not sufficiently utilize the merits of a fiat money system varying from simple personal judgment error to institutional flaw. The major and common reason is the backlash of public opinion against capital injection. The backlash in this case went beyond mere psychological influence on the monetary authorities, and was actually accompanied by an effect. That is, while a central bank does not need to gain approval from the legislature in providing liquidity, capital injection by the government does. Therefore, in a democracy the backlash of public opinion against capital injection by the government affects the political process by possibly seeing a bill in the legislature to inject public capital rejected.

In order to consider the 'institutional deficiency' which may underlie the failure to adequately utilize the merits of a fiat money system, this chapter will question what sort of mistake the US authorities[1] made and why they failed in the face of the financial crisis. According to Hatamura (2006), when we look at the cause and effect, there is a "factor" and "gimmick" (hereafter called 'institutional deficiency') behind the cause of the failure and it is considered that the "factor" leads to "effect" through institutional deficiency. To identify "factor" and institutional deficiency from the "effect" of the failure is called "inverse operation." Such inverse operation is a measure to analyze the failure with hindsight, and is considered a requisite process to improve organization and institutions by learning a lesson from the failure. If inverse operation is conducted on the effect, i.e., emergence of the 2007–09 financial crisis, the "factor" is the emergence and bursting of the bubble in the US, but as for institutional deficiency, in addition to issues regarding financial regulatory oversight over securitization of subprime loans, there is also an institutional deficiency embedded in the political process in a democracy that has to be considered when formulating financial crisis management strategy.

The failure of the US authorities considered in this chapter is the failure of their crisis management amid the financial crisis. According to Ohizumi (2006 <translated from Japanese>), "crisis management is fundamentally risk management," but "while risk management encompasses all risks (risks that accompany damage), crisis management focuses on crisis that inflicts serious damage." In light of the objective of crisis management "to contain damage to a minimum in times of emergency," the

---

[1] 'The US authorities' includes government institutions such as the White House, the Treasury, and, FRS including high-ranking officials of such institutions such as the President, Secretary of the Treasury, and Chairman of the FRS.

US authorities could not reduce the economic loss which could have been achieved by taking advantage of the merits of a fiat money system when faced with the financial crisis stemming from the bursting of the bubble. Therefore, since the US authorities could not achieve the objective of keeping the economic loss to a minimum, we can say that they failed in their crisis management.

Moreover, based on strategy theory, this chapter will consider the US authorities' failure in crisis management as a failure of strategy. "Strategy theory" is "'wisdom to survive', a measure to survive that relates to biology and evolution theory" (Kikuzawa, 2008a <translated from Japanese>). Strategy theory developed in the field of business science, but this chapter will apply Kikuzawa's strategy theory based on economics.

Whether we could avoid the emergence and bursting of the bubble itself is an important theme for macroeconomics, but will not be taken up in this chapter. Rather, this chapter focuses on perspectives such as when an economy faces financial crisis stemming from the emergence and bursting of a bubble what financial crisis management strategy could prevent large economic loss and what sort of system should be in place in order to adopt adequate crisis management strategy.

6.2.2   Outline of Behavioral New Institutional Economics

This section will give an outline of behavioral new institutional economics which will be applied to analyze the US authorities' failure in adopting adequate financial crisis management strategy. The theory has been proposed in various papers by Kikuzawa (in Japanese 2006, 2008a, 2008b, 2009; in English 2009) and is extremely useful in considering the US authorities' failure in their crisis management as the failure of strategy based on strategy theory.

6.2.2.1   Features of Behavioral New Institutional Economics

Features of behavioral new institutional economics are: first, it is a combination of economics and strategy theory. Behavioral new institutional economics regards strategy theory as "wisdom to survive" (Kikuzawa, 2008a). And, in order to survive, it is necessary to behave according to the surrounding world (environment) and, as a behavioral principle, wisdom such as cost minimization in economics is adopted. Therefore, behavioral new institutional economics is not just simple economics but strategy theory based on economic theory.

Second, the world where behavior based on strategy takes place is in a "world" (concept from Kikuzawa) in the sense that three worlds (physical world, mental world, intellectual world) are overlapping one another as suggested by Popper (1972). The specific examples of the three worlds are given below and, from the perspective of strategy theory, it is important to approach them comprehensively.

- *Physical world*: non-living physical objects, living things (biological objects).
- *Mental world*: emotions, desires, mental processes.
- *Intellectual world*: knowledge, theories, technology, ideas and concepts, rights.

Third, respective strategies for the three worlds are based on three different schools of economics (neoclassical economics, behavioral economics, and TCE). Therefore, strategies for the respective worlds can be seen as follows:

- Strategy for *physical world* → neoclassical economics-based strategy
- Strategy for *mental world* → behavioral economics-based strategy
- Strategy for *intellectual world* → TCE-based strategy.

Therefore, behavioral new institutional economics is a strategy theory based on three schools of economics corresponding to three worlds. However, this does not mean that behavioral economics and new institutional economics are directly linked to one another in the same world. Behavioral economics is a basis for strategy in the mental world, whereas new institutional economics is that for strategy in the intellectual world. And, within new institutional economics, only TCE is used and other theories such as agency theory and theory of property rights are not used.[2]

6.2.2.2 Neoclassical Economics-Based Strategy: Direct Approach to Physical World

Of the three schools of economics corresponding to Popper's three worlds, neo-classical economics-based strategy places sole importance on strategy that directly approaches the physical world. In this strategy, advantage in terms of amount of human resources, objects, money is of crucial importance to win. Put simply, 'physical quantity' is all that matters.

The world of neoclassical economics is where only 'production cost (a cost that consumes material and physical resources)' exists. In such a world, neoclassical economics provides an answer to the question 'How can material and physical resources such as human resources, objects, money be distributed to competent persons and used efficiently?' The answer is 'free market transactions.' If there is a place where resources are traded freely (= market), incompetent persons will sell and competent persons will buy, as a result of which resources will flow through free market transactions from incompetent persons to the competent, and thus distributed and utilized efficiently. When this is discussed in terms of strategy theory, only the direct approach strategy such as injecting human resources, objects, and money is all that matters in the physical world which is simply composed of human and material resources.

Two problems can be pointed out with regard to such neoclassical economics-based strategy. One is, according to Popper (1972), humans behave not only in the physical world but also in a complex world where mental and intellectual worlds also take part. We need to understand human behavior from the perspective of such

---

[2]However, Kikuzawa (2007) suggests theory that integrates behavioral economics and agency theory (behavioral agency theory).

a "cubic world" and consider strategy on that premise. However, this is neglected in neoclassical economics-based strategy.

The other is that neoclassical economics considers humans as perfectly rational beings, whereas, in reality, humans are only partly rational. In this regard, free market trade does not necessarily bring about efficient resource allocation as suggested by neoclassical economics. Therefore, in addition to the quantitative aspect of material and human resources as represented in production costs, irrational human behavior taken up by behavioral economics and transaction costs treated in TCE should also be taken into consideration to develop a "cubic grand strategy" (Kikuzawa, 2008a).

6.2.2.3 Behavioral Economics-Based Strategy: Indirect Approach in the Mental World

Among the strategies based on Popper's three worlds, that based on behavioral economics in the mental world is an indirect approach that tries to achieve its objective indirectly by appealing to people's psychological processes and their emotions, unlike the direct approach proposed by neoclassical economics-based strategy of the physical world where human resources, objects, and money are increased. The basis for such a strategy is behavioral economics that studies how people's emotions and psychology influence economic activities. There are numerous theories with regard to behavioral economics, but, in this chapter, the representativeness heuristic and prospect theory are applied.[3]

The representativeness heuristic was first proposed by Kahneman and Tversky (1974). According to Kusumi (2001, p. 278), the gist of the theory is as follows: "When people instinctively judge the probability of some uncertain event, they only use a limited number of examples (samples) to judge its probability. And, when a particular example is recognized as being representative of such an uncertain event (in terms of parent population or category), they deem occurrence probability to be high" (translated from Japanese). That is, it is a theory that considers 'psychological bias.' For example, when there is a prominent example, people will judge it to be a typical case and even for cases that are not necessarily relevant, they judge them to have the same consequence.

Next, with regard to prospect theory, Kikuzawa (2009) explains as follows: When people recognize and evaluate things, a psychological base point exists (this point is called a "reference point") as shown in Fig. 6.2. Based on this reference point, the result that exceeds the estimate (for example point A) will be recognized as 'gains' and when they increase mental value ('satisfaction') also increases. On the other hand, results that are lower than the estimate (for example point B) will be recognized as 'losses' and when such losses increase mental value ('dissatisfaction') also increases. Moreover, since people have psychological biases, increases in gains

---

[3]With regard to behavioral economics that is applied as a basis for strategy of the mental world under behavioral new institutional economics, only prospect theory is used in Kikuzawa (2009, and his other works).

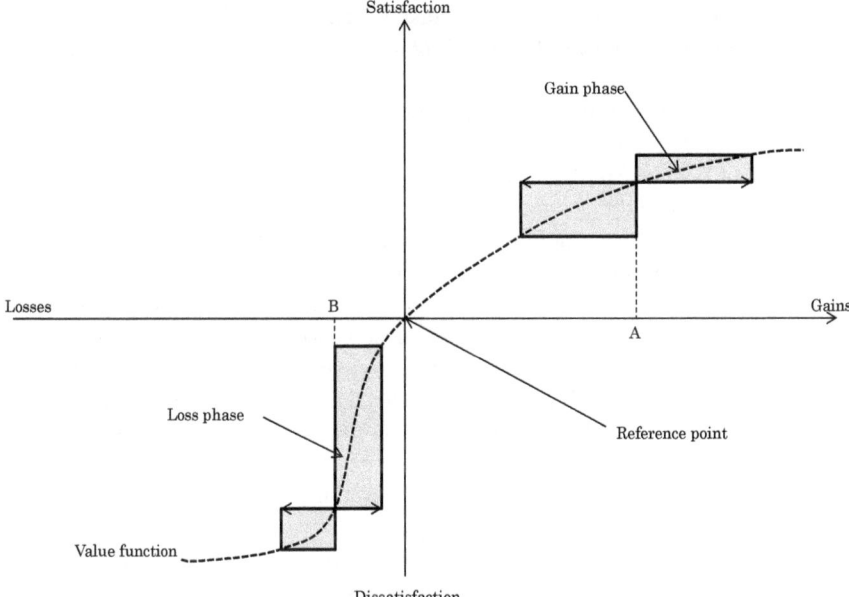

Fig. 6.2 Reference point and value function

and losses are not directly proportional to increases in satisfaction and dissatisfaction. While satisfaction and dissatisfaction diminish, the rate of diminution is faster for the increase in gains than the increase in losses (as shown in the shape of the value function in Fig. 6.2).

According to prospect theory on human psychology, people become 'risk averse' when they are above the reference point ('gains' area, point A) and become 'risk seeking' when below the reference point ('losses' area, point B). Therefore, when they are in the 'gains' area, the degree of satisfaction will not increase even if they venture to seek change and make more gain. Vice versa, the degree of satisfaction will, in comparison, decrease considerably when a change in circumstances brings about a decrease in gains, even if only slightly. Therefore, it is rational to remain in the current position (that is, risk averse). On the other hand, when they are in the 'losses' area, the degree of dissatisfaction will not increase as much as the increase in losses incurred from a change in circumstances. Vice versa, if losses decrease, even if only slightly, the degree of dissatisfaction decreases considerably. Therefore, even if risk is high, it is rational to opt for a change in circumstances (that is, risk seeking).

Strategy based on such human psychology is 'behavioral economics-based strategy' and is one of the three cubic pillars of behavioral new institutional economics.

6.2.2.4 Transaction Cost Economics-Based Strategy: Indirect Approach in the Intellectual World

'TCE-based strategy' is a strategy that acts taking into consideration the transaction costs needed for negotiation and coordination in the intellectual world, one of the three worlds of Popper. Similar to the strategy based on behavioral economics in the mental world, it is an indirect approach to achieve its objective by appealing to one's intellect, rather than directly putting in human resources, objects, and money in the physical world. The basis of this strategy is TCE.

Transaction cost does not appear on a balance sheet, but people have the intellect to grasp it. In the sense that it influences human behavior, it undoubtedly exists. With regard to the content of transaction cost, various costs are pointed out and analyzed in detail in the field of TCE. Based on such analysis, the most important transaction cost related to this chapter's strategy theory is the cost required for negotiation, coordination, and procedures.

On the premise that such transaction cost exists, if the inequality below holds true, no change will occur even if we try to change.[4]

Increase in transaction cost > Decrease in production cost + Decrease in psychological cost.

This inequality shows that even if a decrease in production cost is envisaged in the physical world and a decrease in psychological cost is envisaged in the mental world, if an increase in transaction cost overwhelms the above two decreases, then the current situation would not change. Kikuzawa (2008a, pp. 123–4) states that "even if we understand that the current situation is inefficient, just because our intellect acknowledges transaction cost, we cannot easily shift to the new situation. In other words, if one doesn't shift to a new situation, no transaction cost will emerge, and thus we tend to maintain the status quo" (translated from Japanese). As a result, a strategy that accompanies significant coordination cost among numerous interested parties such as system transfer, is not likely to be realized, and, an inefficient strategy from the perspective of production cost (or even psychological cost) may sometimes be adopted (this is called "absurdity of strategy" (Kikuzawa, 2008b).

Therefore, in order to change the situation, it is necessary to adopt a strategy that lowers transaction cost. According to Williamson (1985), transaction cost is determined by the following three factors: (a) uncertainty and complexity of transactions, (b) frequency of transaction, and (c) asset specificity. Whether any one of the factors can actually be changed depends on the features and situation of the actual transaction.

---

[4]This is a concept similar to Williamson's (2008) "remediableness criterion." This criterion is in contrast to the Pareto criterion. Scheme change accompanies transaction cost that is necessary for negotiation and implementation. If such transaction cost is extremely high, the system will not see any improvement even if the new system is efficient. However, this criterion only compares decrease in production cost and increase in transaction cost, and does not consider decrease in psychological cost as in behavioral new institutional economics.

6.2.3 Failure of Neoclassical Economics-Based Strategy

To clarify the institutional framework which caused the global financial crisis that started in the US, failure analysis will be conducted on the US authorities' financial crisis management strategy during the 'period where crisis management strategy failed' by applying the cubic (three-dimensional) grand strategy based on behavioral new institutional economics as introduced in Sect. 6.2.2.1. The three strategies of cubic grand strategy (neoclassical economics-based strategy, behavioral economics-based strategy, TCE-based strategy) are intertwined with one another, but, assuming that they can be separated, two questions, "What mistakes did the US authorities make?" and "Why did they fail?" will be considered in studying each strategy.

First, in the following, we will conduct a failure analysis of the US authorities' financial crisis management strategy from the perspective of neoclassical economics-based strategy that directly approaches the subject through human resources, objects, and money in the physical world.

6.2.3.1 Failures

The major failing of the US authorities under neoclassical economics-based strategy in the physical world can be summarized as 'they should have injected not only liquidity but also capital at the earliest possible stage.' Specific facts regarding this failure are explained below.

Injection of Public Capital Was Too Late
When we look back to consider what might have been the right period during which to inject capital, that before August 2007 was one that did not necessitate crisis management (as mentioned in Sect. 6.2.1.2) and, therefore, capital injection was unnecessary. However, the authorities should have started to inject capital through various means immediately after the emergence of the financial crisis in August 2007. Nevertheless, it was only after the enactment of the Emergency Economic Stabilization Act in October 2008 that the US authorities implemented capital injection, which was clearly 'too late.' In this connection, the biggest and obvious mistake the US authorities made was to allow Lehman Brothers to fail on the basis that it was impossible to supply liquidity due to lack of collateral. Even though Lehman Brothers lacked collateral, the authorities should have prevented its failure by injecting capital as in the case of saving American International Group (AIG).

The same also applies to other weak financial institutions. It may have been difficult to inject capital to these financial institutions immediately after the emergence of the financial crisis in August 2007, but if the strategy adopted since October 2008 (TARP: Troubled Asset Relief Program included in the Emergency Economic Stabilization Act enacted on October 3, 2008) had been put in place by the beginning of 2008 at the latest, the large-scale financial crisis that followed might have been prevented to a considerable extent.

Types of Funds That Should Have Been Injected

From the perspective of the kind of funds that should have been injected, the FRS provided liquidity but did not inject any capital until enactment of the Emergency Economic Stabilization Act in October 2008.[5] The FRS implemented various liquidity support measures[6] from the emergence of the financial crisis to the failure of Lehman Brothers. Though capital injection was not made, such support measures were considered effective in preventing worsening of the crisis. We could say that the US authorities utilized the merits of a fiat money system in the form of liquidity support by a central bank since the FRS could not have effected such large-scale liquidity support under the gold standard due to there not being unlimited gold reserves.

Nevertheless, as aforementioned in this section, 'liquidity support' differs fundamentally in nature from 'capital injection.' In the case of 'capital injection', the injecting entity provides funds ('risk money') without any guarantee of being paid back. On the other hand, in the case of 'liquidity support,' it does not provide risk money but requires collateral to guarantee payment of principal and interest. Of course, even for liquidity support there are cases where principal and interest are not completely repaid due to a plunge in collateral value. Therefore, strictly speaking, it is not all risk free, but, supposedly, liquidity support is not considered the provision of risk money.[7]

The fact that the US authorities said[8] that they could not support Lehman Brothers due to lack of collateral clearly exhibits their principle to provide liquidity but not to effect capital injection. Also, with regard to the kind of funds that should have been provided, if the US authorities were to take full advantage of the merits of a fiat money system based on neoclassical economics-based strategy, they should have made capital injection rather than limiting themselves to liquidity support.

In line with the above, for example, in a speech given in 2008 at a conference held by the Federal Reserve Bank of Kansas City a month before the Lehman Shock, Yamaguchi (2008, p. 649) said: "In the case of Japan, its systemic stability was restored only when significant capital was injected into the banking system using public funds. In my view, the lesson to draw from the Japanese episode should be, above all, the importance of an early and large-scale capitalization of the financial

---

[5] Strictly speaking, capital injection was decided in the form of guarantee when the US Government placed Fannie Mae and Freddie Mac under its control on September 7, 2008 and when the Treasury provided full value guarantee to money market funds on September 19, 2008.

[6] The specific liquidity support measures during the period specified by the FRS (*Federal Reserve Annual Report* 2009) were (a) lowering of the lending rate at the discount window and easing of screening standard (August 17, 2007), (b) establishment of the Term Auction Facility (December 2007), (c) swap line agreement with the European Central Bank and Suisse National Bank (December 2007), and (d) launch of the Term Securities Lending Facility (March 11, 2008). Also, an FRS loan to Bear Stearns (March 2008) is mentioned in the *Report* as an example of its support to individual financial institutions.

[7] Thus, until the enactment of the Emergency Economic Stabilization Act in October 2008, no clear capital injection had been made. That is, injection was not 'too little' but nil.

[8] For example, Chairman Bernanke (2009b) explains that "the company's available collateral fell well short of the amount needed to secure a Federal Reserve loan of sufficient size to meet its funding needs."

system." In other words, capital injection was 'too little, too late.' The US authorities could not adequately utilize the merits of a fiat money system and burdened the US and global economy with economic losses that could have otherwise been reduced.

Market Liquidity Measure That Should Have Been in Place Earlier
In relation to the above, FRS liquidity support during the failure of Lehman Brothers to the worsening of the financial crisis was limited to the provision of 'cash liquidity' that required good standing collateral such as government bonds. Its direct purpose was not to increase the 'market liquidity' of financial assets such as commercial paper and securitized products. This was because cash liquidity provision to increase market liquidity came with the high risk of a plunge in the prices of the financial assets that were pledged as collateral (or financial assets purchased), which meant the FRS provided risk money that was likely to undermine the soundness of FRS assets.[9]

6.2.3.2 Causes of Failure

With regard to the financial crisis management strategy adopted since August 2007, the reasons why the US authorities such as the FRS and the Treasury Department failed in making large-scale capital injection from the perspective of neoclassical economic-based strategy are as follows:

Failure to Adequately Forecast and Evaluate the Seriousness of the Financial Crisis and its Characteristics
The reason why the US authorities did not effect large-scale capital injection could be that they made a judgment error concerning the scale of the financial crisis and its nature. With regard to why the authorities underestimated the scale of the financial crisis, Henry Kaufman, an American economist, said that "Chairman Bernanke has long been underestimating the subprime loan problem.... What I want to criticize is that the FRB did not adequately forecast the seriousness of the problem and did not take measures in the early stage" (*Nikkei Shimbun,* February 23, 2009 <translated from Japanese>). Indeed, while Chairman Bernanke estimated the loss related to the subprime loan problem to be around $50 billion to $100 billion in his Congressional testimony in July 2007, he revised this figure upward to $150 billion in his testimony in November 2007. On the other hand, the IMF released its forecast of the loss to be around $170 billion to $200 billion as early as September 2007.

---

[9]After the collapse of Lehman Brothers, the FRS adopted market liquidity providing measures. Specifically, creation of the Commercial Paper Funding Facility to reduce turmoil in various markets such as the CP markets and agency bond markets (bonds issued by government sponsored enterprises, i.e., Fannie Mae, Freddie Mac) as well as direct purchase of such agency bonds.

Anna Schwartz also criticized Fed Chairman Bernanke's policy as follows[10] ("Man Without a Plan," *New York Times*, July 25, 2009).

> Last year, when the credit market became dysfunctional and normal channels for borrowing broke down, the Fed misread the situation. It persisted in believing that the market needed more liquidity, even though this was not a solution to the market disturbances. The real problem was that because of the mysterious new instruments that investors had acquired, no one knew which firms were solvent or what assets were worth. At the same time, these new instruments were being repriced in the market. The firms that owned them then needed to restore their depleted capital. When big firms experienced enormous losses, the Fed did not respond in a way that calmed markets. Most of all, Mr. Bernanke ultimately failed to convince the market that the Fed had a plan, and was not performing ad hoc.

Problem in Financial Institution Supervision

Behind the failure of an adequate diagnosis, that is, underestimation of subprime loan problem-related losses, the US authorities may have wanted to give reassurance to the financial markets based on behavioral economics-based strategy which will be mentioned later under Sect. 6.2.4. However, as will be explained, contrary statements were made by Chairman Bernanke and, therefore, we could point out that in addition to his lack of understanding, there was an institutional deficiency concerning financial institution supervision in the US.

That is, no uniform supervisory institution existed in the US and supervision of financial institutions was implemented separately according to type of financial institution concerned. For example, the FRS mainly supervised deposit taking financial institutions, which excluded investment banks and insurance companies such as AIG that triggered the subprime loan problem. Therefore, it may be likely that the FRS could not efficiently collect information on the financial crisis. Indeed, based on such recognition, the Department of Treasury (2009) proposed giving uniform supervisory authority to the FRS as part of its drastic reform plan of financial regulation reflecting the financial crisis (later, in December 2009, the House of Representatives passed a bill to set up a new governmental institution, the Financial Stability Oversight Council, to uniformly supervise financial institutions).

Failure to Provide Risk Money

The basic and direct reason why the US authorities failed in effecting large-scale capital injection at an early stage was that capital injection, meaning provision of risk money, cannot be implemented without approval of Congress and therefore the FRS and the Treasury Department could not inject capital of their own free will. Even if the US authorities had accurately forecast the scale of loss and diagnosed the adequate types of necessary funds, such capital injection would have required legislative approval. As it was, on September 29, 2008, the House of Representatives rejected financial stabilization bills evidencing that Congress was not in the mood to approve large-scale capital injection at that juncture.

---

[10] *The Wall Street Journal* (August 26, 2009) said "As economists Anna Schwartz and John Taylor have noted, Mr. Bernanke misdiagnosed as a liquidity crisis what was principally a bank solvency problem. This is one reason his easing did little to stem the panic throughout 2007 and 2008. A steadier monetary hand might well have avoided autumn panic."

Therefore, as long as the current system concerning capital injection (capital injection requiring legislative approval) exists, a strategy to provide risk money on a large scale suggested by neoclassical economics-based strategy cannot be adopted. This also holds true in deciding to let Lehman Brothers fail, and underlies the comment by Chairman Bernanke that Lehman Brothers is "too big to save."

However, with regard to the provision of risk money by a central bank, even if such provision is possible at a central bank's own discretion, considering the current system of seigniorage (seigniorage is, in principle, returned to the Treasury), the large-scale provision of risk money would erode FRS assets, and, therefore, in reality, it is difficult.

6.2.4 Failure of Behavioral Economics-Based Strategy

According to behavioral new institutional economics, the mental world exists as part of the three worlds and its strategy is based on behavioral economics. When such behavioral economics-based strategy is applied to financial crisis management, in addition to the time and scale of the capital injection in the physical sense, it is important to form a strategy that takes into account the psychological aspect of financial institutions, investors, and other firms.

The US authorities made several critical mistakes in terms of behavioral economics-based strategy in the mental world, and thus burdened the US and global economy with economic losses that would otherwise have been less. We will look at the failure of the US authorities in regard to their behavioral economics-based strategy and then examine the causes.

6.2.4.1 Failures

The following could be pointed out as failures of the US authorities in their behavioral economic-based strategy.

Psychological Impact from the Failure of Lehman Brothers

According to financial crisis management strategy based on behavioral new institutional economics, large financial institutions should not be allowed to fail. The failure of large financial institutions would, even from the perspective of neoclassical economics-based strategy, burden creditors with large losses and aggravate financial crises in the physical world. Moreover, from the perspective of behavioral economics-based strategy, it would have a psychological impact on other financial institutions and the general public, thus worsening financial crisis in the mental world as well. Therefore, a 'too big to fail' (TBTF) policy is normally adopted. However, the US authorities let Lehman Brothers fail, something of a contrarian strategy. However, this was a failure both from the perspective of neoclassical economics-based strategy and behavioral economics-based strategy.

Innocuous Effect of Money on Display

In the past, when a bank faced a bank run, crisis management strategy was adopted whereby banks placed large amounts of cash on counters plainly visible to depositors in the hope it would calm their nerves and put a damper on panic. This is a typical example of behavioral economics-based strategy in the mental world. In light of such an example, the failure of 'too little too late' concerning capital injection from the perspective of neoclassical economics-based strategy was also a failure of financial crisis management strategy based on behavioral economics-based strategy. If large-scale capital injection had been effected at an early stage, it might have played the role of 'money on display' giving reassurance to financial institutions and the general public, thereby avoiding worsening of the financial crisis.

Careless Statements by Chairman Bernanke

In March 1927, Japan experienced the Showa Financial Crisis which is considered to have been triggered by then Finance Minister Naoharu Kataoka misstating in the Diet that Tokyo Watanabe Bank had failed. This implies that in light of behavioral economics-based strategy, officials of the monetary authorities should strictly refrain from making careless comments regarding the financial soundness of any particular financial institution. That is, opinions and forecasts by such officials that are considered to have exclusive information might indeed become a reality as a consequence. However, Chairman Bernanke repeatedly made statements that increased market anxiety during the financial crisis. Some such comments[11] were as follows:

First, in his Congressional testimony on February 28, 2008, he made a statement that admitted the possibility of bank failures. In testimony to Congress on February 28, Fed Chairman Bernanke noted the possibility of the failure of small to medium-sized banks and his anxiety was apparent. Specifically, in reply to a question from Senator Richard Shelby who asked whether there was a possibility of bank failures in the US and whether Chairman Bernanke, as bank supervisor, was concerned about the significant risk that Shelby believed existed because of indulgent real estate financing on the part of banks, Chairman Bernanke admitted that it would not be surprising if there were some bank failure.[12] His insensitive statement that could possibly lead to a bank run caused a stir in financial markets resulting in stock prices falling. Nevertheless, Senator Chris Dodd, Chairman of the Senate Committee on Banking, Housing, and Urban Affairs, highly evaluated the statement, saying "It is the Chairman's duty to accurately present what knowledge he has. I appreciate his frankness" (*Nikkei Shimbun*, March 1, 2008 <translated from Japanese>).

In response to Chairman Bernanke's statement, stock market sales were concentrated on financials. Shares in large securities companies such as Lehman Brothers plunged a considerable 4.8% and those in Merrill Lynch 4.7% (*Nikkei Shimbun* <evening edition>, February 29, 2008). A *Nikkei Shimbun* article (March 5, 2008)

---

[11] Also, in testimony on February 14, 2008, "Chairman Bernanke exhibited cautious business sentiment and stock prices plunged sharply" (*Nikkei Shimbun,* evening edition, February 29, 2008 <translated from Japanese>).

[12] *Wall Street Journal* (February 29), "Fed Chairman Bernanke in his testimony noted that it wouldn't be surprising if there were some bank failure due to the current market crisis."

said the term 'Bernanke risk,' coined from the name of the Fed chairman, began to be whispered among those concerned in the financial community. This was because, as just stated, on February 28, in testimony, Chairman Bernanke mentioned the possibility of the failure of small to medium-sized banks which triggered an unintended plunge in stock prices and weakening of the dollar. The article further said:

> The US financial system is scared of bank failures. Fed Chairman Bernanke stated at end-February that he would not be surprised if there were some bank failures. 'But which bank?' The US financial world began searching for banks with high possibility of failure and some of the banks are revising credit lines to their counterparties. After Chairman Bernanke's statement, the spread between interbank lending rates and government bond interest rates that reflect bank creditworthiness widened by 0.2%. Distrust among banks stemming from the subprime loan problem (housing loans to individuals with low creditworthiness) is increasing. The market expected Vice Chairman Donald Kohn to bring the situation under control, but in his testimony on March 4 he emphasized that 'the US banking system is facing some challenges, but remains in sound overall condition' (translated from Japanese).

Also, on January 13, 2009, Chairman Bernanke (2009c) said in a speech at the London School of Economics that "consequently, more capital injections and guarantees may be necessary to ensure stability and the normalization of credit markets" which invited a plunge in stock prices (the Dow Jones Industrial Average declined 3% from the previous day). With regard to this speech, the *Wall Street Journal* (January 16, 2009) criticized Chairman Bernanke in its editorial titled "Leadership and Panics."

> With Barack Obama about to take the oath of office, this ought to be a moment for fresh, mere consistent economic leadership. Instead, we're getting a new version of the same ad hoc policy and scare tactics that marked 2008. No clear spokesman or leader has emerged with a strategy to rebuild the financial system. Consider Fed Chairman Ben Bernanke, who used a London speech on Tuesday to pat the Fed on the back as the Horatio at the Bridge of this panic. This would have been appropriate for a Princeton seminar a couple of years from now. Amid the current uncertainty, however, he succeeded mainly in suggesting that the financial system is in even worse shape than we thought, the President-elect's 'stimulus' isn't sufficient, and thus more of Mr. Bernanke's policy magic will be needed to save the day.

6.2.4.2 Causes of the Failure

When we think of the causes of the failure of the US monetary authorities, especially Chairman Bernanke's failure in his financial crisis management strategy, the failures are basically due to lack of sufficient consideration being given to behavioral economics-based strategy. Below, we discuss the importance of behavioral economics-based strategy that was not sufficiently acknowledged by the US monetary authorities based on the behavioral economics noted in Sect. 6.2.2.3. Then, we will posit whether Chairman Bernanke's personal failure combined with the necessity of Congressional approval for capital injection led to the authorities' wrong response from the perspective of behavioral economics-based strategy.

Behavioral Economics-Based Strategy and Contagion Effect

Behavioral economics-based strategy does not manage a financial crisis directly such as through capital injection as would be the case with neoclassical economics-based strategy in the physical world, but tries to do so by affecting the psychology and emotions of parties concerned in the mental world. Since a financial system is an organic integration of financial system components such as financial institutions and investors, such strategy is important in managing a financial crisis, as unrest in any of the components will have a spillover effect to other components.

The spillover effect is called 'contagion effect,'[13] and emerges not only through trust in the narrow sense but also through a relationship of mutual trust among financial institutions and investors in the mental world. Looking at the financial crisis of 2007–09, loss of trust in securitized products, mainly those that integrated subprime loans and the solvency of financial institutions that held such products, affected others through the contagion effect and actually brought it about.[14]

Explanation of Contagion Effect by Behavioral Economics

Contagion effect from such loss of trust has two routes: one is the failure of a large-scale financial institution spilling over to other financial institutions, and the other is a particular event such as careless remarks by Chairman Bernanke inviting deterioration in market liquidity. Respective routes can be explained by the 'representativeness heuristic' and 'prospect theory.'[15]

First, according to the representativeness heuristic, the failure of Bear Stearns in March 2008, for example, was accepted by the financial community as an indicator of business conditions at US financial institutions, especially investment banks. And, loss of trust spilled over to many financial institutions without any direct connection with their actual business conditions. Moreover, the failure of Lehman Brothers in September 2009 had a serious contagion effect. That is, the failure invited loss of trust not only in insurance giant AIG that was actually in business difficulties, but in many investment banks that were not necessarily in trouble, thus aggravating the financial crisis.

Next, according to prospect theory, the contagion effect occasioned by Chairman Bernanke's careless statement that caused a plunge in the prices of stocks and securitized products as well as depletion of market liquidity can be illustrated in Fig. 6.3. When the theory is applied focusing on investors (including financial institutions) holding financial assets such as stocks and securitized products, the reference point

---

[13]Other similar terms include 'band wagon effect,' 'herding phenomenon,' 'mob psychology.' So-called 'systemic risk' also includes the spillover of risks through the psychology and emotions of depositors, investors, and financial institutions in addition to risks related to loss of confidence in payment systems and is therefore used in a similar context as contagion effect.

[14]The US authorities' failure to make an accurate forecast which led to the failure of neoclassical economic-based strategy may be due to lack of knowledge on the contagion effect and therefore they could not forecast a rapid and large-scale plunge in market liquidity and deterioration in financial institutions' business conditions.

[15]There are many theories that explain the contagion effect and systemic risks. For example refer to Schoenmaker (1996).

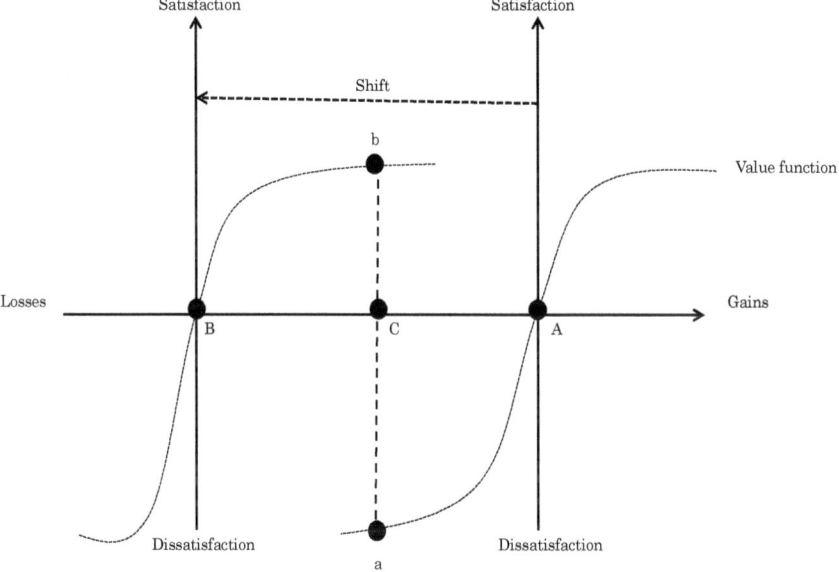

Fig. 6.3   Shift of reference point

had shifted considerably to the right due to euphoria until the outbreak of the financial crisis in August 2007 (point A in the figure). However, with the deflating of euphoria and deterioration in the financial climate, as well as careless statement by Chairman Bernanke, people began to anticipate a plunge in the prices of financial assets. Here, the reference point shifted to the left (point B) since people judged that it would be difficult to continue to make large gains. Under such circumstances, when we consider that the actual selling price of a financial asset is at point C, the gain is in the area of dissatisfaction (point a) based on the value function that passes through the original reference point, but if based on the value function that passes through the new reference point, the gain is in the satisfaction area (point b). As mentioned in Sect. 6.2.2.3, investors will be risk takers when they are in the loss/dissatisfaction area compared to the reference point, and risk averse when they are in the gain/satisfaction area. When the reference point was in point A amidst euphoria, investors took risk and held financial assets. However, considering the severe financial climate, the new reference point shifted to the left (point B), which allowed point C to be in the satisfaction area which made investors sell their financial assets to avert risk.

   That is, just when investors thought that they would make a large loss (reference point at point B) a slightly better price appeared (point C) and in the context that they would not incur the anticipated large loss, they gained satisfaction. Therefore, following the careless statement by Chairman Bernanke, investors became risk averse and sold their financial assets simultaneously. As a result, sellers increased in the financial markets and buyers decreased. The progress of such a phenomenon would cause a vicious cycle of a leftward shift of the reference point and dumping of

they may not have succeeded in persuading Congress. Congress opposed capital injection even at a time when the financial crisis was in a serious phase brought about by the failure of Lehman Brothers, indicating that they would not have agreed to capital injection at the time of the Bear Stearns bailout by the FRS.

6.2.5.2 Causes of Failure

The reasons why the US monetary authorities such as the Treasury Department and the FRS did not pursue TCE-based strategy in the intellectual world are as follows:

High Transaction Cost in Seeking Legislative Approval

With regard to capital injection, the US monetary authorities did not make efforts to build an institutional framework and thus invited rejection of the Economic Stabilization Bill. This suggests that a high transaction cost would have been incurred in convincing Congress to approve the bill, or so the US authorities judged.

Transaction cost here would have basically been the negotiation costs involved for the President and US authorities to convince Congress of the importance of capital injection (which is not popular among the voters) in bailing out a problem financial institution through lobbying activities and approaching Congress. Of course, in the sense that such activities could well prevent negative votes, they might hold down overall transaction cost.

It is not apparent to what extent the US authorities actually made efforts to suppress transaction cost, but if they had judged that Congress could be persuaded to approve capital injection at low transaction cost, the US authorities could have effected large-scale capital injection at an early stage and avoided a situation of 'too little too late.' And, Treasury Secretary Paulson and Chairman Bernanke would not have been criticized by Congress as late as June 2009 for pressuring Kenneth D. Lewis, CEO of the Bank of America (BOA), not to publicize the massive write-down of Merrill Lynch when the BOA bought the company in September 2008.

What can be ascertained from the above facts is that even if capital injection is judged valid from the perspective of neoclassical economics-based strategy (decrease in production cost) and considered useful in preventing the contagion effect from the perspective of behavioral economics-based strategy (decrease in psychological cost), too high a transaction cost concerning Congress from the perspective of TCE-based strategy may have hindered the strategy to inject public funds from an overall standpoint.

Congress Influenced by Short-Term Political Situation

As introduced in Chap. 3, Sect. 3.4.2, based on public economics and with an eye to winning the next election, politicians are, generally speaking, likely to make decisions from a short-term viewpoint. When the financial crisis worsened in August 2007, the US was expecting a presidential election in November 2008 (at the same time, all seats of the House of Representatives and a third of the Senate were up for reelection) and therefore politicians may have been more sensitive to the political situation and public opinion than would have been the case in normal times.

As for the political situation, the Democratic Party may have acted on partisan interests to pester the Bush administration and take advantage of the presidential election. And, since the Republicans were supported by market-oriented voters that dislike political intervention, they were also in a difficult situation vis-à-vis agreeing to capital injection despite being the ruling party. And for both parties, with the possibility of a new president and a new administration looming, business with the then administration would have been made under a high degree of uncertainty (the higher the uncertainty, the higher the transaction cost).

Against such a background, it can be assumed that the transaction cost, centering on negotiation costs for the US monetary authorities (including the President) to convince Congress to approve capital injection, might have been higher than usual. And indeed, rejection by the House of Representatives clearly reflected the situation. Therefore, even if the US authorities had adopted a strategy to reduce transaction cost concerning Congress, it is highly likely that they would not have been able to effect large-scale capital injection at an early stage.

Public Criticism of Capital Injection
In general, even in a period unaffected by politics, politicians have a negative stance toward capital injection and therefore negotiation and transaction costs for the government authorities in pursuing approval from the legislature would be high. This is not just because the capital is ultimately financed by taxpayers' money which makes politicians cautious against its usage, but also because it reflects the fact that voters supporting politicians are essentially critical of capital injection.

That is, it is difficult for the general public to understand an intricate financial system, and, moreover, professional knowledge is necessary to judge the content of financial crisis management strategy. Therefore, until a financial crisis actually affects the real economy and the public realizes its adverse impact on their everyday life, it is inevitable that the public regards capital injection to be a mere bailout of a problem financial institution. Therefore, as Iwata (2009) pointed out, "as apparent from the financial crisis in Japan in the 1990s, many people generally strongly opposed using public funds to bailout financial institutions" (translated from Japanese).

Problem in Obtaining Legislative Approval for Capital Injection
When we analyze the failure of the US authorities' financial crisis management strategy by applying cubic grand strategy based on behavioral new institutional economics, the necessity of obtaining legislative approval for capital injection emerges as an underlying institutional defect. In the face of a financial crisis, whether the situation necessitated capital injection according to neoclassical economics-based strategy in the physical world, and whether capital injection is considered to calm the anxieties of those concerned according to behavioral economics-based strategy in the mental world, if congressional approval is necessary for capital injection which requires overly high transaction cost such as high negotiation cost to gain approval and complicated approval procedures, the US authorities may not, in fact, have been able to pursue such a strategy. In short, the necessity of legislative approval for capital injection is the fundamental cause of "absurdity of strategy" (Kikuzawa, 2008b) with regard to financial crisis management.

6.3   The Importance of Risk Money in Financial Crisis Management

As mentioned in the previous section, the US monetary authorities failed in managing the financial crisis of 2007–09 basically because of the requirement to obtain prior approval from Congress for injecting risk money. Thus, we will take a close look at the importance of risk money in times of financial crisis management. First, we will touch upon the basic understanding from the perspective of the relationship between financial crisis management and the currency system, and then compare liquidity provision and risk money provision, both of which are included in the injection of public money in a broad sense, to discuss the necessity of having a central bank provide risk money.

6.3.1   Financial Crisis Management Strategy

The following offers an outline of financial crisis management strategy. Specifically, the difference in crisis management strategy depending on currency system in place such as whether the gold standard or a fiat money system will be considered, followed by an outline of the global financial crisis that originated in the US.

6.3.1.1   Currency System and Financial Crisis Management Strategy

There is a fundamental difference when formulating financial crisis management strategy under the gold standard and a fiat money system. Here, we discuss the reason behind such difference, and then give a basic understanding of to what extent the monetary authorities are now able to counter economic loss, from, for example, the bursting of bubbles.

Comparison of Gold Standard and a Fiat Money System
Historically speaking, currency systems transitioned from the gold standard to fiat money systems in order to counter the global financial crises of the 1930s. Whether a currency system is based on the gold standard or a fiat money system results in a considerable difference when formulating government/central bank financial crisis management strategy.

Under the gold standard, money supply was limited to the amount of gold reserves maintained at a central bank, and therefore there was a limit to how much support governments/central banks could provide a problem financial institution. Even if a problem financial institution held good standing collateral and was only experiencing a liquidity shortage[17] and not any kind of solvency problem, the central bank

---

[17] 'Liquidity shortage' is a temporary shortage of funds. If given necessary time to sell assets etc., a financial institution in such a situation would not fail. To the contrary, a 'solvency problem' means

concerned could only function as LLR within its gold reserves. Also, even if the central bank tried to buy financial assets to secure market liquidity, there was also the constraint that it could only purchase within its gold reserves.

Similarly, governments were also unable to offer sufficient support to a financial institution with a capital shortage, not to mention fund liquidity shortage. That is, the funds to support a problem financial institution relied only on tax revenue and issuance of government bonds, but, in a financial crisis, the private sector did not have ample funds to shoulder a tax rise and to purchase government bonds. As for a central bank, since the purchase of government bonds brings about an increase in money supply, as long as it needs to hold gold to back the increase in money supply, there is a limit as to the amount of government bonds it could purchase.

In order to overcome such a situation, the gold standard was abolished and a fiat money system adopted. Under a fiat money system, a central bank can function as LLR without any constraints such as imposed by the amount of gold reserves, and the same goes for the purchase of financial assets in the financial markets. Moreover, even if a problem financial institution does not have any good standing collateral and its solvency is problematic, the central bank could shoulder the risk and support the financial institution through capital injection (or support through the purchase of financial assets that could possibly deteriorate) without having to consider its gold reserves.

And, under a fiat money system, apart from the risk of causing future inflation, a central bank can purchase government bonds without considering its gold reserves. Therefore, on the premise that a central bank will purchase government bonds, a tax hike and limited purchase of government bonds by the private sector would not become constraints on the government in supporting a problem financial institution (the same goes for support to provide market liquidity through the purchase of financial assets).

Economic Loss Suffered from Financial Crisis Triggered by Bursting of Asset Bubbles
Therefore, transition from the gold standard to a fiat money system considerably enhanced the ability of the monetary authorities to manage financial crises. However, looking at the response of the US monetary authorities to the financial crisis of 2007–09, it would seem that such enhancement of crisis management capabilities made possible by the transition to a fiat money system was not sufficiently utilized.

Let me explain using Fig. 6.4. First, considering that financial crises stem from the bursting of bubbles, in the gold standard era governments/central banks could do nothing but accept losses as shown in areas (A), (B), and (C). In fact, serious financial crises were often the case under the gold standard.

The adoption of a fiat money system enabled the economic loss corresponding to area (A) to be reduced. That is, the seriousness of a financial crisis is mitigated and ones as serious as those under the gold standard does not occur. And indeed, in the

---

that a financial institution has excess debts and in the sense that time cannot solve a fund shortage, it is insolvent. A solvency problem can only be improved by capital injection.

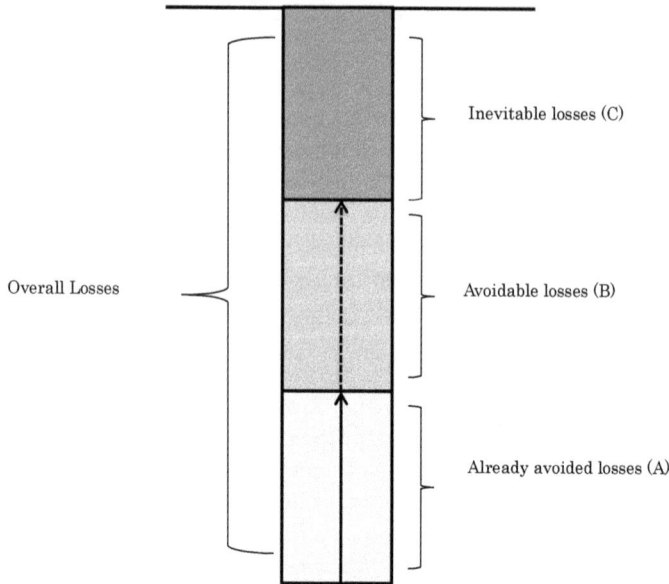

Fig. 6.4 Economic losses from financial crises stemming from collapse of asset bubbles

face of the global financial crisis of 2007–09, the monetary authorities in respective countries, in cooperation with financial institutions, provided tremendous support to the financial markets and prevented the emergence of such serious financial crises.

Despite the fact that they prevented serious financial crises, it is nevertheless true that crises brought considerable economic loss to the real economy. There is a view that such economic loss is inevitable with the emergence and collapse of asset bubbles. However, economic loss corresponding to area (B) in Fig. 6.4 could have been reduced if the authorities had utilized the merits of a fiat money system. Of course, among the losses brought about by the bursting of bubbles, the loss equivalent to area (C) is inevitable regardless of whatever system is in place, and has to be accepted.

Here, I have focused on financial crises stemming from the bursting of asset bubbles and how such losses could be minimized, but crises do not necessarily stem from just the bursting of asset bubbles. This discussion could also be applied to financial crises stemming from a shortage of foreign exchange funds such as was the case with the Asian currency crisis and those emerging from natural disasters such as earthquakes.

6.3.1.2 Financial Crisis Management Strategy Under a Fiat Money System

Here we look at various measures adopted by the monetary authorities in various countries that utilized the merits of a fiat money system to tackle the global financial crisis of 2007–09.

Countermeasures Against Financial Crisis
The authorities in various countries responded to the global financial crisis through countermeasures that utilized the merits of a fiat money system. Such instruments could be categorized as shown in Table 6.1.

The authorities providing such measures would shoulder certain risks and, if such risks materialized, the public purse would eventually have to bear the burden. The size of such risks differs among respective measures. Usually, 'capital injection'[18] is the most risky instrument. Although the risk entailed in 'capital' differs according to how it is invested and the marketability of the instruments chosen, basically, as long as capital injection is an investment, repayment is not assumed. To the contrary, the least risky measure is the 'provision of cash liquidity.'[19] This is, in principle, cash provision backed by collateral—therefore, even if there is no repayment, risk arises only for the portion that cannot be covered by the collateral put up. A measure that exists somewhere between the above two is 'the provision of market liquidity' of a specific asset, such as purchase of commercial paper. In this case, the issuer of the purchased asset bears the risk of non-payment.

Response of the Authorities to the Financial Crisis
Next, let us look at the authorities that provide such measures. Here, the authorities include governments (finance ministry etc.), central banks, and in some countries deposit insurance institutions and government financial institutions. There is a certain relationship between the measures and the providing organizations. That is, while

Table 6.1 Various countermeasures of the authorities against financial crisis

A. Provision of funds
    (a) Provision of liquidity to interbank markets
    (b) Provision of liquidity to specific financial institutions
    (c) Capital injection
B. Purchase of assets from specific markets
    (a) Direct purchase
    (b) Provision of funds to private banks to purchase specific assets
C. Guarantee against bank debts
    (a) Wider coverage of deposit insurance
    (b) Guarantee of large-scale debts such as interbank debts

---

[18] Similar to 'capital,' the term 'public funds' can also be used. However, 'public funds' is a vague term encompassing all instruments explained here, and therefore we do not use it.

[19] 'Cash liquidity' refers to cash and deposits that could be used to make payment, and 'market liquidity' to the ease of selling assets in financial markets. For details of the difference, refer to Chap. 15 of Shirakawa (2008a).

governments and government financial institutions provide risky measures such as capital injection, central banks provide less risky measures such as the provision of liquidity backed by collateral.

And, looking at the decision-making authorities vis-à-vis the riskiness of measures provided, central banks can, in principle, decide at their own discretion. On the other hand, governments and governmental financial institutions need to gain approval, in principle, from the legislature. This is because capital provision is risky and is highly likely to place a burden on the public purse.

As such, the particular measures that can be taken to counter a financial crisis depend on the kind of institution providing them, the framework for which is explained by the so-called 'Bagehot dictum' (see Chap. 1, Sect. 1.2.1). The Bagehot dictum can be summarized as, to avert panic, central banks should lend early and freely (i.e., without limit) to solvent firms, against good collateral and at 'high rates.' This is often interpreted that a central bank should only provide liquidity and should not offer capital to insolvent financial institutions. However, Shirakawa (2009) says, "The very distinction between a liquidity shortage and a capital shortage becomes blurred in a crisis." Therefore, Madigan (2009, p. 186) states that, "Bagehot's precepts need to be interpreted and applied in light of practical considerations, and that application is not necessarily straightforward. In a crisis, the solvency of firms may be uncertain and even dependent on central bank actions; the value of collateral may be depressed to an uncertain degree by liquidity rather than risk premiums; and the extent to which the terms of a central bank facility represent a penalty rate may depend on the circumstances and vary across firms."

6.3.2   Risk Money Provision by a Central Bank

Based on examination of why the US monetary authorities failed in their financial crisis management, it is apparent that the injection of risk money, which plays an important role in financial crisis management, tends to be 'too little, too late' since it needs approval from the legislature. For a central bank to provide risk money in a timely and appropriate manner there needs to be a scheme whereby the central bank can provide it without the necessity of having to obtain such approval. The answer is that adequately utilizing the merits of a fiat money system should enable pursuit of financial crisis management strategy that achieves satisfactory results. In the following, we look at the necessity of risk money provision based on the lessons learned from the failure study of the US monetary authorities and then consider why a central bank is suitable as a provider of risk money.

6.3.2.1   Importance of Risk Money Provision

The failure of financial crisis management strategy by the US monetary authorities in the respective three worlds of behavioral new institutional economics can be summarized in Fig. 6.5. First, from the perspective of neoclassical economics-based strategy, in a physical world where emphasis is placed on physical quantity, the US monetary authorities should have provided not only liquidity but also risk money as quickly as possible.

Second, from the perspective of behavioral economics-based strategy, the US monetary authorities made several critical mistakes in terms of psychological strategy that places importance in calming the anxiety of financial institutions and investors, e.g., psychological anxiety occasioned due to the collapse of Lehman Brothers and also careless comments by Chairman Bernanke.

Third, from the perspective of TCE-based strategy, in an intellectual world where transaction costs increase through negotiation with the legislature to inject risk money (mainly negotiation costs), the US monetary authorities should have adopted strategy to gain approval at an early stage.

That is, behind the failures of the above neoclassical economics-based strategy and behavioral economics-based strategy is the existence of an institutional constraint that necessitates legislative approval for the provision of risk money. And, the legislature needs to take into consideration the public that are against injecting risk money. In short, the main entity that provides risk money is not the central bank (the FRS) but the government, and, for a government to inject risk money, it needs to gain approval

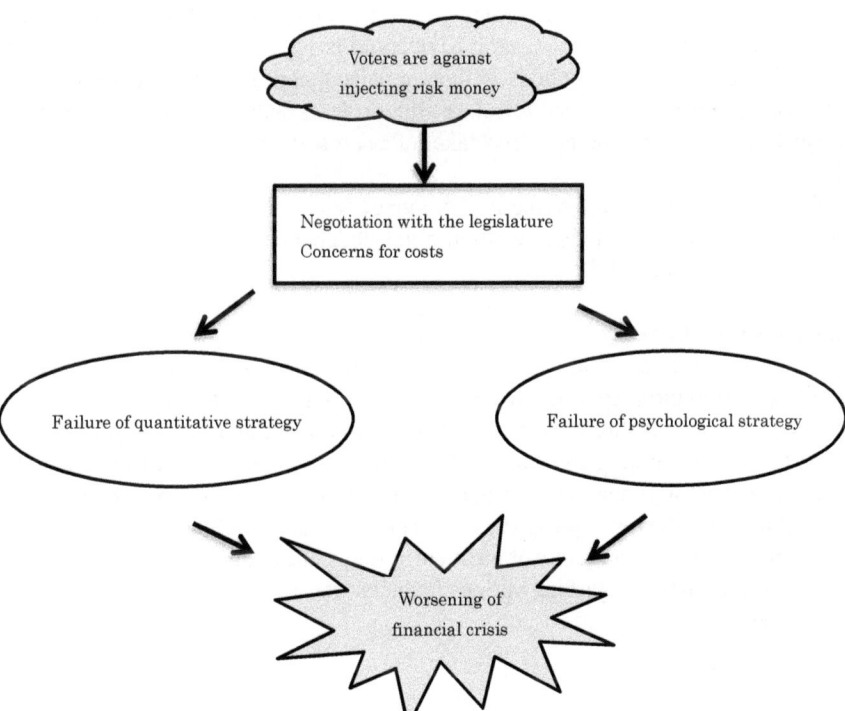

Fig. 6.5   Failure of financial crisis management of the US monetary authorities

from the legislature. It took a while for the US authorities to gain approval and, as a result, the financial crisis of 2007–09 deepened.

Therefore, when we look at the failure mechanism (institutional deficiency) of the US monetary authorities, the fundamental cause is the institutional framework that requires approval from the legislature for injecting risk money. This framework is regarded as a requisite in a democracy, but, as will be mentioned later (Sect. 6.3.3.4), it needs to be reconsidered taking into account the emergency a financial crisis presents. We cannot adopt timely and appropriate financial crisis management strategy if we delegate decisions to inject risk money, the core of crisis management strategy, to politicians who are apt to make decisions based on short-term political considerations.

6.3.2.2   Central Bank as a Provider of Risk Money

Based on Bagehot's dictum, the idea that a central bank should provide liquidity in times of financial crisis became well-established, and, in the global financial crisis of 2007–09, not only the FRS but also other central banks actively provided liquidity. However, central banks provided only a limited amount of risk money as Bagehot's dictum only allows liquidity that is backed by safe collateral.[20]

Learning the lesson from the failure of financial crisis management strategy by the US monetary authorities, the strategy could be conducted more effectively if we could realize a scheme where a central bank could provide risk money swiftly as an independent decision-making body without requiring approval of the legislature. In other words, central banks need to enlarge their role in financial crisis management from just being a LLR to being a 'risk taker of last resort' in that they would provide risk money.

When central banks play a role in risk money injection, there are benefits other than the swift injection of risk money through independent decision-making. The principal benefits are as follows:

Informational Efficiency
Central banks are in an ideal position to efficiently collect and analyze both macro and micro information regarding financial systems. As for micro information about individual financial institutions, central banks can collect and analyze such information through examining and supervising them. As for macro information, central banks can collect and analyze information through daily market operations in the financial markets (this is expressed as 'the central bank in the market'). Moreover, since central banks are operators of payment systems, they could collect and analyze settlement information regarding various financial transactions from both micro and macro aspects.

---

[20] An example of limited provision of risk money by a central bank is when the central banks of the US, Europe, and Japan adopted unconventional monetary policy and bought high risk financial assets.

Group of Experts

Central banks comprise a group of experts on financial systems in both micro and macro aspects. First, with regard to the micro aspect, most central banks conduct the examination and supervision of financial institutions and so are experts on business conditions at individual financial institutions. On the macro side, as central banks conduct daily market operations, they are experts on financial market trends and at the same time well versed in the real economy through research and analysis of business conditions.

Continuous Transition from a Normal Mode to an Emergency Mode

Central banks provide liquidity to financial institutions on a daily basis through daily financial market operations. Therefore, they could shift from a normal mode to an emergency mode smoothly when a problem financial institution needs support. That is, they could start from providing liquidity backed by safe collateral, and, in the face of collateral shortage, could decide on extending unsecured loans or injecting risk money.

And, not only liquidity provision to a financial institution, but the same is true for purchasing financial assets in the financial markets to enhance market liquidity. In times of financial crisis, central banks could just change the type and amount of securities purchased that are used for its daily financial market operations in order to enhance market liquidity and maintain market stability.

6.3.3 Risk Taking by a Central Bank and Seigniorage Utilization

To have a central bank provide risk money as part of financial crisis management strategy means that its assets would be exposed to risk, its capital could be damaged, thus undermining credibility in the value of the currency. To prevent this, a central bank needs to accumulate seigniorage to enhance its ability to shoulder risks in times of financial crisis. The framework will be discussed below.

6.3.3.1 Loss of Risk Money and Central Bank Capital

A central bank is an appropriate body to provide risk money, as mentioned, but, under the current system there is a considerable problem for a central bank in actually providing risk money on a large scale. That is, if the risk does materialize, the central bank would incur loss as a natural consequence of providing risk money. Such provision entails the risk of undermining central bank assets due to a resultant loss, and, if its capital (net assets)[21] is significantly damaged, public confidence in the

---

[21] A central bank's capital is its net assets comprised of capital stock (as discussed in Chap. 2, Sect. 2.5), provisions, and reserves.

central bank would diminish. And, if a central bank's financial conditions deteriorate substantially, there is a risk that it will not be able to pursue its mission of price stability.[22] Therefore, in order to adopt a scheme where the central bank provides risk money as part of financial crisis management strategy, it needs to enhance its capital and its loss bearing ability.

6.3.3.2   Utilization of Seigniorage and Transfer to the National Treasury

As a measure to enhance central bank capital, seigniorage should not be transferred to the national treasury but should be kept at a central bank as its capital. There are two types of seigniorage from the perspective of source of profit: 'seigniorage as issuing profit' and 'seigniorage as investment profit.' The former, 'seigniorage as issuing profit,' is the profit gained by the issuer from the difference between the currency's face value and production costs (i.e., capital gain). On the other hand, 'seigniorage as investment profit,' is the profit gained by the issuer from the difference between interest gained by holding assets acquired to back issued currency and the management fee for the issued currency. In other words, 'income gain.'

Whichever the case, seigniorage gained by a central bank is a profit that should eventually be returned to the public, but intrinsically should be returned through indirect ways such as using it to build up retained profit to prepare for exercise of the LLR function or to enrich the service quality of payment services provided by a central bank (cost of central bank services).

However, the fiscal authority may strongly oppose accumulating seigniorage in a central bank. The government often argues that seigniorage is gained because a central bank is given the monopoly right of banknote issuance from the government.

Therefore, when we consider whether seigniorage actually originates from the government giving a central bank a monopoly right to issue banknotes, such does not necessarily seem to be the case. There is a hypothesis that seigniorage started from gaining the confidence of banknote users and not from the monopoly right of banknote issuance.

Based on this hypothesis, a central bank pursues appropriate monetary policy in order to realize stability in the value of the currency, leading to heightening confidence in the central bank's issued currency, thus calling for greater usage of that currency both domestically and internationally, increasing seigniorage as a result. To the contrary, should a central bank fail in its monetary policy management, and confidence in the currency deteriorates, the public would avoid using and hoarding that currency, resulting in a decrease in seigniorage.

Even if we consider that seigniorage has its roots in the monopoly right of banknote issuance, there is a risk in transferring it to the national treasury. This is because the original purpose to concentrate seigniorage on a central bank is to eliminate the adverse effect of over issuance should the private sector be allowed to issue paper money freely.

---

[22]Milton and Sinclair (2011) discuss these issues in detail from various standpoints.

But, if it is considered that seigniorage should be transferred to the government whatever the case, the government will be tempted to over issue paper money and increase its fiscal revenue (i.e., monetization of government debts), which in turn would increase the risk of pressuring a central bank to conduct inflationary monetary policy.

Whether or not seigniorage is a right given by the government, it is a profit gained by a central bank as a by-product of monopoly banknote issuance under a fiat money system. Under a competitive currency issuing system operated by private banks, inflation would emerge due to over-issuance of currency causing disorder and collapse of the financial system. To prevent this, a central bank was given the monopoly right, resulting in seigniorage unintendedly. Thus, covering fiscal expenditure is not the intended purpose of seigniorage. Therefore, utilizing seigniorage to prevent the collapse of a financial system such as the bankruptcy of financial institutions and deflation in the macroeconomy is in line with the common objective, although it is the opposite reason from preventing chaos and collapse of the financial system due to inflation.

6.3.3.3   Buchanan's Earmarked Tax Theory and Seigniorage Utilization

Seigniorage is a profit gained from the public that holds banknotes, so if we consider seigniorage as 'tax' accompanying banknote usage, accumulating seigniorage and using it to prevent confusion and collapse of a financial system in times of financial crisis can be regarded as 'utilization of earmarked tax.' If we apply Buchanan's (1963) theory of earmarking to consider transfer of seigniorage to the national treasury, the following can be argued.

Buchanan (ibid.) discusses the selection issue with respect to "earmarked tax" (or "earmarking") and "lump-sum tax" (or "general fund budgeting") as a financing scheme for public services. He explicates that earmarking has superior efficiency. To summarize his argument, "earmarking" is defined as the practice of designating or dedicating specific revenues to the financing of specific public services. The restrictions that such practices as earmarking may impose on the independence of a budgetary authority need not produce inefficiency in the fiscal process and can provide a measure to insure more rational individual choice by compartmentalizing fiscal decisions.

In contrast, general fund budgeting allows citizens to vote only on the aggregate outlay for the predetermined 'bundles' of public services, as this choice is presented by the budgetary authorities. The appropriate market analogy to general fund financing is a specific tie-in sale, as opposed to independent quantity adjustment in each market, the analogy to earmarking. Just like the tie-in sale of a monopoly, general fund budgeting will increase overall public outlays. Bureaucracy will be biased toward insuring overall expansion of public services and prefers general fund budgeting, i.e., non-earmarking.

Seigniorage in Japan is used like a lump-sum tax where seigniorage is transferred to the general account of the treasury, from which taxpayer money was injected during the financial crisis with no reference to seigniorage. On the other hand, accumulating seigniorage in a central bank and providing it as risk money in times of financial crisis is like using seigniorage as an earmarked tax. Buchanan's theory of earmarking considers that the latter usage of seigniorage as earmarked tax is more efficient than the former, where seigniorage is used as a lump-sum tax.

With regard to how seigniorage in the US and UK is treated, it is not simply transferred to the general account like in Japan, but usage after being transferred to the treasury is limited. Therefore, their systems are more similar to using seigniorage as an "earmarked tax" than the case of Japan. In the case of the FRS, seigniorage transferred to the Treasury is to be allocated for the redemption of government bonds. And, in the case of the BOE, the Issue Department that issues banknotes is differentiated account-wise from Banking Department that conducts other operations. Seigniorage earned by the Issue Department is transferred to the treasury under the National Loans Fund which is separate from the general account and its usage is limited to national loans.

Nevertheless, the reason why usage of seigniorage in the US and UK is limited is not just to maintain financial system stability, but to prevent the government from conducting inflation-biased monetary policy since the government has an incentive to increase fiscal revenue by over-issuing fiat money.

6.3.3.4   Principle of Democracy and Seigniorage Utilization

Let us say we follow Buchanan's theory of earmarking and accumulate seigniorage to be used in times of financial crisis. In the case of actual financial crisis management, decisions such as how much seigniorage to use, at what point, and how will be left to the central bank's discretion, which gives rise to the question of whether this is contrary to the principle of representative democracy where fiscal expenditure should be approved by the legislature.

First of all, as already discussed in Chap. 3, Sect. 3.3, a central bank itself is subject to public governance through the appointment of its senior officials, and therefore we could say that, though it may not be as direct as a decision made by the legislature, it is in compliance with the minimum requirements of democratic procedure. Moreover, since financial crisis management is one thrust of crisis management, we could apply Congleton's theory on crisis management and democracy under public choice theory and have the following discussion.

Congleton's theory (2005, p. 1) states that "First, a crisis is unexpected, a complete surprise. Second, a crisis is normally unpleasant in that current plans are found to work less well than had been anticipated. Third, a crisis requires an urgent response of some kind." To incorporate these features into the rational choice models of political decision-making, Congleton defined the concept of "ignorance," a form of imperfect information, and, considering it as a missing variable, conducted a model analysis. As one of the conclusions from the analysis, Congleton showed that "the surprise and urgency of policy decisions during times of crisis implies that voters are more likely be mistaken in their assessments of their long-run interests." And as a result, politicians that behave according to the median voters' intentions under democracy (vote-maximizing behavior, see Chap. 3, Sect. 3.4.2) would also not be able to make decisions based on long-run interests. Such a situation will increase "informational asymmetries" between voters and government bureaus, creating a serious agency problem. With the anticipation that "bureaus may secure larger budgets," Congleton proposes effecting routine procedures (manual) to tackle a crisis prior to an actual crisis.

If we apply this theory to financial crisis management, we can clearly explain the behavior of the US Congress in the financial crisis of 2007–09 as well as the behavior of politicians in Japan during the financial crisis that followed the bursting of asset bubbles. That is, in both countries, the public were against the injection of public money and, in line with their opinion, many politicians also opposed such action. Congleton points out the possibility that bureaucrats would also behave separately from the voters' long-run interest. But, considering that organizational behavioral principles that intrinsically realize a national economy's long-run interest attach to a central bank, we could say that a central bank is in a more suitable position than politicians to decide whether seigniorage should be used for maintaining financial system stability in times of financial crisis. In this regard, we cannot say that accumulating seigniorage in a central bank is contrary to the principle of representative democracy.

6.3.4 Case Study of Financial Crisis in Japan

In Japan, the asset bubble that emerged in the latter half of the 1980s collapsed during the beginning of the 1990s. The aftereffects were grave as many banks, credit unions, and securities companies went bankrupt one after another from the mid-1990s to early 2000s. The BOJ provided large scale liquidity and risk money to prevent this domestic crisis from worsening and possibly affecting the global economy. This action on the part of Japan's central bank is significantly different from what happened in the US in the financial crisis of 2007–09 as studied in Sect. 6.2.

Izu (2013) analyzes the providers of bailout funds and the kind of funds extended to 24 financial institutions that the Deposit Insurance Corporation of Japan (DICJ) bailed out in the 1990s. The analysis of the bailouts in this period offers three findings.

First, the response by the Japanese government and the BOJ can clearly be divided into two periods: that until February 1998, and that after. In the former, the general public was strongly against the idea of injecting public money to failed financial institutions as was the case in the US. Therefore, politicians were strongly opposed to capital injection. For example, in 1996, members of the then opposition New Frontier Party set up a picket line inside the Diet to oppose a bill allowing capital injection amounting to 68.5 billion yen for the disposal of the non-performing loans of *Jusen* (housing loan companies) proposed by the government and the then ruling Liberal Democratic Party of Japan. However, when a large bank and securities company (Hokkaido Takushoku Bank and Yamaichi Securities Company) went bust in November 1997, it became clear to everyone's eyes that the default would have a grave impact on the overall Japanese economy. At this juncture, the public understood the necessity of government support and the Diet finally passed the Act on Emergency Measures for Financial Functions Stabilization and the Act on Emergency Measures for Early Strengthening of Financial Functions in February 1998 to enable government support.

As such, the fact that the general public was strongly against government support to the failed financial institutions and that politicians could not adopt effective measures until the crisis worsened was similar to the case of the US in the financial crisis of 2007–09 in Sect. 6.2.

Second, different from the FRS, until government support was authorized, the BOJ provided not only liquidity but also risk money (non-collateralized funds, non-guaranteed funds, and equity finance) which incurred a loss that cannot be collected even to this day (¥11,110 million). This is against "Bagehot's Dictum" (see Chap. 1, Sect. 1.2.1) that says "central banks should lend freely to solvent depository institutions in times of financial crisis only if they have sound collateral" (however loan interest rates were set at a level 0.5% above the official discount rate which is in line with Bagehot's Dictum). Izu (ibid.) criticized the BOJ's strong support stating that "BOJ in the 1990s not only acted as traditional LLR, but also went so far as to substitute/supplement the role which should have been played by the government or DICJ" (translated from Japanese).

However, BOJ's behavior in the 1990s should not be criticized as there are situations where the central bank provision of risk money can be justified even though it is against Bagehot's Dictum, as described in Sect. 6.3.2 in this chapter. Especially in the case of large-scale financial institutions such as Hokkaido Takushoku Bank and Yamaichi Securities Company that actively participated in the international financial markets, namely the New York and London financial markets, risk money provision by the BOJ can be justified as preventing the financial crisis in Japan from spilling over to the global economy and possibly leading to a global financial crisis, as was the case with the US described in Sect. 6.2 (the default of Lehman Brothers).

Third, the BOJ provided emergency liquidity and risk money to not only depository institutions such as banks and credit unions but also to nonbanks such as securities companies and DICJ. However, in the case of the FRS, it provided emergency liquidity and risk money only to banks. Therefore, failing investment banks and insurance companies had to first establish a 'bank holding company' to which the FRS would then provide emergency funds. Such a procedure took time which only aggravated the financial crisis in the US during 2007–09 that developed into a global financial crisis.

6.4 Conclusion

When we analyze the institutional deficiency of the US monetary authorities in financial crisis management strategy, it is clear that the fundamental cause is the scheme that necessitates approval from the legislature to inject risk money. This scheme is considered essential in democracy, but looking at the extent of loss that a financial crisis can cause, it needs to be reappraised. If we leave the decision to inject risk money, which is at the core of financial crisis management, to short-sighted politicians, we cannot adopt timely and adequate financial crisis management strategy.

Learning a lesson from the failure of the US authorities in the global financial crisis of 2007–09, it is necessary to construct a new scheme that sufficiently utilizes the merits of a fiat money system. For example, a scheme utilizing the independence of a central bank, a widely accepted stance in the field of monetary policy, in conjunction with the financial system's stabilization function deserves consideration. That is, the central bank should be permitted to provide an adequate amount of risk money at a suitable time without having to gain approval from the legislature. And, to prevent deterioration of the central bank's capital, it is necessary to construct a scheme that enables central bank seigniorage to be accumulated within the bank and not simply transferred to the national treasury as is presently the case.

Central bank seigniorage was, in the first place, a gain obtained as a by-product of a central bank's monopoly in issuing banknotes under a fiat money system. If private banks were allowed to compete in issuing currency, the financial system would collapse via inflation brought about by the over-issuance of currency. In order to prevent such a situation, a central bank was given the monopoly to issue currency, resulting in seigniorage. Therefore, the intrinsic objective of seigniorage was not to cover fiscal expenditure. Rather, if seigniorage is used to prevent the collapse of the financial system stemming from the failure of private financial institutions, it would be in line with the objective of preventing collapse of the financial system stemming from inflation, and as such can be considered utilization of earmarked tax.

Also, for a central bank to decide whether to use seigniorage to maintain financial system stability in times of financial crisis is not against the principle of representative democracy considering that a central bank is subject to public governance (analyzed in Chap. 3). In particular, according to Congleton's theory of public selection, politicians that pursue vote-maximization behavior (see Chap. 3, Sect. 3.4.2) make biased decisions during a financial crisis and therefore it may be all the more necessary for a central bank to make decisions regarding seigniorage.

Chapter 7
Scope and Governance of Central Bank Payment and Settlement Systems

7.1 Overview

When we look back, central banks have, from the outset, provided payment and settlement systems. Padoa-Schioppa (1991, p. 1) stated "[the] function of monetary policy and bank supervision is derived from provision of settlement services and oversight of payment and settlement systems." Indeed, the provision of payment and settlement services (systems) is a central bank's traditional and intrinsic function. For example, with the Bank of England during the 18th century in mind, Goodhart (1988, p. 34) said "The Bank at the center can also provide various correspondent services and facilitate payments, participations, and introductions to the smaller local bank, and, perhaps services to the local bank's clients that would not otherwise be available." and that "A second main purpose, and function, of the Reichsbank was to improve and to organize the system of countrywide payments." Also, against the background of financial panic that occurred in 1907, disrupting payments throughout the US, the Federal Reserve System (FRS, 2016, p. 120) said that the objective of establishing the FRS was as follows: "Congress creates the Federal Reserve System, giving it the authority to establish a nationwide check-clearing system to eliminate system inefficiencies and inequities."

Currently, a central bank provides a 'retail payment system' through banknote issuance as the 'bank of issue' and also provides an 'interbank payment and settlement system' through direct and indirect funds transfers among the central bank deposits of private banks as the 'bankers' bank.' Moreover, based on its central bank function as 'bank for the government' and historical background, a central bank provides 'securities settlement systems' for government bonds. And, against the backdrop of their role as the 'bankers' bank,' some central banks provide a securities settlement system not only for government bonds but also for private securities as well.

There are two interrelated aspects to the governance structure of interbank payment and settlement systems: the ownership aspect of 'who owns the organization' and the organizational governance aspect of 'how an organization should be governed.' With regard to the ownership aspect of payment and settlement systems,

© Springer Nature Singapore Pte Ltd. 2019
Y. Oritani, *The Japanese Central Banking System Compared with Its European and American Counterparts*, https://doi.org/10.1007/978-981-13-9001-2_7

since a financial system is owned both by private financial institutions and the central bank, there is the question of 'whether ownership belongs to private organizations or the central bank' (private organizations vs. central bank).

The private organization versus central bank question can be analyzed as the study of the optimal scope of payment settlement services provided by a central bank. In this chapter, optimal scope is studied from two viewpoints—one is the diversification of a central bank's payment and settlement systems and the other is the globalization of central bank payment and settlement services.

As for diversification which is studied in Sect. 7.2, two directions are discussed—from real time gross settlement (RTGS) to securities settlement system and from banknotes (paper-based retail payment system) to electronic retail payment systems. As for globalization that is examined in Sect. 7.3, the reasons why central bank payment and settlement services are limited within the confines of a country and also whether such a situation is desirable or not are discussed from the perspective of the ownership question of payment and settlement systems, i.e., 'private organization versus central bank.'

In Sect. 7.4, the organizational governance aspect of interbank payment and settlement systems owned by the central bank is examined. As studied in Sects. 7.2 and 7.3, active provision of payment services by a central bank invites criticism from various perspectives. Looking at such criticism, we can see that the two elements of governance are deeply interrelated with one another, namely, (a) the ownership issue of 'who owns the organization', and (b) the governance structure issue of 'how do stakeholders govern the organization.' This implies that the central bank, a governance structure that can provide more efficient and safer payment and settlement systems, is appropriate as the owner of numerous payment and settlement systems. Nevertheless, while considerable research has been done regarding ownership issues from the perspective of risk management, no research has been made relating them to the organizational governance issue. Taking into consideration that ownership and organizational governance issues are closely interrelated, this section applies organizational economics to investigate the issues of organizational governance.

7.2 Diversification of Central Bank Payment and Settlement Systems

This section discusses the private organization versus central bank question concerning ownership of payment and settlement systems from the viewpoint of the diversification of a central bank's payment and settlement systems. Two directions of diversification, from RTGS to securities settlement system and from banknotes (paper-based retail payment system) to electronic retail payment systems are analyzed.

Organizational economics, especially the theory of diversification under transaction cost economics, is adopted to analyze the issue. 'Diversification' according to this theory refers to, in the narrow sense, 'horizontal integration' that produces multiple products within a single organization. On the other hand, integration of various outputs within a single organization from production of materials to distribution of final products to users is called 'vertical integration,' and, to produce multiple parts of the product within a single organization is called 'lateral integration,' both of which are distinguished from the above narrowly-defined diversification. However, 'diversification' in this Chapter encompasses not only narrowly-defined diversification, but also vertical and lateral integration. That is, diversification in this chapter means to produce goods and services, be they final products, raw materials or intermediate goods, within a single organization. This is because in the financial industry there is no clear demarcation between input and output nor among raw materials, intermediate goods, and final products, as compared to manufacturing industry. In any case, such distinction does not necessarily hold much significance.

This theory states that diversification of an organization should be decided taking into consideration interdependency and economies of scope stemming from multiple goods and services, as well as related transaction costs. In this respect, it is beneficial to apply organizational economics. So far, considerable research has been seen regarding payment and settlement systems using economic theories pertaining to risk, but none that applies organizational economics to payment and settlement system ownership. Since various economic theories encompassed under organizational economics were developed to consider the role of organization, the theory is in line with this chapter's objective of tackling the ownership of payment and settlement systems head-on.

7.2.1 Diversification from RTGS to Securities Settlement System

In this section, we apply organizational boundary theory introduced in Chap. 4, Sect. 4.3 to discussion of the ownership of a securities settlement system, in other words, the question of whether a central bank should diversify into providing a securities settlement system. First, points of contention are introduced and then considered from the perspective of the interdependency of a securities settlement system. Next, the same points are discussed from the viewpoint of common production factors related to securities settlement systems that bring about economies of scope. Then, economies of scope and network externality that diversification from RTGS to securities settlement system enables are discussed. Finally, economic disadvantages behind diversification such as loss of benefit from division of labor (an increase in transaction/coordination costs that accompany division of labor possibly outweighing the benefits) and the concentration of risks (by diversifying into other systems the central bank shoulders more risks) are discussed.

7.2.1.1 Ownership of Securities Settlement System

A securities settlement system is one that delivers securities such as stocks and bonds, and there are various ways to provide such services. Major discussion points in categorizing the variety of services and considering an appropriate design are as follows:

- Securities to be included (especially in the case of a central bank-owned securities settlement system, whether private securities should be included).
- Whether it is a transfer-only system that only transfers ownership of securities (a system that the ECB has developed <T2S>) or a depository system that also provides custody services (the standard central securities depository <CSD>).
- Whether the system is a delivery versus payment (DVP) system that links a securities settlement system and funds transfer system (e.g., RTGS) or a separated system. With regard to DVP system, there is also the question of whether a central bank should become its owner by diversifying into offering a securities settlement system or have another organization become owner. Here, the point raised in above 'securities to be included' is seen from a different perspective.
- Whether the system includes confirmation process which is preprocessing by a securities settlement system and netting (clearing) or just a settlement system (hereafter, a system including netting is called 'central counterparty <CCP> system' which includes both securities settlement and funds transfer).

In the first place, some do not think a central bank should be the owner of a securities settlement system. Advocates of this view consider that a central bank should concentrate on funds transfer and let another organization (e.g., the Depository Trust and Clearing Corporation <DTCC> of the US) handle securities settlement. If a central bank diversifies from RTGS to securities settlement system and becomes the owner, all the above points should be discussed.

7.2.1.2 Interdependencies of Securities Settlement Systems

In considering the above issue, we need to pay attention to interdependency of a central bank securities settlement system. According to firm boundary theory, existence and degree of interdependency are important factors in deciding organizational diversification. It is also important to understand that there are two sides to interdependency. One is interdependency between different payment and settlement systems, in particular that between securities settlement system and RTGS or CCP system. The other is interdependency between securities settlement system and central bank functions other than payment and settlement systems.

The following introduces issues raised by BIS regarding interdependency among typical payment and settlement systems, followed by consideration of interdependency between payment and settlement systems and central bank functions, common production factors related to securities settlement systems, and common production factors between payment and settlement systems and central bank functions. These

considerations ultimately contribute to judging whether a central bank should diversify into providing a securities settlement system. Also, economic advantages and
disadvantages accompanying diversification are given.

**Issues Raised by BIS: Interdependency of Securities Settlement System
with Other Payment and Settlement Systems**
A BIS report (2008, p. 38) entitled *The interdependencies of payment and settlement
systems* warned that payment and settlement systems are increasing interdependencies in the sense that "systems can be interconnected in a variety of ways" and
that "interdependencies can propagate disruptions sequentially from one system to
another."

As a specific case, what is notable when discussing ownership of a securities
settlement system is the (a) interdependency (Fig. 7.1, Arrow (A)) created by connecting a central bank RTGS and the CSD of a central bank or private sector in order
to achieve DVP payment and settlement systems, and (b) interdependency (Fig. 7.1,
Arrow (B)) created by connecting a CSD and CCP system that conducts preprocessing. Arrow (C) in Fig. 7.1 shows interdependency between automated clearing
houses <ACHs> and RTGS noted in 7.2.2.2.

Based on the above, the BIS report (ibid.) recommends "implementing wide coordination among interdependent stakeholders" as one of three suggested actions. As
the reason behind this recommendation, the BIS report (ibid., p. 38) notes that interdependencies among payment and settlement systems have "implication for risk
management" and states as follows:

> Even if these risks are understood, interdependencies may accentuate the externalities and
> collective action problems that can affect the market for payment and settlement services.
> Such market failures could reduce the incentives of systems, institutions and service providers
> to manage risks adequately. Finally, information asymmetries, difficulties in sharing infor-
> mation or coordination challenges are inherently greater between two or more systems and
> their participants than in a single system. These information and coordination challenges
> may hamper risk management.

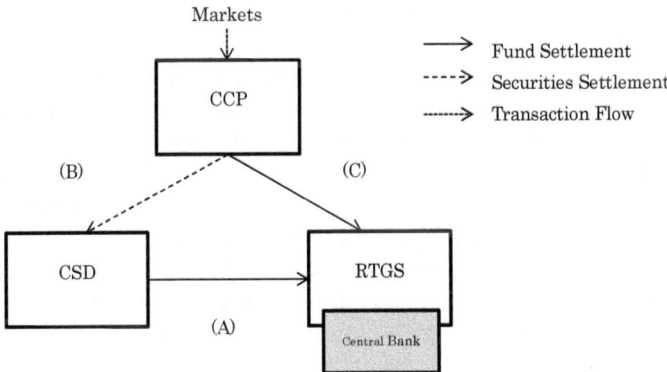

Fig. 7.1 Interdependencies of payment and settlement systems (BIS, 2008)

Interdependencies Between Securities Settlement Systems and Central Bank Functions

Interdependencies mentioned in the previous section are those within payment and settlement systems such as between securities settlement systems and RTGS or CCP system. However, a securities settlement system also has high interdependency with central bank functions other than payment and settlement systems. For example, a securities settlement system has a high degree of interdependence with the monetary policy function as well as regulation and supervisory function. This shows that there are economic benefits for a central bank from diversifying into securities settlement systems.

Interdependency Between Securities Settlement System and Monetary Policy Function

There is considerable interdependency between a securities settlement system and the monetary policy function of a central bank. That is, in implementing monetary policy, a central bank uses securities transactions with private banks as its main instrument (open market operations). In other words, a central bank produces a product (monetary policy function) using a securities settlement system as an ingredient, and so they are in a vertical chain relationship. If a central bank cannot avail itself of securities settlement services, implementation of market operations becomes difficult (or if a securities settlement system is not user friendly, then it becomes difficult to conduct market operations). On the other hand, a securities settlement system does not necessarily need to offer market operation services and customers themselves are not fully dependent on a central bank alone.

Therefore, interdependency between the two according to Chap. 4, Table 4.1 is "high on one side and low on the other." That is, asset specificity is high for a central bank, and low for a securities settlement system. In the case of such a unilaterally interdependent relationship, vertical integration can save transaction costs regardless of the degree of uncertainty and complexity of transactions (vertical integration can also save production costs). Therefore, there is economic benefit for central banks to diversify into securities settlement systems.

Interdependency Between Securities Settlement System and Regulatory and Supervisory Functions

There is also considerable interdependency between a securities settlement system and a central bank's regulatory and supervisory function over financial institutions such as private banks and securities companies. While the fundamental objective of a central bank's regulatory and supervisory function is to maintain financial system stability, the function is also useful for screening the eligibility of participant banks in a securities settlement system ("delegated monitoring").[1]

That is, a central bank can be regarded as utilizing the regulatory and supervisory function as an ingredient to produce services offered by a securities settlement system. On the other hand, by managing a securities settlement system, a central bank

---

[1]Based on Diamond (1984)'s theory of delegated monitoring, information cost to monitor the solvency of settlement counterparties is more efficient when delegated to a specific entity and monitored collectively than monitored individually.

can obtain on-site information and know-how useful for its regulatory and supervisory function ("learning-by-doing"—a concept originally used by Arrow, 1962 and Lucas, 1988 in economic growth theory; see Chap. 5, footnote 5). So, in this case, a securities settlement system becomes the ingredient to produce services offered by the regulatory and supervisory function and hence the two vertical chain relationships overlap.

Therefore, looking at the interdependency between the two, asset specificity is high for both sides as shown in Chap. 4, Table 4.1. Theoretically, integrating securities settlement and the regulatory and supervisory function into one organization can reduce production costs. However, with regard to transaction costs, whether costs can be saved more with a long-term contract (MOU) or organizational integration depends on uncertainty including complexity of transactions between securities settlement system and the regulatory and supervisory function. Thus, when we look at uncertainty and complexity, while uncertainty as to the possibility of a central bank (which exercises the regulatory and supervisory function) falling into default does not exist, we cannot exclude the possibility that it might for a securities settlement system. And, know-how pertaining to both securities settlement and the regulatory and supervisory function is very complex compared to that for general goods and services. Therefore, total organizational integration rather than a long-term contract (involving just the integration of two overlapping vertical relationships) means lower transaction costs. And, in this respect too, we can point out the economic benefits from a central bank diversifying into securities settlement.

7.2.1.3 Common Production Factors Related to Securities Settlement System

Firm boundary theory believes that the economic benefits from a central bank diversifying into securities settlement are not only brought about by interdependence but also by economies of scope realized by common production factors. Four common production factors related to central bank diversification are discussed below—two among payment and settlement systems and two between central bank functions excluding payment and settlement systems.

Common Production Factors Among Payment and Settlement Systems
Common production factors among payment and settlement systems are indivisible tangible assets and technical know-how.

Indivisible Tangible Assets
Both securities settlement and RTGS utilize IT systems and thus such systems, typified by central bank payment and settlement systems, can be considered indivisible tangible assets. The main features of such an IT system are (a) the importance attaching to security rather than efficiency (since a central bank is a non-profit organization) and (b) their being customized for interbank transactions (as counterparties do not include individuals and firms). Such an IT system is the common platform on which specialized systems for securities settlement and RTGS are constructed. It is possible

to construct exactly the same common platform for securities settlement and RTGS individually spending twice the production cost. But, it is impossible to divide one common platform into two systems.

A common platform realizes economies of scope, but, due to its particularity and complexity, trading or leasing usage rights (rental, franchising) requires high transaction costs and is thus not efficient. This means that to realize economies of scope the only way is to integrate RTGS and securities settlement.

Technical Know-How
Among technical know-how related to a central bank RTGS, that which can be used for securities settlement is embedded in the above common platform and so it is difficult to trade or lease the necessary know-how by itself. To utilize economies of scope, RTGS and securities settlement should be integrated.

Moreover, know-how that cannot be embedded in a common platform is accumulated as core competence (in this case, human capital) attaching to central bank management and staff. A central bank provides fiscal agency services for government bonds as bank for the government and related technical know-how includes that which is useful for a government bond settlement system. Know-how can be partially and temporarily traded among relevant organizations by seconding central bank staff to securities settlement systems (leasing contract of human assets) but organizational integration is the only way to realize wide usage of know-how over the long term.

Common Production Factors between Securities Settlement and Central Bank Functions Excluding Payment and Settlement Systems
In relation to securities settlement, other than RTGS, organizational know-how and brand name are important common production factors between a securities settlement system and central bank functions.

Organizational Know-How
Organizational know-how mentioned in Chaps. 4 and 5 can be regarded as a common production factor between central bank functions and securities settlement. The only way to utilize the economies of scope brought about by this common production factor at small transaction cost is for a central bank to diversify into securities settlement.

Brand Name
The brand name of a central bank is credibility of, and trust in, a central bank. Such trust and credibility are common production factors for all services provided by a central bank and also play an important role in a securities settlement system and cannot be leased to other organizations on a long-term leasing contract. Therefore, the only way to utilize the economies of scope brought about by this common production factor at small transaction cost is for a central bank to diversify into securities settlement.

7.2.1.4 Economic Benefits and Disadvantages of Diversification into Securities Settlement

Now we discuss economic benefits and disadvantages of a central bank's diversification into securities settlement that are not related to interdependency and economies of scope.

Economic Benefits

Economies of Scale
Among common production factors in Sect. 7.2.1.3, if a central bank manages not only RTGS but also securities settlement, economies of scale should be seen in the common platform of the IT system. An IT-based payment and settlement system exhibits the typical feature of a corporation equipped with complex equipment consisting of large-scale hardware and a lot of software. That is, the scale of equipment (facilities) and productivity directly lead to competitiveness.[2]

Network Externality
In payment and settlement systems, network externality is realized when the payment settlement network expands and the number of users increases, with the system becoming more useful for each user. This network externality is expected to be seen not only in a single payment and settlement system but also, for example, when a central bank diversifies into securities settlement.

According to Rochet and Tirole (2003), this happens since a payment and settlement system is a "two-sided market." In a two-sided market, the common platform (in this case the payment and settlement system itself) used by multiple service users exists between sellers and buyers, thus creating network externality. As mentioned (Sect. 7.2.1.3), RTGS and securities settlement can share a common IT platform. Therefore, if a central bank diversifies into securities settlement, the number of participants using this common platform would be more than when they use different platforms for RTGS and securities settlement, thus creating network externality.

Economic Disadvantages Regarding Diversification into Securities Settlement
As mentioned above, a central bank's diversification into securities settlement has economic advantages that reduce production and transaction costs based on interdependence and economies of scale. However, at the same time, there is a possibility of an increase in economic disadvantages such as increase in bureaucracy costs and loss of benefit from the division of labor that accompanies expansion of the central bank organization and boundary (an increase in transaction/coordination costs that accompany division of labor possibly outweighing the benefits) and the concentration of risks (by diversifying into other systems the central bank shoulders more risks).

One of the common disadvantages regarding diversification, that is, 'risk concentration,' is not an issue for a central bank in the area of solvency since a central bank

---

[2]Schmiedel, Malkamaki, and Tarkka (2002) conducted an empirical study on 16 central securities depositories (CSDs) and confirmed economies of scale in all cases.

is an organization that does not become insolvent. The only issue is the operational risk related to use of a common platform. This risk and seeking economies of scope by using a common platform are two sides of the same coin and the countermeasure would be to construct a separate IT system so as not to use a common platform. Of course, by doing so, the economies of scope that common production factors bring are lost. Nevertheless, if the economic benefits gained through organizational integration in other aspects are sufficient, it is beneficial for a central bank to diversify its payment and settlement system into securities settlement.

7.2.2   Diversification into Retail Payment Systems

Retail payment systems enable small-value funds transfers among individuals and corporations and are also called 'small-value transfer systems.' Since inception, central banks have played an extremely important role in retail payment systems in the form of the issuance and distribution of banknotes. Nevertheless, as the instruments of retail payment evolved from paper-based currency (banknotes and coins) to computer-based money (electronic money <e-money>) the relative role of central banks have been diminishing. That is to say, with various computer-based retail payment systems (e.g., credit/debit cards) appearing on the scene that substitute for banknotes and coins, central banks now only provide a portion of retail payment services.

Whether the said central bank ownership of such retail payment systems is appropriate from firm boundary theory should be discussed, but before that, retail payment systems that might be candidates for central bank ownership (or are already owned by central banks) are categorized into four: (a) RTGS retail payment systems, (b) clearing retail payment systems, (c) e-money systems, and (d) net position settlement services for clearing retail payment systems. Of the four, (a)–(c) are taken up. We do not discuss (d) since there is no question that such systems are provided by central banks. There is also discussion on whether central banks should provide cross-border retail payment systems but discussion of the CLS Bank in Sect. 7.3 is applicable, so such systems are not considered here.

The following only discusses the economic advantages of central bank diversification into retail payment systems and does not detail the economic disadvantages. That is, while economic disadvantages such as an increase in bureaucracy costs accompany diversification of a central bank into any kind of retail payment system, other disadvantages are not a significant issue as diversification is basically conducted within the same operational arena of payment and settlement systems.

7.2.2.1   Provision of RTGS Retail Payment Systems

RTGS retail payment systems apply RTGS, which is usually used for large-value funds transfers, to small-value payments. Fedwire of the FRS in the US is a typical example of such a retail payment service. Below, we look at economies of scope as the only economic benefit stemming from central bank diversification into RTGS retail payment systems that is occasioned by common production factors such as tangible assets, organizational know-how, and brand name.[3] This is because there is no direct interdependence between such retail payment systems and other central bank payment and settlement systems/central bank functions.[4]

Tangible Assets
Sources of economic benefits accompanying central bank diversification into RTGS retail payment systems are common production factors with existing large-value funds transfer systems, and, central bank money. Technical know-how is also included under common production factors, but cannot be regarded as a pure tangible asset. Of the four common production factors, the most relevant one is tangible assets.

Common Production Factor with Large-Value Funds Transfer Systems
BIS (2003a, p. 11) considers safety, and fair and open access as the rationale for a central bank to provide settlement services. In addition, BIS is of the view that a central bank's large-value payment system (RTGS) brings about economies of scale and scope:

> In some countries, economies of scale and scope are also involved; for example, where a central bank settlement infrastructure exists in any event for large-value payment systems and to facilitate monetary policy operations, it can be argued that the efficiency objective is well served if the settlement infrastructure is also used by retail payment systems.

This refers to settlement of net positions in clearing retail payment systems (this can be included in the category (d) among the four kinds of retail payment systems mentioned earlier) but the same can be said for common production factors between large-value funds transfer systems (RTGS) and RTGS retail payment systems. This is because hardware infrastructure and basic software for large-value RTGS and RTGS retail payment systems can be standardized. There may need to be different specifications in their respective security measures but the only basic difference is the value of funds. In addition to common production factors with large-value RTGS, the common platform shared by central bank payment systems such as securities settlement system and RTGS retail payment system can also be considered a common production factor.

---

[3]We can of course expect economies of scale by sharing existing large-value funds transfer systems. However, network externality is not included as a benefit as while users of such large-value systems are mainly banks, users of RTGS retail payment systems are individuals and corporations. The only economic disadvantage arising from diversification into this system is an increase in bureaucracy costs. Loss of benefit gained from division of labor does not become an issue as there are many similarities between large-value systems and this one.

[4]However, from a broader perspective, we can point out interdependencies with other central bank functions such as realizing financial system stability through an increase in risk free settlement instruments if the central bank provides such settlement services (similar to the discussion of an e-money system to be discussed later) and supporting the effectiveness of monetary policy (by balancing out decreases in banknotes in circulation).

These common production factors are, from a transaction cost standpoint, impossible to lend to private banks and economies of scope can only be utilized by a single organization. In other words, economies of scope brought about by these common production factors represent the economic benefit of a central bank diversifying into RTGS retail payment systems.

Common Production Factors with Central Bank Money
We can point out that central bank money brings a common production factor in the shape of economies of scope between RTGS retail payment systems and other central bank payment systems as well as central bank functions. Central bank money here does not include banknotes but refers to "accounts and deposit money to banks and, in certain cases, to other organizations" as defined by BIS (2003b).

This common production factor is extremely complicated and carries the risk of information leakage. Therefore, it cannot basically exist apart from a central bank. Even from a transaction cost standpoint, to utilize this common production factor, central bank money, RTGS retail payment systems, and other central bank payment systems as well as central bank functions should be integrated into a single organization.

Organizational Know-How and Brand Name
As mentioned in Chap. 5, Sect. 5.3.1.3, four organizational know-how factors attaching to a central bank (behavioral pattern as a public organization, independence, organizational culture, ability to provide credit) are all regarded as common production factors between retail payment systems and other central bank payment and settlement systems. BIS (2003a, p. 11) notes, "In addition, fair and open access for banks to central bank settlement services, as far as is compatible with safety objectives, can provide competitive neutrality and so contribute to efficiency."

And, as mentioned (Sect. 7.2.1.3), a central bank's brand name (credibility of, and trust in it) is one common production factor that brings about economies of scope to central bank retail payment systems. As is the case with securities settlement systems, it is difficult to lease or trade these common production factors and they can only be utilized within a single organization.

7.2.2.2 Provision of Clearing Retail Payment Systems (Automated Clearing House)

Clearing retail payment systems as in the Automated Clearing House in the US, calculate net positions by conducting netting based on small-value payment instructions. Usually, an automated clearing house (ACH) owner fulfills a credit and debit relationship for net positions between participants until settlement and therefore the system is also a central counterparty (CCP) system.

Economic benefits stemming from a central bank providing an ACH are (a) interdependency between the ACH and central bank large-value payment and settlement systems, (b) a common production factor between the ACH and paper-based clearing house, and (c) a common production factor between the ACH and neutrality of a central bank. In addition, we can also add interdependence between an ACH and a central bank's credit provision function[5] as an economic benefit, but, as credit provision to an ACH can also be made by private banks up to a certain amount, we do not include it here.

Interdependency Between ACH and Central Bank Large-Value RTGS
Usually, ACH net positions are settled using a central bank's large-value RTGS and therefore there is strong interdependency between them. BIS (2008, p. 18) notes such relationship (Arrow (C) in Fig. 7.1) as follows:

> These domestic clearing and settlement relationships between systems make the settlement flows of the related systems significantly interdependent. For example, in many instances, balances in the primary LVPS <large-value payment system> (usually an RTGS system settling in central bank money) are used to settle payment obligations in other payment systems (e.g., interbank settlement systems), securities settlement systems and CCPs.

An ACH is unilaterally dependent on central bank RTGS since, for its part, a central bank RTGS does not need it. Based on Chap. 4, Table 4.1 regarding the relationship of determinants of transaction cost and governance mechanism, an ACH should integrate central bank RTGS and become one unified organization. However, while it is possible to integrate an ACH into a central bank, it is impossible to cut off RTGS from a central bank and integrate it with an ACH as a private organization. Additionally, from the perspective of a private sector entity that manages an ACH, transactions with a central bank involve little possibility of it taking opportunistic behavior or falling into default. Therefore, CHIPS and Electronic Payments Network (EPN, a private sector ACH operator) in the US adopt a governance mechanism that does not integrate the two organizations but which settles net positions under a long-term contract.

Nevertheless, we can say that according to firm boundary theory, rather than depending on a long-term contract like the case of the Fed Automated Clearing House (owned by the FRS), integrating an ACH into a central bank would save production costs and transaction costs that arise from interdependency.

Common Production Factors Between ACH and Central Bank Settlement Systems and Functions
Common production factors between an ACH and central bank settlement systems and functions are technical and considered organizational know-how accumulated through operating paper-based clearing houses and central bank independence.

Computerization of Paper-Based Clearing House
Most cases of existing ACHs are the result of paper-based clearing house owners diversifying into such as in the case of the FRS in the US. Since ACHs computerized the functions of a clearing house, technical and organizational know-how acquired through operating a clearing house brings about economies of scope as a common

---

[5]From a broader perspective, there is also interdependency between the monetary policy function and financial system stability maintenance function, similar to an RTGS retail payment system and e-money system.

production factor. According to firm boundary theory, while technical know-how can be transferred to a certain extent to other organizations under a long-term leasing contract, it is extremely difficult to transfer organizational know-how. This is usually explained based on historical reasons (path dependency). Teece's (1994) explanation based on the concept of "coherence" holds true for this case. That is, "A salient attribute of diversification is that firms over time add activities that relate to some aspect of existing activities. They build laterally on what they have got."

The Rivlin Report (FRS, 1998) considers in detail FRS's role in retail settlement systems such as ACHs and recommends that FRS diversify into services such as "cross-border ACH" and financial EDI (electronic data interchange). The objective is to utilize economies of scope within the FRS that are gained from common production factors such as technical and organizational know-how accumulated through operating an ACH.

Economies of Scale and Organizational Neutrality
The abovementioned Rivlin Report (ibid., p. 27) points out the existence of strong economies of scale attaching to an ACH and the possibility of monopoly as a consequence:[6]

> The ACH is characterized by high fixed costs,…The marginal cost of sending an additional ACH transaction is low (less than $0.1), and there are evident economies of scale at current industry volume levels. Hence, with or without the Federal Reserve, the industry is likely to be dominated by one or two large players, much like the market for credit card processing.

Having said this, the Rivlin Report states the need to maintain competition and proposes that the FRS provide an ACH. However, when we turn to existing payment and settlement systems, monopoly cannot be prevented, and it seems more important to think about how an ACH can maintain neutrality/equality towards its participants under monopoly. From this perspective, neutrality embedded in a central bank's organizational know-how is an important common production factor that offers economies of scope for an ACH. Moreover, this organizational know-how cannot be transferred to private organizations through market transactions and a long-term leasing contract. Therefore, one of the economic benefits a central bank offers an ACH is that it can utilize economies of scope with the organizational know-how of 'central bank neutrality' as a common production factor.

7.2.2.3 Provision of Electronic Money

Electronic money (e-money) according to a BIS report (2004, p. 2) on the results of a large-scale survey is:

> Card-based products, also known as multipurpose prepaid cards or electronic purses, are designed to facilitate small-value face-to-face retail payments by offering a substitute for banknotes and coins.… Electronic money continues to be defined as a stored value or prepaid

---

[6]In actuality, there were four private-sector ACHs other than the FRS-operated one in the US in 1987 but the number had fallen to one (Electronic Payments Network) by 2003.

product in which a record of the funds or value available to the consumer for multipurpose use is stored on an electronic device in the consumer's possession.

The report (ibid., p. 2) also notes that:

A number of the central banks which responded to the survey questionnaire stated that there are no plans to introduce e-money schemes in the near future in their respective countries.

However,

The ECB is of the view that the national central banks can maintain the size of their balance sheet if necessary by imposing minimum reserves on e-money issuers or by issuing e-money themselves.

The following section discusses the economic benefits of central bank e-money from two aspects: (a) benefits based on interdependence between e-money and central bank functions such as monetary policy and prudential policy, and (b) benefits based on common production factors between central bank e-money and cash currency system that the central bank has been providing from its outset.

Interdependence Between E-Money and Central Bank Functions
E-money has low linkage with private bank money (deposits at private banks), let alone central bank money, and has weak interdependence with other central bank payment and settlement systems. This is because e-money has direct transferability of value as it is a means of settlement without any direct relation with private bank deposits. However, the ECB in the Appendix of the above BIS report states that "the importance of e-money for monetary policy stems from the fact that it may become a very close substitute for notes and coins" and then raises the issue of how it affects a central bank's monetary and prudential policy functions. This issue points out the interdependence between e-money and central bank functions and implies the necessity to integrate both organizations, that is, issuance of e-money by a central bank.

Interdependence with Monetary Policy Function
The ECB (BIS, 2004, p. 48) raises three specific issues related to the monetary policy function: (a) "There is a need to safeguard the role of money as the unit of account for economic transactions,..." (b) Second, "the effectiveness of monetary policy instruments might be affected by a widespread adoption of e-money. This relates mainly to effects on central bank balance sheets and central banks' ability to steer short-term interest rates." and (c) "The emergence of e-money might have repercussions for the information content of monetary indicator variables."

Similar to the relationship between securities settlement system and monetary policy functions, e-money as a substitute for banknotes and coins is an ingredient of the monetary policy function. A central bank may have difficulty in implementing monetary policy if it does not issue e-money despite a decrease in the issuance of banknotes and coins. On the other hand, e-money does not need monetary policy. Therefore, when we look at interdependence between the two, asset specificity is 'high on one side and low on the other' as in Chap. 4, Table 4.1. Under such a unilateral interdependent relationship, vertical integration can save transaction costs regardless of uncertainty and complexity of transactions (it could also save production costs since it is in a vertical relationship). Therefore, there is a significant economic benefit for a central bank to diversify into the field of issuing e-money.

Interdependence with Financial System Stability Function
The ECB paper (BIS, 2004, p. 49) also points out interdependence between privately-issued e-money that solely focuses on higher efficiency, and the stability function of the financial system:

> E-money development should not jeopardize either the smooth functioning of payment systems or the stability of the financial system….A number of risks can be identified; in particular the intrusion of counterfeit value, major technical failures, float mismanagement and, ultimately, failure on the part of issuers of e-money could have a negative impact on the credibility of various e-money products and possibly even on other electronic payment products. Public confidence in the currency could be undermined if e-money issuers engage in risky investment activities.

To counter these risks, the ECB published *"Report on Electronic Money"* (1998) and *"Opinion on the introduction of e-money institutions"* (1999) that presented a regulatory framework for e-money considering that it is necessary to secure sound management of e-money issuers as well as the security and efficiency of e-money.

As such, secure e-money is an ingredient for maintaining financial system stability, and, in the sense that a regulatory framework covering e-money to maintain such financial system stability is in turn a component for sound and secure e-money, their interdependent relationship is 'high for both sides' as in Chap. 4, Table 4.1. This relationship is similar to that of central bank securities settlement systems and regulatory and supervisory functions. Therefore, most discussions regarding diversification into securities settlement systems apply here, evidencing the economic benefit of a central bank providing e-money.

Common Production Factors with Cash Currency System

It is not odd for a central bank that has historically issued and distributed banknotes and coins (in some countries the central bank prints/mints too) to also provide e-money, similar to the case of a paper-based clearing house evolving to an automated clearing house (ACH). This is just what Teece (1994) stated as a salient attribute of diversification (see Sect. 7.2.2.2). Common production factors between cash and e-money are technical and organizational know-how, and brand name as follows.[7]

Technical Know-How
Over the years, central banks have accumulated technical know-how on anti-counterfeiting measures with respect to cash currency. Not all such technical know-how can be applied to e-money but, considering that e-money is a substitute for cash currency, such technical know-how can be used as a common production factor partially or indirectly. This technical know-how comprises confidential information related to cash currency anti-counterfeiting measures and is therefore impossible to

---

[7] Additionally, between e-money and central bank payment and settlement systems, especially retail settlement systems, common production factors also exist in IT system-related factors such as use of a common platform.

be taken out of a central bank through a long-term contract or selling in the market and can only be used within a single organization, that is, a central bank.

Organizational Know-How

Since e-money is a substitute for cash currency, a central bank that issues and distributes cash currency has abundant organizational know-how that would also be beneficial for e-money. In summary, such know-how comprises the first three of the four aspects of organizational know-how of a central bank mentioned in Chap. 5, Sect. 5.3.1.3 (behavioral pattern as a public organization, independence, organizational culture, ability to provide credit <*Application of Horizontal Integration Theory*>). As for the organizational know-how aspect, that is ability to provide credit, it is difficult to envisage e-money providing credit to participants.

We could also point out the reserve management function for banknotes issued[8] as another form of organizational know-how of a central bank related to the issuance and distribution of cash currency. This function is considered to hold significance should e-money as a substitute for cash currency become widely popular and accumulates to a considerable amount. Whether cash currency or e-money, there are cases that the so-called 'float' emerges until the user completes payment. The float belongs to the issuers of cash currency and e-money, and to prepare assets corresponding to the float amount is thus also a 'reserve management function' on the part of the issuers of e-money. A central bank has organizational know-how regarding asset management that is in line with macro monetary policy based on its behavioral pattern as a public organization (that is, not profit-seeking).

Such organizational know-how cannot exist outside of a central bank and to utilize it as a common production factor for economies of scope there is no other way than for the central bank that issues and distributes cash currency to provide e-money.

Brand Name

Similar to the discussion on diversification to a securities settlement system, considering that the brand name of a central bank is in essence the credibility attaching to, and trust in, the central bank, it has an important role as a common production factor of cash currency and e-money.

If in the future a private issuer of e-money went bust, systemic risk might materialize in which situation the credibility of, and trust in, other private issuing companies might be marred. However, as is the case with cash currency, the credibility of, and trust in, a central bank are virtually inviolate (the public has absolute trust in cash currency provided by a central bank since it does not go bust and, in the same way, the public would trust e-money issued by a central bank). Such credibility and trust is indivisible from a central bank and to take advantage of it a central bank needs to provide e-money.

---

[8]The balance of banknotes issued is a debt of a central bank to holders and therefore the function of determining corresponding assets (reserves for banknotes issued) is a core competence of a central bank. Historically, gold and precious metals comprised a large proportion of reserves but today they also include securities such as government bonds and foreign reserves.

Central Bank Studies of Electronic Retail Payment Systems

'Electronic retail payment system' in this book includes e-money that utilizes traditional technology (such as prepaid card-type e-money) as well as so-called central bank digital currency (CBDC) using blockchain technology that is currently being discussed. To date, no central bank has actually issued e-money or CBDC. However, many central banks have said they have studied or are studying e-money/CBDC such as the Bank of Canada, the Bank of England, the Bank of Japan (BOJ), the Riksbank (central bank of Sweden), and the Monetary Authority of Singapore. This section introduces the experience of the BOJ that conducted a study on e-money more than 20 years ago and also that of the Riksbank which has embarked on a CBDC project.

Study by the Bank of Japan

Nakajima (2017) disclosed in his book that in 1990 the Institute for Monetary and Economic Studies (IMES) of the BOJ had quietly put together a team (inviting a professor of encryption) to study e-money, of which Nakajima himself was a member. The project was titled 'Electronic Cash Project,' and was based on the assumption that "if we use 'eCash' and up-to-date encryption technology, a central bank can issue e-money" (translated from Japanese). The 'eCash' is a network-type e-money proposed by David Chaum.

According to Nakajima (ibid.), the study team found that there were difficulties outlined below, that could not be solved by the level of technology at that time and terminated the project with only writing a study paper.

First is the issue of how to secure the feature of 'direct transferability' that cash enjoys—'direct transferability' is the ability to use cash received to make payments. In this case, once e-money is out of a central bank's hands, it circulates around different holders. Therefore, it would become difficult to detect forgery or duplicate spending in the circulation process.

Second, to what extent should the 'anonymity' attaching to cash be secured? From a security perspective, we need to know where a problem occurs, i.e., at what point did forgery occur, but, to construct such a system, a very high-level and complex encryption scheme needs to be in place.

Third, there is the fact that digital data can easily be copied. A technology called 'tamper resistance' exists to prevent data copying but it is not perfect. If, by any chance, all tamper resistance techniques fail, e-money would be copied unlimitedly. In other words, forged e-money would increase endlessly.

After the project, IMES conducted a joint study with Nippon Telegraph and Telephone (NTT) in 1997 and the results were published under the title *An Electronic Money Scheme—A Proposal for a New Electronic Money Scheme which is both Secure and Convenient* (Nakayama et al., 1997). Nevertheless, the BOJ has not actually issued e-money to date. With regard to CBDC, the BOJ has organized study meetings and conferences with experts, but has not announced any plans to construct an experimental system or to actually issue e-money.

Study by the Riksbank

The Riksbank announced in November 2016 that it had launched a project with the aim of examining whether the krona could be issued in an electronic form of 'e-krona.' This is because "…the use of banknotes and coins is declining in society. At the same time, technological advances with regard to electronic money and payment methods are moving rapidly." (Riksbank website, 2018).

Also appearing on the Riksbank website is "No decision has yet been taking on issuing an 'e-krona' or on what technical solution would be used." Other statements include:

> The project that has been started aims to investigate the legal and technical conditions for the Riksbank to be able to issue an e-krona. It will also entail integrity issues and how an e-krona could be made available to the general public. The inquiry is expected to be finalised in late 2019.

> If the Riksbank later decides to issue an e-krona, it would not be to replace cash, but so that the e-krona could act as a complement to cash.

> The E-krona project published a first interim report in September 2017. With the report, the Riksbank wishes to encourage an open dialogue with various participants in society who may have important points of view and lessons to contribute. In this report you can read more about the reasons why the Riksbank is considering issuing an e-krona, the technical aspects of the design of an e-krona, the role of the Riksbank, the consequences of issuing an e-krona based on, for instance, a monetary policy perspective and a financial stability perspective, and so on.

7.3 Globalization of Central Bank Payment and Settlement Systems

Central banks provide various payment and settlement services within their respective country but none provide 'interbank cross-border payment and settlement services' despite the rapid globalization of financial transactions. This implies that the globalization of central bank payment and settlement systems has not developed to date. In other words, from the perspective of ownership of cross-border systems, some portion of the governance issue of payment and settlement services has been entrusted to private organizations, not to central banks. Based on such awareness, the globalization of central bank payment and settlement services is considered from the perspective of ownership, i.e., 'private organization versus central bank.'

In this respect, it seems beneficial to look into how the Continuous Linked Settlement (CLS) Bank came to be established in New York by major global private banks in 1999. CLS Bank is a cross-border settlement system for multi-currency settlement of interbank foreign exchange transactions.

When examining how CLS Bank came to be established, it seems a theoretical analysis needs to be made in addition to going over the establishment process. For this purpose, it is worthwhile applying transaction cost economics (TCE). Among the various theories within TCE, this section takes up peer group theory by Williamson (1975) introduced in Chap. 1, Sect. 1.6.2.2.

As stated in Chap. 1, Sect. 1.6.2.2, according to Williamson's peer group theory, private payment and settlement system transaction costs are significant. Especially when a private organization starts up a payment and settlement system, the severity of coordination costs becomes all the more evident. The following section considers the coordination costs of cross-border systems by analyzing the establishment of CLS Bank (peer group) applying peer group theory.

7.3.1 Chronology of CLS Bank's Establishment

Eleven major central banks that were members of BIS's Committee on Payment and Settlement Systems (CPSS) played an extremely important role in the process leading to the establishment of CLS Bank. It is not too much to say that without the robust initiative of CPSS, private banks on their own might not have been able to establish such an institution as CLS Bank. On the other hand, if we consider why these major 11 central banks encouraged private banks to provide cross-border settlement services, we should be able to acquire implications for the globalization of central bank settlement systems.

7.3.1.1   From Start of Discussion at BIS to Release of the Noël Report

First, let us look chronologically at how discussion started at BIS which led to the release of the Noël Report as a preparatory stage for establishing CLS Bank. As shown in Table 7.1, the BIS Group of Experts on Payment Systems (GEPS) was assembled in 1980, and then changed to the CPSS (current Committee on Payments and Market Infrastructures), to discuss issues related to payment and settlement systems. Around the same time, the settlement of cross-border foreign exchange transactions increased against the backdrop of the globalization of financial transactions, raising concerns that they were being conducted under netting schemes with high unwinding risk. In light of this, Wayne Angell, member of the Board of the Governors of the FRS, who became chairman of GEPS in 1988, conducted research into netting schemes which led to the publication of the so-called Angell Report (BIS, 1989). In 1989, the G10 governors established the ad hoc Committee on Interbank Netting Schemes, which published the Lamfalussy Report (BIS, 1990) containing minimum standards for the design and operation of cross-border and multi-currency netting schemes or systems.

Later, CPSS enlarged the focus of discussion from risk attaching to netting schemes to all types of settlement risks related to cross-border foreign exchange transactions and published the Noël Report (BIS, 1993). The report gives detailed consideration of measures to reduce settlement risks. Specifically, it details the possibility of a central bank providing direct settlement services with two options.[9] One of the options is called "cross-border links between payments systems" where "direct operational and informational links could be created that would give participating

---

[9]Oritani (1991) also considers various possible linkage patterns of cross-border settlement systems.

Table 7.1   Main events leading to the establishment of CLS Bank

	Main events	Notes
1980	Start of GEPS: Group of Experts on Payment Systems, BIS	
1988	Wayne Angell, member of the Board of the Governors of the Federal Reserve System becomes Chairman of GEPS	
1989	GEPS releases the Angell Report	Considers risks attaching to netting schemes including cross-border transactions
1990	GEPS becomes an official committee of BIS (CPSS). Wayne Angell, member of the Board of the Governors of the Federal Reserve System continues to be its Chairman	
1990	CPSS releases Lamfalussy Report	Lamfalussy standard is made to counter risks attaching to netting schemes including cross-border transactions
1993	CPSS releases Noel Report	Considers options to reduce risks related to cross-border foreign exchange transactions (including central bank offering of multi-currency payment and settlement services)
1994	William McDonough, president of the Federal Reserve Bank of New York, takes over from Wayne Angell as CPSS chairman	
1994	Start of EMI (which later became the ECB) and development of the TARGET system	
1996	CPSS releases Allsopp Report	Proposes establishment of cross-border multi-currency settlement system by private banks (CLS Bank)
1997	Start of CLS Services Ltd (Main body of CLS Bank)	
1997	CLS Services Ltd merges the existing multi-currency netting schemes (ECHO and Multinet)	Against a backdrop of the CPSS's intention
1998	CPSS releases progress report	Implicitly requests private banks to participate in CLS Bank
1999	ECB starts the TARGET system	
2002	Start of CLS Bank	

central banks the joint capability to monitor, control and execute simultaneously final transfers over their respective home-currency payments systems."

The other possible option is the "joint offering of multi-currency payment and settlement services." This option is explained in Noël Report (ibid., p. 4) as follows:

> Multi-currency accounts and settlement facilities might be provided by the central banks of issue through a 'common agent.' Specifically, a central bank controlled common agent could accept deposits in multiple currencies and facilitate final transfers between these accounts. A variant of this arrangement would involve one or more central banks acting as the common agent in providing multi-currency services.

Whichever the option, it is worth noting that the Noël Report implied the possibility of a central bank providing direct cross-border settlement services as follows (emphasis in italics by Oritani): "The goal of the analysis was to identify and promote a common understanding of the advantages and disadvantages of *different payment and settlement services that central banks might offer.*"

7.3.1.2   Encouragement from the Central Banks

In 1994, William McDonough, President of the Federal Reserve Bank of New York, took over from Wayne Angell as CPSS Chairman and discussion of central banks directly providing cross-border settlement services diminished and instead emphasis was placed on encouraging private organizations to provide settlement services. As if to respond to such a shift, Exchange Clearing House (ECHO) organized by 15 international banks from seven countries commenced operations in London in 1995, and in 1996 Multinet operated by banks in the US and Canada began providing cross-border settlement services using netting. Against this background, the Allsopp Report (BIS, 1996) recognized "the G-10 central banks' view that such services (multi-currency settlement mechanisms <Oritani>) would best be provided by the private sector rather than the public sector."

However, at that time, prospects for collective action by the private sector were as follows (Allsopp Report, ibid., p. 17):

> Although some of these industry-wide initiatives are well under way, many banks are skeptical about the business case for committing resources to efforts to reduce FX settlement exposures. As a result, many individual banks have been slow to join these efforts. Without adequate motivation for sufficient number of FX market participants to support and use one or more of these current or prospective industry-wide multi-currency services, their short-term (let alone long-term) viability is uncertain.

And so CPSS proposed that central banks in respective countries reach out to the private sector through inducement such as moral suasion and supervisory measures. The proposal turned out to be effective, and in 1997 major banks in Japan, the US, and Europe established CLS Services Ltd., (CLSS) which in the same year merged ECHO and Multinet, eyeing construction of a cross-border multi-currency settlement system. However, even at this stage, private banks were not coordinating and the number participating in CLSS was, for a while, small.

The Steering Group of CPSS held regular meetings with CLSS and in 1998 CPSS compiled and published the so-called Progress Report (BIS, 1998). The Progress Report reaffirmed that "the private sector, with the active support of the public sector, had the power to contain the risk" and through measures such as "support the lead central banks in analyzing industry group proposals for risk-reducing multi-currency services in the context of the Lamfalussy framework," it decided to "stimulate private sector action" and "strengthen the strategy launched in 1996." Despite such strong encouragement from the central banks, due to the complex mechanism of the framework[10] it was only in 2002 that CLS Bank actually commenced operations.

7.3.2 Implications of Process Leading to Establishment of CLS Bank

The above process leading to the establishment of CLS Bank has various implications concerning debate on private organization versus central bank ownership of payment and settlement systems. We point out major implications such as (a) a peer group consisting of private banks incurs high coordination costs in establishing a payment and settlement system, (b) it is a fact that, in the past, discussions had been held regarding central banks providing cross-border settlement services, and (c) central banks did not provide such services due to bureaucracy costs inherent to a central bank.

7.3.2.1 High Coordination Costs Among Private Banks

As seen in Sect. 7.3.1, the first implication is the high coordination costs in establishing payment and settlement services by a peer group of private banks. CLS Bank was established solely because there was strong encouragement from the central banks. This is evident when we compare CLS Bank and the TARGET system of the ECB.

It took 13 years for CLS Bank to start operating from when its prototype was established (from publication of the Angell Report).[11] On the other hand, ECB's

---

[10]Oritani (1991a) explained that linking private payment and settlement systems (i.e., the CLS Bank) is far more complex than linking payment and settlement systems of the central banks. CLS Bank is not a central bank and therefore cannot directly use central bank money, and is thus unable to secure settlement finality. To reduce risks, there needs to be a complex mechanism. As a result, CLS Bank necessitates more complex arrangements than a central bank system using central bank money.

[11]The Angell Report did not actually propose the establishment of a cross-border multi-currency settlement system by the private sector. However, foreign exchange settlement risks have been recognized in the private sector from around this time. Especially after Herstatt risk materialized on a large scale due to failure of BCCI in 1991, the necessity of multi-currency settlement systems has been widely acknowledged, leading to the establishment of ECHO in 1995. However, ECHO could not gather enough participants (coordination cost issue of a peer group) and failed.

TARGET system started operating only five years after its initial development stage in 1994.[12] From the perspective of transaction costs, unlike CLS Bank, there is a hierarchical relationship among the ECB, respective participating central banks, and private banks which enabled the system to be established with lower coordination costs and in a shorter period of time. Of course, technical factors had a considerable impact since the TARGET system is not a multi-currency settlement service but a single currency system and also one that uses central bank money and has a simple configuration compared to CLS Bank.[13] Therefore, we cannot really make a simple comparison of the two systems. Nevertheless, it is not necessarily misleading to compare the two since if a cross-border settlement system is configured as discussed in the Noël Report, it would be similar to that of the TARGET system that links payment and settlement systems of participating central banks.

7.3.2.2 Central Bank Judgment at the Time of Establishing CLS Bank

The second implication is that central bank judgment at the time of CLS Bank establishment changed from an option that central banks themselves provide cross-border settlement services to that of only encouraging private banks provide such a service. This is a historic policy change on the part of central banks against the background of the globalization of central bank payment and settlement systems. The following section states the basis for such historic policy change and problems accompanying it.

Basis for the Historic Policy Change

The Noël Report which was compiled during the process leading to the establishment of CLS Bank discussed the possibility of central bank provision of cross-border settlement services rather than urging private banks to provide the same. On the contrary, the Allsopp Report, which was published after the CPSS chairman changed from Angell to McDonough, clarified that central banks do not provide cross-border settlement services. This was an historic policy change regarding central bank settlement services against the backdrop of the globalization of financial markets.

As the basis for such historic policy change, the Allsopp Report excluded the risk concern inherent in private payment and settlement systems stating that "These existing and prospective multi-currency services (private sector services) include settlement mechanisms with guaranteed receipts, guaranteed refunds, simultaneous settlement, sequential settlement and different combinations of these features." At the same time, the report also points out that "Market-place competition in providing

---

[12]Development of the TARGET system started at the same time the European Monetary Institute (EMI) was established in 1994. Actually, the EMI (which later became the ECB) agreement states: "to promote the efficiency of cross-border payment and securities settlement transactions in order to support the integration of the euro money market, notably by developing the technological infrastructure (the TARGET system) for the processing of cross-border payments in euro to be as smooth as that of domestic payments." As mentioned in note 15 of Chap. 1, Oritani (1991b) pointed out the importance of payment system linkages among EMU members.

[13]Refer to Oritani (1991a) for a simple framework of a system using central bank money.

multi-currency services would bring important benefits...." and "The test of the market-place could promote competition and ongoing innovation and would make use of continual market pressure to provide cost-effective arrangements." In sum, the report concluded, at least officially, that trust in risk reduction measures embedded in CLS Bank as well as trust in market competition are the reasons why it is sufficient for the private sector and not central banks to provide cross-border multi-currency settlement services.

Problems Related to the Historic Policy Change

When we apply peer group theory to the above reasoning, it does not at all answer the question 'Why choose the private sector that involves high coordination costs as the owner?' There are also other major concerns as follows.

First, consideration of the risk aspect is excluded. As CLS Bank is a user-owned stock company, one cannot deny that there is a possibility that it might default. Also, CLS Bank does not play a direct role if a participating bank experiences a liquidity shortage, and it is up to the pertinent central bank of issue to decide whether to provide liquidity as LLR to participating banks that hold accounts with it. These risks are risks inherent to the private sector that is outside the settlement framework of CLS Bank. Padoa-Schioppa (1991, p. 2) points out concern over the private sector providing cross-border settlement services noting the limitation of a peer group association, that is competition problems (see Chap. 1, Sect. 1.6.2.2):

> Central banks may be challenged at the international level by individual banks or groups of banks supplying the services and organizations typically provided by central banks in national systems. This is obviously a cause for concern from a public policy standpoint. In the past, national financial systems suffered from recurrent crises until some form of public status was given to the clearing houses that were acting as 'quasi-central banks' in several countries. As long as the clearing house was privately run, the clearing process and the stability of the monetary system as a whole, were vulnerable to breaches of the co-operative attitude of the participants, who after all were competitors. Thus, it is not unreasonable to expect that a privately-managed provider of international settlement services might have to resort to central banks in an emergency, raising potentially serious policy problems.

The second issue is related to the technical mechanism. Since CLS Bank is not a central bank, it cannot use central bank money meaning that settlement finality (a settlement which is irrevocable and unconditional) cannot be easily assured. Therefore, as the name CLS suggests, it needs to adopt a complex mechanism called 'continuous linked settlement' with central banks that issue relevant banknotes and coins to reduce related risks. Naturally, the system mechanism for CLS Bank becomes cost inefficient compared to a central bank settlement system.

The third issue is whether we could really expect efficiency through market pressure for an interbank settlement system. As seen in the process leading up to the establishment of CLS Bank, coordination costs for a peer group were a great hindrance and therefore it is unlikely that another similar system will be established. In addition, the system tends to move toward 'natural monopoly' due to factors on the production cost side such as 'economies of scale' and 'network externality.' Of course, whether the system can enjoy monopoly is decided taking transaction costs into consideration.

Moreover, system structure becomes too complex if we try to realize a system that does not use central bank money and at the same time suppresses risk, and so it is considered difficult for several similar systems to co-exist even from a cost perspective. Actually, merger of CLS Services Ltd., ECHO, and Multinet proves the validity of such a perspective. Therefore, if we are to pursue efficiency through market pressure, the only competitor would be central bank settlement services (this meshes with the argument given in the Rivlin Report introduced earlier).

7.3.3 Provision of Cross-Border Settlement Services by Central Banks and Bureaucracy Costs

We first state the necessity for central banks to provide cross-border settlement services and then consider the increase in bureaucracy costs against the backdrop of the globalization of central bank settlement systems in relation to its governance detailed in Sect. 7.4.

7.3.3.1 Need for Central Banks to Provide Cross-Border Settlement Services

Despite various issues stated above (Sect. 7.3.2.2), an historic policy change that central banks themselves should not provide cross-border settlement services was seen. Now that CLS Bank is established, let us consider the role of central banks in cross-border settlement services. For the following reasons, it is still not too late for central banks to provide cross-border settlement services.[14]

- In global financial markets, central banks also need to globalize. In becoming the owner of cross-border settlement systems central banks enjoy the same benefit as becoming owner of a central bank settlement system in respective domestic financial markets.
- Even if central bank settlement systems cannot substitute for CLS Bank, they could at least be a back-up system should CLS Bank face computer system trouble or a financial crisis.
- Central bank cross-border settlement services can act as market pressure on CLS Bank and bring about efficiency for both systems.[15]

---

[14]As a first step towards establishing cross-border settlement services offered by central banks it would be realistic to consider payment versus payment (PvP) linkage which bilaterally links RTGS of major central banks rather than establishing a common agent.

[15]From a market pressure perspective, the following statement in the Noël Report "The study recognizes that central bank services are likely to continue to develop over time in conjunction with, or perhaps as a catalyst for, market developments" deserves attention.

- Technically, as a central bank cross-border settlement system uses central bank money, its structure becomes simple and can be constructed and operated at low cost.

Interestingly, the report (BIS, 2003b, p. 39) later compiled by Tommaso Padoa-Schioppa (the then Executive Board member of the ECB) of CPSS implies the possibility of central banks providing cross-border settlement services as one of the measures to counter a decrease in the use of central bank money due to hierarchy of settlement (see Sect. 7.4) as follows:

> In principle, another option could be for central banks themselves to offer multi-currency settlement facilities, using the accounts most already held with one another. This would provide locally resident institutions with the option of using their local central bank account to settle payments and hold proceeds rather than using a correspondent.

7.3.3.2 Central Bank Bureaucracy Costs

This section provides a clue to the bureaucracy costs of central banks which will be dealt with in detail in Sect. 7.4. This is an answer to the question why central banks was not able to offer cross-border settlement services even though the necessity has been pointed out. First, the Noël Report (1993, p. 24) considers cross-border settlement services offered by central banks themselves to be realized through the cooperation of various central banks as a peer group and not through a hierarchical organization of supranational central banks such as the ECB, and gives its view on coordination costs as follows:

> Establishing and operating central bank multi-currency payment and settlement services would require a high degree of central bank coordination and cooperation. Integrated central bank policies and operational links would be needed to create and run a common agent. Furthermore, in setting up and operating the technical and settlement arrangements, central banks would likely need to share confidential information.

High coordination costs among respective central banks are, indeed, one of the reasons why central bank cross-border settlement services are not realized despite the need. However, the settlement systems of respective central banks are not a pure peer group as in private bank settlement systems. While central banks are in a potential competitive relationship reflecting national interests, they are not in direct competition in the customer market (see Chap. 1, Sect. 1.6.4). And, the relationship between respective central banks and user private banks is hierarchical unlike the customer relationship between direct (large banks) participants and indirect (small to medium-sized banks) participants (see Sect. 7.4).

As such, central banks are superior from a coordination cost perspective compared to the case where private banks establish and operate a cooperative organization. Nevertheless, respective central banks did not try to establish cross-border settlement systems. This seems to be due to the fact that no incentive scheme to make efforts in overcoming coordination costs to respond to the needs of private banks and the public is fully embedded in the organizational governance of respective central banks.

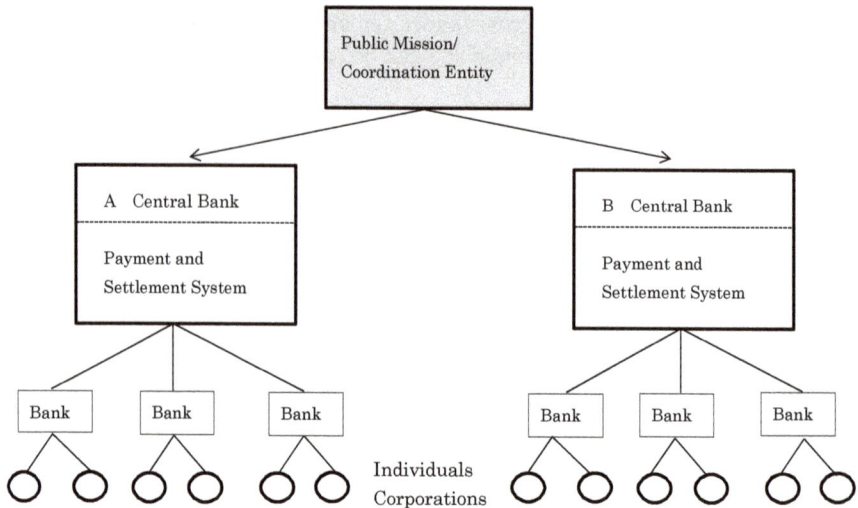

Fig. 7.2 Governance structure of cross-border settlement systems

Transaction costs among central banks may likely arise even for a cross-border settlement system constructed and managed by central banks. Figure 7.2 shows that central banks A and B are equal counterparts and therefore any organization that they jointly establish would be a peer group of central banks, and the issue of transaction costs in such a peer group emerges at a higher tier than that for private banks. Even though there is less transaction costs to reach agreement than would be the case for a peer group of private banks, we can perhaps understand that central banks are not really keen to establish a cross-border settlement system. Not only when establishing a new cross-border settlement system, but also even after its development, considerable transaction costs for negotiation and coordination are necessary to reach agreement among organizations that are on an equal footing (central banks). For example, the clear consent of related central banks is necessary to declare default of a counterpart private bank, which involves significant transaction costs.

7.3.3.3   Bureaucracy Cost Problem and Public Mission Sentiment of Central Banks

To solve or mitigate the issue (reduction of transaction costs) mentioned above (Sect. 7.3.3.2), central banks A and B need to act exhibiting strong commitment to the common public mission or a coordination entity superior to them should be established.

First, the ECB is an example of establishing a coordination entity to construct a cross-border settlement system. When the TARGET system that linked payment and settlement systems of intra-regional central banks was established, the ECB (to be accurate, its predecessor, the European Monetary Institute) was established as a coordination entity over the central banks concerned with the region. Therefore, the TARGET system was established not by a peer group of central banks but through the hierarchical relationship of the ECB and regional central banks that functioned as a coordination entity.

On the other hand, central bank behavior based on a common public mission is the same as changing "atmosphere" in Williamson's theory. According to Williamson (see Chap. 4, Sect. 4.5.1.2), the atmosphere can suppress opportunistic behavior which is the basic cause behind transaction costs. Unlike private banks, central banks do not compete for customer transactions and therefore have an "atmosphere" where it is easier to cooperate with one another. Moreover, there is a serious issue of transaction costs among the private banks of different countries. Such transaction costs emerge from transaction uncertainty such as the lack of credibility of, nor confidence in, counterparty banks due to factors such as differences in legal systems (Chap. 4, Table 4.1). However, among central banks that appropriately recognize their public mission, such transaction costs can be reduced.

7.4 Governance of Central Bank Payment and Settlement Systems

When a central bank actively provides payment and settlement services, it invites criticisms from various perspectives. Major criticisms include: (a) there is a conflict of interest between provision of payment and settlement systems and supervisory function within a central bank, (b) payment and settlement systems provided by a central bank should not compete with those provided by private banks, and (c) the bureaucracy costs of payment and settlement systems provided by a central bank are substantial.

This section looks into these issues regarding the organizational governance of central bank payment and settlement systems applying organizational economics.

7.4.1 Potential for Conflict of Interest Between Provision of Payment and Settlement Systems and Supervisory Function

The point is often made that a conflict of interest occurs within a central bank between payment and settlement system function (as the owner of payment and settlement systems) and supervisory function over private financial institutions. To counter this issue, a governance structure such as building a 'Chinese Wall' within a central bank has often been discussed. We consider this issue below and state that a genuine conflict of interest is unlikely to occur and therefore does not pose a significant problem to the governance of central bank payment and settlement systems.

7.4.1.1 Assertions of a Conflict of Interest

There has often been discussion that there actually is, or there is a possibility of, a conflict of interest between the regulatory and supervisory functions of central banks and their payment and settlement services giving examples of settlement services provided by the FRS as a past case and securities settlement system provided by the ECB as a recent example. For example, Tucker (1990) stated that there was a conflict of interest between the "services provider" function and "regulator" function within FRS. At that time, the FRS Automated Clearing House was in fierce competition with a privately-owned one and it was pointed out that FRS might be using its regulatory and supervisory function to its advantage. Based on such recognition, Tucker (ibid., p. 228) asserted that "A second procedural step the Fed needs to take is to establish formal rules for coping with its internal conflict of interest in payment services, perhaps something akin to Chinese Wall procedures."

And, in 2006, when the ECB announced the development plan for TARGET 2-Securities: T2S,[16] an industry group of regional central securities depositories (ECSDA, 2007) considered that the ECB's securities settlement system would compete with their central securities depositories (CSDs) and asserted that:

> The proposal risks a blurring of responsibilities between the accepted role of the ECB as a public authority and its proposal to become a monopoly supplier of IT-infrastructure for CSDs regarding their settlement services to the securities industry. It is essential that the implications of such a potential conflict of roles, and the possible strategies for managing those conflicts, should be considered in greater detail.

In contrast, Jean-Michel Godeffroy of the ECB (2007) refuted that:

> The first point you focus upon is a possible conflict of interest, between the operational function and oversight function of central banks. This subject is not new to us…. In the field of payment systems we have developed tools to deal with this issue, such as the need to strictly separate the oversight and operation functions in distinct units. I believe we have a good track record for managing this potential conflict of interest.

In addition, he states that the privately-managed settlement systems themselves should pay more attention to conflict of interest and stated (ibid.):

> This leads me to highlight that possible conflicts of interest are not limited to public authorities. We are following very carefully how CSDs will address possible conflicts of interest between their corporate interests, and the interests of their users in this debate.

---

[16]T2S is a securities settlement system; the ECB announced a development plan in 2006, development was formally approved in July 2008, and launch was in June 2015.

7.4.1.2 Principal-Agent Relationship of the Central Bank and Conflict of Interest

To see which of the above arguments is persuasive, let us consider whether a conflict of interest actually occurs in central bank payment and settlement systems, and whether the possibility of such occurrence is relatively larger than in privately-managed payment and settlement systems.

In considering the matter, we need to distinguish a broad-sense conflict of interest and a narrow-sense conflict of interest based on Boatright (1992) while taking into consideration whether the two entities have a principal-agent relationship or not (see Chap. 5, Sect. 5.4.1). According to this categorization, the conflict of interest pointed out in central bank payment and settlement systems does not fall under a narrow-sense conflict of interest in Boatright's definition. Looking at the principal-agent relationship with respect to a central bank's two services, the principal that the central bank needs to obey is the same, and basically a conflict of interest does not arise. Specifically, the principal for the regulatory and supervisory function of a central bank is the public that uses the financial system including payment and settlement systems. On the other hand, the direct principal for payment and settlement services are users of private banks. The principal for the former and the latter may seem different at a glance, but in both cases end-users and principal are the public.

Listfield (1990, p. 233) commented on a paper by Tucker entitled "*The Conflicting Role of the Federal Reserve as Regulator and Services Provider in the U.S. Payment Systems*" as follows: "The Fed uses its regulatory authority in general banking matters to ensure safety and soundness, while using both regulatory and operational means to achieve the same objectives for payment services." "The same objectives" here can be interpreted as a common principal in the principal-agent relationship.

In this way, a narrow-sense conflict of interest does not exist in central bank payment and settlement systems. On the other hand, a narrow-sense conflict of interest may exist in privately-managed payment and settlement systems as pointed out by Godeffroy of the ECB. Such a conflict of interest cannot be avoided, especially if the privately-managed payment and settlement system becomes an outsider-owned stock company. That is, the owner of the system who is the agent, needs to obey two principals who have conflicting interests (stockholders who pursue profits and users that pursue efficiency and safety). However, in the case of a user-owned stock company, principals are relatively the same and therefore conflict of interest can be mitigated to a degree.

In addition, we need to understand that the relationship between central bank payment and settlement systems and the regulatory and supervisory function plays a significant role in payment and settlement systems, rather than causing a conflict of interest. Specifically, the relationship between the central bank and private banks is hierarchical and not a peer group, and, based on the theory of delegated monitoring (see Sect. 7.2.1.2), the regulatory and supervisory function contributes to making central bank payment and settlement systems efficient and safe and at the same time contributes to reducing coordination costs that arise in establishing such a system.

7.4.2   Possibility of Achieving Governance of Payment and Settlement System Through Competition

Issues discussed in Sect. 7.4.1 are deeply related to competition among payment and settlement systems, and, while it is generally said that such issues should be solved through competitive pressure on payment and settlement systems, below we show that the effect of such solution is dubious and clarify that it is basically impossible to realize governance of central bank payment and settlement systems through competitive pressure.

7.4.2.1   Possibility of Abuse of Superior Bargaining Position

While central bank payment and settlement systems do not have a conflict of interest, if a competitor is a payment and settlement system owned by an organization that is under the supervision of a central bank, there is a possibility of 'abuse of superior bargaining position' forbidden under fair trade law. So, the major discussion point is whether a privately-owned payment and settlement system can really be a competitor of a central bank payment and settlement system.

Listfield (ibid., pp. 232–3) stated that "The Fed does not compete directly with the private sector in making loans or taking deposits" and regards the interbank settlement service of the FRS and deposit/lending operation to be equal. However, this argument is not really plausible and we cannot deny that there is potential competition. Usually, a central bank's business operation regarding deposits and loans is limited to interbank transactions in a two-tiered financial system and therefore does not compete with private sector customer transactions (see Chap. 1, Sect. 1.6.4). In contrast, a private financial system is, though 'private', in the same tier market as a central bank's payment and settlement system which deals with interbank transactions.

Therefore, in order to prevent abuse of its superior bargaining position, a Chinese Wall is necessary depending on degree of competition between payment and settlement systems of a central bank and the private sector. As mentioned in Sect. 7.4.1.1, we can interpret that the ECB "developed tools to deal with this issue, such as the need to strictly separate the oversight and operation functions in distinct units" (Godeffroy, 2007) in order to prevent abuse of superior bargaining position, rather than to prevent a conflict of interest. The possibility of competition is low but, given even a slight possibility, a central bank needs to be ready for any criticism from the outside.

7.4.2.2   Plausibility of Competition Between Payment and Settlement Systems

In the first place, is competition between interbank payment and settlement systems plausible? Intrinsically, such competition is not possible. Significant coordination costs are incurred in constructing interbank payment and settlement systems as mentioned in Sect. 7.3, and, moreover, payment and settlement systems enjoy economies of scale and network externality which tend to lead to strong monopoly. In actuality, major interbank payment and settlement systems such as CLS Bank and CHIPS in the US enjoy a monopoly in the industry.

Therefore, while there is an argument that, "The optimum for achieving efficiency in payment services is a mix of public and private, with open competition between them." (Tucker, 1990, p. 225), there is a limit to the effect of competitive pressure.

In addition, it is also important not to sacrifice the safety of payment and settlement systems under competitive pressure. Too often, an improvement in efficiency through competitive pressure is achieved by sacrificing a system's safety. Tucker (ibid., p. 226) criticized the FRS for its "anti-competitive mindset" saying "The problem is that pursuing this goal of controlling systemic risk also provides a wonderful cloak for hiding a strong anticompetitive bias." However, it may be possible that the FRS took such behavior deliberately recognizing, at the back of its mind, that competitive pressure does not have a desirable effect and only heightens systemic risks.

7.4.3 Bureaucracy Costs and Countermeasures of Central Bank Payment and Settlement Systems

As mentioned in the previous section, we cannot expect competitive pressure to enhance efficiency of central bank payment and settlement systems. Even if it does, it is highly likely to sacrifice safety of the system which is not desirable. The only way is to improve or add a little twist to the governance mechanism of central bank payment and settlement systems. Such a measure is extremely important. Transactions between a central bank and private banks within the tier-structure of a financial system (composed of private banks and a central bank) have fewer market transaction features compared to those within a peer group, but at the same time have stronger internal organization transaction features (see Chap. 1, Sect. 1.6.3). Therefore, while there is the benefit of low transaction costs in the area of coordination costs, there is the question of an increase in transaction costs in the area of internal organization transaction costs, such as bureaucracy costs.

Also, private banks, which are users of central bank payment and settlement systems, have a weak incentive to demand a central bank improve its system, and thus do not necessarily respond to the needs of end-users (individuals and corporations). The same issue exists in private payment and settlement systems.

The following examines the bureaucracy costs of central bank payment and settlement systems and incentive problem on the part of users of interbank payment and settlement systems. We then consider measures to reduce bureaucracy costs and mitigate the incentive problem for interbank payment and settlement system users.

7.4.3.1 Bureaucracy Costs of Central Bank Payment and Settlement Systems

Let us look at bureaucracy costs, a kind of internal organization transaction cost, of central bank payment and settlement systems in comparison with private organizations. Bureaucracy cost is an important concept in Williamson's transaction cost economics (1996) and is a kind of internal organizational transaction cost that emerges since "As compared with market organization, internal organization displays a differential propensity to manage complexity, to forgive error, and to engage in logrolling."

Such relationship is illustrated in Chap. 1, Fig. 1.6. As the degree of hierarchy increases from flat peer group organization (private payment and settlement systems) to a tier-structure organization (central bank payment and settlement systems), costs related to peer group organization (such as information cost, supervisory and monitoring cost, competition cost between members), shown by line P, decrease. In contrast, bureaucracy costs shown by line H increase. This is because the relationship between private banks and a central bank is not simply a relationship between user and service provider, but also one between supervised and supervisor which infers a diminution in the sense of participation among private banks (see Chap. 1, Sect. 1.6.3). The fact that the central bank does not try to respond to the needs of members can be included in such diminution in the sense of participation.

Similarly, when we consider degree of diversification on the horizontal line instead of degree of hierarchy (that is, the same organization providing several payment and settlement services, or providing services other than payment and settlement services), as the degree of diversification increases from an organization that provides a single product (private payment and settlement systems) to an organization that provides multiple products (central bank payment and settlement systems), the cost shown by line P in Chap. 1, Fig. 1.6 decreases due to economies of scope, but bureaucracy costs shown by line H increase.

Bureaucracy costs here include bloated organization, conflict of organizational cultures, and decrease in benefit from specialization, all of which emerge from providing multiple products. Conflict of organizational culture within a central bank is especially a large problem (see Chap. 4, Sect. 4.5.2.2). This includes issues that surface from a conflict of organizational culture between the section that conducts operational tasks such as providing payment and settlement systems, and the section that conducts policy-oriented tasks such as implementing monetary policy, and, regulatory and supervisory functions. This is because a central bank has the tendency to favor tasks related to monetary policy and regulatory and supervisory functions and tries to avoid those that require hard work such as developing and operating payment and settlement systems.[17]

---

[17]Bureaucracy costs related to central bank payment and settlement systems should take into consideration the cost that is incurred as the degree of hierarchy and diversification heightens as well as slackness of organization that may emerge from being a central bank (having payment ability backed by banknote issuance authority) that is not exposed to market pressure and does not fall into default.

7.4.3.2   Incentive Problems in Interbank Payment and Settlement Systems

With regard to interbank payment and settlement systems such as central bank managed systems, in addition to bureaucracy costs within the central bank as explained above, there is another basic issue on the part of user private banks. That is, private banks have a weak incentive to encourage a central bank to improve payment and settlement systems owned and operated by the central bank. This incentive problem relating to private banks is not directly related to the bureaucracy cost issue of central bank payment and settlement systems (in the narrow sense) but is nevertheless discussed here.

From the private banks' side, all private banks use the same central bank payment and settlement systems as their basic system. Therefore, payment and settlement services provided by private banks to their customers using central bank payment and settlement systems are more or less the same, and it would be difficult for them to find any strategy to make themselves stand out from one another. It is an uncontested situation. So, private banks have a weak incentive as users to encourage the central bank to improve its systems.

Allen, Christodoulou and Millard (2006) of the BOE consider that such an incentive problem on the part of direct users that emerge from a two-tiered structure of payment and settlement services is similar to the 'double marginalization problem' discussed in the theory of industrial organization.[18] According to Tirole (1988), a double marginalization problem occurs when a chain of monopolies exists. For example, as in Fig. 7.3, if goods and services are provided through a two-tiered structure of wholesaler and retailer, and both are monopolist, a chain of monopolies emerges. In this case, the monopolist wholesaler sells to the retailer at a monopoly price exceeding marginal cost (gaining excess profits) and, in turn, the retailer sells to consumers at a monopoly price that exceeds marginal cost taking into consideration the buying price that includes excess profit of the wholesaler (that is, the pricing of monopoly price that exceeds market price is conducted twice). As a result, the consumer price that consumers pay increases compared to a case when price is determined by one monopolist that integrates wholesaler and retailer.

If we apply this to payment and settlement services, an interbank payment and settlement system is the equivalent of wholesaler, and individual banks that are members of payment and settlement systems are retailers. That is, interbank payment and settlement systems usually enjoy monopoly, and, moreover, individual banks also enjoy monopoly as regards customer interbank payment and settlement services. Therefore, the problem of double marginalization may emerge where interbank payment

---

[18] Allen, Christodoulou and Millard (2006) discuss the governance of financial infrastructure, especially payment and settlement systems, based on a formal microeconomics model. The feature of this model is that it takes up a two-tiered structure and includes not only ownership but also organizational governance among various governance issues. As a result, the model tackles the issue of reflecting end-users' needs in interbank payment and settlement systems (incentive issue of a two-tiered structure) regarding the former, and, as for the latter, the model can be used to consider oversight of payment and settlement systems as well as the importance of having outside directors on the Board of Directors.

Fig. 7.3 Double
marginalization problem

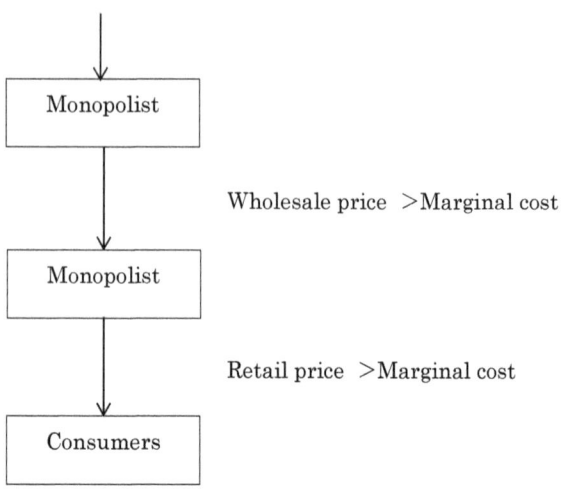

and settlement systems provide services to individual banks at a price that exceeds marginal cost (price) and, in turn, individual banks provide services to consumers also at a price that exceeds marginal cost. As a result, the price offered by a two-tiered payment and settlement system would exceed that offered by a single-tiered payment and settlement system that integrates interbank payment and settlement systems and individual banks (high cost here also includes low level of service).

Such issue is embedded in all monopolistic interbank payment and settlement systems in the private sector such as CLS Bank and CHIPS, and is not limited to central bank payment and settlement systems. Also, interbank payment and settlement systems have the tendency to move towards natural monopoly due to economies of scale and network externality in addition to coordination costs within the industry at time of establishment. As such, this poses a basic and serious problem when we consider measures to counter bureaucracy costs.

7.4.3.3 Countermeasures Against Bureaucracy Costs of Central Bank Payment and Settlement Systems

Next, let us consider countermeasures that solve or ease the issue related to central bank payment and settlement systems. Basically, from a user perspective (private banks), the organizational feature of central bank payment and settlement systems needs to move from being an 'outsider-owned organization' to a 'club organization.' Specifically, it is important to introduce a multiboard system and to establish cooperative mechanisms between the central bank and private financial institutions.

Transition from Outsider-Owned Organization to Club Organization
As the degree of hierarchy and diversification increases, so do bureaucracy costs as mentioned (Sect. 7.4.3.1). If countermeasures are taken to address this issue, central

bank payment and settlement systems may become superior to privately-managed payment and settlement systems. As can be seen in Chap. 1, Fig. 1.6, bureaucracy costs in line H shift towards H′, the intersection with line P shifts to the lower right, the degree of optimum hierarchy and diversification shifts to the right (h to h*), and at the same time total cost decreases (c to c*).

What do we need to do to prevent bureaucracy costs from increasing even if the degree of hierarchy and diversification heightens? The answer is to improve or re-design the organizational governance of a central bank. That is, to improve transparency and accountability of central bank payment and settlement systems, and, in addition, increase the sense of participation on the part of private banks who are users of central bank payment and settlement systems (i.e., to have a central bank respond to the needs of members) and have private banks participate in the organizational governance of central bank payment and settlement systems. In other words, we need to shift the feature of a central bank from being an outsider-owned organization to a club organization.

As explained in Chap. 2, Sect. 2.3.1.2, central bank governance structure has two features: public governance and corporate governance. If emphasis is placed on public governance, a central bank is distanced from private banks and thus becomes an outsider-owned organization for private banks just like the open stock company in privately-managed payment and settlement systems. As a result, the sense of participation on the part of users diminishes and the central bank fails to respond to user needs, thus increasing bureaucracy costs. On the other hand, if emphasis is placed on a central bank's corporate governance, and has private banks participate in central bank governance, central bank payment and settlement systems become a user-owned corporation where features of a club organization owned by users are strengthened, thus suppressing bureaucracy costs.

Historically, in many central banks, private banks participated in their governance structure as stockholders, and, therefore, central banks had the feature of being a private banks' club organization. Central banks with such a feature still remain to this day. One example is the FRB in 12 Federal Reserve districts as explained in Chap. 2, Sect. 2.5.1—all of their stock is held by member banks in the respective districts that are users of FRB payment and settlement services, and, in this sense, the FRB can be said to be a user-owned corporation (nevertheless, there is a limit to stockholder authority).

However, even if a central bank transits from being an outsider-owned organization to a club organization, the incentive issue (double marginalization problem) on the part of users of interbank payment and settlement systems cannot be solved. Countermeasures discussed in this section consider organizational governance that can reflect the needs of private banks (direct users) in central bank payment and settlement systems. Countermeasures such as utilization of a multiboard structure and cooperation between the central bank and private banks as noted below are necessary to achieve organizational governance that reflects the needs of private banks' customers that are end users of central bank payment and settlement systems such as individuals and corporations.

Utilization of a Multiboard Structure

A multiboard structure is considered effective in terms of central bank governance structure to shift the feature of a central bank from being an outsider-owned organization to a club organization by having private banks participate in the organizational governance of central bank payment and settlement systems. And, a multiboard structure may also contribute to easing the incentive problem of private banks that are users of central bank payment and settlement systems. The following gives the reasons and considers the effectiveness of a multiboard structure (see an example of RBA in Chap. 2, Sect. 2.4.2).

Separation of Monetary Policy Board and Payment System Board for the Purpose of Avoiding Conflict of Organizational Cultures

The first reason why a multiboard structure contributes to suppressing the bureaucracy costs of central bank payment and settlement systems is that by separating the decision-making boards of monetary policy and payment systems, conflict of organizational cultures can be prevented. A single-board structure is likely to invite conflict of organizational culture as in the case of the BOJ where only the Policy Board exists as the sole decision-making body. A multiboard structure that realizes governance that secures autonomy and independence by separating the decision-making roles of monetary policy and payment systems is better able to enhance efficiency and adequacy of decision-making in each field and enhance incentive on the part of respective staff. As discussed in Chap. 4, Sect. 4.5.2.2, it is a fact that in each field of monetary policy and payment systems, different organizational cultures exist and required competence varies. For example, economic theories relating to monetary policy and payment systems differ. Monetary policy is based mainly on macroeconomics, while payment and settlement systems are based on microeconomics, jurisprudence, and computer science.

Nevertheless, monetary policy and payment systems are in an interdependent relationship and economies of scope can exist between the two. Therefore, it is extreme and inappropriate to outsource payment and settlement systems (or monetary policy) to an organization outside of a central bank.

Reflecting the Needs of Private Banks Efficiently

The second reason why a multiboard structure contributes to suppressing the bureaucracy costs of central bank payment and settlement systems is that by having a decision-making body for payment and settlement systems separate from that for monetary policy, the needs of user private banks can be adequately reflected in central bank payment and settlement systems. User private banks are regulated and supervised by a central bank, and thus they need to send a representative to the top hierarchy of the central bank governance structure to ensure that the central bank seriously endeavors to reflect the needs of private banks.

However, while it is beneficial to shift the organizational feature of central bank payment and settlement systems from being an outsider-owned organization to a club organization of private banks as much as possible, it is not adequate to do away with the regulatory and supervisory function of a central bank and eliminate the feature of hierarchical organization altogether. This is because the uniqueness of a central bank payment and settlement system lies in that it can supervise and monitor private banks that are system participants, and also because of its LLR function to assist them. This can also be regarded as a conflict of interest issue within the representative bank of member private banks (of central bank payment and settlement systems). The representative of private banks acts as an agent for private banks and at the same time also becomes the agent for a central bank. Thus, it is torn between its role as the representative of private banks and role of central bank agent. However, with regard to regulation and supervision, the principal differs for private banks and a central bank. While private banks wish moderate regulation and supervision, a central bank pursues strict regulation and supervision in the interest of financial system stability.

Therefore, the actual governance structure of a central bank needs to strike a balance between economic benefit (low production costs brought about by economies of scale) and disadvantage (increase in transaction costs within an organization). To strike an adequate balance, a multiboard structure is in the end an appropriate governance structure in the sense that it does not completely separate the central bank by outsourcing payment and settlement systems nor concentrate authority under a single-board structure. There are varieties of multiboard structure as explained in Chap. 2, Sect. 2.4.1, but, in order to prevent conflict of interest, it is necessary to at least separate the board responsible for regulation and supervision and that for payment and settlement systems.

Reflecting Needs of End-Users

A multiboard structure not only contributes to suppressing bureaucracy costs of central bank payment and settlement systems, but may also contribute to easing the incentive issue of private banks that are users of central bank payment and settlement systems. This can be realized by inviting the representative of private banks as well as representative of individuals and corporations that are end-users to participate in the board responsible for central bank payment and settlement systems. This is deeply related to the issue of public governance of a central bank discussed in Chap. 3, Sect. 3.3.4 and its relation to the discussion on a multiboard structure is considered below.

Perspective from Public Governance

As explained in Chap. 2, Sect. 2.4.1, there is a variety of multiboard structures. A multiboard structure where boards are established for each central bank function—'monetary policy board' and 'banking board' (including matters related to payment and settlement systems)—is desirable in this chapter's discussion (Chap. 2, Fig. 2.3, Prototype B). However, when the objective is to lessen pressure from the government concerning personnel matters such as appointment of central bank senior officials, then a multiboard structure Type A-1 as in Chap. 2, Fig. 2.3 would be desirable. But, the latter multiboard structure cannot achieve the objective of separating monetary policy and payment and settlement systems policy discussed in this chapter.

Therefore, a desirable multiboard structure that fills both objectives would be Type C as in Chap. 2, Fig. 2.3, that is, a 'three-board system.' In this structure, while the monetary policy board and banking board are separated, there is an upper board, the 'personnel committee,' that presides over them and appoints board members. Here, the government conducts public governance indirectly through the appointment of the board of directors.

Cooperation Between the Central Bank and Private Banks

Another measure is to construct a cooperative framework between the central bank and private banks to reduce bureaucracy costs embedded in central bank payment and settlement systems. This is an unofficial governance structure compared to a multiboard structure, but can shift the feature of central bank payment and settlement systems from being an outsider-owned organization to a club organization as seen from user private banks. Specifically, let us introduce BIS's recommendation on constructing such a cooperative framework.

BIS (2006, p. 35) compiled a report entitled "*General guidance for national payment system development*" that includes 14 guidelines. Guideline 8 recommends to "involve relevant stakeholders." The main idea is as follows:

> Encourage the development of effective consultation among relevant stakeholders in the national payment system…Consultations can take place in both structured groups and less formal arrangements. Structured bilateral and multilateral consultations are powerful tools for developing consensus on the common goals and broad directions of reforms…Various types of payment advisory groups have been established in many countries. They usually function as a high-level, forward-looking, strategic group to: (i) organise background information and research on payment system issues; and (ii) advise on policy initiatives to resolve these issues and facilitate ongoing development in the national payment system.

7.5 Conclusion

As for diversification studied in Sect. 7.2, numerous economic advantages exist for a central bank to diversify from RTGS and paper-based retail payment systems into securities settlement and electronic retail payment systems. First, looking at diversification from RTGS to securities settlement system, various interdependencies exist between them. According to diversification theory, this alone has economic advantage for a central bank to diversify into a securities settlement system. Moreover, a common production factor that brings about economies of scope exists between a securities settlement system and the central bank's existing payment and settlement systems as well as other central bank functions. And, transaction costs can be saved if these interdependencies and common production factors are consolidated within a single organization.

Next, with regard to diversification from RTGS into electronic retail payment systems, systems that have the possibility of central bank ownership (or are currently owned by a central bank) can be classified into four: (a) RTGS retail payment system, (b) clearing retail payment system (automated clearing house <ACH>), (c) e-money, and (d) settlement service for net position of the clearing retail system. Of the four, the first three were considered. As a result, with regard to (a), the existence of a common production factor that realizes economies of scope with RTGS, especially for large value settlements, became clear. Moreover, since integration of organization is the only way to utilize common production factors at low transaction costs, it became apparent that diversification into an RTGS retail payment system would be a perfectly natural step. As for (b), we can point out the economic advantage the central bank can enjoy if it diversifies into an ACH. For example, as in the case with the FRS, economies of scale and scope are realized by common production factors with the clearing houses, and we could also point out the interdependency between Automated Clearing House and the FRS's large-value RTGS. Concerning e-money (c), central banks have so far played an important role with regard to paper- and metal-based retail payment systems in the form of supplying and managing cash (such as banknotes and coins) that has direct transferability of value with no direct relation with bank deposits. Nevertheless, against the background of the rapid development of e-money in the private sector, no central bank offers e-money that substitutes for cash. Central banks are not fully adapting to the changes in the institutional environment surrounding retail payment systems with direct transferability of value. They need to change from being paper- and metal-based to being IT-based.

And, not only from the risk perspective as generally discussed, but also from the perspective of transaction costs, central banks are, essentially, the most adequate organization to offer e-money. That is, central banks provide a cash system (such as banknotes) which is the same type of payment instrument as e-money in the sense that it has direct transferability of value. In doing so, central banks have accumulated common production factors such as technical and organizational know-how and brand name, which would bring about economies of scale and scope. In addition, the fact that e-money is highly interdependent with central bank monetary policy and stability of the financial system implies that a central bank should offer e-money.

As for the globalization of central bank payment and settlement services studied in Sect. 7.3, from the perspective of organizational economics, CLS Bank was established at high coordination costs since it is a private peer group. And apparently, coordination costs need to be paid continuously in the future. Nevertheless, provision of interbank cross-border payment and settlement systems has been entrusted to private organizations. The following points illustrate why the globalization of central banks does not progress.

First, there seems to be a misperception concerning the word 'private.' That is, the ownership of interbank settlement services belongs, in most cases, to a club organization (membership organization) and not to a pure private organization (stock company) owned by outside stockholders. In short, when we say 'private' organization in the context of payment and settlement systems, it is not a private firm in the perfect competitive market envisaged by microeconomics. Therefore, it takes huge coordination costs for the private banks' peer group to establish and manage interbank settlement systems. Nevertheless, it is strongly argued that ownership should be entrusted to a private organization based on a simple anti-intervention dogma that is backed by efficiency of a perfect competitive market. However, such necessary coordination costs incurred by entrusting to a private banks' peer group can be saved by using the hierarchical relationship between a central bank and private banks in the financial system, and so interbank funds transfers should first be considered to be entrusted to the central bank.

Second, if we utilize such hierarchical relationship and enlarge the scope and scale of the business, central banks will, like other organizations, face increasing bureaucracy costs, which is one type of transaction cost of internal transactions. If central banks are to provide cross-border payment and settlement systems in addition to their current business operations, other things being equal, bureaucracy costs should increase. And, the fact that central banks are not perceived to have the adequate organizational governance to suppress such increase in bureaucracy costs may perhaps be one of the reasons why there is strong opposition to central banks providing cross-border settlement systems.

Third, there is the issue of central banks' organizational governance. In providing cross-border settlement systems, a peer group of various central banks needs to cooperate which will in fact incur related coordination costs, albeit not as high as those of a private organization. To overcome such coordination costs, an incentive mechanism in the place of the profit seeking motivation of private organizations needs to be embedded in the organizational governance of respective central banks. Such an incentive mechanism is an element of organizational governance to suppress the above bureaucracy costs but is only realized by the ECB and yet to be established by other central banks. As for BIS, a member of the central bank peer group, it does not have the authority to supervise or order central banks.

As for the organizational governance aspect of interbank payment and settlement systems owned by the central bank studied in Sect. 7.4, two major conclusions became apparent. One is that it is necessary to have the central bank provide wide-ranging payment and settlement systems as argued in Sects. 7.2 and 7.3. There are three reasons. First, with regard to the issue of conflict of interest between the supervisory function and provision of payment and settlement services within a central bank, we can see that the issue does not lie in conflict of interest but rather in the abuse of dominant position. Second, hierarchy of payment and settlement systems implies cutback on payment and settlement services offered by the central bank (i.e., this is a net settlement system where netting is first conducted among private banks <e.g., CHIPS in the US> and then settlement of each bank's net position is carried out by the central bank) which raises considerable issue with regard to how payment and settlement systems and financial systems should be managed. Third, although there are proposals that the above issues should be solved through competitive pressures on the payment and settlement systems, such solution does not seem to be realistic.

The other conclusion that became apparent was that in the case where the central bank provides wide-ranging payment and settlement services, an increase in bureaucracy costs within the central bank organization is likely to occur, and, in order to avoid such an increase, it is necessary to bolster organizational governance. Specific measures include: first, with a view to shifting the characteristics of the central bank from being an outsider-owned organization to a club organization by having private banks participate in the organizational governance of central bank payment and settlement systems, central bank governance structure should apply a multiboard system that has a separate decision-making body for payment and settlement systems apart from that for monetary policy. Second, in order to achieve the same objective, it is necessary to establish a cooperative framework between a central bank and private banks. Third, it is necessary to urge private banks to work on improving central bank payment and settlement systems. This could be done by inviting the representatives of end-users such as individuals and corporations to take part in the organizational governance of central bank payment and settlement systems.

Chapter 8
Epilogue

The three objectives of this book mentioned in the Preface were to discuss various issues regarding central banks based on new institutional economics (NIE), to show that NIE has the same analytical viability when applied to central banks as applied to various systems and corporate organizations and to apply NIE to central banks in Europe and in the US to be able to make comparative analysis with the Bank of Japan. Those objectives have been fulfilled. Nevertheless, NIE is still developing and if new theories are to be applied in the future, there is every likelihood that different conclusions may be drawn. For this book, I chose theories from NIE that I believed would be efficacious in studying topics relating to the central bank arena. As such, all main subjects regarding central banks that needed to be considered were analyzed applying existing theories. It should be noted that theories were adopted for their ability to efficiently convey my views rather than just to support them.

Moreover, we need to recognize that there is a limit to an economics-based approach to institutional issues. That is, this book provides specific opinions and arguments for a desirable central bank in the real world based on analytical results. However, any approach to central banking systems also needs a viewpoint from sociology that place emphasis on historical background and political science that looks at power games. Therefore, we need to understand that while a certain central bank model may be desirable from an economic-based viewpoint, it may not be so from an overall standpoint. And, though desirable in theory, it may not lead to actual reform of central banks.

Lastly, there is a need to take into consideration the actual details of central banks that are discussed in this book. The central bank to which economic theories are applied in this book is not a specific central bank like the Federal Reserve System or European Central Bank, but one based on Max Weber's "idealtypus" (ideal type or pure type). Actual existing central banks are not necessarily uniform, but quite different in their makeup. Therefore, the central bank adopted in this book is an abstract version of intrinsic characteristics taken from observing various central banks. In other words, it is a model or working hypothesis. The book also gives explanation of actual specific central banks. The objective is to see whether the conclusions and

© Springer Nature Singapore Pte Ltd. 2019   311
Y. Oritani, *The Japanese Central Banking System Compared with Its European and American Counterparts*, https://doi.org/10.1007/978-981-13-9001-2_8

implications drawn from applying NIE to an "idealtypus" central bank indeed apply to actual central banks.

As above, another reason why the book takes up actual central banks is to create an "idealtypus" central bank from them. However, the basic functions of future central banks may well be different. The most important change would be the disappearance of demand for banknotes through development of IT as discussed by Goodhart (2002). He proposes that a central bank should issue electronic money, but there are no central banks in the world that are moving decisively towards such issuance. If central banks do not issue electronic money (in place of banknotes), and banknotes do disappear, the "idealtypus" central bank would change considerably. That is because banknotes are the core of payment and settlement services provided by central banks and, moreover, a central bank's lender of last resort function and monetary policy are largely dependent on the fact that central banks have a monopoly right to effect banknote issuance. In this case, many of the conclusions drawn in this book would have to be changed significantly.

References

Akerlof, G., & Kranton, R. (2010). *Identity economics: How our identities shape our work, wages, and well-being.* Princeton University Press.

Alchian, A., & Demsetz, H. (1972). Production, information costs, and economic organization. *American Economic Review, 62*(5), 777–795.

Allen, H., Christodoulou, G., & Millard, S. (2006). *Financial infrastructure and corporate governance* (Bank of England Working Paper No. 316). Bank of England.

Arrow, K. (1951). *Social choice and individual values.* Wiley.

Arrow, K. (1962). The economic implications of learning by doing. *Review of Economic Studies, 29*(3), 155–173.

Bagehot, W. (1873). *Lombard street: A description of the money market.* Henry S. King & Co.

Beck, N. (1982). Does there exist a business cycle?: A Box-Tiao analysis. *Public Choice, 38*(2), 205–209.

Beck, N. (1987). Elections and the Fed: Is there a political monetary cycle? *American Journal of Political Science, 318*(1), 194–216.

Bernanke, B. (2009a). *Financial reform to address systemic risk.* Speech at the Council on Foreign Relations, Washington, DC.

Bernanke, B. (2009b). *Reflections on a year of crisis.* Speech at the FRB of Kansas City's Symposium.

Bernanke, B. (2009c). *The crisis and the policy response.* Speech at the Stamp Lecture, London School of Economics, London.

Bevir, M. (2007). *Public governance.* Saga Publications.

BIS. (1989). *Report on netting schemes.* Report prepared by the group of experts on payment systems.

BIS. (1990). *Report of the committee on interbank netting schemes of the central banks of the group of ten countries.* CPSS report.

BIS. (1993). *Central bank payment and settlement services with respect to cross-border and multi-currency transactions.* CPSS report.

BIS. (1996). *Settlement risk in foreign exchange transactions.* CPSS report.

BIS. (1998). *Reducing foreign exchange settlement risk: A progress report.* CPSS report.

BIS. (2003a). *Policy issues for central banks in retail payments.* CPSS report.

BIS. (2003b). *The role of central bank money in payment systems.* CPSS report.

BIS. (2004). *Survey of developments in electronic money and internet and mobile payments.* CPSS report.

BIS. (2006). *General guidance for national payment system development.* CPSS report.

BIS. (2008). *The interdependencies of payment and settlement systems.* CPSS report.

© Springer Nature Singapore Pte Ltd. 2019

Y. Oritani, *The Japanese Central Banking System Compared with Its European and American Counterparts*, https://doi.org/10.1007/978-981-13-9001-2

BIS. (2009). *Issues in the governance of central banks*. A report from the central bank governance group.

BIS. (2011). *Central bank governance and financial stability*. A report by the study group.

Boatright, J. (1992). Conflict of interest: An agency analysis. In N. E. Bowie & R. E. Freeman (Eds.), *Ethics and agency theory* (pp. 187–203). Oxford University Press.

Boylan, D. (2001). *Defusing democracy: Central bank autonomy and the transition from authoritarian rule*. University of Michigan Press.

Breton, A. (1974). *The economic theory of representative government*. Aldine.

Brousseau, E., & Glachant, J. M. (2008). *New institutional economics: A guidebook*. Cambridge University Press.

Buchanan, J. (1963). The economics of earmarked taxes. *Journal of Political Economy, 71*(5), 457–469.

Buchanan, J. (1965). An economic theory of clubs. *Economica, 32*(125), 1–14.

Buchanan, J. (1991). *The economics and ethics of constitutional order*. University of Michigan Press.

Buchanan, J., & Tullock, G. (1962). *The calculus of consent: Logical foundation of constitutional democracy*. The University of Michigan Press.

Buchanan, J., & Wagner, R. (1977). *Democracy in deficit: The political legacy of Lord Keynes*. Academic Press (Reprinted from *The Collected Works of James M. Buchanan* (Vol. 8), 2000. Liberty Fund, Inc.).

Chang, K. (2003). *Appointing central bankers: The politics of monetary policy in the United States and the European Monetary Union*. Cambridge University Press.

Coase, R. (1937). The nature of the firm. *Economica, 4*(16), 386–405.

Congleton, R. D. (2005). Toward a political economy of crisis management: Rational choice, ignorance, and haste in political decision making. *Dynamics of Intervention, Advances in Austrian Economics, 8*, 183–204.

Cukierman, A. (1992). *Central bank strategy, credibility, and independence: Theory and evidence*. MIT Press.

Demsetz, H. (1991). The theory of the firm revisited. In O. Williamson & S. Winter (Eds.), *Nature of firm: Origins, evolution, and development* (pp. 159–179). Oxford University Press.

Department of Treasury. (2009). *Financial regulatory reform, a new foundation: Rebuilding financial supervision and regulation*. U.S. Department of Treasury.

Diamond, D. (1984). Financial intermediation and delegated monitoring. *Review of Economic Studies, 51*(3), 393–414.

Dixit, A. (1996). *The making of economic policy: A transaction cost politics perspective*. MIT Press.

Douma, S., & Schreuder, H. (2002). *Economic approaches to organizations* (3rd ed.). Pearson Education.

Downs, A. (1957). *An economic theory of democracy*. Harper and Row.

ECB. (1998). Report on electronic money. https://www.ecb.europa.eu/pub/pdf/other/emoneyen.pdf.

ECB. (1999). Opinion on the introduction of e-money institutions. https://www.ecb.europa.eu/ecb/legal/.../en_con_2004_37_f_sign.pdf.

ECSDA. (2007). A letter from ECSDA to ECB on TARGET 2 securities. https://www.ecb.europa.eu/paym/t2s/pdf/.../T2SECSDAletter.pdf.

Epstein, D., & O'Halloran, S. (1999). *Delegating powers: A transaction cost politics approach to policy making under separate powers*. Cambridge University Press.

Fama, E., & Jensen, M. (1983). Separation of ownership and control. *Journal of Law and Economics, 26*(2), 301–325.

Fama, E., & Jensen, M. (1983). Agency problems and residual claims. *Journal of Law and Economics, 26*(2), 327–349.

Federal Reserve System. (1998). *The Federal Reserve in the payments mechanism*. Committee on the Federal Reserve in the Payments Mechanism.

Federal Reserve System. (2009). *Federal Reserve initiatives to address financial strains*. Federal Reserve annual report.

Federal Reserve System. (2016). *Purposes and functions* (10th ed.). Federal Reserve System.

French, K. R., et al. (2010). *The Squam Lake report: Fixing the financial system*. Princeton University Press.

Friedman, M. (1986). Monetary policy: Theory and practice. In E. F. Toma & M. Toma (Eds.), *Central bankers, bureaucratic incentive, and monetary policy* (pp. 11–35). Kluwer Academic Publishers.

Friedman, M., & Schwartz, A. J. (1965). *A monetary history of the United States*. Princeton University Press.

FSA. (2011). *The report on Incubator Bank of Japan*. The Committee on the Review of Administrative Actions, Financial Supervisory Agency (in Japanese).

Fujita, Y. (1987). *Historical development of the Bank of England*. Tagashuppan (in Japanese).

Godeffroy, J. M. (2007). Letter to ECSDA. www.ecb.europa.eu/paym/t2s/pdf/feedback/ECB-012.pdf.

Goodhart, C. (1988). *The evolution of central banks*. MIT Press.

Goodhart, C. (2002). Can central banking survive the IT revolution? In R. Pringle & M. Robinson (Eds.), *E-money and payment systems review* (pp. 271–289). Central Banking Publications.

Goodhart, C. (2010). *The changing role of central banks* (BIS Working Papers No. 326).

Goodhart, C., & Schoenmaker, D. (1993). Institutional separation between supervisory and monetary agencies. In C. Goodhart (Ed.), *The central bank and the financial system* (pp. 333–413). MacMillan Press.

Greenspan, A. (2007). *The age of turbulence*. Penguin Press.

Hart, O., Sheifer, A., & Vishny, R. (1997). The proper scope of government: Theory and an application to prisons. *Quarterly Journal of Economics, 12*(4), 1127–1161.

Hatamura, Y. (2006). *Study of failure*. Natsumesha (in Japanese).

Hayek, F. A. (1945). The use of knowledge in society. *American Economic Review, 35*(4), 519–530.

Hayek, F. A. (1976). *Denationalisation of money: An analysis of the theory and practice of concurrent currencies*. Institute of Economic Affaires.

Henderson, R., & Clark, K. (1990). Architectural innovation: The reconfiguration of existing product technologies and the failure of established firms. *Administrative Science Quarterly, 35*(1), 9–30.

Hermalin, B. E. (2001). Economics and corporate culture. In C. L. Cooper, et al. (Eds.), *The international handbook of organizational culture and climate* (pp. 217–261). Wiley.

Hillman, A. (1978). The theory of clubs: A technological formulation. In A. Sandmo (Ed.), *Essays in public economics* (pp. 29–47). Lexington Books.

Hirayama, K. (2006). Development of monetary theory in England. *Keizaigaku kenkyu, 59*(3), 77–118. University of Kansai-gakuin (in Japanese).

Holmstrom, B., & Milgrom, P. (1991). Multitask principal-agent analyses: Incentive contracts, asset ownership, and job design. *Journal of Law, Economics, and Organization, 7*(Special Issue), 24–52.

Holmstrom, B., & Milgrom, P. (1994). The firm as an incentive system. *American Economic Review, 84*(4), 972–991.

Ito, H. (2002). Separation of regulation entity based on contract theory. In H. Imai & A. Okada (Eds.), *New development of game theory* (pp. 153–174). Keisoshobo (in Japanese).

Ito, H. (2003). *Economic theory of contract*. Yuhikaku (in Japanese).

Ito, M. (1982). *The constitution*. Kobundo (in Japanese).

Iwata, K. (2009). *Economics of financial crisis*. Toyokeizai (in Japanese).

Izu, H. (2013). The resolution of financial institutions and the Bank of Japan. *Shoken Keizai Kenkyu, 84*, 83–102. Japan Securities Research Institute (in Japanese).

Jackson, P. M. (1982). *The political economy of bureaucracy*. Philip Allan.

Kahneman, D., & Tversky, A. (1974). Judgement under uncertainty: Heuristics and biases. *Science, New Series, 185*(4157), 1124–1131.

Kanai, Y. (1989). *Evolution of monetary policy by the Bank of England*. University of Nagoya Press (in Japanese).

Kanemoto, Y. (1991). Political economy of the public sector. In Y. Kanemoto & H. Miyajima (Eds.), *The public sector* (pp. 3–29). University of Tokyo Press (in Japanese).

Kiewiet, D. R., & McCubbins, M. (1991). *The logic of delegation*. University of Chicago Press.

Kikuzawa, K. (2006). Psychological accounting analysis of manager behavior. *Mita-Shogaku kenkyu, 49*(4), 131–147. (in Japanese).

Kikuzawa, K. (2007). Behavioral agency analysis of corporate governance. *Mita-Shogaku kenkyu, 50*(3), 165–179. (in Japanese).

Kikuzawa, K. (2008a). *The theory of strategy*. Diamond Press (in Japanese).

Kikuzawa, K. (2008b). The possibility of behavioral new institutional economics. *Mita-Shogaku kenkyu, 51*(4), 59–79. (in Japanese).

Kikuzawa, K. (2009). *Toward behavioral new institutional economics* (Keio University Discussion Paper Series No. FY09(1)).

Klein, P. (2004). *The make-or-buy decision: Lessons from empirical studies* (Working Paper No. 2004(7)). Contracting and Organizations Research Institute, University of Missouri at Columbia.

Kreps, D. M. (1990). Corporate culture and economic theory. In J. Alt & K. Shepsle (Eds.), *Perspectives on positive political economy* (pp. 90–143). Cambridge University Press.

Kusumi, T. (2001). Heuristics. *Handbook of social recognition* (p. 278). Kitaojishobo (in Japanese).

Laffont, J. J., & Martimort, D. (2002). *The theory of incentives: The principal-agent model*. Princeton University Press.

Langlois, R., & Robertson, P. (1995). *Firms, markets and economic change: A dynamic theory of business institutions*. Routledge.

Lave, J., & Wenger, E. (1991). *Situated learning: Legitimate peripheral participation*. Cambridge University Press.

Levacic, R. (1990). Public choice: The economics of politics. In J. R. Shackleton (Ed.), *New thinking in economics* (pp. 141–159). Edward Elgar.

Listfield, R. J. (1990). Commentary. In D. Humphrey (Ed.), *The U.S. payment system: Efficiency, risk and the role of the Federal Reserve* (pp. 232–243). Kluwer Academic Publishers.

Lucas, R. (1988). On the mechanics of economic development. *Journal of Monetary Economics, 22*, 3–42.

Lupia, A., & McCubbins, M. (1994). Designing bureaucratic accountability. *Law and Contemporary Problems, 57*(1), 91–126.

Madigan, B. F. (2009). Bagehot's dictum in practice. In *Proceedings of Symposium at the FRB of Kansas City*. Federal Reserve Bank of Kansas City.

Martin, J. (1992). *Cultures in organization: Three perspectives*. Oxford University Press.

Maxfield, S. (1997). *Gatekeepers of growth: The international political economy of central banking in developing countries*. Princeton University Press.

Mayer, T. (1990). *The political economy of American monetary policy*. Cambridge University Press.

McCrakin, B. H. (1994). Federalism and the Fed: The role of Reserve Bank presidents. *Economic Review, 79*(5), 12–23. Federal Reserve Bank of Atlanta.

Meyerson, D. E., & Martin, J. (1987). Cultural change: An integration of three different views. *Journal of Management Studies, 24*(6), 623–647.

Milgrom, P., & Roberts, J. (1992). *Economics, organization and management*. Prentice Hall.

Milton, S., & Siclair, P. (2011). *The capital needs of central banks*. Routledge.

Moe, T. (1984). The new economics of organization. *American Journal of Political Science, 28*(4), 739–777.

Moe, T. (1990a). The politics of structured choice: Toward a theory of public bureaucracy. In O. Williamson (Ed.), *Organization theory* (pp. 116–153). Oxford University Press.

Moe, T. (1990b). Political institutions: The neglected side of the story. *Journal of Law, Economics, and Organization, 6*(Special Issue), 213–253.

Moe, T. (1991). Politics and the theory of organization. *Journal of Law, Economics, and Organization, 7*(Special Issue), 106–129.

Moe, T., & Caldwell, M. (1994). The institutional foundation of democratic government: A comparison of presidential and parliamentary system. *Journal of Institutional and Theoretical Economics, 150*(1), 171–195.

Morimiya, Y. (1985). *Risk management theory*. Nippon-hyoronsha (in Japanese).

Mueller, D. (1989). *Public choice II*. Cambridge University Press.

Mullins, E. (1993). *Secrets of the Federal Reserve*. Bankers Research Institute.

Munger, M., & Roberts, B. (1990). The Federal Reserve and its institutional environment: A review. In T. Mayer (Ed.), *The political economy of American monetary policy* (pp. 81–96). Cambridge University Press.

Nakajima, M. (2017). *After bitcoin*. Shinchosha (in Japanese).

Nakayama, Y., et al. (1997). *An electronic money scheme: A proposal for a new electronic money scheme which is both secure and convenient* (IMES Discussion Paper No. 97-E-4). Bank of Japan.

Ng, Y. K. (1973). The economic theory of clubs: Pareto optimality conditions. *Economica, 40* (159), 291–298.

Nicholl, P. (2009). What is the role of the board in a central bank? In J. Mendzela & N. Carver (Eds.), *Central bank management* (pp. 25–39). Central Bank Publications.

Nishimura, Y. (2003). *Financial reform in Japan*. Toyokeizai (in Japanese).

Niskanen, W. A. (1971). *Bureaucracy and representative government*. Aldine-Atherton.

Nonaka, I., & Konno, N. (1998). The concept of "*Ba*": Building a foundation for knowledge creation. *California Management Review, 40*(3), 40–54.

Nordhaus, W. D. (1975). The political business cycle. *Review of Economic Studies, 42*(2), 169–190.

Ohizumi, K. (2006). *The theory of crisis management*. Minerva Shobo (in Japanese).

Ohnuki, M. (2006). *Bank of Japan network and financial market integration: From the establishment of the Bank of Japan until the early 20th century* (IMES Discussion Paper Series No. 2006-E-27). Bank of Japan.

Ordeshook, P. (1990). The emerging discipline of political economy. In J. E. Alt, et al. (Eds.), *Perspectives on positive political economy* (pp. 20–36). Cambridge University Press.

Oritani, Y. (1991a). Globalization of payment network and risks. In E. H. Solomon (Ed.), *Electronic money flows: The modeling of a new financial order* (pp. 115–125). Kluwer Academic Publishers (Reprinted from *The globalization of financial services*, pp. 553–563, by M. K. Lewis, Ed., 1998. Edward Elgar).

Oritani, Y. (1991b). A Japanese central banker's view of the EMS. In C. Wihlborg, et al. (Eds.), *Financial regulation and monetary arrangements after 1992* (pp. 335–337). Elsevier Science Publishers.

Padoa-Schioppa, T. (1991). Foreword. In Banca d'Italia (Ed.), *Proceedings of the Workshop on Payment System Issues in the Perspective of European Monetary Unification* (pp. 1–3). Banca d'Italia.

Padoa-Schioppa, T. (2007). Financial supervision: Inside or outside central banks? In J. Kremes, et al. (Eds.), *Financial supervision in Europe* (pp. 160–175). Edward Elgar.

Palmer, M. (1995). Toward an economics of comparative political organization: Examining ministerial responsibility. *Journal of Law, Economics, and Organization, 11*(1), 164–188.

Popper, K. (1972). *Objective knowledge: An evolutionary approach*. Clarendon Press.

Quintyn, M., & Taylor, W. (2007). Robust regulators and their political masters: Independence and accountability in theory. In D. Masciandaro & M. Quintyn (Eds.), *Designing financial supervision institutions: Independence, accountability and governance* (pp. 3–40). Edward Elgar.

Riksbank. (2018). https://www.riksbank.se/en-gb/financial-stability/payments/e-krona/.

Rochet, J., & Tirole, J. (2003). Platform competition in two-sided markets. *Journal of the European Economic Association, 1*(1), 990–1029.

Sakashita, A. (2002). *Organizational symbolism.* Hakutoshobo (in Japanese).

Samuelson, P. A., & Nordhaus, W. D. (2010). *Economics* (19th ed.). McGraw-Hill.

Sandler, T., & Tschirhart, J. (1980). The economic theory of clubs: An evaluative survey. *Journal of Economic Literature, 18*(4), 1481–1521.

Sayers, R. S. (1957). *Central banking after Bagehot.* Oxford University Press.

Schein, E. H. (1999). *The corporate culture: Survival guide.* Jossey-Bass Inc.

Schein, E. H. (2000). Sense and nonsense about culture and climate. In N. M. Ashkanasy, et al. (Eds.), *Handbook of organizational culture and climate* (pp. 23–30). Saga Publication, Inc.

Schmiedel, H., Malkamaki, M., & Tarkka, J. (2002). *Economies of scale and technological development in securities and settlement systems* (Bank of Finland Discussion Papers No. 2002-26). Bank of Finland.

Schoenmaker, D. (1996). *Contagion risk in banking* (Discussion Paper Series No. 239). LSE Financial Markets Group.

Shepsle, K., & Weingast, B. (1981). Structure-induced equilibrium and legislative choice. *Public Choice, 37*(3), 503–519.

Shirakawa, M. (2008a). *Monetary policy in today.* Nikkei Press (in Japanese).

Shirakawa, M. (2008b). *Liquidity and payment systems.* Speech at the University of Tokyo (in Japanese).

Shirakawa, M. (2009). *International policy response to the financial crisis.* Speech at the FRB of Kansas City's symposium.

Shirakawa, M. (2011a). *150 years of innovation and challenges in monetary control.* Speech at Goethe-Universität Frankfurt am Main in Celebration of the 150th Anniversary of German-Japanese Diplomatic Relations, Bank of Japan.

Shirakawa, M. (2011b). *The task of public policy implementation.* Speech at the University of Kyoto (in Japanese).

Shirakawa, M. (2018). *Central banking: The 39 years experienced by a central banker.* Toyokeizai (in Japanese).

Smith, V. C. (1936). *Rationale of central banking.* P.S. King & Son Ltd. (Reprinted from *Rationale of central banking and the free banking alternative,* 1990. Liberty Press).

Stevens, J. (1993). *The economics of collective choice.* Westview Press.

Takahashi, M. (2006). *Organizational symbolism.* Dobunkan (in Japanese).

Takeishi, A. (2002). Knowledge partitioning in the interfirm division of labor: The case of automotive product development. *Organization Science, 13*(3), 321–338.

Taylor, J. (2009). *Getting off track.* Leland Stanford Junior University.

Taylor, M. (1995). *Twin peaks: A regulatory structure for the new century.* CSFI: A Pamphlet.

Teece, D. (1994). Understanding corporate coherence. *Journal of Economic Behavior and Organization, 23*(1), 1–30.

Tirole, J. (1988). *The theory of industrial organization.* MIT Press.

Tirole, J. (1994). *The internal organization of government* (Oxford Economic Papers No. 46). Oxford University.

Tognato, C. (2012). *Central bank independence: Cultural codes and symbolic performance.* Palgrave Macmillan.

Toma, E., & Toma, M. (1986). *Central bankers, bureaucratic incentives, and monetary policy.* Kluwer Academic.

Toma, M. (1982). Inflationary bias of the Federal Reserve System: A bureaucratic perspective. *Journal of Monetary Economics, 10*(2), 163–190.

Tucker, D. (1990). The conflicting role of the Federal Reserve as regulator and services provider in the U.S. payment system. In D. Humphrey (Ed.), *The U.S. payment system: Efficiency, risk and the role of the Federal Reserve* (pp. 223–231). Kluwer Academic Publishers.

Turnbull, S. (2000). Why unitary boards are not best practice: A case for compound boards. In *Proceedings of the First European Conference on Corporate Governance*. http://ssrn.com/abstract=253803.

Waldrop, M. (1992). *Complexity: The emerging science at the edge of order and chaos* (p. 243). Simon & Schuster.

Wall, L. D., & Eisenbeis, R. A. (2000). Financial regulatory structure and the resolution of conflicting goals. *Journal of Financial Services Research, 17*(1), 223–245.

Walsh, C. (1995). Optimal contracts for central bankers. *American Economic Review, 85*(1), 150–167.

Weingast, B. (1994). The congressional-bureaucratic system: A principal agent perspective with applications to the SEC. *Public Choice, 44*(1), 147–191.

Weingast, B., & Moran, J. (1993). Bureaucratic discretion or congressional control?: Regulatory policy making by the Federal Trade Commission. *Journal of Political Economy, 91*(5), 765–800.

White, L. H. (1984). *Free banking in Britain*. Cambridge University Press.

Willett, T., & Keen, E. (1990). Studying the Fed: Toward a broader public-choice perspective. In T. Mayer (Ed.), *The political economy of American monetary policy* (pp. 13–26). Cambridge University Press.

Williamson, O. (1975). *Markets and hierarchies: Analysis and antitrust implications*. Free Press.

Williamson, O. (1985). *The economic institutions of capitalism: Firms, markets, relational contracting*. Free Press.

Williamson, O. (1996). *The mechanism of governance*. Oxford University Press.

Williamson, O. (1999). Public and private bureaucracies: A transaction cost economics perspective. *Journal of Law, Economics, and Organization, 15*(1), 306–342.

Williamson, O. (2000). The new institutional economics: Taking stock, looking ahead. *Journal of Economic Literature, 20*(12), 1087–1108.

Williamson, O. (2008). Transaction cost economics. In C. Menard & M. Shirley (Eds.), *Handbook of new institutional economics* (pp. 41–65). Springer.

Williamson, O. (2013). *The transaction cost economics project: The theory and practice of the governance of contractual relations*. Edward Elgar.

Yamaguchi, Y. (2008). Commentary: Central banks and financial crises. In *Proceedings of Symposium at the FRB of Kansas City*. Federal Reserve Bank of Kansas City.

Young, P. H. (1996). Economics of convention. *Journal of Economic Perspectives, 10*(2), 105–122.

Young, P. H. (1998). *Individual strategy and social structure*. Princeton University Press.

Index

© Springer Nature Singapore Pte Ltd. 2019
Y. Oritani, *The Japanese Central Banking System Compared with Its European
and American Counterparts*, https://doi.org/10.1007/978-981-13-9001-2

Lightning Source UK Ltd.
Milton Keynes UK
UKHW021814220719

346630UK00003B/159/P